Puzzles of Economic Growth

DIRECTIONS IN DEVELOPMENT
Public Sector Governance

Puzzles of Economic Growth

Leszek Balcerowicz and Andrzej Rzońca, Editors

WORLD BANK GROUP

Contents

Boxes

Figures

Preface

Observation of economic reality brings remarkable facts to the surface and prompts numerous questions. Why, for example, has Australia gotten so much ahead of New Zealand, in spite of the latter being held up as a paragon of free market reform? How is it possible that Austria, with its persistently oversized state enterprise sector, has managed to (nearly) catch up with Switzerland, which in the early 1970s boasted per capita national income that was more than 50 percent higher? How can we account for the differences in economic growth between Estonia and Slovenia, and which of these two countries has been more successful at systemic transformation? Why is Mexico so much poorer than Spain, despite having been wealthier all the way into the 1960s? Why has República Bolivariana de Venezuela, which in 1950 had a per capita income higher than that of Norway and remains a major exporter of oil, slipped behind Chile? How is it possible that its currency, considered one of the most stable currencies in the world until the 1970s, has lost its luster even for Venezuelans? How has Chile, blighted by acute crises in the 1970s and 1980s, managed to overtake other South American countries in terms of income per head? Why is Costa Rica lagging behind Puerto Rico, even though in the 1970s the U.S. territory's fast development slowed to a crawl and is now far below other comparable island economies? Why has "communist" China outstripped "capitalist" India? Why has Pakistan's growth lagged behind that of Indonesia, even though the latter was exposed to recurrent bouts of state interventionism, and suffered one of the deepest crises in world economic history in the years 1997–98? Why, even before the 2010 earthquake, the Dominican Republic has been visited by tourists many more times than Haiti, despite being situated on the same island? To what extent are humans responsible for Haiti's exposure to the hurricanes occurring in this region?

This book strives to answer these (and many other) questions. They are all part of a broader question that we wish to address: How do differences in economic growth arise?

To explain the causes of these differences is one of the fundamental tasks of empirical economics. It is a task of crucial importance both from the analytical and practical points of view. Economic growth is the only sure path to lifting nations out of poverty and raising their living standards. As long as a nation's economy grows, the income of all its citizens can grow as well. To quote but one example, the poorest one-fifth of the Republic of Korea's population—the

Republic of Korea being an economic tiger—earn an income four times larger than the income of the wealthiest one-fifth of Korea's population before the country's division and seven times larger than the income of an average citizen of today's the Democratic People's Republic of Korea. Our book will present more such striking instances of swift economic growth, or—conversely—lack thereof.

Without economic growth, the only way to acquire wealth is to divert it from others. What is more, the very strife for available wealth may shrink it. There are currently many countries in the world whose income per head is lower than it was a few decades ago. Our book provides an opportunity to have a closer look at two such countries—República Bolivariana de Venezuela and Haiti. Both post per capita income below the 1950 level.

Although there is ample literature on economic growth, much remains to be explored. Proponents of a particularly influential trend, growth theory, focus on shallow causes of economic growth such as capital accumulation, employment growth, and improvement in the productivity of capital and labor. This theory does not, in our opinion, convincingly account for differences in growth rates, as the shallow causes it focuses on themselves require explanation. To this end, more and more studies focus on underlying factors—institutions and systems—as they seek to explain diverging growth rates over time and across countries. Our book subscribes to this strand of economic literature.[1] Yet, readers will also find in it references to key works of growth theory. Before proceeding to describe our research, in chapter 1 we offer an overview of other studies of this issue—crucial to both economic theory and economic policy.

The overview warrants our claim that the book we are submitting is fundamentally different from other works on economic growth. Most examine either a large group of countries or focus on a single one. In the process, they may concentrate predominantly either on steady growth factors (those at work over a long period) while ignoring economic collapses, or else analyze various kinds of shocks without considering their relation to long-term growth. Or they may devote themselves entirely to shallow growth factors, such as labor and capital outlays and changes in factor productivity, or their underlying influences, such as institutions.

Our book stands out from these studies in three respects:

- First, we describe carefully selected pairs of countries (or, as in the case of Costa Rica and Puerto Rico, pair a country with a territory). Owing to this approach, we can avoid many faults—described in more detail in chapter 1—found with the standard methods of analysis, that focus either on single country or large group of countries.

- Second, growth forces and the impact of shocks are examined in combination. This is because, as it turns out, susceptibility to shocks is of crucial importance to the average growth rate even over a very long period. In all the pairs of countries covered by our study, inferior growth performance was observed in the country that had experienced more frequent or more powerful shocks. Further, the weakest overall performance in the analyzed sample was seen in

Haiti and República Bolivariana de Venezuela, two countries characterized by the most frequent crises, while the best performance was posted by China and India, which have enjoyed stable growth since the 1980s.

- Third, we focus on the factors underlying growth, and institutions in particular. We start with growth accounting wherever it might *help identify shallow causes of growth*. We also point out situations where such accounting serves no purpose. But later we go deeper looking for the factors underlying growth.

The book comprises 12 chapters.

Chapter 1 serves as an introduction to the problem of economic growth. In this chapter, we highlight the significance of economic growth in raising living standards. We describe the diversification of the long-term growth rate over time and across countries—and point to the impact of shocks on this rate. We systemize methods of research into economic growth. Finally, we familiarize readers with the research methods applied in this book and its conceptual framework.

Chapter 2 deals with the influence of institutional frameworks upon an economy's driving forces. In this chapter we distinguish between two kinds of growth mechanisms. The first—potentially universal and sustainable—is based on innovation, necessary for sustainable, long-term growth. The second is transitional and is present only in situations shaped by particular types of institutional frameworks or a distortionary economic policy. We introduce the notion of institutional barriers to growth. We present the typologies of institutional systems incapable of steady long-term growth. At the same time, we point to situations in which such growth can be attained. Finally, we define and analyze which reform packages best enable growth.

In chapters 3–11, the authors analyze the periods and points in time when differences arose in the pace of growth—and, consequently, in the level of per capita income between: Australia and New Zealand, Austria and Switzerland, Estonia and Slovenia, Mexico and Spain, Chile and República Bolivariana de Venezuela, Costa Rica and Puerto Rico, Haiti and the Dominican Republic, China and India, and Indonesia and Pakistan. Most were paired because of their similarities, at least at the starting point of the analysis, including in such difficult-to-measure factors as culture. By selecting the pairs in this manner, we have been able to isolate the impact of institutional differences on economic growth. At the same time, the economies under review are sufficiently varied as to indicate several key determinants of long-term per capita income growth.

In chapter 12, we summarize the key findings of the comparative studies and draw conclusions from the entire research project. Key findings include the following points:

- Shocks—of various strength and frequency—significantly impacted the economic performance of almost all the economies under review.
- These shocks do not result exclusively, or even chiefly, from bad luck. In almost every instance, they had been caused or amplified by domestic economic policy.

- Institutional weakness comes at a considerable cost to society. Yet there is little consensus on how to strengthen (or create) institutions so that they mitigate both the frequency and strength of shocks.
- Of the reforms and policies considered in this book, only some strengthened institutions; in some countries reforms and policies only weakened them. The occurrence of shocks and their intensity does not diminish the significance of propelling institutions for economic growth. How these institutions are advanced in large part decides whether income per capita will rise or fall.
- The most important propelling institutions are those whose diversification or change results in differences in the long-term rate of growth. They, include:
  - An economy's ownership structure and, in particular, the share of state ownership in enterprises.
  - The structure of property rights and the degree of freedom of private entrepreneurship.
  - The level of protection of property rights (and of persons), including against corruption, which can be seen as a factor curtailing these rights.
  - The intensity of competition between suppliers, which depends heavily, for example, on the economy's openness to foreign trade and foreign direct investment (FDI).
  - The fiscal position of the state, which deteriorates mainly as a result of growing social transfers in relation to gross domestic product (GDP).
- In some cases, the condition of key propelling institutions condemns a country to slow growth (or even stagnation or GDP decline) irrespective of the condition of other institutions.
- Particularly fast economic growth is observed in those countries that, having inherited an institutional framework that has a serious distortionary effect on the economy, not only quickly remove the distortions but also introduce a reform package extensive enough to trigger the fundamental growth mechanism, that is, innovation-based growth.

We wish that this book reaches a broad circle of readers: teachers and students of economics, policy makers, and also those who benefit (or not) from policy—that is, the public. We hope that this work will help such readers better understand the causes of economic growth.

We thank Professor Stanisław Gomułka for numerous and valuable comments on our book. We also extend our words of gratitude to Aleksander Łaszek, who helped us in the editing work. Obviously, any weaknesses or errors this book might still contain are solely and fully our responsibility.

Note

1. Incidentally, institutions are increasingly present in growth models, albeit still in a very simplified manner—most frequently as a single parameter in a single equation, whereas in reality they have a (complex) impact upon the many economic choices made by enterprises and households.

Abbreviations

CACM	Central American Common Market
CAP	Common Agricultural Policy
CCSS	Costa Rican Social Security Institute
CEEC	Central and Eastern European Countries
CIT	corporate income tax
CPI	consumer price index
EEA	European Economic Area
EEC	European Economic Community
EFTA	European Free Trade Association
ERS	Economic Research Service
EU	European Union
FDI	foreign direct investment
GATT	General Agreement on Tariffs and Trade
GDP	gross domestic product
GNP	gross national product
ICE	Costa Rican Electricity Institute
ILO	International Labour Organization
NAFTA	North American Free Trade Agreement
NDP	net domestic product
OECD	Organisation for Economic Co-operation and Development
ODA	official development assistance
OPEC	Organization of the Petroleum Exporting Countries
PIT	personal income tax
PPP	purchasing power parity
SME	small and medium-sized enterprise
SNB	Swiss National Bank
TFP	total factor productivity
TVE	township-village enterprise
VAT	value-added tax

CHAPTER 1

The Significance of Economic Growth

Leszek Balcerowicz and Andrzej Rzońca

The pace of long-run economic growth is of fundamental importance to living standards. Growth is an irreplaceable mechanism for lifting people out of poverty. In East Asia, the fastest-growing region in the world, the number of people forced to live on less than $2 a day has declined by a quarter of a billion in recent years alone (since 2000); in other words, it has been shrinking by about a million people every week (Gill and Kharas 2007). Around the world, the incomes of the poorest track the rise in average incomes (see, for example, Dollar and Kraay 2001).[1]

Higher income levels (a benefit of economic growth) enable people to better satisfy their material needs. Differences in per capita income correspond to consumption (see, for example, Acemoglu 2009, 7). Also, as their incomes rise, people may adopt healthier lifestyles (including a better diet) and gain wider access to health services. Thus, average life expectancy is also closely correlated with the level of income per capita (see, for example, Weil 2005, 156–7).[2]

Lifting people out of poverty by boosting economic growth does not necessarily imply that the gap between the rich and poor will lessen. In East Asia, such differences actually widened in the previous decade by almost a quarter, mostly because of China (Gill and Kharas 2007). If income inequality increases in tandem with economic growth, this is not because growth pushes a part of society into poverty, but because it does not lift everyone out of poverty at the same moment. At first, only a few people invest in the modern sectors and find employment there. These sectors develop mainly in the cities, because densely populated areas are more conducive to the cooperation that allows people to benefit from both specialization and economies of scale. With time, as more people relocate from villages to cities, where there are more jobs in modern economic sectors, inequalities tend to gradually diminish (see, for example, Kuznets 1955).[3] Overall, income discrepancies in individual countries are currently smaller than before the advent of modern economic growth—that is, growth enabling a visible improvement in the living standards within the lifespan of one generation (see, for example, Weil 2005, 19).[4]

Even though when the modernization begins income inequalities initially increase, we should remember that in the longer term it is better to have a smaller stake in a fast-growing income than a large share in a slowly expanding one (or, worse still, one that is contracting). In the Republic of Korea, for example, the poorest one-fifth of the population earns an income almost four times the size of the income of the wealthiest one-fifth before the Korean War and the country's division. The income of the poorest one-fifth is approximately seven times the income earned by an average citizen in the Democratic People's Republic of Korea, where accumulating wealth is frowned upon for ideological reasons.

Long-Term Growth

A glance at the world's economic history shows that long-term growth rates, and, in effect, average living standards, have fluctuated widely over time. Until the year 1000, growth wavered around 0 percent. The differences in per capita income between the richest and the poorest regions of the world did not exceed 10 percent. Between 1000 and 1820, global per capita income growth amounted to 0.05 percent a year on average, ranging from 0 percent in the poor regions of Africa to 0.14 percent in the wealthiest regions of Western Europe. On the eve of the Industrial Revolution, per capita income in the world's wealthiest regions was roughly three times the income in its poorest areas (Galor 2005, 174, 180, based on data from Maddison 2001). Between 1820 and 1870, per capita income growth picked up to 0.5 percent in annual terms. In the period 1870–1950 it was running at 1.1 percent a year, to exceed 2 percent in annualized terms after 1950 (Weil 2005, 16, based on data from Maddison 2001).

Modern economic growth, which we tackle in this book, did not start at the same time everywhere. It was first observed in Great Britain. Some economists date its beginning back to the 18th century. In the 19th century, it engulfed the countries of Western Europe as well as Australia, Canada, New Zealand, and the United States. In Latin America, it started in the early 20th century, and in Asia, around 1950 (with the exception of Japan, where it had begun at the end of the 19th century). In Africa, with a few exceptions, modern economic growth has not yet occurred (Parente and Prescott 2005, 1373). Cross-national differences in the moment when modern economic growth took off are today reflected in the vast per capita income differences across those same countries. In 2006 the income of the world's 20 wealthiest countries was on average 57 times higher than that of its poorest (IMF 2009).

Also, the pace of modern economic growth was not uniform everywhere. Great Britain initially needed 100 years to double its per capita income. In the 20th century, the countries of Western Europe achieved the same in as little as 35 years; in the second half of the century, this period shrank even further. After 1950 Asian countries (such as Singapore; Hong Kong SAR, China; Taiwan,

China; and the Republic of Korea) required only 10 years or fewer to double their income per head (Parente and Prescott 2005, 1373). Other examples of equally fast growth—that is, the case of China, India, and Chile in the 1980s and Estonia from the mid-1990s until the outbreak of the recent financial crisis—are analyzed in this book.

All countries that got a later start did not necessarily enjoy higher growth rates than their predecessors, however. Consider, for example, the countries of Central and Eastern Europe and Latin America—cases given ample space in this book. In the former group, per capita income in 1950–90 decreased from nearly a half to approximately a third of the level observed in Western Europe. In the latter, the process of catching up with the richest countries was also interrupted toward the end of the first half of the 20th century. Over the next 50 years, their per capita income in relation to Western European countries sank by almost half, to approximately the same level as that seen at the start of modern economic growth (Maddison 2001).

In recent years, the number of countries which have managed to speed up growth has decreased, while more countries have been able to sustain a high growth rate. Stabilization in the composition of the group of fast-developing countries versus the stagnant ones may be demonstrated by a rising (if still low—see the section on A Brief History of Economic Research) correlation in per capita income growth rates across adjacent decades (Durlauf, Johnson, and Temple 2005, 568–71).

Shocks and Periods of Relatively Stable Growth

Looking at the long-term paths of economic growth in various countries, we see more or less stable dynamics—from, say, a slow decline in gross domestic product (GDP), through stagnation, to fast growth—punctuated by the aberrations of usually brief downturns and occasionally sharp declines. Generally, in most cases the past growth rate (whether of the past 15 or even 50 years) is of little assistance in predicting the future (see, for example, Easterly and others 1993; Easterly and Levine 2001; Easterly 2002; Durlauf, Johnson, and Temple 2005). Often, fast growth in a given period contains the seed of a collapse to occur in ensuing years. Moreover, the volatility of growth paths varies greatly across countries (Easterly and Levine 2001). Some countries expand at a steady rate—although this rate may differ considerably across countries—while others undergo frequent and deep collapses.

A sudden slowdown, even if followed by a quick return to the growth path, may stem a country's average growth rate in the long term in comparison with more stable growth paths. Recent research shows that in a group of low-income countries that developed fastest in the 1990s, 18 were characterized by small fluctuations in their growth rate (World Bank 2005). In another study, Hnatkovska and Loayza (2003) came to the conclusion, based on an analysis of 79 countries in the period 1960–2000, that "macroeconomic volatility and long-run economic growth are negatively related" and that this negative relationship is not the effect of small cyclical variations, but of "large drops below the output trend." Such drops occurred very often in Africa, a fact reflected in the highest standard deviation of GDP growth per employee in 1960–2000 among all world regions. As a result of the collapses, growth on that continent was episodic in nature (Fosu 2007). Also, in all the country pairs discussed in this book, poorer performance was observed in those that had experienced more frequent or deeper downturns (see, for example, the chapters comparing the economic performance of New Zealand and Australia, Switzerland and Austria, Mexico and Spain). Among the examined countries, the worst results were observed in Haiti and República Bolivariana de Venezuela—two countries where the crises were most frequent and deepest. China and India—also with fast growth paths—were, in contrast, characterized by more stable growth.

Differences in the frequency and depth of growth collapses resulted, in part, from differences in the external shocks experienced. But many shocks originate domestically; these are not part of cyclical variations in economic activity but are prompted, after periods of serious disequilibrium, by the inevitable correction of the market mechanism. How such shocks affect long-term growth also depends on countries' differing ability to address them. Those differences account not only for the depth of collapses but for their very occurrence, once a shock hits. In many countries, collapses have been preceded by positive shocks, that is, shocks leading to faster short-run economic growth to which those countries failed to respond properly (they assumed that the boom would continue to last—see, for example, the chapters on Costa Rica, República Bolivariana de Venezuela, and Mexico). Finally, vulnerability to external shocks—resulting from, for example, an economy's structure—is an important variable, possibly of a domestic origin (contrast the experiences of Indonesia, Mexico, and República Bolivariana de Venezuela with those of Australia—all described in this book).

The occurrence and pace of stable economic growth patterns also vary considerably across countries. The forces behind them are long term or even permanent; thus, they can be termed sustained growth drivers. Chapter 2 deals with their nature and determinants. At this juncture, we will present the approaches to economic growth that prevail in the economic literature. This will enable us to better describe the research methods as well as the conceptual and analytical frameworks used in this book.

A Brief History of Economic Research

The causes of economic growth mark the most important area of economic study since its birth. The father of modern economics, Adam Smith, first published *An Inquiry into the Nature and Causes of the Wealth of Nations* in 1776. Since then—and even though economists' interest in the issue has occasionally waned—economic growth has attracted the most space of any topic in the literature (in the past 20 years, more articles than on growth have been written only on inflation—see, for example, Weil 2005).

Following a 1982 article by Nelson and Plosser, the idea that shocks may have a lasting effect on economic growth has been gaining ground (Fatas 2002); still, the relevant literature shows a strong bias toward sustained growth drivers, with little attention given to shocks. Only a few address the question of why collapses can have a long-lasting effect: why, instead of prompting renaissance, do they so often devastate an economy?[5] This research problem entails other, more detailed questions: Is a collapse with a long-term adverse effect always to be considered destructive, or has it only triggered mechanisms long inherent in the economy? Does the short-run economic growth rate have any limits—even following a deep decline—preventing full recovery of output level after a collapse? Finally, are growth opportunities time dependent, which would mean that a country affected by a collapse may lose some of these opportunities? The literature has not been able to address any of these questions convincingly.

Economic collapses, and financial crises in particular, have been studied within a separate stream in economics. Since John Maynard Keynes, the focus has been on an economy's capability to restore equilibrium—on its own, and under one institutional system: free-market capitalism. Much effort has been put into both highlighting the serious flaws of the system and debunking the very proposition that such flaws exist. One neglected issue is that of instability in various institutional systems, although there is no major doubt that the worst collapses in modern economic growth have been observed in noncapitalist countries and those where the free market was seriously hampered.

The empirical studies contained in this book attempt to carry out a comprehensive analysis of how both sustained growth drivers and shocks impact long-term economic growth.

Existing research into economic growth, which (as we have already pointed out) focuses on sustained growth drivers, disagrees over which factors are to be considered drivers, and applies varying methods of analysis to the problem. The most influential and extensive research trend in the literature is often dubbed "growth theory." It strives to account for the differences in the economic growth rate by referring to three factors: labor, capital,[6] and their combined productivity. These are factors of a quantitative nature. In this framework, it is only natural to apply, as is usually done, mathematical and econometric methods.

The foundations of growth theory were laid in the works of Solow (1956) and Swan (1956). These works changed the way quantitatively inclined economists thought about economic growth. Before this change—and based on the work of Harrod (1939, 1948) and Domar (1946, 1947)—the economies of developed countries were expected to see long periods of either rising unemployment or falling utilization of capital inputs. Both phenomena occurred, it was assumed, because a scarce factor of production could not be substituted by one that was abundant. According to the Harrod-Domar model, the inputs of capital and effective labor (that is, taking into account increasing productivity) had to be used in production in a steady (assumed) proportion; when the input of a given production factor exceeds the amount given by that proportion, it became completely useless. Both rising unemployment and falling utilization of capital input could be prevented by the state—in the first instance by increasing and in the second instance by decreasing the investment rate by so much as to keep the pace of capital input growth strictly in line with growth in the labor input and with labor productivity. The model implied that less-developed countries with high employment in agriculture (characterized by low labor productivity) may quickly catch up with developed countries by launching heavy industrialization initiatives. The possibility of labor flows from agriculture to industry was supposed to allow the labor input to be fully utilized at any level of investment.

The Solow-Swan model challenged the conclusions of the Harrod-Domar model (Solow 1994). First, by admitting the possibility of substitution between the inputs of capital and labor, it gave the capital intensity of production the character of a variable. The relation of output to capital ceased to be a parameter. The capital input growth rate, regardless of the investment rate, adjusted automatically to the growth of the labor input and its productivity, thus eliminating the need for state intervention in mutual adjustment of these growth rates and full utilization of production factors. Second, the model showed that the long-run economic growth rate was not determined by the capital input, which is characterized by decreasing marginal productivity (that is, the increments in output are increasingly smaller as the input rises),[7] but by drivers of factor productivity. It can hence be inferred that the recipe for development includes *effective* rather than *heavy* investment and innovation. This was confirmed by the growth accounting proposed by Solow (1957), who used 1909–49 data for the United States and broke down the growth rate into components attributable to— respectively— factor inputs and the increase in their productivity. Solow found that an increase in factor productivity is the key source of economic growth, even ignoring the fact that a large part (and on the balanced growth path—the whole) of any increase in capital input per person employed is driven by an increase in productivity—which in turn raises the return on investment.[8] Growth accounting in itself proved to be a very useful tool in empirical studies of economic growth.[9] We also use it in this book, although only to identify the causes of economic growth, mindful of the tool's limitations (to be discussed further).

The Swan-Solow model, as well as subsequent generations of neoclassical models, while emphasizing the significance of productivity gains to economic growth, did not indicate the source of those gains. They assumed that technological progress was exogenous. Hence, the forces determining longer-term economic growth were not explained by these models. They attached no material role to economic policy,[10] only inferring that policy makers should strive to ensure a high savings rate[11] and a high level of education in society (see, for example, Mankiw, Romer, and Weil 1992). Most often, however, they did not indicate how these goals were to be achieved. At the same time, it followed from the models that whether these goals were achieved or not had only a passing influence on the economy, and one that materialized slowly. Both the passing character and the slow emergence of the influence were related to the same point: economic policy could only influence the capital input (physical or human), the growth of which, given the prevailing technology, would lead to increasingly smaller output increments. Capital formation requires time, whereas factor productivity requires growth—and the only thing that could drive economic growth infinitely while undergoing substantial changes in the short run was assumed by proponents of the neoclassical models to be *a priori* and thus outside the scope of economic policy influence.

The neoclassical models also implied conditional convergence (that is, faster economic growth in countries with low per capita income versus more developed countries) under the assumption that the only difference between both types of countries is per capita income and capital. Controversies around the issue of convergence in developed countries (see, for example, Baumol 1986; Baumol and Wolff 1988; De Long 1988) prompted researchers to compile comparable national accounts data for a large group of countries over a long period. The effort laid down by, among others, Summers and Heston (1991) in the creation of such time series enabled the development of empirical research into economic growth. Updated figures collected by Summers and Heston (1991) are also used in this book.

Proponents of the neoclassical models pointed to a convergence mechanism: the higher marginal productivity of capital in the poorer countries, which they attributed to the smaller amount of capital relative to the number of employees in those countries. Assuming instant adoption of the latest technologies around the world, including the poorer countries, those models excluded from their scope of interest the differences in technology advancement between the richer and poorer countries and—in effect—the significance of reducing these differences through technology transfer. Yet differences in openness to imports of technology and in the capacity to use them are the most important factors explaining the diversity of growth rates in poorer countries (see, for example, Gomułka 2008). In the scenario that identical technologies were applied in all countries, differences in the marginal productivity of capital between countries with a high and low per capita income strayed far from those observed in reality.[12] Differences as large as those indicated in the models should trigger flows of capital (both physical and human) from the richer to the poorer countries, whereas in reality these are limited and tend to run in the opposite direction. The fallacy of the assumption that the same technology is used by all countries has also been confirmed when neoclassical growth models were calibrated to data from many countries. Such approach showed that the differences in per capita income mainly result from differences in the technology applied and not in the inputs of production factors.[13]

Discrepancies between the assumptions and findings of the neoclassical models on the one hand and well-documented facts on the other have contributed to the creation of endogenous[14] growth theory (Romer 1994), in the process reviving economists' interest in economic growth. Under the theory, an increase in factor productivity—the source of long-run economic growth—is not assumed, but is modeled. The first models of this kind were created in the 1960s and 1970s—see, for example, the studies by Arrow (1962); Frankel (1962); Uzawa (1964, 1965); Nelson and Phelps (1966); Nordhaus (1969); Gomułka (1970);

and Nelson and Winter (1982). Yet, a strong impulse for their development arrived later. It was provided by the work of Romer (1986, 1987, 1990), Lucas (1988), Grossman and Helpman (1991), as well as Aghion and Howitt (1992).[15] According to the models explored in these studies, factor productivity growth is either a by-product of productive activity (acquisition of knowledge through practice) and human capital formation, or of profit-oriented, targeted research and development (R&D) activity. This activity can increase the variety of intermediate goods, thus offsetting the impact of the decreasing marginal productivity of a single production factor. It can also result in an expanded range of final goods, raising the utility households derive from their consumption. Finally, it can introduce new, more productive generations of intermediate goods, owing to which final goods can be manufactured at a lower cost than their earlier generations (and squeeze those earlier generations out of the market). Factor productivity growth, contingent on the profitability of, respectively, production activity, human capital formation, or dedicated R&D activity becomes—regardless of the source assumed in the model—susceptible to the influence of economic incentives. This proposition is in line with many earlier empirical studies of technical progress.

The responsiveness of productivity-boosting actions to economic incentives observed in endogenous growth models confers a much greater significance on economic policy than is done under the neoclassical models. Policy can influence not only the level of per capita income in the long run, but also its pace of growth (see, for example, Temple 2003 or Easterly 2005).[16] A greater number of channels through which economic policy influences growth under the endogenous growth models versus the neoclassical ones justifies extending the analysis of its impact beyond any influence on the saving rate or human capital formation rate (see, for example, Shaw 1992; Sala-i-Martin 2002).[17] Generally speaking, the scope of possible applications of the new growth theory models is much broader than that of neoclassical models.[18] For example, introducing externalities to such models potentially explains the direction of capital flows between countries and the differences in remuneration that cause those flows. If new technologies are developed only in selected countries, and in effect only the conditions observed in those countries are taken into account (for example, surrounding capital stock), differences may arise in the effectiveness of applying the same technology in different countries (see, for example, Basu and Weil 1998). Meanwhile, specialization increases in significance (see, for example, Young 1991). Extending the analysis to more than one sector allows us to look into structural changes in the economy, which are driven by the changing structure of demand as per capita income increases (see, for example, Kongsamut, Rebelo, and Xie 2001 or Matsuyama 2002) and by productivity growth differences in individual sectors of the economy (see, for example, Acemoglu and Guerrieri 2008). Assuming the possibility that some types of activity might result in increasing returns to scale helps explain the potentially positive impact of financial sector development on an economy (see, for example, Acemoglu and Zilibotti 1997). But increasing returns of scale in some industries may also result in a poverty trap;

that is, they may become a self-reinforcing mechanism preventing a country from utilizing modern technologies, and, in consequence, plunging it into stagnation at low-income levels (see, for example, Durlauf 1993). Exceeding the assumption of perfect competition, which is the condition for profitable research activity when its result—the knowledge of how to manufacture more efficiently—is of nonrival nature, allows one to analyze[19] the significance of the intensity of competition to the rate of economic growth (see, for example, Aghion and others 2005).[20] It is also a *sui generis* return to the roots of economics. Economists such as Adam Smith (1776 [2007]) emphasized "market imperfections" interpreted in a modern manner, that is, as any departure from the assumption of perfect competition. They did not claim that all consumers and businesses have access to perfect information or that benefits from a given type of activity are accrued in their entirety to the persons who undertake it, or that there are no differences in the features of the goods created by different entrepreneurs, or that all entrepreneurs are price takers.

Yet, in endogenous growth models—as in neoclassical models—nonzero and nonexplosive long-term growth rates are obtained practically only under the assumption that any increase in a selected variable that determines factor productivity growth in a unit of time depends—in a linear manner—on the level of that variable (see, for example, Jones 2005). This assumption follows from the construction of growth models, both of which require that—at least in the long run—the product be characterized by a 1-for-1 elasticity with respect to this variable, that is, that it should grow at the same pace. If this elasticity were less than 1, growth would gradually disappear; if, on the other hand, it exceeded unity by even a small margin, the rate would accelerate from one period to another. The strictness of this assumption hampered the development of endogenous growth models for a long time, in spite of the fact that the first models of this kind came about—as we have already mentioned—back in the 1960s (see Jones 2005). The development of endogenous models took off only after researchers had stopped attaching so much weight to this assumption.

A vast majority of both neoclassical and endogenous growth models refer exclusively to the shallow causes of growth rate diversification, that is, to differences in employment levels, the rate of formation of various kinds of capital, and the technical progress as well as efficiency of use of factors of production (studies such as those by Parente and Prescott 2000 or Acemoglu, Antras, and Helpman 2007 are an exception rather than the rule). Under both types of models, those shallow causes are most often determined exclusively by the assumed shape of the households' utility function and the production function(s), along with the value of their parameters, which in themselves require explanation. Even though these models are employed to analyze the consequences of various economic policies, these policies tend to be narrowly defined (as certain types of taxes or public expenditures), without addressing the problem of what determines the shape of a certain policy. Models of both types are in principle totally ahistorical.[21] The elements (for example, market structures) whose changes in reality exert a huge influence upon economic performance are merely assumed in these models and thus, not depending on anything, remain constant. Finally, it is not quite clear which countries' growth can be analyzed on this basis. Yet a mere glance at the assumptions tells us that, for example, a centrally planned economy does not conform with them. Consequently, such an economy should not be analyzed with these models. But by the same token we could eliminate subsequent groups of countries. If one wishes to apply these models to examine growth in a large number of countries, it has to be accepted that the basic assumptions of the model are incompatible with the reality observed in those countries. Such a broad application would be tantamount to assuming something rather dubious: that all economies are alike, irrespective of, for example, the socioeconomic system. The significance of the socioeconomic system to economic performance cannot thus be assessed with growth models alone.

A sensitivity analysis would require going beyond the shallow determinants of growth and looking into deeper-lying reasons, in particular institutions (more on the concept of institutions to follow). Attempts to analyze how relevant conditions affect economic growth are made within other research strands. Two contrasting approaches to the issue can be discerned: a free market and a statist one (Balcerowicz 2006).

The free market approach goes back to Adam Smith and classical economics. This book also subscribes to this tradition. Smith (1776 [2007]) emphasized the beneficial effect of market competition—one of the consequences of economic freedom—on development. On the other hand, he was critical of monopolies. He pointed to the "unproductive" nature of the public sector and was skeptical about state regulation of the economy. Smiths' principal observations can also be traced in the work of his successors, including Mill (1909), according to whom the despotism of the state, including predatory or arbitrary taxation, poses a far greater threat to the growth of nations than almost any degree of lawlessness or other turbulence in the "freedom system."

In the statist approach, the free market is considered to be a fundamental obstacle to the path to economic growth. As a consequence, anti-market state interventionism is seen as the key to development. Mercantilists, heavily criticized by Adam Smith, subscribed to this line of reasoning, but its best-known and somewhat paradoxical proponent was Karl Marx. Despite appreciating the technical dynamism of capitalism, he augured its decline, pointing to, among other things, the destructive role of "production anarchy"—that is, market competition. Marx's key recommendation has been embodied in the centrally planned economy. According to North (1998, 100–1) it is a particular irony that Marx, who was the first to point to the need to make changes in the structure of societies in order to utilize the potential of new technology, is responsible for the emergence of economies that failed exactly in this respect. Statist leanings, if not that obvious, can also be seen in Schumpeter's work. He proposed that certain incentives for entrepreneurship may function under noncapitalist systems, and the capitalistic profit motive can be substituted by other incentives (Schumpeter 1934 [1983]). Later, he went even further, claiming that industry managers in socialism could be instructed to produce in the most economical manner possible.

According to him, in effect, "in the socialist order, every improvement could theoretically be spread by decree and substandard practice could be promptly eliminated" (Schumpeter 1942 [1962], 196).

The influence of the statist approach, both in research and economic practice, increased together with the rising popularity of the view that interwar economic growth in the Soviet Union on the one hand, and the 1930s Great Depression in capitalist countries on the other, proved the superiority of wide-scale state intervention over the free market. Its impact started to weaken as anti-market systems' spectacular failure to stimulate growth became increasingly apparent, particularly following the crisis, and subsequently the decline of socialism in the Soviet Union and the countries of Central, Eastern, and Southern Europe.

Natural experiments involving the introduction of diametrically different institutional systems in countries such as the Federal Republic of Germany and the German Democratic Republic or North and South Korea showed that institutions are of key significance to growth. The shift toward analyzing institutional variables occurred on the grounds of such research trends as the analysis of property rights (Furubotn and Pejovich 1972; Alchian 1977), the public choice theory (Niskanen 1971; Buchanan 1989; Tullock 1998), constitutional economics (Hayek 1960; Buchanan 1989), the pressure group theory (Olson 1965; Becker 1985), and economic history (North 1998).

Growth models have started to be used to analyze effects of some institutions on growth. Those institutions include, among others, regulations undermining competition by restricting the ways in which a given technology can be applied on the one hand, and the very choice of this technology on the other (Parente and Prescott 2000); another area examined is contract viability (Acemoglu, Antras, and Helpman 2007). Such studies can be seen as an important step toward analyzing economic growth. In practice, however, their analysis boils down to examining, within the framework of growth models, the impact of taxation that reduces investment profitability (or other productive activity). The assessment of that impact depends—as we have already mentioned—on whether neoclassical or endogenous growth models have been applied and how the parameters have been calibrated. There is no agreement among economists on which of the two groups of models offers a better fit with reality, or what values should be ascribed to the parameters of fundamental importance to the outcome. Arbitrary decisions are practically inevitable, especially with respect to the parameters describing institutions. Thus, even under one and the same model there is no convincing manner in which to rank institutions by their importance to growth. Studies of the topic, while taking advantage of quantitative methods, are far from being capable of quantitatively determining the role of a particular institution. They can, however, be helpful in interpreting the findings obtained through other methods (for example, they may help prove that the sign of the correlation need not correspond with the direction of the relationship between the variables). They should also be used more widely in constructing econometric models (further examined in this section).

Puzzles of Economic Growth • http://dx.doi.org/10.1596/978-1-4648-0325-3

In the early empirical research on the impact of institutions on economic growth, econometrics was applied on a restricted scale. In the first estimated equations, looking at a large number of potential sources of economic growth, it is hard to find any—narrowly understood—institutional variables (see, for example, Kormendi and Meguire 1985; Barro 1989, 1991; Levine and Renelt 1992; Barro and Lee 1993). They did, however, take account of variables related to institutions (such as the fiscal deficit, various public expenditure items, economic openness indices, the difference between the black market and official currency exchange rate, lending growth, political instability, and wars).

Institutional variables were first introduced into estimated equations in the mid-1990s (see, for example, Knack and Keefer 1995; Mauro 1995; Barro 1996; Keefer and Knack 1997; Ayal and Karras 1998; Hall and Jones 1999; Chong and Calderon 2000; Acemoglu, Johnson, and Robinson 2001; McArthur and Sachs 2001; Acemoglu and Johnson 2005). This progress in research, involving a look at the deeper-lying determinants of growth, was related to the creation of measures of institutional variables and databases on this subject. Initially, this research drew on the data published by the Political Risk Service, a private firm providing assessment of investment expropriation risk in various countries. Subsequently, other measures were created, among them those constructed by the Fraser Institute (Economic Freedom of the World Index—published since 1996), the Heritage Foundation (Index of Economic Freedom—calculated since 1995), the European Bank for Reconstruction and Development (the EBRD Transition Indicators—presented for the first time in 1994), and the World Bank (the Governance Matters and Doing Business measures—published since 1999 and 2003, respectively). Overall, there are over 30 organizations busy gauging differences between institutions around the world (Kaufmann, Kraay, and Mastruzzi 2008). The indices they have developed, despite many shortcomings (discussed below), have enabled considerable progress on the path to identifying and determining the impact of the deeper-lying determinants of growth. They are also employed in this book.

The weaknesses of these measures involve, in the first place, the fact that what is taken into account in their construction is often not the shape of a given type of institution itself—since this is difficult to quantify—but its easily quantifiable effects. This may render biased findings when applied in empirical research, reflecting the subjective judgment of the constructors of the various institutional indices rather than actual impact of institutions on growth. Second, these measures offer little analysis of institutional changes over time. Their time series are generally short, whereas institutional changes in most countries occur rarely and over an extended period of time. Even where measures date back to periods preceding the start of the indices' publication, the comparability of data is limited—among other reasons, on account of the differences between the sets of variables used to determine the index readings in a given year (see the sub-indices of the Fraser Institute). Some indices are changed only in one direction, which, given their upper limits, results in increasingly smaller increments (for example, the EBRD indices). In studies taking account of the time dimension this property may result in a spurious regression (Rzońca and Ciżkowicz 2003). Some indices, owing to their annual standardization (for example, Governance Matters) exclusively allow an assessment of the relative changes in the quality of the institutions versus the sample mean. Third, cross-country comparisons are complicated by the arbitrariness of the scales applied in measuring institutional quality. By making such comparisons, we can ascertain whether the quality of a particular institution differs significantly across individual countries; what we cannot determine precisely is the extent of the differences. As a result, the indices may help resolve whether certain institutions increase differences in economic performance across countries, but they do not clarify the specific institutional changes needed to improve a country's performance. Fourth, the complexity of most indices makes it difficult to determine what they actually measure. As a consequence, if empirical research distinguishes various kinds of institutions at all, the distinction tends to be very general. Such broadly defined indexes allow to show that institutions affect growth, but are too general to analyze effects of particular institutions. On the other hand, some indices identify the measured area precisely (for example, those comprised by Doing Business). In this case however, the problem lies in the too narrowly delineated area to be measured, which does not necessarily reflect the quality of the institutions in a country.

The weaknesses of institutional variable measures should be seen in perspective. Measurement difficulties are not restricted to these variables alone. To a similar degree they apply to the measures of shallow economic growth determinants. In most countries, the stock of physical capital—not services rendered—is estimated. In addition, the estimation is done in a mechanical manner using two simple formulae and data on the share of investment in GDP and GDP itself. Thus, not only are intertemporal differences in the quality of capital goods ignored, but so are differences in how investment projects are implemented (economical, or, on the contrary, wasteful); an arbitrary assumption is adopted for the capital depreciation rate—that is, the portion used up in a unit of time (assumed to not vary either across periods or countries)—and for the initial stock of capital.[22] Finally, the very data on the share of investment in GDP and GDP itself used in the estimates are, for most countries, affected by measurement bias, as evidenced by disparities between databases sponsored by various agencies, as well as subsequent versions of the same databases (see, for example, the chapter on Estonia and Slovenia). In the case of human capital, there is no consensus on how it should be approximated (data typically used involve the percentage of the population of productive age who have completed secondary education, the average number of years of formal education completed by persons of 25 years of age or more, life expectancy, average daily intake of calories, and so on). The following differences are usually not taken into account: the quality of formal education between countries[23] and over time; the level of education, lifestyle, and access to health care of both the employed and unemployed; the intensity and quality of extracurricular education; the age structure of the productive-age population, and so on. These weaknesses show that research focused on shallow drivers of growth has not yet exhausted its potential. Yet progress—both in the intellectual and practical sense—should be sought, above all, in the analysis of growth's deeper-lying determinants.

The sign that precedes the institutional variables (and those variables related to institutions)—reflecting the direction of their influence and their statistical significance—has usually been as expected. But in cases where these variables were tested for robustness to changes in the specification of the estimated equation (see, for example, Levine and Renelt 1992; Sala-i-Martin 1997; Doppelhofer, Miller, and Sala-i-Martin 2000; Kalaitzidakis, Mamuneas, and Stengos 2000), they failed to be robust, whether wholly or in part (depending on the particular study).[24]

Poor robustness of the estimates of effects of institutions on growth indicates, on the one hand, the need for a wider application of the theories and findings of other studies while specifying the estimated equations, and on the other, the shortcomings of theory. Theory suggests which mechanisms are potentially responsible for economic growth, but this is not sufficient to build structural models whose choice of explanatory variables reflect the deeper-lying conditions for that growth. There is no agreement among economists on the variables' channels of influence—or even on the list of variables themselves. As a consequence, both shallow determinants of growth and variables approximating deeper-lying causes are introduced into the model.[25] Even if those deep causes were fully independent of one another, and economists had perfect tools for measuring them—as each influences growth through shallow determinants but not necessarily the same ones, and practically never with the same impact as others—the outcomes might not be robust to changes in the specification of estimated equations. If, on the other hand, we take into account only the variables meant to reflect the deeper-lying growth drivers in the estimated equations, we run the risk of replacing the variables that have a better-documented impact on growth[26] and a longer measurement history with variables only spuriously related to growth or subject to greater measurement bias. Moreover, even if the variables used in the estimation of the model accurately reflected some of the deep-growth drivers and were, additionally, free from significant measurement bias, they would not necessarily fully capture the significance to growth of at least some of its shallow determinants. Thus, their inclusion in the estimated equation may not provide ground for exclusion of the shallow determinants.

Using econometrics to study the factors of economic growth—whether shallow or deep—also entails other problems: the dependence of the explanatory variables not only on one another but also on the explained variable, changes in both the explained variable and the explanatory variables resulting from a third variable not included in the model, nonincidental gaps in the data (because of, for example, the fact that governments may be loath to publish data that could show them in a bad light), potentially nonlinear dependencies between the explained variable and the explanatory variables, the instability of these relationships over time, their diversification across countries, and so on.[27] The constant progress in econometrics mitigates the impact of these problems but is unable to eliminate them entirely—even as it proceeds to expose subsequent problems. As a result, the list of problems is becoming longer rather than shorter.[28]

Even if this list were becoming progressively shorter, the (traditionally understood) historical studies would continue to play a major role in the analysis of forces driving economic growth. Historical studies provide a large part of the information for further analysis with other tools.[29] They also provide many hypothesis to be later verified with the use of quantitative methods.

Empirical research into economic growth may also be categorized by the number of countries covered. Most studies of the issue provide either (a) an analysis of a broad range of countries, or (b) case studies focused on single countries.

The first approach enables us, thanks to the (relatively) large number of observations included, to apply quantitative analysis, and thus determine the importance (statistical significance and, at least, the direction of impact) of the selected determinants of economic growth. Those determinants may include institutional variables. Although measured only recently, the large number of countries, given differences in institutions across them, provide a sufficient range of observations. This approach can do much to further understanding causes of economic growth. However, it will necessarily be characterized by numerous weaknesses. In spite of the quantitative methods used, its ability to compare the relevance of various variables for growth is limited. Looking at the bulk of research done in this area, we see that a myriad variables of different natures have been included (for instance, Durlauf, Johnson, and Temple [2005] describe the findings of studies of a total of 145 variables, that is, a larger number of variables than countries covered by most studies—see Durlauf and Quah 1999). Yet, because of the limited availability of comparable data for the same groups of countries, and also because different variables are used—at least in part—to measure the same phenomena, only a small number of potential sources of growth are taken into account in a single study. Many such studies ignore the direction of causality. Those that include the time dimension or instrumental variables in their analysis estimate this direction but in a highly imperfect manner because of the reduced form of the estimated equations (and difficulties in finding the appropriate instrumental variable). Equally, this approach does not allow us to fully factor in the conditions specific to a given country (and in the case of cross-sectional studies it does not account for such conditions at all). Finally, research based on this approach is usually ahistorical in character. The passing of time, if it changes anything at all, changes only single parameters (meanwhile, it is assumed that a change in a given parameter occurred at the same moment in all the countries studied).

The second approach—case studies of specific countries—allows room for specific, historical knowledge on the sources of economic development and thus raises important questions for studies within the first approach. But given that the measures of potential growth determinants are usually limited—both in time and scope—case studies tend to take on a descriptive character that makes it difficult to determine the significance of any one factor. If, on the other hand, analysis based on this approach is quantitative, it is restricted to only a few potential determinants of growth over a short time period. Thus, it only provides a fragmentary picture of the sources of economic growth. Institutional arrangements tend to be overlooked in this context, because (a) attempts to measure the quality of institutions are recent (b) changes are often imperceptible over the short periods for which data are available. These problems can be circumvented by underpinning research with sector- and firm-level data. But this solution entails the many challenges of data aggregation (for example, the conclusions obtained may not necessarily lend themselves to generalizations at the all-economy level), as well as those typical of the first approach.

In the present study, we apply a third method: a comparative study of specially selected pairs of countries. Owing to this we will be able, as we explain in the next section, to avoid some of the shortcomings listed earlier.

Research Methods Applied in This Volume

The research basis of this book has three features that set it apart from the vast majority of empirical studies of economic growth. It is our conviction that these distinguishing features allow a better determination of the deeper-lying determinants of growth.

First, as has already been mentioned, the studies presented in this book consider, among potential determinants of growth, both shocks and sustained growth drivers. They also attempt to determine the relative significance of growth collapses to long-term growth.

Second, sustained growth drivers are analyzed at two levels. First, wherever it is reasonable, growth accounting is conducted to determine the relative significance of labor and capital inputs and the change in factor productivity. Next, an attempt is made to explain the levels of these magnitudes by referring to the deeper-lying forces—in particular, institutions.

Third—and this in particular makes the present book different from the vast majority of work devoted to economic growth—the studies herein compare specially selected pairs of countries. In each pair, income per capita was equal or very similar at a certain point in time, to subsequently diverge in a very visible manner.[30] Our study examines the periods during which the differences in the growth rate—and, in effect, in the per capita income—emerged in: Australia and New Zealand, Austria and Switzerland, Estonia and Slovenia, Mexico and Spain, Chile and República Bolivariana de Venezuela, Haiti and the Dominican Republic, Puerto Rico and Costa Rica, China and India, and Indonesia and Pakistan. A comparative analysis of countries paired in this manner has allowed us to eliminate many factors that may appear to be significant determinants of growth when only a single country is analyzed, but in fact are not.[31] The majority of paired countries had—at least at the starting point—possibly a lot of similarities, especially in terms of factors that are difficult to measure, such as culture. At the same time, the whole sample is sufficiently diverse to afford certain generalizations regarding the key determinants of long-run per capita income growth. The study countries are: large and small, insular and landlocked, rich in natural resources and deprived of them, inhabited by followers of all major religions, situated on all continents but Africa,[32] with aging as well as young populations who are highly educated and not, characterized by low and high income per capita.

Each chapter has three parts. In the first, the long-run growth path of per capita income is analyzed and two questions asked:

- Whether the countries under review have experienced periods of collapses in their economic growth.
- To what extent these potential downturns account for the differences in the per capita income of both countries.

Next, for the periods during which no deeper downturns occurred, a typical growth accounting calculation is conducted. In contrast to past practice, we have deemed it pointless to conduct it for economic downturns as this procedure implicitly refers to sustained growth drivers. During economic collapses, on the other hand, there are other forces at play—such as those linked to a sharp slump in the terms of trade, a considerable fall in external demand, a collapse in domestic demand, and so on. Besides, the outcomes of growth accounting—applied to periods of economic downturn—can be easily predicted; inputs of labor and capital are naturally characterized by low variability, so the collapse must be reflected mainly in sinking levels of factor productivity. Yet, this obvious fact does not add to our knowledge of the deeper causes of the collapse, or—even worse—it may erroneously suggest the need to seek the causes among the sustained growth drivers, not the shocks.[33]

In some chapters, growth accounting has been supplemented by two kinds of analysis:

- In cases where growth accounting indicated that employment changes had a material impact on the pace of economic growth, it was attempted—depending on the availability of suitable data—to break these changes down into components resulting from changes in (a) the portion of the total population that is of productive age and (b) the ratio of working persons to the productive-age population. It was assumed that the first change results from demographic factors (which the state can directly influence almost exclusively through changes in the retirement age); the second, from other factors (analyzed in the second part of each chapter).

- To identify the sources of (and barriers to) productivity growth, labor productivity and its changes in various sectors of the economy have been compared, as well as changes in the shares of these sectors in total employment. Such analysis helped, firstly, identify those sectors with a positive (or impeding) effect on the economy and secondly, determine mobility of production factors in sectors characterized by different efficiency of their use.

The latter part of each chapter describes deeper causes of the different levels of per capita income in the respective pairs of countries, including the institutional solutions in place and the related manner in which economic policy is conducted.

In cases where differences in income were found to result from variation in the depth or frequency of collapses in economic growth, attempts were made to identify the sources of those collapses and the causes of their depth in one of the countries, as well as to determine why the other country was capable of avoiding such (deep) collapses. To this end, the following was assessed for each country:

- Shocks independent of the economic policy adopted—such as, on the one hand, a sharp drop in terms of trade, a dramatic decline in external demand for goods produced, a sudden and large increase in interest rates in international financial markets, or in risk aversion among investors, and, on the other hand, natural disasters and political coups.
- Shocks caused by economic policy, including, in particular, fiscal and monetary policy implemented in the country.

Furthermore, the following was examined:

- How the country was prepared for the occurrence of a given shock.
- How, in response to the shock, it adjusted its economic policy—that is, how it went about managing the crisis, and what sort of conditions for growth it created following the crisis.

To the extent in which the differences in the growth rate for the entire period examined were not determined by the crisis years, but by growth rate differences in the periods that were relatively stable in both countries, growth accounting is carried out and the latter part of the respective chapters is devoted to seeking factors underlying growth accounting results. Depending on those outcomes, the authors depend on barriers to both employment and investment growth and the effective use of production factors as well as technical progress.

Each chapter concludes with key findings of the analysis. The most important of these are also presented in the last chapter of the book.

Conceptual and Analytical Framework

As presented in this book, the study of economic growth, its breakdowns, and periods of relative stability is based on a clear conceptual and analytical framework (Balcerowicz 2006, 2008), the key elements of which are depicted in figure 1.1.

In economic literature, the terms *institutions* and *economic policy* crop up frequently, yet their definitions vary depending on the author. In the present study, they are of central importance and, considering the diverse definitions adopted in the literature, need to be specified.

Institutions are understood to be any intangible and relatively lasting factors external to a person and capable of influencing behavior (Balcerowicz 1995);

Figure 1.1 Determinants of Short-Term Growth

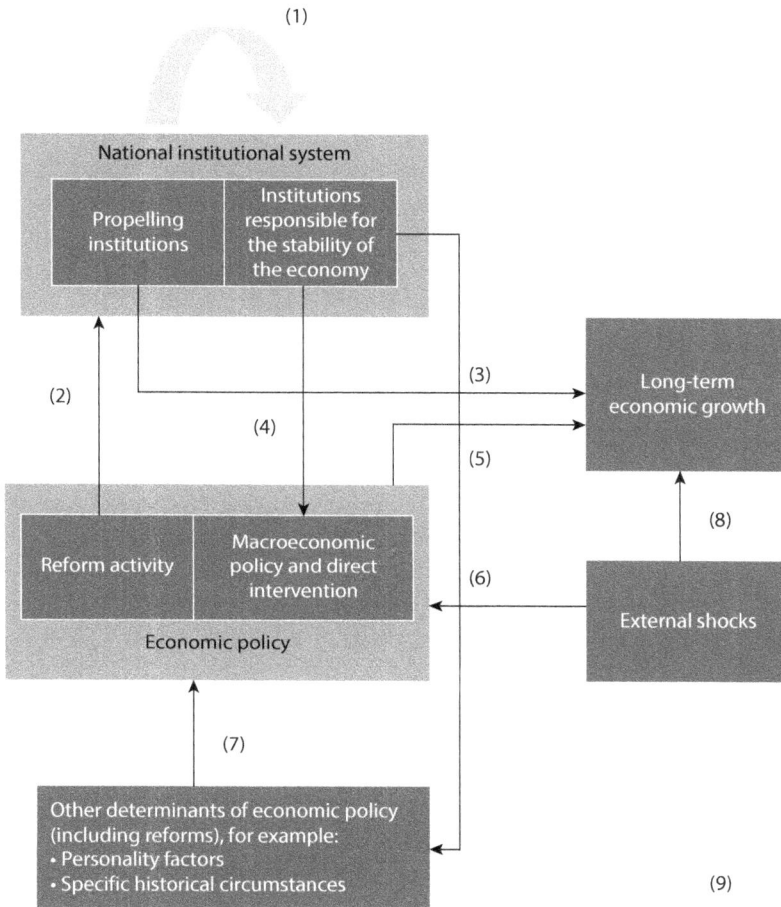

Source: Based on the argument presented in Balcerowicz (2008).

a similar definition can be found in Greif (2006). Institutions shape people's actions, and in particular their interactions (transactions); sufficiently large differences or changes in institutions cause large differences in those activities and interactions, and in effect, in economic performance.[34]

Institutions are usually divided into formal ones, that is, those connected with the existence of the state and considered "official," and informal ones, that is, those existing independent of the state. The latter are various social norms as well as groups and networks of links between people (for example, the caste system in India). Informal institutions are roughly identical to culture, narrowly defined. In this book, we focus on formal institutions in the analyzed countries and their effects on people's behavior.[35]

By international policy we mean all activities—undertaken by individuals vested with political power—that have an impact on the economy, including its stability and growth. In contrast to many earlier studies,[36] we do not include variables such as the exchange rate regime or the degree of domestic market protection. According to our definition, these and similar factors fall under a country's institutional system. They are, beyond doubt, intangible factors—defined by the rules of play in a given area of economic life.

Within economic policy, we focus on reform activity: that is, any activity undertaken by persons with political power that changes—for better or worse—any parts or aspects of the national institutional system. Key examples involve (a) liberalization, or the removal of legal and administrative constraints to economic freedom, and (b) privatization, or a change in the ownership structure of businesses such that persons and organizations directly benefiting from political power are replaced by persons not directly benefiting from this power. Yet, reforms also comprise changes in the opposite direction—toward regulation and nationalization.

Reforms may—depending on their direction, extent, and temporal structure—trigger two kinds of growth mechanisms (Balcerowicz 2008).

The first one is the special mechanisms of growth, whose availability depends on the starting conditions, and which expire after a period of time—sometimes a long one. Examples are accelerated growth in the post-socialist countries resulting partly from the removal of all-pervading wastefulness typical of central planning or from the expansion of sectors whose development was previously blocked. Owing to these particular mechanisms, economic growth can accelerate even at the early stage of reform, that is, before the institutional system has attained its final shape.[37]

The other mechanism is innovation-based growth (including technology transfers from abroad). In contrast to others, this is a potentially universal and lasting mechanism. But in order for it to function, reform activity must give the institutional system a proper shape (arrow 3), that is, remove any barriers to growth driven by innovation or other factors. Meanwhile, reforms that remove institutional barriers to innovation-based growth also trigger some special growth mechanisms. These two can add up to exceptionally quick growth in the early stages.

We give both mechanisms and barriers to growth a much more detailed treatment in chapter 2.

The remaining elements of economic policy are mainly macroeconomic in nature—fiscal, monetary, and, under a managed system, the exchange rate policy—as well as financial supervision. These elements determine the extent of economic imbalance and its changes, which may have a bearing on long-term growth (arrow 5). Under systems characterized by state intervention, policy may include direct decisions by the country's authorities allotting investment funds (and, sometimes, funds intended to finance current needs of the economy) to specific areas and applications. Direct intervention naturally also influences fiscal policy and, more broadly, macroeconomic policy.

It is obvious that the relative significance of both reform activity and economic policy in general depends greatly on the institutional system. Under a stable system with extensive economic freedom (as that under the metal-based monetary regime prevailing in the latter half of the 19th century in, among others, Great Britain), economic policy was chiefly reduced to fiscal policy, which, in turn, was subject to the informal but very deeply ingrained doctrine of the balanced budget. The role of top-down reforms was limited (arrow 2 in figure 1.1). On the other hand, extensive economic freedom created ample space for bottom-up institutional innovations: the new organizational structures of enterprises and new forms of contracts (see arrow 1). The limited scope of economic policy and the capability to generate bottom-up institutional innovation is a property of systems characterized by individual freedom. Under a centrally planned economy, the emphasis was, not surprisingly, on direct intervention in the command form, amid a lack of reforms. Macroeconomic policy, exposed to direct allocation decisions by the state could, as experience shows, vary widely: from utter chaos (as in Poland in the 1970s) to relative macroeconomic stability (as in the former Czechoslovakia). Finally, economic policy in the post-socialist countries contained a very large reform component (which comprised the dismantling of direct intervention) and stabilizing macroeconomic policy.

While attempting to account for economic growth, its collapses, and periods of relative stability, this books also distinguishes two types of national institutional systems (Balcerowicz 2008):

- Those that largely determine the economy's susceptibility and resilience to shocks (institutions responsible for the stability of the economy).
- Those that mainly influence the intensity of sustained growth drivers (propelling institutions).

The institutions responsible for the stability of the economy influence the shape of macroeconomic policy (arrow 4, which, in combination with direct state intervention exacerbates or mitigates [arrow 5] the effects of external shocks on long-term growth [arrow 8]). The destabilizing or stabilizing character of this policy depends on the interaction between the force of the institutions responsible for growth and other factors, including the personality and skills of the people in power, as well as the economic doctrines accepted in scientific circles and the practice of economic policy.[38] Well-developed institutions responsible for stability are not always capable of preventing economic shocks, as the recent financial crisis in developed countries has shown.

The institutions responsible for the stability of the economy can be divided into shallow and deep ones. The shallow ones include:

- The financial and foreign exchange system, determining the stability of the currency as well as the exchange rate risk.
- Constraints on government expenditure and the public debt related to the risk of a financial crisis.
- Financial supervision and the admissible scope of self-discipline among financial markets, which influences financial institutions and the risk of a financial crisis.

Some variables may be considered related to both the institutions in charge of the stability of the economy and those that propel it. Bank ownership affects both risk and efficiency. State-owned banks are saddled with more bad debts (see, for example, World Bank 2001), since while granting loans they are more exposed to political pressures of all sorts (see, for example, the studies of Mexico, Indonesia, China, or India). Institutional rigidities in the labor market have an impact on both the adjustment of the economy to shocks and long-term unemployment and the speed with which innovations are introduced in the economy. Fiscal institutions impact the fiscal position of a country, which determines the risk of fiscal crises (see, for example, Mexico, Costa Rica, República Bolivariana de Venezuela, Pakistan, and India, which all experienced a fiscal crisis), but it also plays an important role among sustained growth drivers. The monetary and currency system helps decide the risk of galloping inflation, but may also induce a less spectacular price growth, which does not entail a crisis but undermines sustained growth drivers (see, for example, Fischer 1993 or Li and Zou 2002).

Besides, there are significant interdependencies among the variables linked to the institutions responsible for economic stability. For example, the development of the financial sector curbs the negative impact of procyclical macroeconomic policy (Aghion and others 2004), but is not possible in itself amid a policy conducive to macroeconomic imbalances such as inflation (see, for example, Boyd, Levine, and Smith 2001).

The shape and force of shallow institutions responsible for stability depends on key characteristics of the political system: whether it imposes constraints upon political power, and the nature of those constraints. When political authorities are not constrained in any way, these institutions must be very weak. Prudence—or, conversely—recklessness in economic policy is then a function of the personality traits of the rulers, and not impersonal institutional limitations (arrow 7; see, for example, the chapter on Pakistan and Indonesia in the section comparing macroeconomic policy of the two countries until the 1960s). Only if political power is limited is there space for institutions responsible for economic stability (see, for example, the segment on Indonesia concerning the balanced budget rule established by President Suharto). The degree to which this space is used for institutionalizing limitations on macroeconomic policy, or—to put it differently—their depolitization, depends on the history of a given country.[39]

The political system influences macroeconomic stability and, in effect, growth, not only by affecting the institutions in charge of economic stability, but also through other channels. Unrestrained political power attracts ambitious people, yet ones not necessarily equipped with high ethical standards (arrow 9). It may result in frequent shocks within the ruling bodies and ensuing economic turbulence (see the chapter on Haiti). Or, conversely, power may end up, for extended periods of time, in the hands of people conducting disastrous economic policy. Lenin and Stalin in the USSR, Hitler in Germany, Mao in China, Kim Ir Sen in the Democratic People's Republic of Korea, and Mugabe in Zimbabwe are shocking but scarcely isolated examples of this threat.

The division of political systems into those with limited versus unlimited political power is not identical with the division into democratic and undemocratic countries. Democracies with soft constitutional constraints may also be susceptible to irresponsible economic policies (for example, Chile under Allende; see also the studies of Costa Rica and República Bolivariana de Venezuela). But it must be added that economic shocks brought about by dictators have been far more damaging.

Institutional constraints on political power are thus a fundamental security feature protecting the public against reckless economic policy—by, on the one hand, reducing the risk of economic madness and, on the other, enabling the construction of specialized institutions responsible for the stability of the economy.[40] Such institutions are difficult to establish and yet more difficult to keep alive, even in countries with stable constitutional democracies.

Let us now proceed to discuss the propelling institutions, that is, those elements of a country's institutional system that determine the level of sustained growth drivers. In other words, these are institutions responsible for whether—disregarding periods of shocks—the economy is stagnant or expanding; and if it is expanding, at what pace (arrow 3). What kind of institutions are covered by this definition is a fundamental empirical question that will be dealt with in more detail in chapter 2 of this book. While referring readers to that chapter, we want to take this early opportunity to list the most important of those institutions:

- The structure of property rights—that is, whether private enterprise is allowed by law and the extent of regulatory and tax-related limitations to economic freedom.
- The level of property rights protection: whether state authorities guard or threaten property rights (as well as the life/health of citizens).
- The degree of competition between manufacturers, dependent in part on the structure and level of property rights protection and the extent of protectionist policies.
- The fiscal position of the state in the economy, defined as the relation of government expenditure and—in effect—taxes as well as the fiscal deficit to GDP.

The absence of sustained growth can be explained by the operation of systems in specific countries and periods, described in chapter 2, that have impeded innovation-driven growth. Naturally this in itself does not explain why such systems operated widely in Western Europe until modern times and why they have subsequently been so common in other regions of the world.

On the other hand, triggering growth based on innovation (and usually also on special mechanisms of growth) has in most cases required specific reforms. Almost every country has been affected, for longer or shorter period of time, by a system hostile to growth. Where the absence of sustained growth is the result of the stable operation of anti-development systems, releasing such growth involves their destabilization. That is, reforms remove institutional barriers to growth and replace them with key institutional factors that open the door to

Puzzles of Economic Growth • http://dx.doi.org/10.1596/978-1-4648-0325-3

constant innovation. Arrow 7 in figure 1.1 signals the dependence of those reforms being implemented (or not) on various forces, an issue handled by political economics of reforms and—more broadly—the study of institutional dynamics. We will revisit this issue in chapter 2.

In examining the relationships between propelling institutions and the pace of economic growth one must focus on variability in those institutions—and its consequences, including the implementation of specific reform packages. This is a more important focus than the static states of those institutions (that is, some kind of average of the institutions' initial or final state during the analyzed period). The subsequent chapters show that institutional variability was of major consequence to economic dynamics in the examined economies.

Notes

1. Moreover, by breaking up the extant structures, economic growth may lift persons out of low-income categories to higher ones in subsequent periods. This may also apply to their children. The scale of this upward movement depends on social mobility, which in turn fuels economic growth (see chapter 2).

2. Some economists observe that the weaker health statistics of poorer societies versus more affluent ones are a consequence rather than a cause of their poverty (see, for example, McArthur and Sachs 2001).

3. An argument against this proposition involves rising income inequality in the most developed countries, observed since the 1970s (see, for example, Bourguignon and Morrison 1992, as cited in Aghion and Howitt 1997). Yet this growing inequality can be explained with a similar logic, that is, by reference to productivity growth, which initially occurs in a small number of sectors and subsequently extends to other sectors.

4. It needs to be remembered, though, that a certain degree of inequality in incomes is necessary, because without it, fast economic growth would be impossible, leading to poverty shared by all. If all people earned the same income regardless of their contribution to aggregate output, there would be no incentive for effort. The size of the aggregate output in an economy depends on the effort each person contributes to its creation. Yet, the effort itself has a nonobservable magnitude, and hence one difficult to monitor directly (see, for example, Mirrlees 1971).

5. For example, practically only one chapter out of the 28 in a study edited by Aghion and Durlauf (2005), which presents an overview of the key trends in economic growth research, deals with the influence of shocks on growth.

6. In some models, capital is given a narrow meaning—machinery, the factory floor, that is, human-produced goods utilized in manufacturing other goods. In other models, the concept is defined more broadly and includes, besides physical capital, also human capital (that is, the knowledge and skills employees apply in the generation of goods) as well as employees' health, attitude, and so on (that is, anything that is not material but helps boost labor productivity).

7. The decreasing marginal productivity of capital can be explained in the following manner. If, for example, we equip someone with a spade, the length of the ditch he or she is able to dig will increase dramatically over what is possible using only bare hands. If we add another spade, the possible ditch length will increase again, because the digger can use the second spade when the first has gone blunt. Yet the increment

of increase will be far smaller. If the digger is given a tenth or a hundredth spade, the distance dug will no longer increase (it might actually decrease, as the digger will now be saddled with the obligation of looking after and maintaining the spades).

8. According to Solow, factor productivity growth accounted for 87.5 percent of the increase in output growth per unit of labor in the United States in 1909–49, while the increase in the capital input per unit of labor, accounted for 12.5 percent of this growth. Improvement in the methods of measuring the input of production factors considerably reduced the significance of increases in their productivity as the source of economic growth—a role ascribed by growth accounting—yet only to the extent that the productivity increase was independent of the size of the factor inputs (see, for example, Jorgenson and Griliches 1967, according to whom productivity accounted for as little as 3.3 percent of output growth in the United States in 1945–65). When considered as a whole, the proposition that factor productivity growth—without distinguishing whether it was independent of factor inputs or whether such inputs were required—is of crucial significance to economic growth remains valid. It is worth pointing out at this stage that the very same Solow (1957, 316) admitted that "obviously much, perhaps nearly all, innovation must be embodied in new plant and equipment to be realized at all."

9. For example, the part of the study by Aghion and Durlauf (2005) dealing with empirical studies of economic growth devotes more space to growth accounting than to econometric studies, in spite of the latter including more variables explanatory of economic growth, with the qualifying parameters not assumed but resulting from calculations aimed at achieving a smallest possible difference between the model results and the real data on growth. At least to some extent, this results from the fact that the theory of growth, to which the study edited by Aghion and Durlauf (2005) is devoted, focuses on shallow determinants of economic growth rather than root causes (to be discussed further in this chapter).

10. Besides, the treatment of economic policy under these models is extremely simplified. Most frequently it is stripped down to a selected type of tax or public spending on a specific purpose.

11. The savings rate should not, however, be too high—that is, at a level triggering investment so large that its marginal productivity should fall short of the rental cost of capital and its depreciation. In such conditions, raising income through investment would reduce the level of consumption. Neoclassical growth models, however, differ in their assessment of whether this so-called dynamic inefficiency is at all possible in a free market economy (see, on the one hand, the Diamond model [1965], which finds it possible, and on the other hand, the Ramsey [1928]-Cass [1965]-Koopmans [1965] model, which excludes such a possibility). Empirical research indicates that savings in a free market economy at a level causing dynamic inefficiency are a theoretical curiosity (see, for example, Abel and others [1989] or Romer [2000, 106], who summarizes the effects of the first work).

12. It follows from the Solow model that with the share of capital remuneration in output at 40 percent, the marginal product of capital in India—where per capita income is 15 times lower than in the United States—should be 58 times the level of the United States (Lucas 1990). Estimates of the real scale of differences in capital productivity across countries can be found, among others, in Caselli and Feyrer (2007).

13. Neoclassical models verified their observations of relationships in the economy mainly on the basis of U.S. data, reinforcing the inclination to focus on sustained drivers while ignoring the significance of shocks to growth. The United States is characterized by

an exceptionally stable economic growth rate (see, for example, Jones 1995). Yet in contrast with the aforementioned flaws, this one did not provide a stimulus for developing endogenous growth theory.

14. The term *endogenous growth* is meant to emphasize that growth is being explained within the model, thus highlighting the difference from the neoclassical models, where growth is the result of the operation of forces outside and not addressed by the model. In reality, in both categories of models, nonzero growth in the long run is the exclusive result of one and, in terms of mathematical notation, the same assumption (see further in this section).

15. It should noted, however, that many findings of such models also find no corroboration in empirical studies.

16. For this reason, and considering a far higher diversification in the poorer than well-developed countries (see, for example, Gomułka 2008), endogenous growth models seem potentially more useful in examining growth in the first group of countries, and neoclassical models in the other. In reality both endogenous growth models and neoclassical models are used more frequently to examine growth in the developed rather than the poorer countries.

17. But endogenous growth models do not differ much from the neoclassical ones in the way economic policy is modeled. Most often economic policy continues to be equated with a selected type of tax or specific public expenditure. The major difference between how it is portrayed in the two types of models is the greater number of potential forms of taxation and ways of spending public funds. Moreover, even though the conclusions are less trivial than in the neoclassical models (for example, spending more on activities which have a bearing on economic growth is not necessarily the best policy—see for example, Sala-i-Martin 2002), they are at the same time less consistent—they may vary considerably depending on the type of endogenous growth model, both justifying extensive state intervention and the lack thereof.

18. The term *new growth theory* has been used synonymously with the theory of endogenous growth. We have used it here, since in the works quoted factor productivity growth is not always (and need not be) endogenous by nature. In all of them, however, at least one assumption characteristic of the neoclassical growth theory has been waived (that of the absence of differences in the efficiency of technology use, constant returns to scale, perfect competition, and so on).

19. Yet, it continues to be far from perfect—see chapter 2.

20. Endogenous growth models, in which—let us say it again—changes in factor productivity are not assumed but modeled, have enabled us to gain more insight into the relationship between long-term growth and shocks than was possible using neoclassical models (see, for example, Kydland and Prescott 1982). According to the growth models, any shock ultimately affecting factor productivity has a lasting influence on output level. But without any additional interference, and amid the regularly recurring shocks characteristic of real-life economies, these models may render a negative relation between growth and shocks only when negative shocks are on average larger than positive. Yet, empirical studies show that such a negative relationship occurs also when this asymmetry is missing, and that asymmetry enhances this relationship only to a limited degree, if at all. In sum, although growth models, including endogenous growth models, do not allow us—without introducing additional assumptions—to accurately reflect the empirically significant dependence of long-term growth on shocks, this has failed to add significance to the research into this relationship so

crucially important in developing growth models (see footnote 5). More examples of applications of endogenous growth models can be found, for example, in Aghion and Howitt (1997) or Acemoglu (2009).

21. This does not mean that we do not see the progress that has been made in growth theory in this respect—for example, models have been constructed enabling the illustration of the fact that throughout most of the history of mankind, per capita income remained stable, to subsequently—in some countries—take off at a steep angle (for example, Galor and Weil 1999; Galor and Moav 2002; and Hansen and Prescott 2002; see also Galor 2005).

22. To be more precise—the arbitrary assumptions are about the long-term growth rate of income per unit of labor, the share of investment in output and the depreciation rate, that is, the parameters determining the steady-state capital-output ratio (see, for example, King and Levine 1994).

23. In this respect, labor poses an exception; see Hanushek and Kimko (2000). The measure adopted for the quality of human capital is students' scores in standardized international tests. Such a measure can be helpful in evaluating the quality of formal education in a given period, but it need not be directly linked to the quality of formal education in the past, and, in effect, the quality of formal education of the majority of the productive-age population.

24. It has to be noted, though, that these tests are so strict that they may exclude the true determinants of growth from the set of its explanatory variables (Hoover and Perez 2004; see also Durlauf, Johnson, and Temple 2005, 611–612).

25. Such construction of the equation was popularized by Barro (1989); hence it is often called the Barro equation (Durlauf, Johnson, and Temple 2005, 580–581).

26. This strong relationship can, however, reflect the problem of the endogenous character of shallow determinants of economic growth (if not necessarily in terms of statistics, then in terms of economics; see next paragraph).

27. Most of these problems are analyzed in, among others, Durlauf, Johnson, and Temple (2005).

28. This does not mean that econometrics has more weaknesses today than in the past. Owing to progress in this discipline, the situation is quite the contrary. Yet progress in econometrics has also consisted in discovering its subsequent limitations. In other words, all the current limitations to econometrics have existed before, yet not all of them were realized.

29. The study by Acemoglu, Johnson, and Robinson (2001), notwithstanding all the reservations voiced about it, may serve as an example of such a positive influence of historical research on econometrics-based research. These authors took the death rate observed among the first European settlers in the former European colonies as the instrumental variable to represent today's institutions in these areas.

30. In some cases the difference in the per capita income between the countries in the selected pair diminished notably in the period under review.

31. See, for example, Bergoeing and others (2002). While comparing Chile and Mexico, the authors challenge the explanations for Chile's sound economic performance and Mexico's poor performance prevailing in the literature.

32. The fact that African countries are not covered by the analysis does not mean that the principles of economics do not extend to the continent. Fast economic growth is also possible in Africa, which can be exemplified by Botswana—a country that in 1960

belonged among the poorest in the world, yet today boasts a per capita income on par with Poland.

33. Limited variability of labor and capital inputs is indicated by, among others, Kehoe and Prescott (2002). Yet—strangely—these authors find it surprising that during downturns it is mainly the statistical measure of factor productivity that breaks down.

34. According to another definition, institutions are "limitations generated by man which shape the interactions between people and influence stimuli of economic, political, or social character" (North 1998, 95). The set of factors that are isolated as "institutions" based on the first definition is similar to that distinguished by the other definition.

35. The institutional systems of various countries may have similar components, that is similar laws. This concerns, for example, the countries of the European Union. What can generally be considered as the common part of various countries' institutional systems is any international law that is reflected in a given country's law or directly binds its citizens or institutions.

36. A broad understanding of economic policy and a corresponding narrowing down of the scope of institutions may of course lead to an increase in the significance of the first variable to economic performance and a decrease in the significance of the other (see Glaeser and others 2004).

37. Another factor which may speed up growth at the early reform stages is the expectations of enterprises of a further improvement in the business environment. Therefore, it is crucially important for the pace of economic growth to maintain a clear direction of reform while these are being implemented.

38. So, for example, how Keynesian doctrine contributed to the 1970s stagflation in Western Europe. The doctrine—attributed to Greenspan—of nonintervention in the face of a growing speculative bubble in the asset market and focusing macroeconomic policy on offsetting the aftermath of its bursting could—as is currently believed—have played a part in exacerbating the financial crisis that broke out in 2007 in the United States.

39. For example, in West Germany the independence of the central bank was guaranteed as early as in 1950, whereas in the United Kingdom this did not happen until the 1980s (see also the chapter on New Zealand).

40. Such limitations are also necessary for the existence of strong propelling institutions.

Bibliography

Abel, A. B., N. G. Mankiw, L. H. Summers, and R. J. Zeckhauser. 1989. "Assessing Dynamic Efficiency: Theory and Evidence." *Review of Economic Studies* 56 (1): 1–20.

Acemoglu, D. 2009. *Introduction to Modern Economic Growth*. Princeton, NJ: Princeton University Press.

Acemoglu, D., P. Antras, and E. Helpman. 2007. "Contracts and Technology Adoption." *American Economic Review* 97: 916–43.

Acemoglu, D., and V. Guerrieri. 2008. "Capital Deepening and Non-Balanced Economic Growth." *Journal of Political Economy* 116: 467–98.

Acemoglu, D., and S. Johnson. 2005. "Unbundling Institutions." *Journal of Political Economy* 113: 949–95.

Acemoglu, D., S. Johnson, and J. A. Robinson. 2001. "The Colonial Origins of Comparative Development: An Empirical Investigation." *American Economic Review* 91: 1369–401.

Acemoglu, D., and F. Zilibotti. 1997. "Was Prometheus Unbound by Chance? Risk, Diversification, and Growth." *Journal of Political Economy* 105: 709–55.

Aghion, P., M. Angelatos, A. Banerjee, and K. Manova. 2004. "Volatility and Growth. The Role of Financial Development." Department of Economics, Harvard University.

Aghion, P., N. Bloom, R. Blundell, R. Griffith, and P. Howitt. 2005. "Competition and Innovation: An Inverted-U Relationship." *Quarterly Journal of Economics* 120: 701–28.

Aghion, P., and S. N. Durlauf, eds. 2005. *Handbook of Economic Growth*, Vols. 1A and 1B. Amsterdam: Elsevier B.V.

Aghion, P., and P. Howitt. 1992. "A Model of Growth through Creative Destruction." *Econometrica* 60 (2): 323–51.

———. 1997. *Endogenous Growth Theory*. Cambridge, MA: MIT Press.

Alchian, A. 1977. *Economic Forces at Work*. Indianapolis, IN: Liberty Press.

Arrow, K. J. 1962. "The Economic Implications of Learning by Doing." *Review of Economic Studies* 29: 155–73.

Aslund, A., and M. Dąbrowski. 2008. *Challenges of Globalization: Imbalances and Growth*. Washington, DC: Peter G. Peterson Institute for International Economics.

Ayal, E. B., and G. Karras. 1998. "Components of Economic Freedom and Growth: An Empirical Study." *Journal of Developing Areas* 32 (3): 327–38.

Balcerowicz, L. 1995. *Socialism, Capitalism, Transformation*. Budapest, Hungary: Central European University Press.

———. 2006. "Concluding Comments." In *Living Standards and the Wealth of Nations: Successes and Failures in Real Convergence*, edited by L. Balcerowicz and S. Fischer. Cambridge, MA: MIT Press.

———. 2008. "Institutional Systems and Economic Growth." In *Challenges of Globalization: Imbalances and Growth*, edited by A. Aslund and M. Dąbrowski. Washington, DC: Peterson Institute for International Economics.

Balcerowicz, L., and S. Fischer. eds. 2006. *Living Standards and the Wealth of Nations. Successes and Failures in Real Convergence*. Cambridge, MA: MIT Press.

Barro, R. J. 1989. "A Cross-Country Study of Growth, Saving, and Government." NBER Working Paper 2855.

———. 1991. "Economic Growth in Cross Section of Countries." *Quarterly Journal of Economics* 106: 407–43.

———. 1996. "Democracy and Growth." *Journal of Economic Growth* 1 (1): 1–27.

Barro, R. J., and J. W. Lee. 1993. "Losers and Winners in Economic Growth." Proceedings of the World Bank Annual Conference on Development Economics, 267–314. Washington, DC: World Bank.

Basu, S., and D. Weil. 1998. "Appropriate Technology and Growth." *Quarterly Journal of Economics* 113: 1025–54.

Baumol, W. J. 1986. "Productivity Growth, Convergence, and Welfare: What the Long-Run Data Show." *American Economic Review* 76: 1072–85.

Baumol, W. J., and E. N. Wolff. 1988. "Productivity Growth, Convergence, and Welfare: Reply." *American Economic Review* 78 (5): 1155–9.

Beck, T., R. Levine, and N. Loayza. 2000. "Finance and the Sources of Growth." *Journal of Financial Economics* 58 (1–2): 261–300.

Becker, G. S. 1985. "Public Policies, Pressure Groups, and Dead Weight Costs." *Journal of Public Economics* 28 (3): 329–47.

Bergoeing, R., P. J. Kehoe, T. J. Kehoe, and R. Soto. 2002. "Policy-Driven Productivity in Chile and Mexico in the 1980's and 1990's." *American Economic Review* 92 (2): 16–21.

Bourguignon, F., and C. Morrison. 1992. "The Kuznets Curve and the Recent Evolution of Income Inequality in Developed Countries." Paris.

Boyd, J. H., R. Levine, and B. D. Smith. 2001. "The Impact of Inflation on Financial Sector Performance." *Journal of Monetary Economics* 47: 221–48.

Buchanan, J. 1989. *Explorations into Constitutional Economics*. College Station, TX: Texas A&M University Press.

Caselli, F., and J. Feyrer. 2007. "The Marginal Product of Capital." *Quarterly Journal of Economics* 123: 535–68.

Cass, D. 1965. "Optimum Growth in an Aggregative Model of Capital Accumulation." *Review of Economic Studies* 32 (3): 233–40.

Chong, A., and C. Calderon. 2000. "Causality of and Feedback between Institutional Measures and Economic Growth." *Economics and Politics* 12 (1): 69–81.

De Long, B. J. 1988. "Productivity Growth, Convergence, and Welfare: Comment." *American Economic Review* 78 (5): 1138–54.

Diamond, P. 1965. "National Debt in a Neoclassical Growth Model." *American Economic Review* 55: 1126–50.

Dollar, D., and A. Kraay. 2001. "Growth Is Good for the Poor." World Bank Policy Research Working Paper 2587.

Domar, E. 1947. "Expansion and Employment." *American Economic Review* 37 (1): 343–55.

Domar, E. D. 1946. "Capital Expansion, Rate of Growth and Employment." *Econometrica* 14: 137–47.

Doppelhofer, G., Miller, R. I., and X. Sala-i-Martin. 2000. "Determinants of Long-Term Growth: A Bayesian Averaging of Classical Estimates (Bace) Approach." NBER Working Paper 7750.

Dorn, J. A., S. H. Hanke, and A. W. Walters. eds. 1998. *The Revolution in Development Economics*. Washington, DC: Cato Institute.

Durlauf, S. N. 1993. "Nonergodic Economic Growth." *Review of Economic Studies* 60: 349–66.

———. 1996. "A Theory of Persistent Income Inequality." *Journal of Economic Growth* 1: 75–94.

Durlauf, S. N., P. A. Johnson, and J. R. W. Temple. 2005. "Growth Econometrics." In *Handbook of Economic Growth*, Vols. 1A and 1B, edited by P. Aghion and S. N. Durlauf. Amsterdam: Elsevier B.V.

Durlauf, S. N., and D. Quah. 1999. "The New Empirics of Economic Growth." In *Handbook of Macroeconomics*, edited by J. Taylor and M. Woodford. Amsterdam: North-Holland.

Easterly, W. 2002. *The Elusive Quest for Growth, Economists' Adventures and Misadventures in the Tropics*. Cambridge, MA: MIT Press.

———. 2005. "National Policies and Economic Growth: A Reappraisal." In *Handbook of Economic Growth*, Vols. 1A and 1B, edited by P. Aghion and S. N. Durlauf. Amsterdam: Elsevier B.V.

Eastely, W., M. Kremer, L. Pritchett, and L. Summers. 1993. "Good Policy or Good Luck? Country Growth Performance and Temporary Shocks." *Journal of Monetary Economics* 32: 459–83.

Easterly, W., and R. Levine. 2001. "It's Not Factor Accumulation. Stylized Facts and Growth Models." *World Bank Economic Review* 15: 177–219.

Fatas, A. 2000. "Endogenous Growth and Stochastic Trends." *Journal of Monetary Economics* 45 (1): 107–28.

———. 2002. "The Effects of Business Cycles on Growth." In *Economic Growth: Sources, Trends, and Cycles*, edited by N. Loayza and R. Soto. Santiago: Central Bank of Chile.

Fischer, S. 1993. "The Role of Macroeconomic Factors in Growth." *Journal of Monetary Economics* 32: 485–512.

Fosu, A. K. 2007. *Wider Angle*. World Institute for Development Economics Research, 1–3.

Frankel, M. 1962. "The Production Function in Allocation and Growth. A Synthesis." *American Economic Review* 52: 995–1022.

Furubotn, E. G., and S. Pejovich. 1972. "Property Rights and Economic Theory: A Survey of Recent Literature." *Journal of Economic Literature* X.

Galor, O. 2005. "From Stagnation to Growth: Unified Growth Theory." In *Handbook of Economic Growth*, Vols. 1A and 1B, edited by P. Aghion and S. N. Durlauf. Amsterdam: Elsevier B.V.

Galor, O., and O. Moav. 2002. "Natural Selection in the Origin of Economic Growth." *Quarterly Journal of Economics* 117: 1133–92.

Galor, O., and D. N. Weil. 1999. "From Malthusian Stagnation to Modern Growth." *American Economic Review* 86: 374–87.

Gill, I., and H. Kharas. 2007. *An East Asian Renaissance. Ideas for Economic Growth*. Washington, DC: World Bank.

Glaeser, E. L., R. La Porta, F. Lopez-de-Silanes, and A. Shleifer. 2004. "Do Institutions Cause Growth?" *Journal of Economic Growth* 9 (3): 271–303.

Gomułka, S. 1970. "Extensions of Golden Rule of Research of Phelps." *Review of Economic Studies* 37 (1): 73–93.

Gomułka, S. 2008. "Mechanizm i źródła wzrostu gospodarczego w świecie." In *Wzrost gospodarczy w krajach postsocjalistycznych: Konwergencja czy Dywergencjam*, edited by R. Rapacki. Warsaw: PWE.

Greif, A. 2006. *Institutions and the Path to the Modern Economy. Lessons from Medieval Trade*. Cambridge, U.K.: Cambridge University Press.

Grossman, H., and E. Helpman. 1991. "Quality Ladders in the Theory of Growth." *Review of Economic Studies* 68: 43–61.

Hall, R. E., and C. I. Jones. 1999. "Why Do Some Countries Produce So Much More Output per Worker than Others?" *Quarterly Journal of Economics* 114 (1): 83–116.

Hansen, G. D., and E. C. Prescott. 2002. "Malthus to Solow." *American Economic Review* 92: 1205–17.

Hanushek, E., and D. Kimko. 2000. "Schooling, Labor Force Quality, and the Growth of Nations." *American Economic Review* 90: 1184–208.

Harrod, R. F. 1939. "An Essay in Dynamic Theory." *Economic Journal* 49: 14–33.

———. 1948. *Towards a Dynamic Economics*. London: MacMillan.

Hayek, F. A. 1960. *The Constitution of Liberty*. Chicago, IL: Chicago University Press.

Hnatkovska, V., and N. Loayza. 2003. "Volatility and Growth." World Bank Policy Research Working Paper 3184. Washington, DC: World Bank.

Hoover, K., and S. Perez. 2004. "Truth and Robustness in Cross-Country Growth Regressions." *Oxford Bulletin of Economics and Statistics* 66 (5): 765–98.

IMF (International Monetary Fund). 2009. World Economic Outlook Database. IMF, Washington, DC, April.

Jones, C. 2005. "Growth and Ideas." In *Handbook of Economic Growth*, Vols. 1A and 1B, edited by P. Aghion and S. N. Durlauf. Amsterdam: Elsevier B.V.

Jones, C. I. 1995. "Time Series Tests of Endogenous Growth Models." *Quarterly Journal of Economics* 110 (2): 495–525.

Jorgenson, D. W., and Z. Griliches. 1967. "The Explanation of Productivity Change." *Review of Economic Studies* 34 (3): 249–83.

Kalaitzidakis, P., T. Mamuneas, and T. Stengos. 2000. "A Non-Linear Sensitivity Analysis of Cross Country Growth Regressions." *Canadian Journal of Economics* 33 (3): 604–17.

Kaldor, N. 1957. "A Model of Economic Growth." *Economic Journal* 57: 591–624.

Kaufmann, D., A. Kraay, and M. Mastruzzi. 2008. "Governance Matters VII: Aggregate and Individual Governance Indicators 1996–2007." World Bank Policy Research Working Paper 4654.

Keefer, P., and S. Knack. 1997. "Why Don't Poor Countries Catch Up? A Cross-National Test of an Institutional Explanation." *Economic Inquiry* 35 (3): 590–802.

Kehoe, T. J., and E. C. Prescott. 2002. "Great Depressions of the 20th Century." *Review of Economic Dynamics* 5 (1): 1–18.

King, R., and R. Levine. 1993. "Finance, Entrepreneurship, and Growth: Theory and Evidence." *Journal of Monetary Economics* 32: 513–42.

King, R. G., and R. Levine. 1994. "Capital Fundamentalism, Economic Development, and Economic Growth." World Bank Policy Research Working Paper 1285.

Knack, S., and P. Keefer. 1995. "Institutions and Economic Performance: Cross-Country Tests Using Alternative Institutional Measures." *Economics & Politics* 7 (3): 207–27.

Kongsamut, P., S. Rebelo, and D. Xie. 2001. "Beyond Balanced Growth." *Review of Economic Studies* 48: 869–82.

Koopmans, T. C. 1965. "On the Concept of Optimal Economic Growth." In *The Econometric Approach to Development Planning*. Amsterdam: North-Holland.

Kormendi, R., and P. Meguire. 1985. "Macroeconomic Determinants of Growth: Cross Country Evidence." *Journal of Monetary Economics* 16 (2): 141–63.

Kuznets, S. 1955. "Economic Growth and Income Inequality." *American Economic Review* 45: 1–228.

Kydland, F. E., and E. C. Prescott. 1982. "Time to Build and Aggregate Fluctuations." *Econometrica* 50 (6): 1345–70.

Levine, R. 1997. "Financial Development and Economic Growth: Views and Agenda." *Journal of Economic Literature* 35: 688–726.

Levine, R., N. Loayza, and T. Beck. 2000. "Financial Intermediation and Growth: Causality and Causes." *Journal of Monetary Economics* 46: 31–77.

Levine, R., and D. Renelt. 1992. "A Sensitivity Analysis of Cross-Country Growth Regression." *American Economic Review* 82 (2): 942–63.

Li, H., and H. F. Zou. 2002. "Inflation, Growth, and Income Distribution: A Cross Country Study." *Annals of Economics and Finance* 3 (1): 85–101.

Loayza, N., and R. Soto. eds. 2002. *Economic Growth: Sources, Trends, and Cycles*. Santiago, Chile: Central Bank of Chile.

Lucas, R. E. 1988. "On the Mechanics of Economic Development." *Journal of Monetary Economics* 22: 3–42.

———. 1990. "Why Doesn't Capital Flow from Rich to Poor Countries?" *American Economic Review* 80: 92–6.

Maddison, A. 2001. *The World Economy: A Millennial Perspective*. Paris: Development Centre.

Mankiw, G. N., D. Romer, and D. N. Weil. 1992. "A Contribution to the Empirics of Economic Growth." *Quarterly Journal of Economics* 107: 407–37.

Matsuyama, K. 2002. "The Rise of Mass Consumption Societies." *Journal of Political Economy* 110: 1035–70.

Mauro, P. 1995. "Corruption and Growth." *Quarterly Journal of Economics* 110: 681–712.

McArthur, J. W., and J. D. Sachs. 2001. "Institutions and Geography: Comment on Acemoglu, Johnson and Robinson." NBER Working Paper 8114.

Mill, J. S. 1909. *Principles of Political Economy with Some of Their Application to Social Philosophy*. London: Ashley.

Mirrlees, J. 1971. "An Exploration in the Theory of Optimum Income Taxation." *Review of Economic Studies* 38 (2): 175–208.

Nelson, Ch. R., and E. S. Phelps. 1966. "Investment in Humans, Technological Diffusion and Economic Growth." *American Economic Review* 56: 66–75.

Nelson, Ch. R., and C. I. Plosser. 1982. "Trends and Random Walks in Macroeconomic Time Series." *Journal of Monetary Economics* 10 (2): 139–62.

Nelson, Ch. R. and S. G. Winter. 1982. *An Evolutionary Theory of Technological Change*. Cambridge, MA: Belknap Press.

Niskanen, W. 1971. *Bureaucracy and Representative Government*. Chicago: Aldine/Atherton.

Nordhaus, W. D. 1969. "An Economic Theory of Technical Change." *American Economic Review: Papers and Proceedings* 59: 18–28.

North, D. C. 1998. "Institutions, Ideology, and Economic Performance." In *The Revolution in Development Economics*, edited by J. A. Dorn, S. H. Hanke, and A. W. Walters. Washington, DC: Cato Institute.

Olson, M. 1965. *The Logic of Collective Action: Public Goods and the Theory of Groups*. Cambridge, MA: Harvard University Press.

———. 1982. *The Rise and Decline of Nations: Economic Growth, Stagflation, and Social Rigidities*. New Haven, CT: Yale University Press.

Parente, S. L., and E. C. Prescott. 2000. *Barriers to Riches*. Cambridge, MA: MIT Press.

———. 2005. "A Unified Theory of the Evolution of International Income Levels." In *Handbook of Economic Growth*, Vols. 1A and 1B, edited by P. Aghion and S. N. Durlauf. Amsterdam: Elsevier B.V.

Rapacki, R. ed. 2008. *Wzrost gospodarczy w krajach postsocjalistycznych: Konwergencja czy Dywergencja*. Warsaw: PWE.

Ramsey, F. P. 1928. "A Mathematical Theory of Saving." *Economic Journal* 38: 543–59.

Romer, D. 2000. *Advanced Macroeconomics*. Warsaw, Poland: Polish Scientific Publishers (PWN).

Romer, P. M. 1986. "Increasing Returns and Long-Run Growth." *Journal of Political Economy* 94: 1002–37.

———. 1987. "Growth Based on Increasing Returns Due to Specialization." *American Economic Review* 77: 56–62.

———. 1990. "Endogenous Technological Change." *Journal of Political Economy* 98 (I): S71–102.

———. 1993. "Idea Gaps and Object Gaps in Economic Development." *Journal of Monetary Economics* 32: 543–73.

———. 1994. "The Origins of Endogenous Growth." *Journal of Economic Perspectives* 8: 3–22.

Rzońca, A., and P. Ciżkowicz. 2003. "A Comment on the Relationship between Policies and Growth in Transition Countries." *Economics of Transition* 11 (3): 743–48.

Sala-i-Martin, X. 1997. "I Just Ran Two Million Regressions." *American Economic Review* 87 (2): 178–83.

———. 2002. "Fifteen Years of New Growth Economics." In *Economic Growth: Sources, Trends, and Cycles*, edited by N. Loayza and R. Soto. Santiago: Central Bank of Chile.

Schumpeter, J. 1962. *Capitalism, Socialism and Democracy*. New York: Harper Torchbooks [originally published in 1942].

———. 1966. *Invention and Economic Growth*. Cambridge, U.K.: Cambridge University Press.

———. 1972. *Patents, Invention, and Economic Change. Data and Selected Essays*, edited by Z. Grilliches and L. Hurwicz. Cambridge, MA: Harvard University Press.

———. 1983. *The Theory of Economic Development*. Oxford, U.K.: Oxford University Press [originally published in 1934].

Shaw, G. K. 1992. "Policy Implications of Endogenous Growth Theory." *Economic Journal* 102: 611–21.

Smith, A. 2007. *An Inquiry into the Nature and Causes of the Wealth of Nations* [originally published in 1776]. Warsaw: PWN.

Solow, R. M. 1956. "A Contribution to the Theory of Economic Growth." *Quarterly Journal of Economics* 70: 65–94.

———. 1957. "Technical Change and the Aggregate Production Function." *Review of Economics and Statistics* 39: 312–20.

———. 1994. "Perspectives on Growth Theory." *Journal of Economic Perspectives* 8: 45–54.

Summers, R., and A. Heston. 1991. "The Penn World Table (Mark 5): An Expanded Set of International Comparisons, 1950–1988." *Quarterly Journal of Economics* 106: 327–68.

Swan, T. W. 1956. "Economic Growth and Capital Accumulation." *Economic Record* 32: 334–61.

Taylor, J. B., and M. Woodford, eds. 1999. *Handbook of Macroeconomics*. Amsterdam: North-Holland.

Temple, J. R. W. 2003. "The Long Run Implications of Growth Theories." *Journal of Economic Surveys* 17 (3): 497–510.

Tullock, G. 1998. *On Voting: A Public Choice Approach*. Cheltenham, U.K.: Elgar.

Uzawa, H. 1964. "Optimal Growth in Two-Sector Model of Capital Accumulation." *Review of Economic Studies* 31: 1–24.

Uzawa, H. 1965. "Optimal Technical Change in an Aggregative Model of Economic Growth." *International Economic Review* 6: 18–31.

Weil, D. 2005. *Economic Growth*. Boston, MA: Pearson.

World Bank. 2001. *Finance for Growth. Policy Choices in a Volatile World*. Washington, DC: World Bank.

———. 2005. *Economic Growth in the 1990s: Learning from a Decade of Reform*. Washington, DC: World Bank.

Young, A. 1991. "Learning by Doing and the Dynamic Effects of International Trade." *Quarterly Journal of Economics* 106: 369–405.

CHAPTER 2

Institutional Systems and Economic Growth

Leszek Balcerowicz and Andrzej Rzońca

In chapter 1, we pointed out that long-term economic growth paths usually consist of short periods of collapse and longer periods of relatively stable growth—although patterns and paces vary significantly from country to country.[1] Collapse is triggered by various shocks, some from outside and others caused or magnified by domestic economic policy. Economic policy, in turn, is shaped not only by the personal choices of political decision makers but also by the institutions that impose stronger or weaker limits on their power. We consider these institutions ultimately responsible for economic stability.

This chapter is devoted to such institutions and the drivers behind them. Our analysis is divided into eight sections.

In the section on innovation-based growth and special growth mechanisms, we demarcate two types of growth mechanisms. The first, based on innovation, is potentially universal and sustainable. The second consists of special growth mechanisms that are situation specific and transitional.

In the section on determinants of individual choice, we present a general model of individual choice and, in the section on Institutional Systems and Individual Decisions, use it to define barriers to innovation-based growth created by (lack of) information and incentives. In the section on Information Barriers to Innovation-Based Economic Growth we discuss information barriers, emphasizing that under present conditions they are mainly created by factors that simultaneously create incentive barriers.

In the section on institutional barriers, we categorize institutional systems that create barriers to innovation. Because innovation-based growth is a basic and irreplaceable growth mechanism, such institutional systems are incapable of systematic long-term growth.

In the section on cases of accelerated economic growth, we focus on national institutions that enable innovation-based growth. A small group of countries have had such institutions over their entire history. Much larger group of countries has had institutional systems that at some point blocked long-term growth.

Subsequent reforms to activate the innovation-based growth mechanism then prompted a stage of accelerated growth in these countries.

In the section, which is on successful reform packages, we define and analyze successful reform packages, focusing on their direction, scope, and time structure. We also introduce the concept of institutional barriers to growth and discuss their main types and special growth mechanisms.

The last section provides the chapter summary.

Innovation-Based Growth and Special Growth Mechanisms

Sustained economic growth is possible only as long as innovations increase the productivity of the factors of production.[2] On their own, such factors (speaking in technical terms) are observed to have decreasing marginal productivity, with limited possibility that their use—without further innovation—will become more efficient. In this book we define innovation, following Schumpeter, as the use of new ideas—innovative proposals introduced into economic activity.[3] Some of these proposals may result from the research of independent inventors or research and development (R&D) units in enterprises and other organizations. Others originate in the course of business itself. Innovations are various in nature: Some relate to a production process, not only in a narrow sense, but also to transport, communication, and organization (for example, just-in-time logistics systems). These reduce the production costs of manufactured goods.[4] Others contribute to an increase in the number of types of goods that can yield direct utility to individuals (see, for example, Grossman and Helpman 1991).

Many innovations require investment. According to some estimates, new machines may be responsible for well over half of the world's technical progress (see, for example, Geenwood, Hercowitz, and Krusell 1997; Jorgenson 2005). Therefore, serious barriers to investment block innovation-based growth (see the chapter on Haiti and data included therein about investment rates in that country). Innovation may be blocked by other types of barriers, as well (see the section on Institutional Barriers). Without it, capital expenditure has diminishing marginal productivity, eventually negating any positive impact of capital on economic growth.

Innovation-based growth necessitates structural changes. Resources must be reallocated to new production processes and to the manufacturing of new products; otherwise innovation cannot spread through an economy. Therefore, barriers to the more efficient use of resources may also bar innovation-based growth. That said, not all structural changes are connected with innovation. Many occur as a result of differences in the income elasticity of demand for particular goods. What is more, changes in the demand structure that accompanies income growth per capita may also change the economic structure in ways that constrain the productivity of factors of production.[5]

Innovations may originate in a given country or may be adopted from abroad, usually following successful implementation.

Technical progress in small and medium-sized open economies—even if they have high per capita income—is most often due to the transfer of foreign technologies. According to some estimates, in countries with a low or moderate growth rate the transfer of technologies accounts for up to 90 percent of technical progress (Keller 2004). This transfer is accomplished not only through foreign companies that invest in domestic companies or through licenses purchased overseas, but also through international trade—paradoxically, not so much exports as imports (although any transfer necessitates the adoption of foreign standards). Imports give enterprises access to machines as well as components and semi-finished products that no domestic entity would be able to manufacture as cheaply or well (Keller 2004).[6]

Gaining the technology edge in a given field limits opportunities for borrowing foreign technology. The further development of the leaders in the field will depend on a shift in the world technology frontier through invention activity. Although this problem is relevant to few countries, a country's own R&D activity may be necessary for a successful transfer of foreign technologies (or at least helpful in the process) (Griffith, Redding, and Van Reenen 2005).

Since successive innovations increase the productivity of factors of production—and the utility derived from consumption of new types of goods—countries on the technological frontier also lead in income per capita, whereas those that are technologically behind are characterized by poorer living conditions. The poorer nations can, however, catch up with highly developed countries by adopting technologies used by those countries.[7]

Technology transfer enables convergence—a process whereby countries with lower income per capita catch up with countries with higher income per capita. As such, transfer is cheaper and requires less time than does shifting the technological frontier by countries already technologically advanced (Barro and Sala-i-Martin 1997).[8] Meanwhile, the costs of transfer are declining thanks to the ongoing information revolution. Enterprises may copy and customize solutions previously tested in distant areas of the world never visited by enterprise representatives.

But even in the globalized world, being poor does not guarantee economic growth, let alone faster growth than in highly developed countries. A country may be in the wrong "convergence club" (Durlauf and Johnson 1995), that is, it may copy inferior solutions and, as a result, instead of catching up with highly developed countries, its lag may widen. There are still many countries where income per capita today is lower than it was in the highly developed countries in the early 19th century (and lower than in the 1950s or 1960s, when a large number of them gained sovereignty). So, although their poverty does not trigger economic growth, neither does it condemn them to be poor forever. For instance, in 1950 the Republic of Korea was poorer than Liberia or Niger. Now, ranking among the industrialized economies, it boasts an income per capita that is approximately 48 times higher than those countries (and more than 16 times higher than that of the Democratic People's Republic of Korea; if there were any differences between the two Koreas in the 1950s, they favored the Democratic

People's Republic of Korea). Much as in the Republic of Korea, fast economic growth in Taiwan, China, spurred that country's income per capita to rise from twice as high as China's in 1950 to six times as high at present (although in 1950 poverty in Taiwan, China was only slightly less severe than on the mainland)—this, despite the fact that in the late 1970s China became one of the fastest-developing countries in the world.

Factors that push countries backward must be eliminated and replaced by conditions that enable technology transfer or other growth mechanisms. These conditions are often defined as "social capability" (see, for example, Abramovitz 1986), which is usually reduced to domestic capability to learn and adapt foreign technologies.[9] In a review of the literature on technology transfer, Keller (2004), for example, focuses on this factor alone and omits the problem of incentives.

Only continuous innovation enables sustainable economic growth, but other growth mechanisms do exist. One is Ricardo's comparative advantage, that is, the improved allocative efficiency achieved as international trade increases. In other words, even if domestically produced technologies and goods do not change, opening up to foreign trade will usually spur economic growth. This mechanism may explain the improved living conditions in European countries that opened to foreign trade in the 16th to 18th centuries. When activated, this and other special growth mechanisms result in a temporary increase in the growth rate.[10]

The special mechanisms of greatest importance differ from country to country, because the factors constraining growth differ, too. For instance, the system of central planning is characterized by extremely inefficient use of factors of production. Factors are wasted and their flow is blocked to certain sectors (for example, agriculture in China, services in the USSR—see the chapters on China and Estonia). Some countries are characterized by a low percentage of (officially) employed individuals among their working-age population (see the chapter on Puerto Rico); in others, a low investment rate is a problem (see the chapter on Haiti).[11] Since these weaknesses are usually much more serious in developing countries than in highly developed ones, their elimination is conducive to convergence.

Elimination of these weaknesses is related to the basic mechanism of convergence, that is, investment-based growth. It is hard to imagine a situation in which a developing country's uninhibited operation of investment-based growth is not accompanied by the activation of special growth mechanisms. But while free operation of investment must always activate special mechanisms (provided that they are embedded in the initial conditions of a given country), the latter do not necessarily trigger innovation—and as a result economic growth slows after some time. This simple rule helps us to understand why so many countries have failed to catch up with the world's richest and also why, when success is achieved, it is often spectacular—that is, characterized by an economic growth rate that has never been achieved even by those countries with the highest income per capita (see, for example, Parente and Prescott 2005, 1403–6).

Puzzles of Economic Growth • http://dx.doi.org/10.1596/978-1-4648-0325-3

Determinants of Individual Choice

Aggregate outcomes in the economy—for example, its growth rate—ultimately depend on individual decisions. Those decisions can be seen as an effect of the interactions between individual personalities and the circumstances surrounding the decision (for more on this issue, see Balcerowicz 1995, 4–15).

Personality—or how an individual views and chooses among various options—is slow to change. It can be further divided into motivational and cognitive dispositions. Motivational disposition is expressed in the utility that an individual assigns to various objects and actions, whereas cognitive disposition determines knowledge-related abilities, including the ability to learn.

A choice may be made between more than one physical (or technological) option (Greif 2006). It may also be made in a situation where one option is seen as *so* far better than the others that the individual, in effect, feels there is no choice.

The sum total of an individual's dispositions constitutes his or her "motivational potential." This, in turn, determines which variables an individual perceives as motivators—that is, values whose change the individual perceives as a reward or punishment in a psychological sense. The expected differences in values adopted by the motivators, connected with the various options in a given choice situation, create positive or negative incentives.

Most individuals experience four main categories of motivators. Their general utility function may be given as follows:

$$U = U(EM, ES, IM, E).$$

EM stands for external motivators of a pecuniary nature, for example, income or wealth as a source of consumption. ES represents external motivators of a social nature, including reputation, social position, prestige, power, the need to belong, and so on. These stem from the emotional needs of an individual and the natural tendency to seek to maintain or improve self-esteem (Madsen 1968). External motivators of a social nature relate to the power of social norms—that is, the values enforced by the informal reactions of other members of a given group rather than by a specialized enforcement apparatus (Elster 1989). Some variables are both EM and ES. For example, income and wealth are for many individuals not only a source of consumption, but also an indicator of social position. IM stands for intrinsic motivators that include, for instance, achievement (McClelland 1961) or a pleasure derived from intellectually stimulating activities. Such activities are rewarding because of a felt need for sensory and intellectual stimulation (Hebb 1960). Finally, E denotes the unpleasant effort related to boring or excessively stressful activities.[12] This motivator helps to explain the innovative deficiency of a monopoly in relation to enterprises facing competition (see the section on Institutional Barriers).

An individual's cognitive and motivational dispositions translate each decision-making scenario into a mental representation of the options, namely a set of feasible solutions. These solutions have two dimensions: (1) activities that an individual perceives as feasible, and (2) the utility allocated to these activities, by which the individual ranks them in accord with individual preferences.[13]

From this discussion of how an individual utility function is formed, we move on to discuss barriers to innovation. An individual will not introduce innovations:

- If innovative proposals are outside the individual's set of feasible solutions (Elster 1989).
- If they are feasible but, in light of the individual's motivational disposition, their expected utility is low relative to alternative options (such as routine activities, rent-seeking, or robbery).

In the first case, the individual encounters an information barrier to innovation; in the second, an incentive barrier.

Moving from the individual to society, an information barrier occurs where a given innovative option is not to be found among the feasible solutions of any decision maker in society. An incentive barrier, on the other hand, occurs when an innovative option is considered feasible by at least some decision makers but has low expected utility in comparison with other possibilities.

Institutional Systems and Individual Decisions

The literature on economic growth, reviewed in chapter 1, increasingly recognizes that direct determinants of growth—such as the accumulation of capital, employment growth, and the improved productivity of factors of production—depend on underlying factors such as institutions.[14]

The effects of institutional systems on individual decisions may be categorized into three different types (Balcerowicz 1989):

- *Situational*, which is a derivative of the differences between institutional systems in terms of the types of positions that they allow a given individual to hold (positions are here defined as the categories of typical choice situations faced by an individual).
- *Selectional*, resulting from differences between institutional systems in terms of the degree to which they allow individuals with certain dispositions to reach decision-making positions.
- *Formative*, which is connected with specific dispositions (the beliefs, attitudes, and skills of society members) generated under the influence of the institutional systems operating in a given society over a long period of time.

The situational impact, as pointed out earlier, consists of the positions (roles) that exist in a given institutional system. Their defining features are the typical decision-making scenarios connected with these positions. Examples of such positions (roles) include those of a private entrepreneur under competition, a private monopolist, a manager of a state-owned company, a deputy in a democratic parliament, a member of the ruling group in a dictatorship, an employee in a private company, an employee in a state-owned enterprise, a member of a specific caste, and so on. Individuals may play different roles in different areas of their lives. For example, an individual may be a member of a voluntary association and an employee of a public agency. Sets of positions related by common origin and common rules are usually called organizations.

Differences between countries (in terms of legal framework, property rights, competition, political system, and so on) may be expressed as differences in the sets of available individual roles. Seeing things in this way helps us understand the relationship between the activities of individuals and institutions or institution-dependent variables. Since roles by definition differ in terms of typical decision-making scenarios—and such scenarios determine human behavior, decisions made by identical individuals will differ depending on the institutions that decide their roles.

In this context, a crucial characteristic of institutional systems is the extent to which they offer productive positions (roles) that allow and encourage work, research, the implementation of innovation, as well as savings and investments.

Of particular importance are the features of those positions from which decisions of particular relevance to society as a whole are made. Such positions are usually part of a political system. Constraints (if any) imposed on individuals who exercise power in a given country are of key importance to economic growth. These constraints determine both the type and degree of protection of property rights and also, as discussed in chapter 1, the shape of economic policy—and the frequency and intensity of economic shocks caused by this policy. In this sense, the basic features of a political system and that system's most important economic institutions are two sides of the same coin. In general, individual liberties, including economic freedom, are determined by constraints actually imposed on political powers (rather than by their formal enumeration).[15]

The more the decision-making process is concentrated at the top, the less room remains for voluntary action, and especially for free interactions between individuals.[16] Free interactions can yield spontaneous development of new institutional solutions, that is, new types of contracts and new forms of organizations. As a result, institutional systems with a highly concentrated decision-making mechanism are deprived of the capacity for bottom-up institutional innovation; in other words, they are characterized by institutional rigidity. In contrast, systems in which power is limited can spontaneously evolve, offering individuals numerous chances to interact. This difference in the extent of free interaction is of fundamental importance to institutional dynamics and innovation-based growth.

When analyzing the situational impact of institutional systems on human actions, scholars usually assume that institution-dependent positions (roles) change while human dispositions remain constant. These invariants include a general utility function and certain informational capabilities.[17] Assuming constancy in human dispositions is a typical procedure in social sciences, especially economics, convenient because it enables researchers to isolate the impact of institutional—or more broadly, situational—variables on individuals' actions.

But although individuals share certain features, they also differ in many respects, such as talent, ambition, intelligence, character, propensity to take risks, and so on. One can assume that in every (large) society there exists a wide spectrum of psychological features.[18] Because individuals differ, it matters who holds particular positions, especially positions with decision-making power.

At this point we come to the *selective* impact of institutional systems on individuals' actions. Institutional systems differ from one another not only with respect to the positions (roles) they offer, but also in terms of the mechanisms that define access to positions connected with making important decisions—in other words, mechanisms that define upward mobility, both political and economic. Institutional systems differ in the extent to which positions in the two spheres overlap. In fact, that difference is one of their most important variable dimensions. For example, in a centrally planned system, political and economic powers are concentrated, while in democratic capitalism important political and economic positions are usually separated, and the political and economic power that they offer is decentralized.

The importance of differences among individuals and, in consequence, the importance of the selection mechanism at work in the institution varies by institution, depending on the types of positions that exist therein.

Among top political positions, succession may occur by election, co-optation, appointment of a successor by the incumbent, or *coup d'état*. Differences in the personality features of individuals who hold decision-making positions will affect how they use their power. The various forms of political succession also have different effects—some, for example, prompting more instability than others—which can affect economic performance. The greater the concentration of power in a given country, the stronger the impact of succession. In other words, the weaker the constraints on the power of those in top political positions, the more important become the personality features of those who occupy them (and thus the larger the potential change in policies which may occur after the succession). This being so, the psychological profiles of dictators should be included in any analysis of the economic performance of dictatorships. The leaders' psychological features also affect institutional rigidity: Individuals who assume positions vested with concentrated power have the option of acting to reduce that power, that is, of fundamentally changing the system that put them in power.[19] Whether they choose that option or choose to preserve the system depends on their personality[20]—and on external circumstances.

Institutional barriers may also limit access to positions that carry economic decision-making power. Such barriers can (as under the caste system or slavery, for example) block the mobility of large groups of individuals or even most of society, regardless of the personality features of individual members. Less drastic barriers to the mobility of individuals with similar features include unequal access to education, financial services, and protection of the laws. It is possible to assume, other things being equal, that the economic performance of societies with serious barriers to mobility must be worse than that of societies closer to the ideal of equal opportunity. For example, free enterprise amid social mobility produces better results than does free enterprise without social mobility. Thus, the impact of upward social mobility on efficiency once again depends on the types of positions (roles) that exist in particular institutional systems. The greater the number of productive positions in a given system, the stronger the impact of upward mobility. In systems that combine a great number of productive positions (roles) with social mobility, individuals can choose positions (roles) best suited to their psychological profile. Positive self-selection forces are activated[21] as a result, and these strengthen the potential for spontaneous evolution of the institutional system.

Certain types of institutional systems exclude the most productive positions (roles) (see the section on Institutional Barriers). In such systems, the degree of social mobility matters much less for efficiency because, even if it exists, talented and hard-working individuals cannot assume highly productive positions (because they do not exist). Entrepreneurial potential is wasted in such societies. Their situation is equivalent to that in which productive positions actually exist, but rigid institutional barriers prevent anyone from accessing them. A conclusion can be made based on this equivalence: The long-term economic performance of institutional systems without productive positions, irrespective of their degree of social mobility, will be much worse than of systems in which such positions exist but where access to them is limited[22] because even the most talented individuals in unproductive positions usually cannot outperform less talented individuals in productive positions.

Finally, two very different institutional systems operating for a long time in two otherwise similar societies will lead to differences in people's skills, attitudes, beliefs, and so on. A definition of the formative impact of institutional systems on the actions of individuals itself does not say much about its importance or durability. Comparative psychological research, for example, on East and West Germans, or on North and South Koreans, would facilitate a better understanding of this issue. The psychosocial legacy of a given regime may be especially important when an attempt is made to replace it with a different one. The most-often-quoted example of a struggle with such a legacy is the transformation from socialism to capitalism in Central and Eastern Europe.[23]

The bulk of economic research on institutions and economic growth focuses on the situational impact of institutional systems on growth. The situational impact seems to be the most important of the three types discussed here, in addition to being much easier to model and investigate empirically than the other two.[24] It is therefore the one discussed most extensively in this chapter. But it must be noted that there are many interesting research problems relating to the other two impacts. For example, early development in the West is often associated with the emergence of productive positions (roles), such as that of a private entrepreneur operating under competition. It would be worthwhile to investigate the role played by the reduction of institutional barriers to entry into these positions (for example, the abolition of serfdom), in initiating this development. Another example relates to measuring the scope of economic freedom using indicators. Such indicators deal mostly with the administrative barriers

Puzzles of Economic Growth • http://dx.doi.org/10.1596/978-1-4648-0325-3

that an average entrepreneur intending to take up a certain type of activity must overcome. But an important question remains unanswered: What is the impact of specific barriers on individuals with varying psychosocial legacies? The issue of psychosocial legacy is a subject of much speculation but very little empirical research, and most of that concentrated on the psychosocial legacy of communism.[25] Such research would be of great interest if it were to compare, for example, the attitudes of employees at state-owned and privatized enterprises.

Information Barriers to Innovation-Based Economic Growth

A sufficient reason not to implement innovations in a given society is the absence of innovative proposals in the set of decision makers' feasible solutions.

There are three situations in which information barriers result in an absence of innovation:

- Innovative proposals are not produced at all and, in consequence, are unknown to a society.
- Innovative proposals are not produced in a given society, but exist in other societies.
- Innovative proposals are produced in a given society, but are unknown to the appropriate decision makers in this society.

The first situation characterizes the distant past, when individuals organized themselves into small hunter-gatherer groups. Technology did not change much at that time. How some of these groups evolved and implemented major innovations (for example, enabling them to live off sedentary agriculture) is beyond the scope of this book.

In the second and third cases, the absence of innovative proposals is a consequence of broadly conceived communication barriers (including a limited capacity to understand innovative ideas). Such barriers can be external (rendering communication with other societies impossible) or domestic (existing, for example, between researchers and rulers or between universities and enterprises).

Until recently external isolation was mostly due to geographical location. In the modern world, however, it is determined by institutions and takes the form of politically imposed bans on contact with foreigners. Such bans are typical of regimes with a heavy concentration of political power in society (for example, China under Mao, the Democratic People's Republic of Korea, and Cuba).

Systems that impose external isolation on societies often display features that also produce barriers, weakening incentives to innovation. As a result, even if the isolation were to be reduced, the incentive barriers would continue to block innovation. For example, following the opening of Poland in the 1970s, Western technologies were either poorly selected or inefficiently implemented, as there were no incentives for productive behaviors.

Both types of barriers occur jointly, among others, because each type of behavior depends on incentives. This rule applies to the presentation of innovative proposals, how these proposals are communicated to decision makers, as well as the search for innovative ideas. If the implementation of innovative projects is blocked by institutional solutions, few people will waste their time and energy to present, communicate, and search for them. Thus, an information barrier may result from factors that weaken incentives for productive action.

But there is also a reverse influence—of external isolation on incentives. Isolation not only blocks the inflow of foreign technologies but also reduces competition, the intensity of which affects the utility of innovation compared with routine activity (see the section on Institutional Barriers). Isolation also limits the scope of the market and reduces the rate of return on innovation in two additional ways. First, it reduces possible benefits from large-scale production and specialization. Second, it raises the costs that must be incurred to implement innovation. These costs consist of expenditure on the creation (acquisition) of new technology (whether the costs of new research or of imitation) and the start-up costs—including costs of learning by doing—in the early phase of use (see, for example, the chapter on Costa Rica and Puerto Rico, specifically a comparison of the two nations' factors of production in 1961–72, when Puerto Rico pursued a liberal trade policy and Costa Rica implemented a strategy of import substitution). Obviously, the negative effects of external isolation on incentives to implement innovation are much more serious in small than in large economies (see, for example, the chapter on Spain and Mexico and a comparison of their factors of production in 1961–77—that is, following the opening of Spain to foreign countries and the implementation of stricter anti-import restrictions in Mexico—cases that may be compared to Costa Rica and Puerto Rico).[26]

Institutional Barriers

In this section we consider institutional systems that reduce the relative utility of innovation (or of related activities) for decision makers, to such an extent that innovative proposals are rejected in favor of alternative options. In other words, we analyze the situational impact of institutional variables on the actions of individuals.

Institutional systems (and the scenarios they generate) create barriers to innovation by altering its utility function. The most important and most researched impact of institutional systems relates to pecuniary motivators (EM, in the equation offered earlier). It is usually implicitly assumed that social norms (ES in the equation) do not constitute a barrier to innovation and that wealth cannot be increased by noneconomic actions, such as the conquest or exploitation of subjected territories.

In the modern world, pecuniary motivators most often block innovation-based growth. In line with most literature, we will focus on these. We will also present the impact of institutional systems on incentives to innovate through tedious or unpleasant effort (E in the equation). At the end of the section we list examples of institutional systems that have blocked innovation because of social norms or because possibilities to increase wealth by noneconomic actions existed.

Puzzles of Economic Growth • http://dx.doi.org/10.1596/978-1-4648-0325-3

Systems that block innovation-based growth because of their impact on EM and E may be divided into two groups:

- Systems that to a great extent block investment and thus indirectly block innovation, which frequently requires investment.
- Systems that create direct barriers to innovation.

The first group of systems reduces the investment rate to a very low level. Their negative impact on economic growth and convergence results mainly from the fact that they reduce not only routine investment but also the accumulation of capital that embodies technical progress.[27] What is more, innovative investment in these systems (or at least in some of them) faces more serious barriers than routine investment (therefore these systems comprise elements of systems from the second group).[28] Systems that belong to the second group— that is, those that create direct barriers—may display a high investment rate; they block innovation-based economic growth by reducing the utility of innovation in comparison to routine activity or nonproductive innovation.

The low investment level in the first group of systems may be caused by a low (or highly uncertain) rate of return on individual investment or low domestic savings and limited access to foreign savings (see figure 2.1).

The return on private investment and the level of related uncertainty depends on a crucial institutional variable: property rights. The literature on this important issue is huge and growing. The explanation provided in the following paragraphs pertains to property rights in their relation to innovation-based economic growth.

It is important to distinguish between the structure of property rights and the level of security (protection). The structure determines whether private business activity is allowed or banned and—if it is allowed—then the conditions for starting up and conducting the activity, and the way the returns are divided

Figure 2.1 Institutional Systems That Block Economic Growth

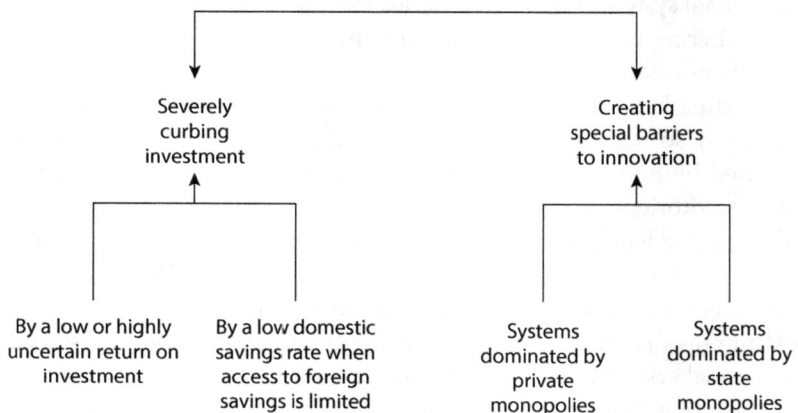

Severely curbing investment		Creating special barriers to innovation	
By a low or highly uncertain return on investment	By a low domestic savings rate when access to foreign savings is limited	Systems dominated by private monopolies	Systems dominated by state monopolies

Puzzles of Economic Growth • http://dx.doi.org/10.1596/978-1-4648-0325-3

between the entrepreneur and other individuals. This definition indicates that the structure of property rights is, among other factors, formed through economic regulations, contract laws, and taxation. The security of a property may be defined by the extent of uncertainty connected with the return on investment for an entrepreneur.[29]

Generally speaking, barriers to investment result either from the improper structure of property rights that are effectively enforced, or from insufficiently protected property rights that have a proper structure.[30]

An illustration of the first case would be of small, traditional tribal communities with collective property rights that strive to equalize the incomes of all their members irrespective of individual efforts. Such redistribution discourages other group members from productive actions, capital accumulation included. Only the assumption of strong altruism or a sense of community can change this conclusion, but given the results achieved by these societies, such an assumption is not realistic.[31]

A more common illustration of the first case would be systems that allow private property rights, but impose very high taxes on returns on private investment. This practice may be due to ideological reasons (as in the case of the private sector in centrally planned economies). Another possible reason includes the vast needs of the public finance sector overextended by an oversized bureaucracy or by excessive (and usually badly targeted)[32] social spending. State-enforced redistribution may have the same effects as redistribution among tribal communities. Analysis of its economic consequences is not complicated; high general taxes with especially high prohibitive taxation will reduce private investment. If an investment is to be made, returns on it cannot be lower than the cost of borrowing the capital needed for its financing. Some projects that would be profitable if taxes were low are not undertaken when taxes are high, because the return that they generate is not high enough to cover costs after the taxes are paid.[33] Tax rates affect not only the investment of domestic enterprises, they also have a significant impact on foreign direct investment (FDI). The mechanism is exactly the same as in the case of domestic investment. Since taxes reduce the profits of foreign enterprises, the enterprises invest in those countries, where, with the same revenues, they will incur lower costs and pay lower taxes.[34]

The political economy question of why such socially dysfunctional systems have come into being and persisted is more difficult to answer than the effects of prohibitive taxation on investment. It seems that such effects usually owe their origin to politico-ideological breakthroughs. The very existence of such breakthroughs calls for an explanation as well. Such systems, once created, reproduce their own clientele that supports their continued existence and resists reforms.

Returns on investment are reduced by all forms of forced payments—including not only regular taxes but also "corruption tax"—imposed on entrepreneurs. While taxes are minimal in many countries (or rather inadequately collected),[35] the costs of corruption may be very high. As a result, total forced payments are large (and uncertain), which discourages and constrains investment.[36]

Puzzles of Economic Growth • http://dx.doi.org/10.1596/978-1-4648-0325-3

From the analytical point of view, widespread corruption is not just due to the reprehensible behavior of a few officials, but has specific institutional roots. Both official and corruption taxes are paid by entrepreneurs when officials use credible threats of exercising state power to enforce their collection. In the case of official taxes, the officials have the ultimate instrument of the penal and fiscal code. This cannot, however, be used to enforce corruption taxes since the actions of the officials are illegal. The instrument of pressure in this case is the threat of forcing the entrepreneur to comply with all official regulations, which would reduce his return on investment even more than corruption taxes. In this sense, bribes, in contrast to purely private pillage, owe their existence to the state or, to be more precise, to any regulations that seriously reduce profits from business activity. These regulations must be eliminated if the very source of corruption—that is, the credible threat of using state power—is to be eliminated as well.[37]

Widespread corruption may be regarded either as a manifestation of improperly structured property rights (connected with excessive regulation) or of poor protection of official property rights. This second explanation is more useful, because corruption is associated with a higher degree of uncertainty with regard to some returns on investment received by an entrepreneur than in the case of other factors (for example, official taxes[38]) that affect the content of property rights. Regardless of how corruption is treated, its impact is clear: the greater the level of corruption, the more private investment shrinks.

Finally, in theory, if property rights are properly structured but not protected, investors are in danger of being pillaged by nonofficial agents. This is the case of weak or failed states that do not perform their fundamental functions: the protection of individuals and their property, including the enforcement of contracts.[39] The huge uncertainty generated by such a situation reduces private investment to a low level (see, for example, the chapter on Haiti and data on investment rates in that country). In such circumstances it is rational not to own a large number of fixed assets that could be easily pillaged, as it is difficult to hide them or escape with them. Thus, a weak or failed state has an impact similar to that of the egalitarian redistribution observed in tribal communities or the high prohibitive taxes exacted by some efficient but predatory states.

Some institutional systems may combine the aforementioned features. For example, pillage by officials may be accompanied by poor protection of property against pillage by nonofficial agents. High official taxes, if spent on a bloated bureaucracy or oversized social transfers, may not guarantee law and order.

Systems that reduce the rate of investment in effect discourage the introduction of new, more efficient technologies. Innovative investment is usually more visible, because of its large scale and lack of precedent, than noninnovative investment.[40] In systems where property rights are inadequately protected, returns on innovative investment may be more easily appropriated by officials or other individuals[41] than routine investment (Gonzales 2005). Entrepreneurs will then avoid the innovative investment that enables large-scale production. Inadequate protection also forces them to avoid deferred payments and to

enter into business contacts with clients they do not know well. The first feature reduces the volume of individual transactions, whereas the latter reduces
the number of business partners. They both heavily hamper economic growth
because they require depersonalized transactions (see, for example, North 1993).
Uncertain that property rights will be protected, investors are unlikely to conclude the long-term contracts that would guarantee the recovery of at least some
expenditure needed for the application of high-efficiency technology.[42]

In some countries investment may be limited by low domestic savings. Despite
the high profitability of investment in these countries, the investment rate is low.
A prominent example of this is Brazil (Hausman, Rodrik, and Velasco 2005).
Domestic savings may act as a constraint on investment because of the imperfect
international mobility of savings.[43] Although it has significantly increased over
the past dozen or so years (see, for example, Blanchard and Giavazzi 2002),
knowledge of the local situation still makes individuals keep their savings in their
own countries, even if they could achieve higher returns abroad (see, for example,
Mussa and Goldstein 1993). Countries that have experienced macroeconomic
crises encounter particular difficulties in attracting foreign savings (the news
of crises spreads to foreign countries much faster than does information about
changes in economic policy or the institutions determining that policy). Such
crises may also reduce domestic savings for a long time (see, for example, the
chapter on Mexico and data on changes in the savings ratio during the period
of economic stabilization following crises in the 1980s). Another factor that
may limit savings, despite high return on private investment, is an overextended
welfare state. Excessive welfare payments reduce forethought, which in turn is a
basis for savings (see, for example, the chapter on China, where the abolition of a
welfare state in the 1970s caused the savings ratio to rise to a very high level).[44]
Finally, a fiscal deficit is an important factor that reduces savings. In theory, individuals reacting to a budget deficit may increase their savings to pay higher future
taxes imposed on them to pay off the public debt incurred at present (Barro
1974). In such a case the deficit would not reduce the savings that finance investments of enterprises. But, if savings are to increase by the same amount as the
deficit, everyone would have to (1) be aware that today's deficit means higher
taxes in the future, (2) already start worrying today about future higher taxes,
and (3) have high enough incomes to freely increase savings (Rzońca 2007).[45]

We now come to the second group of institutional systems that block
innovation-based economic growth: that is, systems that create barriers that
diminish incentives to innovation without necessarily affecting the rate of investment. Their common characteristics, as subsequently pointed out, are serious
deficiencies in the structure of property rights rather than in the level of their
protection.[46]

One such system is analyzed by Parente and Prescott (2000).[47] These authors
identify widespread and persistent working practices that perpetuate the use
of inefficient technologies by preventing the shifting of labor force within sectors and between them. They illustrate this with an example of India under
British rule.[48] The country was incapable of introducing more advanced British

technologies into the textile industry, although it was open to British capital inflow and British technologies were successfully implemented in countries at a similar level of development as India—for example, in Japan. They stress that if working practices are to be an effective barrier to innovation,[49] they have to be protected by the state.[50]

Such protection includes constraints on domestic and foreign competition, so as to secure a monopoly position for crippled domestic enterprises. Otherwise, the entry of domestic or foreign companies would undermine the profitability of enterprises that use rigid, anti-innovative working practices and would push them out of the market. This point may be generalized. An element of every institutional barrier to efficiency is, by virtue of functional necessity, protection against competition (understood broadly, this includes subsidies paid to inefficient enterprises).[51] One example of such an institutional barrier is state property. On the one hand, the state does not ensure that its labor and capital resources are used in full. State decision makers are not affected by incentives that would make them care about profits generated by supervised enterprises. On the other hand, the state may save persistently loss-making enterprises (enterprises whose products are worth less to customers than the cost of the resources they use) from bankruptcy. Without state subsidies or tax remission, the capital and employees of these enterprises would shift to companies whose products are so valued by customers that their payments alone can finance the capital and employees involved.

The phenomena described by Parente and Prescott include rigid working practices and, as their necessary complement, the monopoly rights granted to domestic companies crippled by these practices. The authors stress in their conclusions (1999, 1,231) that "Until now, support for the view that monopoly rights can lead to large inefficiencies and impede economic growth has been empirical in nature. Theory provided no economic mechanism by which monopoly could have a serious impact. In this paper, we present a mechanism causing monopoly rights to have large effects upon aggregate output." But Parente and Prescott deal with a special case where monopoly rights complement rigid working practices. This case does not allow us to determine the impact of those rights on economic growth when there are no rigid working practices or to identify mechanisms by which they affect incentives to innovation. Theoretical literature on this important issue is surprisingly scarce. It mainly deals with the static costs of monopoly. Further in this section we distinguish two types of institutional systems with monopolistic product markets and we identify mechanisms by which these systems block innovation.

One of these types may be called the private monopoly system. In this system producers have private property rights but do not face competition. Competition is another concept that, although extensively described, requires further clarification. It is perceived as a mechanism of incentives for productive action and the reallocation of factors of production. Incentives and reallocation, being the functions of competition, are organically linked: competition acts on enterprises as an incentive mechanism only if they can attract the factors of production to achieve their purpose. If competition is to exist in this sense, three conditions must be met concurrently (Balcerowicz 1995):

- Buyers must be able to freely choose between alternative products.
- Producers must include enterprises capable of and willing to undertake actions that result in outcomes that attract demand, and thus exercise pressure on other producers.
- Changes in demand must have a significant impact on incentives that affect producers experiencing these changes.

If even one of these conditions is not met, competition cannot function as an incentive-reallocation mechanism. There are several institutional systems where at least one of these conditions is not fulfilled.

Buyers cannot choose between alternative products if there are strong barriers to entry in individual sectors (see, for example, the chapter on Indonesia, whose economy in the 1970s was dominated by private conglomerates), or if the economy is small and isolated from external competition (see, for example, the chapter on Costa Rica, which until the crises of the 1980s pursued a strategy of import-substitution). But even with many producers operating in a given market, there may be no competition when producers are limited by restrictive price or quality regulations. This was the case with medieval guilds. It is also true of many services markets, as well as highly developed countries (see, for example, the chapter on Switzerland, whose slower growth in the productivity of factors of production is compared to Austria in the years 1991–2003). Competition will not function properly when enterprises cannot expand because of rigidity in factor markets (see, for example, the chapter on India, where enterprises had to struggle with rigid labor market regulations and huge restrictions on investment, as well as obstacles in obtaining external financing because of the delayed liberalization of financial markets). Finally, competition will be constrained if a failure in the market does not entail serious consequences (if only because of the absence of an effective bankruptcy law—see, for example, the chapter on Slovenia).

Some of the aforementioned cases result from the same mechanisms as the rigid working practices analyzed by Parente and Prescott (1999, 2000). For example, efficiently enforced restrictive price and quality regulations impose such a threat of penalties, in terms of EM, on innovative proposals or require such a huge additional E that the expected utility of those proposals falls below the utility of continuing the routine activity.[52] But from an analytical point of view, the case of long-term monopolies that are fully free to innovate (that is, are not subject to any regulations restricting their implementation) is more interesting.[53] The analysis of the institutional system dominated by such monopolies allows the conclusion that this system limits or impedes at least two important channels of creating and implementing innovation. First, the chances to invent or adapt new technologies may be related not only to the amount of expenditure on R&D (as is often assumed in endogenous growth models), but also to the number of individuals involved in the research and testing of new possibilities

(Gomulka 1990). A large number of those individuals, which is a distinguishing mark of competition, should speed the process of detecting problems in a new technology, to the point that its use is so efficient that the productivity of factors of production can rise. Second, radical innovation is often implemented by new enterprises (Jovanovic and Rousseau 2005, 1200–2),[54] which, while making decisions about the directions of search for new technological solutions, are not restricted by thinking about the technologies used so far and do not take into account the impact of innovation on the profits/value of capital used by the companies previously operating in a given market (see, for example, Arrow 1962). For these two reasons private monopolies should be less innovative than a system where competitors have free entry to individual sectors. But if this statement is to be true, monopolies must not demonstrate a greater tendency and ability to innovate than an average enterprise exposed to competition. Some economists such as Schumpeter (1942), however, claim that a certain degree of monopoly power (but not a lasting monopoly) can be conducive to innovation. We come now to the least-explored link between the extent to which an economy is monopolized and its innovativeness. Empirical research explicitly proves that private enterprises operating under competition are more innovative than monopolies (see, for example, Nickell 1996), but finds it hard to explain why. On the one hand, the innovation incentives of monopolies should be enhanced by the extraordinary profits that monopolies may obtain from innovation (see, for example, Aghion and Howitt 1992). On the other hand, since factors of production are typically rewarded with marginal products under perfect competition, inventive activity cannot be financed without incurring losses (see, for example, Jones 2005).

One (theoretical) explanation of why monopolies are less innovative than enterprises operating under competition is the assumption that they have a certain aspiration level of EM that can be easily achieved without innovation and without the related effort and risk. This explanation, in the spirit of Herbert Simon, may accurately describe some real-life situations, but it does not specify how the aspiration level is determined.

Some mechanisms that reduce incentives to monopolies innovating can be identified without reference to the concept of satisfactory profit or aspiration.

A lasting monopoly is often institutionally based, and the political powers that grant this privilege are likely to impose some obligations as well. In other words, to explain the monopoly's behavior one must remember that it is a political fact that may have certain political consequences. One such likely consequence is the responsibility of the monopolist for an uninterrupted supply of goods that it has a monopolistic privilege to supply. By granting the monopoly, the rulers take the responsibility for its supply to society. Innovation, in contrast to a technological *status quo*, may end in technical failure. The more radical it is, the greater the risk of failure. Therefore, the risk of interrupted supply may exceed the pecuniary rewards of successful, radical innovation to such an extent that the status quo is maintained or given only cosmetic changes.

Even if a monopoly were not responsible for the continuity of supply, there are other mechanisms that diminish its incentives to innovate. The expected utility of alternative activities depends not only on EM but also on other motivators, including E (see the section on Institutional Systems and Individual Decisions). Innovations require extra effort over and above routine activity. This effort is likely to grow with the degree of an innovative proposal's technical novelty. It is possible to assume that the effort is the same in the case of both monopoly and competition. But only in the case of competition does effort reduce the risk of the enterprise being overtaken by a competitor in the course of implementing the innovation. The risk increases as time elapses since implementation of any earlier innovation, reducing the expected utility of routine actions. This gradual decrease in the expected utility of routine actions may at some point reach below the expected utility of innovation, despite the effort required for its implementation. Furthermore, the more different a new technology is from its predecessors, the smaller the risk that it will be copied by competitors at low cost.[55] In the case of a monopoly, continued use of the same technology is not risky at all. The scale of technological progress due to innovation does not help a monopoly keep its edge, since there is no competition. Yet, the greater the progress, the bigger the risk that some production assets and the related know-how will become useless, reducing the expected utility of radical innovation for the monopoly due to both a decrease in EM and an increase in E.[56] On the other hand, if innovation is delayed to collect more information about its potential consequences, the risk of monopolies making a mistake can be reduced, which increases the expected utility in terms of EM. All these factors diminish the monopoly's incentives to implement innovation, especially radical innovation, which requires a lot of effort and may render previously accumulated capital useless.

The difference between the expected utility of innovation for a competing enterprise and a monopoly would be bigger if we assumed that enterprises were not neutral but, like households, displayed a certain aversion to risk and, as a result, were willing to give up potential profits in exchange for a higher degree of certainty regarding future profits. As indicated earlier, innovation allows competitors to reduce certain types of risk, whereas for a monopoly it only becomes a source of risk. This difference becomes even bigger on the assumption that enterprises can get accustomed to risk if they experience changes. In other words, potential aversion to risk among enterprises affected by competition should be smaller than for monopoly, which to a great extent can control both the number and scale of the changes it undergoes.

All in all, given the various possible channels of a monopoly's impact on innovation, the institutional systems of private monopolies must be characterized by barriers that reduce innovation incentives and, in consequence, impede innovation-based growth in contrast to systems that ensure market competition.

Moving on to an analysis of the centrally planned economy, it is possible to point out two basic features that distinguish it from the private monopoly system. First, monopolistic enterprises are owned by the state, not by private investors. Second, central planning replaces the market as the coordination mechanism.

A glimpse at the history of economic thought leads to a puzzling observation: while no prominent economist has regarded the (long-term) private monopoly system as conducive to innovation and economic growth, many of them did not doubt the innovative potential of a centrally planned economy. Since they did not treat long-term monopolies, either private or state-owned, as a driving force of innovation, their optimism about the innovative performance of a centrally planned economy must have stemmed from the belief that market competition is not necessary for innovation-based economic growth and can be effectively replaced with the command mechanism. This was the view expressed by Schumpeter (1962), who maintained that (as pointed out in chapter 1) under socialism innovation could be spread by instructions issued by authorities to the managers of state companies.

Early critics of socialism—for example, Brutzkus, von Mises, and Hayek—did not have such illusions and warned that the centrally planned economy would struggle with bureaucracy and dissuade risk taking. And experience has indeed shown that the command mechanism, instead of being an effective substitute for market competition, is a source of additional problems that make the centrally planned economy even less innovative than private monopoly systems (Balcerowicz 1995). First, greater effort is needed to implement innovation in a centrally planned economy than in the private monopoly system—if nothing else, because of shortages and social rigidity. Second, the command mechanism induces managers to prepare plans that do not cause any problems at the implementation stage; thus they are reluctant to include innovation in the plans, since its effects are often difficult to predict. Given information asymmetry to the disadvantage of central planners, the latter are incapable of counteracting the effects of the disincentives affecting their subordinate managers. As a consequence, the plans do not encourage innovation, leading instead to avoidance of innovation and mass inefficiency—an incomplete use of factors of production, which ensures that present and future plans will be executed—as well as macroeconomic crises (see, for example, the chapters on Indonesia in the early 1960s and Chile and Pakistan in the early 1970s). Contrary to the assumptions made in models, central planners are neither omniscient nor disinterested (which is clearly illustrated in these examples).

So far, we have focused on institutional systems that impede innovation-based growth either because they limit investment (including the investment required for innovation), or because they create an incentive structure such that the expected utility of innovation is lower than that of routine actions. The systems described include most institutional solutions that impede economic growth in the modern world. But to complete the analysis, another two sources of barriers to innovation need to be mentioned:

- Options other than innovation may include not only business as usual but conquest, the exploitation of conquered territories, and making a living from public money.
- Social norms may discriminate against business activity, including in particular the implementation of innovation.

Puzzles of Economic Growth • http://dx.doi.org/10.1596/978-1-4648-0325-3

These two additional reasons for a low level of innovation may be present separately or jointly, compounding each other.

Baumol (2002) suggests, with reference to the historical literature, that both alternative options to innovation and social norms dissuading it were present in Ancient Rome. Roman elites were not interested in business activity (except for land holding) because more lucrative options (in terms of EM) were open: conquest and administration of conquered territories. In addition, business was not considered a particularly reputable activity by members of the ruling elite, which, as a result, did not introduce innovation. This leaves open the question of why other individuals did not engage in innovative business activity to acquire wealth and, as in 19th-century Great Britain, become members of the elite. To prevent such an expansion of the elite (and innovation-based economic growth), some barriers to social mobility and other barriers to innovation must have been present in Rome. In Imperial China, on the other hand, ambitious individuals were better off becoming imperial officials rather than innovators; having plodded through the required examinations, they could prey upon innovators with impunity (Baumol 2002).

In some systems social norms emphasized the value of order and the *status quo*, while hampering innovation. Changes brought about by innovative competition were regarded as immoral. The idea of progress was alien to many cultures. The fascinating question of how such social norms originated and what influences brought about their change lies beyond the scope of this chapter and book.

Cases of Accelerated Economic Growth

Economists believe that before 1500 there were only slight differences in the quality of life across countries and over time (Parente and Prescott 2000); such differences increased slowly until the early 19th century. In 1500 income per capita in the richest region of the world was twice as high as in the poorest one. Three hundred years later income per capita in the world was on average only a fifth higher than in 1500 (Ventura 2005), and in the richest region no more than three times the income of the poorest region (Galor 2005). This can be attributed to institutional factors: for most of their history, all societies had some variety of the innovation-blocking systems we have described. And systemic change, when it occurred, was scarcely conducive to innovation. The common features of historic systems were:

- Improperly structured property rights, that is, ones that excessively taxed individual benefits of ownership, heavily restricted freedom of private actions, and created monopolies.
- No protection of properly structured property rights.

An additional role may have been played in some cases by: (1) the availability of lucrative noneconomic options and social norms that penalized entrepreneurship and (2) the implementation of innovation in particular.[57]

Puzzles of Economic Growth • http://dx.doi.org/10.1596/978-1-4648-0325-3

As long as societies lived under innovation-blocking institutional systems, modern (that is, fast and sustainable) economic growth could not begin. It only appeared in Britain in the 18th century, followed by the colonies inhabited by British citizens, and later other European countries. Why innovation-blocking systems prevailed everywhere until that time and why Great Britain or, more generally, Western countries managed to escape the forces that supported them are among the most-important and most-often-debated questions of history, political science, and institutional economics (see, for example, Kuznets 1971; Rosenberg and Birdzel 1986; North 1990; Mokyr 2005). Finding answers to these questions lies beyond the scope of this chapter or this book.

The appearance of modern economic growth sparked a new era of divergence and convergence in the long-term growth paths of countries around the world. Over the past 200 years particular countries have separated themselves from others by the length and distribution of their periods of stagnation, economic growth acceleration, and slowdowns (see, for example, Maddison 1991). Periods of accelerated growth in less developed countries brought them temporarily closer to the world leaders in terms of income per capita, while periods of stagnation and serious slowdowns widened the gap. Meanwhile, the world leader also experienced growth acceleration periods (for example, the United States in the 1990s); and some countries saw their income per capita fall by comparison, even when their growth did not decline (for example, Puerto Rico in the 1990s, described in this book).

Looking at the distribution of countries' growth rates over time we can conclude that long-term growth may accelerate at various initial levels of income. Income levels may start out low (as in China in the late 1970s), moderate (as in Estonia in the second half of the 1990s), or high (as in Ireland in the late 1980s). The same refers to periods of slow (or negative) growth. They occurred in poor countries (for example, Haiti) and countries with moderate income per capita (for example, República Bolivariana de Venezuela in the late 1970s) and also high-income countries (such as New Zealand in the 1970s and 1980s). And finally, the growth paths of individual countries displayed enormous variation: for example, until the late 1970s China increasingly lagged behind the richest countries, only to close the gap quickly over the past 30 years. Indonesia and Pakistan experienced recurrent periods of stagnation, even economic growth collapse and acceleration. In the 1950s República Bolivariana de Venezuela was no poorer than Norway, but beginning from the late 1970s its economy started to contract rather than develop. In the 1970s and 1980s Chile experienced two tremendous crises but as a result of subsequent rapid development, it has become the richest country in South America. During the past 30 years Mexico has experienced repeated periods of economic slump, which explain to a great extent its enormous per capita income difference in relation to Spain—a difference that didn't exist before the 1960s. Until the end of the 1960s Puerto Rico had been among the world's fastest-developing countries but then it became an economic tortoise, unable to shorten the distance that separated it from the highly developed countries. Until the mid-1990s Estonia and Slovenia (like other socialist countries) had developed more slowly than their Western European neighbors, but later managed to bridge much of the gap in per capita income. In the past 40 years, whenever economic conditions in the world deteriorated, Switzerland suffered more and longer than other developed countries.

The universal existence of institutional systems that blocked innovation-based growth until the 19th century, explains, as noted earlier, why economic growth during that period was slow and differed little across countries and time. But with the onset of modern economic growth, these systems did not merely become a historical curiosity. They still are the main explanation for periods of stagnation.[58]

A slowdown in growth may result not only from the prolonged operation of innovation-blocking systems but also from the short-term operation of any such system, even if it is not introduced in its full-fledged form. An innovation barrier may take the shape of a serious deterioration in ownership-related incentives through increased forced payments, the introduction of regulatory restrictions on domestic and foreign competition, or the reduced protection of property rights. The impact of systemic changes of this kind—leading to the establishment of a predatory, overregulated, or failed state—has been widely described in the empirical literature (see, for example, Scarpetta and others 2002; Lewis 2004). Such changes may, of course, only occur in countries that previously had a better structure of property rights (in terms of incentives to productive behavior) or more efficiently protected these structures. This book shows that these structures are sometimes introduced in countries at every level of development, although in highly developed countries they mostly relate to the structure of property rights (that is, they take the form of official taxes or regulations that limit competition) rather than the level of protection.

We now turn to the institutional determinants of fast-growth periods, which fall into two categories:

- Periods that extend over the entire growth path of a given country.
- Periods when growth is rapid only along a segment of that path.

Fast-growth periods of the first category occur in countries that from the beginning have maintained strong (and properly structured) property rights, sufficient protection of these rights, and the competition needed to fuel progress. The constitutional features of their underlying systems provided strong incentives not only for technological innovation, but also for bottom-up institutional changes that manifested themselves, for example, in the introduction of new types of organizations or contracts. These systems—let us call them liberal—are capable of bottom-up evolution thanks to their invariable fundamentals (a large scope of economic liberties and the resultant relatively free and flexible markets that operate as prescribed by law). Few countries belong to this category. We can name only two: Hong Kong SAR, China, and, somewhat hesitantly, the United States. This should not be interpreted as an argument against liberal systems—one must not confuse value with incidence. Rather, it begs the question: why has economic freedom been so difficult to achieve historically and why, once achieved, has it proved so fragile?

The economic performance of countries that have managed to maintain a somewhat liberal system shows that they implement reforms aimed at rapid innovation-based economic growth. A qualitatively different model that, in the light of experience (and the theory of institutional economics) could play this role equally effectively does not exist. Centrally planned economies have failed everywhere. German corporatism has shown its limitations as well (Phelps 2006), and Germany has been liberalizing its economy in recent years. France, another example of a constrained market economy, is also making such attempts. Japan, which 20 years ago was expected to overtake the United States and become a world leader in the not-too-distant future, proved to be a dual economy whose export sector is subject to intense market competition and thus is characterized by high innovation, while the service sector that displays low productivity because of anticompetitive regulations (Lewis 2004). Sweden, another country presented as an alternative to the liberal system, achieved the status of a wealthy country under a liberal system. Subsequently, when its welfare state and regulations expanded, the rate of its economic growth declined below the level observed in other highly developed countries. Economic problems induced the state authorities to deregulate and reform the welfare sector. Various so-called unconventional institutional solutions (some of them are subsequently described) were either functional equivalents of liberal solutions or had a negative economic impact.

The second category of fast-growth periods relates to a far greater number of countries. They occurred in countries that moved away from innovation-blocking institutional systems and replaced them with systems closer to liberalism.

Successful Reform Packages

A reform package expected to permanently accelerate economic growth should, first of all, have an adequate direction, scope, and time structure.[59] Those issues constitute the subject matter of the economics of reform, which examines relations between various institutional systems, individual behaviors, and the economic performance achieved, including long-term economic growth as the main goal of institutional change. Second, a reform package with a proper structure cannot be reversed. This issue is examined by scholars of the political economy of reforms, who analyze relations among sociopolitical factors (protests, pressures, interest groups, and so on) and the sustainability of reforms (that is, whether they take hold, or, on the contrary, weaken or are rejected).

The direction, scope, and time structure of a reform package—which may (given initial conditions) permanently improve economic performance if continued—need to be defined in the first place. There is no point in introducing reforms not capable of improving people's quality of life. Such reforms, if sustained, would only play a negative role, leaving no room for changes leading to improved economic performance). Reforms that promise to improve social conditions, meanwhile, may or may not be sustained depending on their extent and timing or sequencing. For example, changes that (at the early implementation stage of the reform package) reduce the power of organized groups that may oppose them, boost the chances of their own continuation. Successful reforms aimed at the sustainable acceleration of economic growth must often have a political ingredient—that is, they must alter the set of forces influencing the shape of institutional solutions. This proves that the economy of reforms and the political economy of reforms are interconnected. The better the reforms' results (stemming from their appropriate direction, scope, and time structure), the higher the possibility that they will be continued and extended.

But the sustainability of reforms cannot be limited to a simple function of their construction. It is not possible to reduce the political economy of reforms simply to the economy of reforms: the economic results influencing reforms' sustainability depend not only on their direction, scope, and time structure, but also on the economic conditions in which they are introduced. As a result, a similar package of reforms may have varied results and chances for continuation depending on initial economic conditions. The reforms introduced in China at the end of the 1970s and in Russia at the beginning of the 1990s are a good example. Apart from this, the sociopolitical situation has its own dynamics, independent of economic results, specific to every country and any given point of time. For example, depending on a country's history and geopolitics, there are various way of connecting reforms to other factors perceived as positive or negative by the population. Market reforms could be positively related to the future accession of Central European countries to the European Union (even if this very membership entails the necessity to undo some of those reforms—see the chapter on Estonia). On the other hand, for example, in Russia, such a relation could not occur; what is worse free market reforms could actually be blamed for the fall of the Soviet empire. The development of the political situation influencing reforms also depends on the personality of the people who introduce these reforms and the leaders opposing them. This factor also differs from country to country and from one period of time to another. For example, in Chile the political breakthrough and transition to democracy did not lead to a retreat from the radical free-market reforms introduced during the Pinochet dictatorship, but to their expansion; on the other hand, in República Bolivariana de Venezuela, attempts to introduce such reforms were inconsistent, and the weakness of the reformers was the reason Hugo Chávez rose to power in the late 1990s. Finally, differences in natural resources in various countries have various impacts on the implementation of reforms—in countries rich in natural resources politicians have weaker incentives for improving institutional solutions than in countries devoid of natural resources. For example, in Mexico, República Bolivariana de Venezuela, or Indonesia, periods of unexpectedly high income from exports of crude oil were accompanied by deterioration in the quality of economic policy, sometimes to the point of recklessness; if free market reforms were introduced in these countries, it was under the pressure of a poor economic situation.[60]

This section focuses on the economy of reforms: the direction, scope, and time structure of those reforms that promise a sustainable acceleration in economic growth (assuming that the reforms are not be reversed). We also mention relevant problems in the field of political economy.

Successful reforms should serve to liberalize the institutional systems they address. This may involve changes in the structure of property rights (for example, abolishing the prohibition on private property) and a move toward privatization, deregulation, reduced taxes, and the decentralization of fiscal policy. Reforms may also further protect rights with an appropriate structure. There is no example of a successful reform that moves away from liberalism rather than toward. Institutional economics may explain why anti-market reforms cannot improve economic results: they weaken incentives for labor, inventiveness, and the savings and investment needed to support innovation (see the sections on information barriers to innovation-based economic growth and institutional barriers).

But there are authors[61] who see alternatives to liberal (classic) reforms in solutions they call unconventional. For example, they underline that openness to international trade may be achieved not only by reducing customs duties and removing para-tariff and nontariff barriers, but also by the return of duty fees, export subsidies, special economic zones, and so on. They claim that the quasi-private enterprises (township-village enterprises, TVEs) in rural areas in China constituted an efficient substitute to open privatization (Rodrik 2006). Moreover, they praise the Chinese system of double prices (in operation until 1985) as a way to liberalize without stirring up social tensions. In general, they claim that different institutional solutions may bring about similar economic results.

However, such a claim raises two questions:

- How much are those unconventional solutions different from the classical ones?
- Can considerably different institutional solutions bring about similar results?

If considerably different institutional solutions could, in identical conditions, lead to similar individual behaviors and results, then those solutions, would be devoid of significance. But experience denies such institutional nihilism. It seems that supporters of unconventional approaches, without directly saying so, are implying that certain differences in institutions are not important; some institutions that differ in their nominal (legal) categories are functionally equal, that is, they form incentives in a similar manner and, in effect, generate the same behaviors and economic results (in similar conditions).[62] Such a possibility cannot be denied, though its empirical confirmation is a challenge. Yet proponents of unconventional solutions usually take their possible success for granted. This is the case of Rodrik's (2006) various manners for opening the economy to international trade. It is obvious that the examples he has quoted are real-life situations, but it does not mean that they are functionally equivalent to the reduction of custom duties and the removing of para-tariff and nontariff barriers to international trade. They differ at least in one respect: unconventional manners of opening to international trade are more complex than a typical liberalization of trade and, as a result, they lead to higher transaction costs and are more prone to corruption.

If they were in fact functionally equivalent to classical liberalization, supporters of unconventional solutions would not criticize such liberalization.

We may seriously doubt whether unconventional solutions in areas other than foreign trade are indeed functionally equivalent to direct, liberal reforms. For example, TVEs in China, praised by Rodrik (2006, 479) for their capacity to "trigger exceptionally high private investment," led to immense corruption and the abuse of farmers' rights (Woo 2006). On the other hand, postponing the privatization of state enterprises in China created strong incentives and possibilities for managers to take assets out of the enterprises. Finally, the system of double prices, presented as a step toward market prices while avoiding social tensions, in fact led to staggering corruption and social tensions serious enough for the system to be rejected (Woo 2006; see also the chapter on China in this book).

It seems that individuals praising unconventional solutions for their alleged effectiveness not only disregard some of their actual results, but also the impact of the specific conditions in which they were introduced. For example, rapid economic growth in China in the 1980s was largely possible owing to the initial structure of the economy: agriculture (which was easy to privatize) comprised a large share of gross domestic product (GDP) generation and employment (see the chapter on China in this book). The initial structure of the economies of the Central and Eastern European countries was completely different, and this precluded a similar effect on the growth of their economies (see, for example, Balcerowicz 1995; Aslund 2007; and the chapter on Estonia and Slovenia in this book). While comparing the results of different reform packages, we need to control for the impact of other factors on economic results. This basic requirement is often neglected in discussions of reforms.[63]

The scope of a reform package intended to speed up economic growth obviously depends on initial conditions, including the inherited institutional system. In examining relations between initial conditions, and the scope of reforms and growth, we will consider both barriers to and special mechanisms of growth. The idea is that barriers to growth are useful in specifying the scope of reforms needed to sustainably accelerate economic growth. On the other hand, special mechanisms of growth will help us explain how growth might accelerate prior to completion of the reforms.

The idea of barriers to growth is very old.[64] Here, we apply it to the institutional system. Let us assume that the set of institutional variables $(I_1, I_2, ..., I_n)$ corresponds to various dimensions of the institutional system in a given country. Every variable may assume various states. For example, the variable concerning the structure of property rights comprises state, cooperative, and private property rights. Every institutional system is a combination of interrelated dimensions of various institutional variables, that is, dimensions that may coexist even if they produce poor results.[65] A coordination mechanism by order cannot, for example, coexist with the freedom to enter particular sectors; it requires that an economy have a stiff, multilayered organizational structure (Balcerowicz 1995).

Both simple observation and empirical examinations indicate that particular institutional variables do not influence the long-term development of the economy in an additive manner. At least some of them may assume factors that, if they occur, push the economic development rate to a very low level independent of the shape of other institutional variables. Those particular factors may be called institutional growth barriers.[66] Each growth barrier is, by definition, a sufficient cause for slow growth or even no growth at all (the section on Institutional Barriers presents a description of the institutional systems characterized by such barriers).

The maximum rate of economic growth with such barriers—B_1, B_2, ..., B_n— may be the same, or, more likely, may differ. The second case is presented in figure 2.2. In this figure, r stands for the average long-term growth rate achieved with increasingly hard barriers, B_1, B_2, and B_3. Points A and B represent various initial states and, consequently, the varying scope of reforms necessary for r to exceed r_3. Starting from point A, the r rate of growth may be achieved earlier (path $A \rightarrow C_1$) or later (path $A \rightarrow C_2$). Selection of the slower path results in increasing the cost of slow growth for the period of time, T. Therefore numerous barriers to growth in the initial state constitute an argument for a broad package of reforms introduced in a short period of time rather than for a gradual approach. Obviously, this claim does not encompass problems in the area of the political economy of reforms.

Figure 2.2 Reforms and Paths of Economic Growth

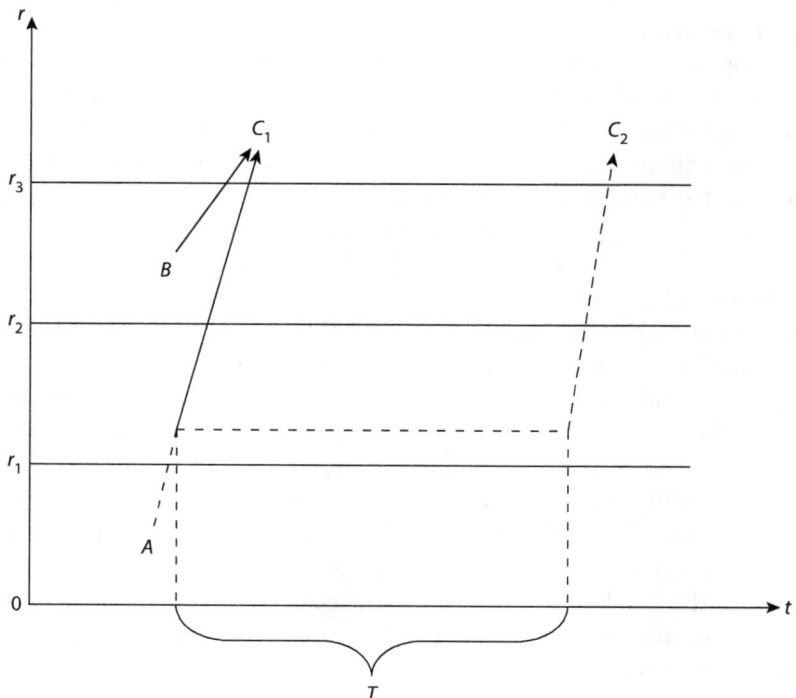

A successful reform package may be defined as a package that removes all growth barriers existing in the inherited institutional system. On the other hand, an unsuccessful package leaves certain barriers; as a result, economic growth is still slow, despite certain reforms.[67] This situation often leads to reforms themselves being blamed, instead of their inadequate scope, for poor economic results (see, for example, the chapter on República Bolivariana de Venezuela). An empirically oriented institutional economics should specify more precisely the states of institutional variables constituting growth barriers, and the diagnosis should indicate the sorts of reforms that are likely to be successful.

The problem of specifying a successful reform package does not only boil down to identifying growth barriers. Another important issue is how much r might increase as a result of further improvements in the particular institutional variables forming the institutional system of a given country—at the moment when those variables are no longer growth barriers. In other words, reforms that are most productive in the r category in initial conditions need to be found. Another question is whether an improvement in the various dimensions of institutional systems is characterized by a drop-off in extreme productivity in the r categories. If this is the case (which seems probable), reforms should concentrate on those institutional variables that, despite an appropriate state, are closest to the state of growth barriers—that is, changing them by a particular value would trigger the highest increase of r. But this claim also disregards issues in the area of political economy; for example, it does not consider why a given institutional variable is closer to the state of a growth barrier than other variables.

Moreover, we should remember that some reforms may complement one another to a considerable degree. For example, competition as a mechanism of incentives and reallocation, necessary for economic growth based on innovations, may work only when (as already mentioned) three conditions are fulfilled: the buyer enjoys freedom of choice among alternative goods, producers attract demand and thus create pressure on other producers, and any changes in demand considerably influence the producers who experience them. If in the initial state the economy is, for example, centrally planned, any permanent introduction of competition requires mass liberalization (of entry to particular sectors, prices, and foreign trade) and systemic change (for example, the introduction of bankruptcy procedures and the privatization of state-owned enterprises). In such a situation, one should analyze the productivity of the whole package of closely interrelated (complementary) reforms and not its single components.

Reform packages that transition an economy from very slow to rapid long-term growth are particularly interesting. Such a transition may be called an economic miracle. Obviously, in such cases at least one barrier to growth must exist (and be removed). But it remains less clear what factors increase r to a high level. Yet this is one of the most important questions in the theory of development, requiring further detailed research. It may be safely claimed that such a package must radically and permanently increase the rate of technology transfer from abroad. To make this achievable, depending on the initial conditions and growth barriers in a given country (see the chapters on China, Estonia, Chile, and also Puerto Rico in the initial period covered in the chapter), a reform package should: radically open foreign trade, deregulate, involve fiscal reforms clearly increasing the rate of savings and investment, strengthen private property rights, and so on.

In the economic literature there is no consensus concerning which initial conditions may provide the backdrop for an economic miracle. According to some authors, an economic miracle is most likely to occur in the poorest countries, since they have the largest amounts of foreign technologies to adopt, and they may initiate the process starting from technologies ensuring the highest growth of r (see, for example, Barro and Sala-i-Martin 1997).[68] Other economists claim that the best conditions for economic growth are in countries with a moderate level of income per capita, as they are better equipped with the human capital necessary for the adoption of foreign technologies (see, for example, Gomulka 1990). Their economic structure is also closer to that of highly developed countries, and consequently they have a high rate of growth in sectors with the largest potential to leap forward, thanks to new technology—a condition that strongly influences the growth rate of the entire economy (see, for example, Parente and Prescott 2005). The example of Ireland in the 1990s shows that even a highly developed country may become a tiger. To achieve high income per capita, it needs to display relatively rapid growth for a long period of time, that is, it has to be free from growth barriers. Next, one (several) of the growth determinants must deteriorate to the degree that it becomes a barrier reducing the rate of economic growth to a very low level, despite the fact that the shape of other institutional variables fosters rapid development. In such conditions, restricted reforms (transforming the critical variable from a growth barrier into a factor fostering growth) release the whole power of all the forces of growth—making an economic miracle.[69] This example shows once again that the extent of successful reforms depends on initial conditions or, to be more precise, on the initial weak points of a system. There is no point in treating a disease that the patient does not have.

If in a given country there are many growth barriers, any reform package expected to permanently accelerate economic growth must be broad. But in many cases economic growth has accelerated prior to a complete introduction of the package of reforms—that is, rapid growth has occurred in an institutional system undergoing changes but still far from the model liberal system and presumably still constrained by growth barriers.[70] This apparent paradox may be explained by the following: to achieve the permanent acceleration of economic growth in a country with numerous growth barriers, a broad and adequately structured package of reforms is needed. But it is also possible to experience temporary growth acceleration resulting from more modest reforms (prior to the completion of complex reforms) if these launch the needed special growth mechanisms.

Growth based on innovation is the only potentially universal mechanism ensuring sustainable growth. Special growth mechanisms depend on the situation and they are transitional, even if some of them are in operation for many years. Several examples of such mechanisms are subsequently given.

The first two mechanisms are related to incomplete use (in initial conditions) of human capital, whether specific (knowledge of how to use particular technologies) or general (conditions allowing one to acquire such knowledge).

Destruction resulting from World War II deteriorated the quality of life in Western Europe; at the same time it disturbed the relation between physical and human capital. Western European countries with surplus human capital could thus develop rapidly when the war machine came to a stop and the market economy was restored.[71] The impact of this special mechanism of growth ceased when reconstruction, restoring balance between both types of capital, ended. The system of education in socialist countries was much better than their economic system. They accumulated relatively rich human capital resources, which (because of restrictions of the centrally planned economy) were not fully utilized. When these restrictions were lifted, human capital (which was previously dormant) could start to operate as a force accelerating technology transfer from abroad (see the chapter on Slovenia and Estonia). This mechanism, however, was gradually exhausted as the competences of educated people were to an increasing degree fully employed in the new system.[72]

The third mechanism is based on widespread waste. Such waste in centrally planned economies occurred both in particular enterprises and in the relations among them. The first type of waste may be expressed as a very low level of efficiency X (Leibenstein 1957), and is characterized by a very low level of use of physical capital, wastage of time at work, neglect of renovation and maintenance, and so on.[73] The second was the widespread, chronic breaks in trade relations among enterprises, causing standstills and breaches in the technical requirements of production (reducing the quality of manufactured goods) and discouraging specialization. This was an inevitable result of the command-based coordination mechanism,[74] but some Western economists (among others, Nelson 1981) believed that it is the market mechanism that may suffer from this type of inefficiency.

The fourth mechanism is also related to a move away from socialism. This political system was characterized by an ideological hostility toward sectors recognized by Marxism as "unproductive." Services were in this category—especially trade, which is the condition for specialization. As a result, the tertiary sector was subject to drastic restrictions. Removing those restrictions also released the previously constrained demand, ensuring an exceptionally high rate of return on investment in the tertiary sector and its rapid growth—up to the moment when it reached the significance similar to that observed in countries at a comparable stage of development. In countries that are uniformly underdeveloped, such a potential source of temporary acceleration of economic growth does not occur.

In certain sectors, another type of restriction imposed incentives that broke off any relation between individual effort and remuneration. Consider the Maoist communes that employed the majority of productive-age people in rural China. These were, at the same time, poorly equipped in physical capital, a fact that facilitated their privatization. When communes were dissolved and replaced with what was known as the "system of responsibilities," there was a sharp growth in the productivity of agriculture. This in turn released a large part of the labor force and halted the growth of labor costs in other sectors, at the same time increasing their profitability and capacity and willingness to invest (see, for example, Crafts 1998, and also the chapter on China in this book). This special growth mechanism could not operate in the Central and Eastern European countries, as agriculture generated a much smaller share of employment in these countries. In countries where agriculture was relatively important, it was equipped with machines that could be fully employed only at a large scale of production (see chapter on Slovenia and Estonia).[75] This mechanism worked in many African countries (not analyzed in this book), despite the fact that state monopsony imposed unfavorable nominal prices on private agricultural holdings. Funds raised in this way were wasted on ineffective public projects (see, for example, Schultz 1980; Bauer 1998).

The mechanisms discussed in the preceding two paragraphs are similar to the next one to a certain degree. In all developing economies, sectors with low productivity of production factors have a large share in employment, and a low share of employment characterizes sectors with high productivity.[76] These economies have a high capacity for structural changes to strengthen economic growth. The changes may be triggered by an accelerated transfer of technologies from abroad, as growth of the more productive sectors is based on exactly this factor. Obviously, the transfer of technology from abroad cannot be recognized as a special growth mechanism. But releasing production factors, including labor, that were previously wasted in sectors of low or even negative productivity (for example, in a bloated bureaucracy) is a special growth mechanism.

Some economies are characterized by a low employment rate. This is tantamount to zero productivity among an important part of the working-age population.[77] Raising this rate—that is, increasing the productivity of this share of people from zero to positive values—constitutes yet one more growth mechanism.[78] The low share of working people in the productive-age population is caused by factors other than the sources of inefficiency described earlier. Its increase requires the application of another recipe: weakening incentives to remain unemployed or nonemployed, mainly through reforms of social transfer systems (see the chapter on Puerto Rico).[79]

Finally, a special growth mechanism may accompany an increase in an initially low investment rate. As the operation of this mechanism is related to investment that does not generate innovation, but adds to the scale of operation at a given technological level, it can be triggered not only by free market reforms but also by institutional changes in the opposite direction. The distinguishing feature of many centrally planned economies was, as already mentioned, a high share of investment in GDP. Raising the investment rate in a command economy inevitably led to mounting difficulties both in the cost-efficient implementation and full employment of the capital resulting from the investment. In other words, the higher the investment, the less of it actually increased the capital stock—and the larger the capital stock, the more was left unused.[80]

Puzzles of Economic Growth • http://dx.doi.org/10.1596/978-1-4648-0325-3

Owing to those two effects, this special growth mechanism resulted in weaker acceleration of growth in centrally planned economies compared with more liberal systems; in addition, it was faster exhausted. Launching it under the influence of free market reforms that remove barriers for private investment may be accompanied by a significant growth acceleration, since such reforms also strengthen innovation-based growth, while simultaneously triggering other special growth mechanisms (connected, for example, to eliminating waste, removing barriers that hinder the development of sectors seen as "unproductive" for ideological reasons, or removing distortions in the system of incentives). Even if those other growth mechanisms (which may be triggered by the same set of reforms) are disregarded, the scale of growth acceleration caused by the higher investment rate, or the period of time in which this faster growth may be maintained, are potentially more important than the scale and persistency of growth acceleration caused by changes in employment (see, for example, the chapter on China). The possibilities of a much stronger influence on economic growth of changes in the investment rate, rather than in the employment rate, result mainly from a considerably wider range of possible changes in the former than in the latter. In countries with the highest investment rate, it is six times (and even more) higher than in countries with the lowest investment rate (compare, on the one hand, the investment rate in China and, on the other, in Haiti). To compare, the difference between countries with the highest and the lowest employment rate slightly exceeds half (see data from the chapter on Puerto Rico comparing its employment rate with that of the United States). However it is worth remarking that according to some studies (see, for example, Dowrick 1992), in the Asian tigers (i.e., countries in which modern economic growth has reached the highest rate so far) raising the employment rate was of no lesser importance for accelerating the economic growth than increasing the investment rate, the only exception being Japan.[81]

Countries with many special growth mechanisms may achieve accelerated growth for a certain period of time, yet they pay a high price for this opportunity. These mechanisms are the result of previous distortions which hampered growth, that is, of severely constrained sectors, mass waste, low employment rate, and so on. Though the existence of a simple, linear relationship between income per capita and the force of those mechanisms may be questioned,[82] they seem to affect the pace of convergence.

Different types of reforms trigger different growth mechanisms. Some may be released by restricted reforms, which do not strengthen the fundamental growth mechanism: systematic innovation. For example part of a bureaucracy may be reallocated to more productive tasks or agriculture may be decollectivized, even as most of the economy remains closed to market competition. Such restricted reforms may increase the economic growth rate temporarily, but it will fall back in time (see figure 2.3).[83] We consider such reforms unsuccessful.[84]

Other special growth mechanisms may be launched by complex reforms aimed at strengthening innovation-based growth. Thanks to the operation of such growth mechanisms, growth may accelerate even prior to the full

Figure 2.3 Changes in the Economic Growth Rate in Time Resulting from Restricted Reforms

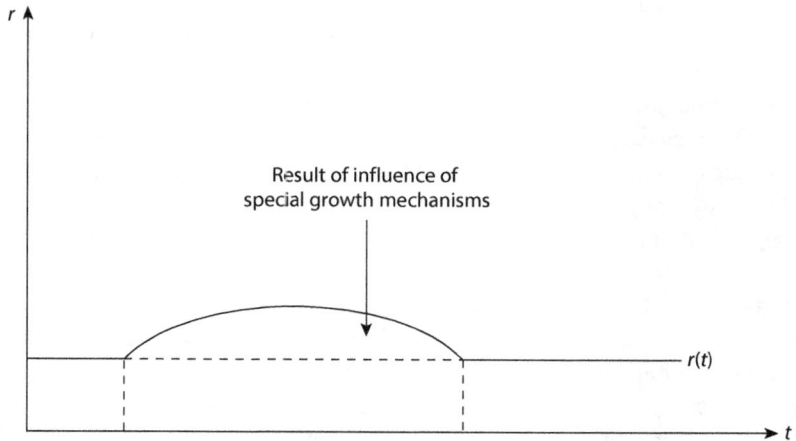

implementation of the reform program. For example, market competition is necessary to curb waste in enterprises and in the relations among them; however, it requires a broad scope of reforms to strengthen incentives for innovation.

Figure 2.4 presents acceleration r in time period t_0–t_1, which is caused by special growth mechanisms, launched by comprehensive reforms that, when completed, strengthen innovation-based growth. Since the t_1 moment, only the mechanism of innovation-based growth is operating. The economic growth rate is much higher than prior to the launch of the reforms; however, it may be lower than over the transition period when as special growth mechanisms are operating.

Moving on to the time structure of a successful reform package, that is, the distribution of its components in time, we may distinguish two principal variables:

- The moment of launching the particular reforms (cumulative or sequential).
- The rate of introducing the reforms—in other words, the period between the launching of the reforms and the manifestation of their results.

While analyzing and determining the time structure of a reform package, the sequence of introducing particular reforms is of decisive importance. Developing a new law—even liberalizing and stabilizing the economy—requires less time than constructing new organizations or reconstructing existing ones. Reforms differ in two other important aspects: their direct influence on economic performance and their significance to the success of other reforms. Obviously, any reforms that pave the way for success in either of these two dimensions should be launched first and introduced quickly. For example, a reform of the product market (deregulation) should be introduced together or prior to a reform of the labor market, as the former reduces producers' margins, and, as a result, weakens

Figure 2.4 Changes in the Rate of Economic Growth Influenced by Comprehensive Reforms

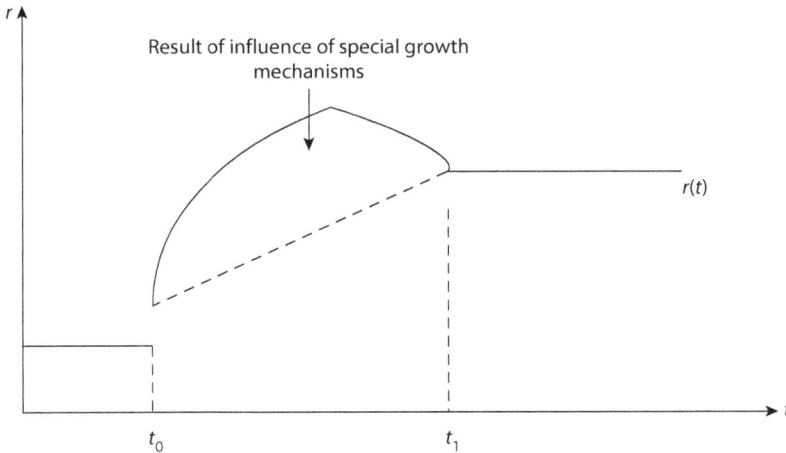

employees' resistance to making the labor market more flexible (Berger and Danninger 2005). Any reform to liberalize the setting up and running of business operations should be conducted comprehensively and radically.[85] this should be combined with a deep liberalization of foreign trade, which constitutes one of the most important mechanisms not only of technology transfer but also of exerting pressure on state-owned enterprises to compete (see the chapter on Estonia, which at the beginning of its transformation removed all barriers to international trade apart from an excise tax on certain goods).[86] Partial liberalization may only preserve an immature market economy suffering from unproductive factors and waste, including a lack of competition due to the use of private political connections. This threat stems from the fact that people who benefit from partial liberalization may hinder further reforms in order to preserve their privileges (Hellman 1998; Aslund 2007; see also the chapter on Indonesia, where liberalization after the fall of Sukarno in the 1970s was reversed to a large extent to protect the private interests of conglomerates).

The need for comprehensive and rapid liberalization does not mean that other reforms need be postponed until the process of liberalization is complete. If initial conditions effect deep macroeconomic instability, then efforts toward stability should begin together with liberalization and be conducted in a decisive manner. Tolerating instability is risky (see, for example, the chapters on República Bolivariana de Venezuela, Mexico, and Costa Rica in this book). Apart from this, there are important connections between stabilization and liberalization (see, for example, Balcerowicz 1995).

Organizational reconstruction (for example, the construction of an independent central bank and financial supervision system, privatization of enterprises, reorganization of the judicial system) is decisively important for long-term economic growth, but takes much more time than liberalization—and changes to the law in general—and macroeconomic stabilization (see, for example, the chapters on Mexico, Chile, Estonia, and Slovenia). These factors speak in favor of the early and rapid introduction of reforms that involve reconstruction. Thus we arrive at the general conclusion that in countries with restricted competition, deep macroeconomic instability, and organizational structures that hamper growth, all types of reforms should be launched more or less at the same time and introduced as quickly as possible. This strategy allows for the launch of both special growth mechanisms and innovation-based growth mechanisms, guaranteeing that economic growth will accelerate faster than is likely under other strategies. It also simplifies the introduction of subsequent reforms even as it narrows the field for unproductive actions.[87]

Summing up the differences between unsuccessful reforms and reforms capable of a permanent acceleration of economic growth,[88] we may claim that all reforms that uphold the status quo are unsuccessful—that is, reforms that exchange one system constraining innovation-based growth for another with similar features. For reforms to be successful, they need to move toward liberalization. But while this is a necessary factor, it is not adequate on its own. Many unsuccessful reforms were in the right direction but were incomplete. Some of them left specific barriers to growth (for example, reforms to socialism kept the structure of incentives that hampered innovation, Balcerowicz 1995; see also the chapter on República Bolivariana de Venezuela: free market reforms introduced in the late 1980s and early 1990s did not set the country on the path of permanent growth). Other reforms, while removing most of the old barriers, introduced new ones (for example, after the fall of socialism, East Germany received from West Germany not only an efficient legal system but also a social safety net that proved destructive in an area with low productivity; see also the chapter on Puerto Rico, where a similar system, in qualitative terms, was introduced). Successful reforms remove all inherited barriers for growth and do not form new ones. But permanent acceleration of growth may be undermined not only by vestigial barriers to growth but also by susceptibility to shocks. Certain characteristics of an institutional system will sooner or later lead to a macroeconomic crisis (see the chapters on Mexico, Chile, and Estonia, which after the introduction of radical free market reforms experienced deep crises). Successful reforms eliminate such features without introducing new ones; conversely, unsuccessful reforms leave some of them or form new ones.

Summary

This chapter outlines several concepts that, in our opinion, are useful in explaining differences in the rate of long-term economic growth.

The authors distinguish mechanisms of growth based on innovation (with the transfer of technologies from abroad as the main driver of convergence) and special growth mechanisms. The first is potentially permanent and may occur everywhere, but special mechanisms depend on a given situation and their influence is transitional.

The institutional system is treated as a set of variables composed of (1) various types of positions (roles) affecting decisions (we define positions in terms of typical situations of choice) and (2) various mechanisms of access to those positions. The first determines the system's situational influence on the economic performance of the country (with the influence depending on the typical situations of choice offered to decisions makers). The second determines the selective influence resulting from the mechanisms that govern access to decision-making posts in the system, including the most important ones. We concentrate on the first type of institutional influence on economic performance, at the same time indicating reasons why the second type of influence also requires detailed research.

Innovation-based growth may be blocked either by information barriers or by barriers to growth incentives. The first occur when innovative proposals are not included in the set of possible solutions considered by the people making decisions in a given society. In today's world such a situation is caused by institutional isolation, which also creates barriers to incentives for innovation (among others, by reducing the size of the market and the extent of market competition).

Incentives to innovate are barred when the expected utility of introducing innovation (and investing in it, as needed) is low compared to alternative options. Two types of institutional systems contribute to such barriers. The first does so by drastically reducing investment, including in technical progress. It may allow a lack of profit motive (because of, for example, the uncertainty of private investments) and a low savings rate (as when access to foreign savings is restricted). Or the connection between remuneration and individual effort may be cut (by, for example, community property rights or the prohibitive taxation of profits). Returns on investment may be uncertain for unofficial reasons, as well, due to bribes exacted in return for necessary services (characteristic of a predatory or failed state). On the other hand, the reason for a low savings rate, despite the high profitability of private savings, is most often an inflated welfare state and lack of fiscal discipline.

The second type of institutional system to obstruct innovation-based growth directly reduces the expected utility of innovations to a level lower than the utility of routine actions, even as it may not necessarily reduce investment rates. It may allow monopolies—subject to detailed analysis in the economic literature—or set constitutional and other institutional restrictions on competition. Many such systems are dominated by private monopolies or state monopolies (as in the case of a centrally planned economy).

With the occurrence of innovation-based growth in Great Britain at the turn of the 18th century, the world faced a new era. As increasingly globalized markets rose and fell, growth accelerated and slowed at different rates in different countries, and growth paths converged and diverged. Slow growth almost always resulted either from institutional systems that blocked innovation-based growth or a trend toward such systems.

Puzzles of Economic Growth • http://dx.doi.org/10.1596/978-1-4648-0325-3

Meanwhile, accelerated growth occurred in two groups of countries. The first, a very small one, are those that maintained a system affording a large scope of economic freedom and good protection of property rights from the beginning. The second group, much larger, started out with a system obstructing growth but eventually released their growth potential through a successful package of reforms.

A reform's success (or lack thereof) depends on initial conditions, including the shape of the inherited institutional system. Institutional systems differ from one from another in the number and type of growth barriers they pose. We define such barriers as specific institutional variables that obstruct permanent growth independently of the shape of other variables.

The more barriers to growth a given institutional system posits, the broader the reform package needed to achieve permanent economic growth. But aside from the conditions needed to support innovation, so-called special mechanisms of growth may be introduced, depending on the situation and with transitional influence. Thanks to those mechanisms, growth may accelerate prior to the completion of a comprehensive package of reforms, or, temporarily, as a result of restricted reforms. They allow a country to achieve spectacular rates of economic growth for a certain period of time.

In this chapter we also indicate certain topics calling for further research. Among them are mechanisms of social mobility and their interactions with various decision-making positions (roles), and the resulting influences on innovation-based economic growth. Moreover, economists' knowledge of major barriers to growth requires broadening, as does, more generally, an understanding of how long-term economic growth performance is affected by changes in selected institutional variables and various initial conditions. This task would be easier if, for their analysis, economists could use models that include a diverse array of variables influencing enterprises' decisions as they operate under various market structures (from competition to full monopoly). Despite recent progress in this field, there is still no convincing formalized theory that would explain why competition is, in practice, *always* more innovative than a monopoly. It would also be worthwhile to analyze, in more detail, how special mechanisms of economic growth operate under different initial conditions.

Notes

1. This chapter is based on Balcerowicz (2008).
2. Two caveats must be made on this point. First, the limited possibility of improving the efficiency of factors of production does not mean that they are exhaustible. Second, changes in the efficiency of use of factors of production may permanently change the economic growth rate if they influence stimuli to innovation and the possibility of their introduction.
3. Thus understood innovations comprise, in our opinion, all sources listed in the literature that help avoid a decrease in the marginal productivity of factors of production and, in consequence, maintain growth. Therefore, they also comprise positive external effects connected with the accumulation of different types of capital. Depending on

the model, these effects either facilitate formation of new knowledge on how to produce more effectively than in the past or spread this knowledge across the economy. The one or the other eventually leads to new ideas being introduced into business activity—that is, to innovation.

4. As pointed out in chapter 1, innovation relating to the manufacturing process may consist not only in "creative destruction"—that is, goods hitherto used in production being superseded by new goods of greater efficiency (see, for example, Aghion and Howitt 1992)—but may also take place through an increased number of types of such goods. Introduction of new types of indirect/capital goods reduces production costs, because it hampers the operation of the right of diminishing marginal productivity of factors of production (see, for example, Rivera-Batiz and Romer 1991).

5. This is how a slowdown in the productivity growth rates of factors of production is sometimes explained in highly developed countries, but this explanation lacks strong empirical grounds.

6. The fundamental importance of imports for technology transfer underlies the importance of free international trade for innovation-based growth. One of the first studies in which the impact of technology imports on economic growth was modeled is an article by Gomułka (1970).

7. According to Weede (2006), thanks to possible transfers of technologies, benefits from the smooth operation of institutions in highly developed countries (that build extensive technological knowledge) are not only limited to these countries, but spread to less developed countries as well.

8. Some models of endogenous growth can be interpreted as questioning the second assumption, and, as a result, convergence based on technology transfer. But as pointed out by Sachs and Warner (1995), they are not supported by international experience.

9. The insufficient size of a suitably qualified workforce in poor countries is perhaps a barrier to the foreign technology transfer that is a feature of so many formalized growth models. It constitutes a specific case of a more general problem that developing countries face: that is, they have a *different* variety of factors of production than are found in highly developed countries, which develop technologies suitable to their own factors (see, for example, Basu and Weil 1998). The resulting mismatch of foreign technologies to the individual factors of production in developing countries may explain why an especially high growth rate is characteristic of those that have not only opened to foreign technology transfer but also maintained a high rate of physical and human capital accumulation. Thanks to this capital, they can quickly reduce differences in the proportions of imported factors of production. It is also complemented, usually, by other types of productive behaviors.

10. Over the long term their effect on the average economic growth rate is close to zero. For instance, the average growth rate in the years 1500–1820 in Great Britain and Holland, on the one hand (that were the most open to international trade), and the rest of Western Europe, on the other hand, differed by only 0.13 percentage points (see, for example, Maddison 2001). In the contemporary world the benefits of international trade are dynamic rather than static, at least for those countries that are not at the technological frontier. Even if the countries with the most advanced technologies cannot shift this frontier faster under the conditions of a global economy than an autarky, other countries systematically benefit from the adaptation of more and more modern technologies developed elsewhere. Meanwhile, because no country is a leader in all types of technologies, all countries dynamically benefit from free international trade. In addition, it is doubtful that the technological frontier would shift in the

same way under a global economy as under an autarky is highly doubtful. Not all technological knowledge is specific, and openness to foreign countries is equivalent to knowledge extension—which facilitates other potential innovations. Finally, the static benefits from of international trade may at present be much larger than those resulting from a better allocation of factors of production; low-technology countries benefit from the transfer of more advanced foreign technologies and all countries benefit from a larger market that enables large-scale production and a higher degree of specialization (see, for example, Ventura 2005).

11. Of course an insignificant investment rate has not been the only problem caused by political instability in Haiti.

12. Particular activities differ in the degree to which they are rewarding in themselves (at least for some individuals), and in the amount of unpleasant effort that they require. It is understandable that activities rewarding in themselves require fewer external motivators than activities accompanied by unpleasant effort.

13. The process of ranking need not be comprehensive. In reality, some activities (or types of activities) are preferred, given individuals' motivational dispositions, over others that are left off the "list" rather than being ordered by declining utility. Thanks to the incomplete ordering of feasible solutions individuals can make decisions quickly, but omission is also one of several sources of possible errors in the decision-making process.

14. Apart from institutions, underlying factors include the physical environment. But it seems that, today, differences in institutions result in much bigger differences in economic performance (consider, for example, the Democratic People's Republic of Korea and the Republic of Korea) than does the physical environment. Besides, institutions may be changed while geographical factors are basically unalterable.

15. That is why, for example, James Madison, a coauthor of the United States Constitution and a proponent of these liberties, was not enthusiastic about the Bill of Rights but insisted on constraints on political powers.

16. This scope depends not only on institutional factors but on geographical distance from the political center. For example, in czarist Russia, people in Siberia had more actual freedom than those who lived in Moscow (though this did not mean that their standard of living was necessarily better). But modern transport and exchange of information have reduced the importance of physical distance to the exertion of political control.

17. For further information on this issue, see Balcerowicz (1995). Research in psychology provides increasing information on the unalterable aspects of individuals' dispositions. These findings, applied to economics, promise a better understanding of many economic decisions. One example of such a useful application is behavioral finance.

18. This assumption should prove true at least in societies created by birth and not by self-selection (as, for example, in the case of monasteries and Israeli kibbutzim).

19. For example, Gorbachev and Yeltsin in the USSR.

20. But it is not the only reason: Dictators may in effect be prisoners of their own power apparatus, which defends the dictatorship as a source of privilege for its members. This was the case of some czars in 19th-century Russia.

21. In systems with concentrated political power, negative self-selection may operate. As noted in chapter 1, it is highly likely that the power apparatus will attract individuals with reprehensible moral characteristics.

22. For example, success at the earliest stages of business activity may depend on political connections. Keefer and Knack (1997) suggest that people who become entrepreneurs thanks to such connections may have lower entrepreneurial potential than entrepreneurs who operate in conditions of free competition.

23. If socialism left any psychosocial legacy, it would be an additional argument for a radical system transformation (Balcerowicz 1995). The theory of cognitive dissonance (Festinger 1957) shows that individuals have more chance to adapt to new conditions if a change is radical and, consequently, perceived as irreversible.

24. Cultural differences, including the formative impact of institutional systems on actions of individuals, are studied more thoroughly by sociology and anthropology.

25. There is much talk of "homo sovieticus" but wherever radical reforms have been introduced, the scale and pace at which individuals adapted to their new conditions have been amazing.

26. For further reading on the benefits and costs resulting from the size of an economy (as well as on correlations between the size of countries and foreign trade), see Alesina, Spolaore, and Wacziarg (2005).

27. If world technology were stagnant, then the negative impact of low investment on economic growth would be reduced to a decreased product level in the long term. This is the basic conclusion from the growth theory discussed in chapter 1. But technologies change, and the most productive technologies require large investments (Abramovitz 1993).

28. The proportion of innovative investment in such systems is lower than in innovation-friendly ones. But even if it were the same, the volume of innovative investment in systems with a low investment rate would be smaller than in innovation-friendly ones (due to a higher investment rate in the latter).

29. The uncertainty may be expressed by the parameters (for example, standard deviation) of the statistical distribution of possible returns or by subjective measures based on investors' perceptions.

30. The effects of the structure of property rights and the level of their protection are not additive. If the content of property rights is improper (for example, they protect private or public monopolies), it is doubtful that their effective enforcement can have a positive impact on the overall efficiency of factors of production in the economy, as it would imply harsher prosecution of competitors that encroach upon monopoly privileges (and favor efficiency).

31. The communal nature of property rights is not the only reason for the low level of economic development observed among traditional tribal communities. Some of them have more individualistic property rights; however, the scope of private transactions is limited by the protection of property rights that does not extend beyond the members of a small group (see, for example, Greif 2006).

32. For example, in the European Union 20 percent of the poorest households receive on average 19.6 percent of the social spending, whereas 20 percent of the wealthiest households receive 22.8 percent. In France, where these proportions are especially distorted to the disadvantage of the poor (and social spending is the most oversized), the former receive 17.2 percent of the social spending, whereas the latter receive 27.4 percent (Collado and Iturbe-Ormaetxe 2006).

33. Profitability of investment may be reduced not only by taxes on profits and their distribution. It is also reduced by taxes on labor, if employees (who find employment

thanks to investment) manage to transfer at least some of this burden on to the enterprises. Finally, it is also reduced by taxes on consumption, if enterprises cannot increase their prices by the amount equivalent to tax. Both higher labor costs (not accompanied by suitably increased efficiency of labor) and payment of taxes on consumption (not fully included in the price), reduce enterprises' profits and therefore their capability and willingness to invest.

34. Excessive public spending often reduces investment and economic growth through an additional channel—a chronic fiscal deficit. It absorbs private savings and causes microeconomic instability and related uncertainty, sometimes leading to a crisis (see later in this section for more information on this issue; see, for example, Rzońca 2007).

35. High corruption "taxes" are usually accompanied by low tax revenues for the state, but not necessarily by low official tax rates (see, for example, the chapter on República Bolivariana de Venezuela and data on the scale of corruption and tax rates). If official tax rates are high or, worse still, determined at the discretion of officials, then they give officials yet more leverage in pressuring entrepreneurs to give bribes (see later in this section). This may activate a vicious circle, eventually leading to a crisis (and political transformation): high official taxes increase the possibility of bribes being demanded; bribery lowers the collection of official taxes; tax revenues, insufficient to cover public spending, prompt an increase in official taxes; bribery becomes even more common, and reduces official tax collection; the state resorts to inflation financing of public spending; and hyperinflation shifts the economy back to the primitive condition, where exchange only takes place in the event of a mutual convergence of needs, that is, only when two parties to a potential transaction have the goods of the quality and quantity desired by the other party (see, for example, the section in the chapter on Indonesia relating to the outcomes of Sukarno's policies).

36. The simple correlation between official tax rates and investment and economic growth is weak. A different picture emerges if actual tax burdens (including the corruption tax) are collectively taken into account. For more information on the links between private investment and corruption, see Frey (2001).

37. Two additional comments are needed at this point. First, not all regulations that produce higher compliance costs can and should be eliminated. For example, sanitary and safety regulations are usually justified and need not produce corruption. Second, corruption is not only related to official regulations, but may also be present in the public procurement and legislative process. The best remedies for these kinds of corruption are transparent procedures as well as a strong and efficient judicial apparatus.

38. This does not mean that official taxes may not be a source of uncertainty as well. If tax burdens are large, economic entities are strongly motivated to find loopholes in the tax system, which is easier the more complex that system. Because of such efforts, tax revenues calculated by governments are often incorrect. To obtain the planned level of revenues, parliaments have to hastily amend tax bills. Hasty amendments in turn produce other loopholes in the system. Simultaneously, as pointed out by Adam Smith (1776 [2007 is the year of the second Polish edition, vol. 2, p. 585]): "The certainty of what each individual ought to pay is, in taxation, a matter of so great importance, that a very considerable degree of inequality [in tax burdens], it appears, I believe, from the experience of all nations, is not near so great an evil as a very small degree of uncertainty."

39. We leave aside a fundamental question about the extent to which private protection (either contractual or self-help) can replace state protection. This issue, in its

philosophical dimension, relates to the rationale of the very existence of the state. For an in-depth analysis thereof, see Nozick (1974) and also Greif (2006).

40. Changes in the investment structure due to innovative investment being more sensitive to institutional solutions than noninnovative investment, may explain why there is much less inertia in economic growth than in investment rate (Easterly and Levine 2001).

41. Worse still, even if the pillager only intends to deprive an entrepreneur of a portion of his investment returns, this portion in the case of innovative investment may actually prove much bigger than in the case of routine investment, due to the pillager's problems with the estimation of the scale of return on innovative investment (see Baker 2004; quoted after Aziaradis and Stachurski 2005).

42. Therefore high official taxes not accompanied by pillage may be less detrimental to innovation-based economic growth than low taxes and unprotected property rights. But this does not mean that taxes only reduce investment and are not likely to disturb its structure to the detriment of innovative investment. The state that, thanks to taxes, has a share in profits from successful projects—but does not have any in loss—directs investors' activity to traditional (thus, safer) forms of activity at the expense of innovative (and more risky) projects. Imposing taxes on profits without subsidizing the losses reduces the difference in the expected profitability of projects. Some entrepreneurs prefer not to take the risk of investing in new, potentially more efficient production methods, as the benefits are not high enough. Furthermore, an increase in taxes strengthens incentives not to pay them, thus discouraging innovative investment, which is more difficult to hide than routine investment. On the other hand, the more important the low investment sectors (where tax evasion is easy) in the economy, the higher the taxes the state has to impose on high investment sectors to achieve specific revenues. This further discourages from innovative investment in favor of investment facilitating tax evasion.

43. In addition, there are at least two problems connected with the financing of investment from foreign savings. First, foreign capital holders, like all others, expect a return. Therefore, when investment is financed from foreign savings, in the long run only a part of the income that has increased thanks to such savings remains in the country. It is the part designated for the remuneration of employees working in production launched as a result of the new investment. On average it amounts to approximately two-thirds of the total revenue achieved in the economy; the remaining one-third goes to foreign holders of savings (see, for example, the chapters on Puerto Rico and Estonia and also the data on GDP and net domestic product [NDP] in these countries). Second, foreign holders can, if the situation in a given country becomes unfavorable, withdraw their capital faster than domestic holders, which deepens the scale of primary economic problems (see, for example, the chapter on Mexico, in which sudden outflows of capital and stops in inflow led to repeated currency crises). Withdrawal of foreign direct investment (FDI) is the most difficult, but its level cannot be high without huge domestic savings (see, for example, Aghion, Comin, and Howitt 2006). What is more, research shows that foreign investment is most beneficial for the economy when financed from domestic savings, since then it simply involves the import of more advanced technologies and does not cause any considerable exchange rate fluctuations.

44. Following the abolition of the welfare state, forethought was obviously not the only factor responsible for an increase in the savings ratio in China. An even greater role has been played in recent years by increased corporate savings, but this, at least in part, was also caused by the elimination of most social spending (as well as the labor

market's increased flexibility). Such measures allowed enterprises to keep labor costs low and, in consequence, to post high profits that provided grounds for savings.

45. These are not the only conditions that are critical to achieving the Ricardian equivalence. Others include, for example, nondistortionary nature of taxation. Most empirical research shows that in developed countries, where households find it easier to set aside a part of their income, their savings increase by an amount equivalent to 20–50 percent of the deficit increase (see, for example, Gale and Orszag 2003). *Ipso facto*, the savings that can finance investment decrease by the amount equivalent to 50–80 percent of the deficit. Economists still argue about the issue of Ricardian equivalence (see, for example, Elmendorf and Mankiw 1998).

46. This may explain why, in the light of empirical research, the content of property rights is more important to long-term growth than their protection (which does not mean, of course, that property rights protection is insignificant to economic growth). See, for example, Acemoglu and Johnson (2005). Admittedly these authors introduce a slightly different division of institutions: they divide them into property rights and contract institutions. But their definitions of both groups of institutions are close to how the content of property rights and the level of their protection are understood in this chapter.

47. The formalized model that they present is relatively simple—for example, it does not include capital. Its more complex version does not change the conclusions in terms of quality, but results in an intensified negative impact of monopoly rights on economic efficiency (see, Herrendorf and Teixeira 2003; cited after Parente and Prescott 2005, 1395).

48. Rigid working practices still hamper economic development in India; see the chapter that compares its economic performance with China's.

49. This barrier may be interpreted as a factor that either eliminates more efficient technologies from feasible sets, or charges their introduction with such an effort that their utility becomes lower than the continued use of inefficient technologies.

50. There can of course be certain specific cases, where a more efficient technology does not replace a less efficient one, although the use of the latter is not supported by the state. Such a situation may take place, for instance, when the benefits of a technology depend on its widespread use; in such a case the date of its implementation may determine which technology will be used (see, for example, Arthur 1996). It must, however, be emphasized that even if market forces block the implementation of more efficient technologies in some specific cases, the state can do it at any time.

51. On the other hand, noninstitutional barriers (for example, collusion of enterprises using old technologies or protests of their employees) to efficiency in general, and to the implementation of new technologies in particular, most often prove to be inefficient (see, for example, Mokyr 2005, 1167–68; Mokyr demonstrates the accuracy of this statement in the context of the Industrial Revolution in Great Britain).

52. The impact of these regulations on innovation depends on the effectiveness of their enforcement. For example, the diminishing power of guilds resulted in a declining importance of guild regulations as a barrier to innovation. This example once again shows that the impact of changes in the effectiveness of law enforcement on economic performance depends on its content.

53. But it must be noted that the granting of monopoly power by the state to an enterprise is often followed by various regulations that limit its activity (for example, price or rate of return), the introduction of which is justified by an intention to

reduce this power. Thus, there is a double link between restrictive regulations and monopolies: on the one hand, such regulations require that the enterprises covered by the regulations should be protected from competition and, on the other, established monopolies are often subject to regulations intended to protect the clients of a monopoly against its power.

54. This argument should be enough to advocate market competition in developing countries. Even if we assume, contrary to experience, that new technologies are mainly developed by monopolies, this is of no importance to those countries mainly interested in the fast implementation of technologies developed and tested elsewhere. Such imports can be guaranteed by a continuous inflow of new companies to the market that, by nature, do not care about the costs sunk in previous technologies.

55. Boldrin and Levine (2002) claim that costs of copying innovations are large enough to make intellectual rights protection socially undesirable. Such protection was completely nonexistent, for instance, in 19th-century Holland and Switzerland, and this did not have any negative impact on their technical progress (see, Schiff 1971; cited after Mokyr 2005, 1166). A review of the pros and cons of intellectual rights protection, however, lies beyond the scope of this chapter and book. The only possible conclusion is that its importance for economic growth is the subject of a growing, rather than a subsiding, controversy in economics.

56. Since enterprises do not take into account the impact of innovation on profits or the value of capital accumulated by other enterprises, the pace of innovation implementation under competition may be theoretically *too* fast from the point of view of social utility maximization. This issue is not analyzed further because this book focuses on economic growth analysis. In contrast to social utility it is an observed parameter and also, generally speaking, has a positive impact on social utility. What is more, estimates of the social rate of return on R&D activity, which are much higher than the private rate of return, show that a potentially rapid pace of innovation is not a problem that exists in practice (see, for example, Jones and Williams 1998). In other words, the pace of innovation implementation is nowhere fast enough for possible negative external impacts—such as rendering the assets previously accumulated by a society useless—to outweigh the positive external impacts that include, for example, the diffusion of more efficient production methods.

57. A modern version of an innovation-blocking system is the centrally planned economy. But as a matter of fact, it was not basically different from the older systems that did not allow private ownership or competition.

58. This does not mean that they are the only reason why such periods occur. Wars may have similar consequences. An economy may also be derailed by strong shocks, though many shocks have domestic, institutional roots.

59. We use the term time structure and not, for example, sequence, as the distribution of reforms in time does not have to be sequential.

60. But another two examples of countries exporting natural resources, Australia and Chile, described in this book, show that large natural resources do not have to be a calamity and periods when their sale generates extraordinary income can be used for introducing reforms.

61. Rodrik (2006) is a prominent representative of this group.

62. It is worth emphasizing that analyzing the relations among nominal and functional differences in institutional solutions (including the issue of which nominally different

institutions lead to similar individual behaviors and aggregated results) constitutes one of many important tasks of the institutional economy.

63. This problem concerns not only discussions of reforms after the fall of socialism. For example, the Dutch system of "flexible protection" is often presented as an alternative to the Anglo-Saxon flexible labor market. It is claimed that both systems assure low unemployment and high employment rates, but the systems disregard differences in the growth in the number of productive-age people. In Denmark this number practically remains unchanged, and in the United States it is rapidly growing. Therefore, the Dutch system in the United States would have to be much more expensive and surely less efficient from the point of view of the employment rate than current U.S. solutions.

64. Recent application may be seen in Hausman, Rodrik, and Velasco (2005).

65. The capacity to co-occur, that is, to persist as a system, should be distinguished from the results achieved. The set of institutional variables may form a system, that is, it can persist even if it produces poor economic results. What is more, poor institutional solutions may not only persist, but also deteriorate. For example, systems characterized by corruption may form incentives for increased corruption.

66. Not all barriers to growth are institutional. For example, a chronic fiscal deficit is not directly an institutional barrier, but it depends on institutional factors; in other words, it is a reflection of a lack of adequate restrictions imposed on people responsible for conducting fiscal policy. Certainly, there are extrainstitutional barriers to growth (for example, unfavorable locations) that do not depend on institutions. The significance of those barriers decreases alongside the development of technology. For example, a location in the tropics was important for the productivity of technologies used in agriculture, but it does not have much importance in the case of industrial technologies.

67. A successful package of reforms also removes all major sources of macroeconomic crises; on the other hand, an unsuccessful package of reforms leaves at least some of them.

68. This factor, even though it may not be sufficient for an economic miracle (see later in this section), may explain why latecomers to the path of modern economic growth often grew faster than their predecessors (that are now highly developed economies) when their income per capita had been equally low.

69. It seems that the poor condition of public finances posed a growth barrier in Ireland in the 1980s, while other factors fostered growth—well-protected private property, an economy open to international trade and the flow of capital, few institutional restrictions of particular markets (including the labor market), and a well-qualified labor force at its disposal; for more information on the Irish miracle, see Rzońca 2002. The aforementioned mechanism does not explain why Hong Kong SAR, China and Singapore remained economic tigers after reaching a high level of income per capita. Here we reach another interesting topic—the maximum rate of growth in countries of various sizes, various degrees of urbanization, and so on.

70. This state of affairs leads certain authors (see, for example, Eckhaus 2004) to question the significance of institutions to growth. They claim that as growth can accelerate under very imperfect institutions, these do not have a decisive role in explaining growth.

71. An additional growth factor was the liberalization of international trade, which reversed the economic isolation of the 1930s. The resulting acceleration of growth was

only partly permanent in part it was exhausted with the depletion of opportunities to improve the efficiency of the use of production factors.

72. This mechanism may be overturned by freedom of migration. The most talented and energetic people are likely to leave a country if they do not see any prospects for an improvement in their economic situation. Mass emigration may in turn reduce the quality of education, on which the growth of human capital depends in the long term.

73. This type of inefficiency probably occurs in every organization not subject to market competition. The force of incentives for removing this inefficiency, which affect the individuals in a given organization, depends on the force of incentives these organizations are subject to. Market competition does not have good substitutes in terms of putting pressure on organizations.

74. For more information concerning the subject, see Balcerowicz (1989).

75. Apart from this, Chinese agriculture in Maoist times was subject to high taxes, while agriculture is the USSR was subsidized (Rozelle and Swinnen 2004; see also the chapter on Estonia in this book).

76. But differently structured economies do not fully explain why poor countries are poor and why rich countries are rich. Poor countries are characterized by lower productivity in all sectors: in sectors where productivity is on average low all over the world and in those in which it is high. The main reason of their underdevelopment is that they differ from highly developed countries most in terms of productivity in sectors in which the highest share of people work, that is, in sectors in which productivity is on average low worldwide (Caselli 2005, 723). Once again, a conclusion may be drawn that the only mechanism that could push poor countries out of poverty is the mechanism of growth based on innovation, even if we assume that changes in the structure of the economy are possible independent of changes in the productivity of its particular sectors (or, in other words, that the mechanism of growth based on innovation has no crucial significance for structural changes).

77. A portion of formally unemployed people may be employed in informal sector, at the same time receiving various social benefits. Therefore, a low rate of employment may be accompanied by a large informal sector.

78. Increase in employment rate may have a permanent or at least a stronger influence on economic growth than it is implied by the change in productivity of people who used to be professionally passive from zero to a positive value. The number of the employed may be related to the pace or at least the quantity of innovation. Empirical research confirms this relation, characteristic of many models of endogenic growth. But identifying a positive relation between the level of GDP per employee and the size of the labor force (see, for example, Jones 2005), this research indicates a positive influence of the employment rate on the quantity rather than the pace of innovation. This result of empirical research does not qualitatively alter the previous conclusion, according to which increase in employment rate cannot permanently accelerate economic growth; in other words, it is a special mechanism of growth.

79. Of course, a high rate of employment may be also achieved by the commands of central planner But in such a case, the productivity of many formally employed people still remains nil (and will even have a negative value if employment grows, for example, in secret police or other repressive institutions). Moreover, a zero productivity of a portion of the employed may corrode the discipline of their colleagues. This (at best) ambiguous influence of increase in employment rate achieved by the

commands of central planer on economic growth makes it hard to consider such type of employment growth to be a special growth mechanism.

80. This manner of interpretation may be applied to the results of growth calculations conducted for the USSR, for example, by Easterly and Fischer (1994).

81. Another issue is that this considerable growth in the proportion of the employed since the 1960s resulted more from a rise in population than from a shift in actual employment ratios. In other words, it resulted from demography rather than from reforms motivating people to seek work. But we have to emphasize that demographic changes increasing the share of productive-age people in the population do not necessarily result in an increase in the number of the employed. This depends, to a considerable extent, on the flexibility of the labor market. If the market is made stiff by excessive regulations, high margins on labor costs, or inflated social expenditures directed toward productive-age people, the potential of demographic changes cannot be realized. This is the experience of, for example, free Poland.

82. The mechanisms may be related more to particular features of systems hindering growth rather than to income per capita. For example, centrally planned economies can gather more excessive human capital than countries at a similar level of development free from the experience of central planning.

83. Certainly, the change of the rate of growth under the influence of special mechanisms does not have to be continuous. Figure 2.3 is only an illustration of an example. This comment concerns also figure 2.4.

84. Their introduction, despite the fact that it only partially accelerates economic growth, improves living conditions as it increases the level of production over a longer period of time.

85. Such reforms have crucial significance for post-socialist countries (see, for example, the chapter on Estonia in this book). They launch mechanisms of growth, remove deficiencies, and narrow the possibility of undertaking unproductive actions in the future.

86. Membership in international organizations may help strengthen freedom of international trade, which in turn makes it impossible to block the introduction of new technologies. Without such membership, national enterprises may, instead of introducing necessary adjustments, try to convince politicians to protect their particular interests (see, for example, Parente and Prescott 2005, 1408–13). But membership in international organizations may be detrimental to economic growth if it restricts economic freedom in general and the freedom of international trade in particular (see, for example, the chapter on República Bolivariana de Venezuela, specifically its participation in the Andean Pact in 1973). In such a case, to accelerate economic growth it is necessary to withdraw from an international organization (see, for example, the chapter on Chile, which, despite the fact that it was the founding state of the Andean Pact when it liberalized its economy, withdrew in 1976).

87. In countries in which a political breakthrough is taking place, there are also other arguments for launching all reforms at once and implementing them rapidly. Directly after such a breakthrough, social support for radical reforms is easier to achieve (Balcerowicz 1995). Moreover, the theory of cognitive dissonance indicates, as has already been mentioned, that the radicalism of reforms increases the chance that people will see them as irreversible and will more quickly adjust to the new conditions. It is more complicated, from the point of view of the political economy of reforms, to specify the timing of reforms in countries in which the initial institutional system does not contain barriers to growth, and the economy does not have features whose removal would mean launching special growth mechanisms. In such systems,

reforms that strengthen incentives for productive behaviors (for example, decreasing progression of income taxes) may accelerate growth after a period which goes far beyond even a few terms of the parliament (see, e.g., Li and Sarte 2001).

88. Here, we should consider the situation of a country whose initial institutional system blocks economic growth based on innovations.

Bibliography

Abramovitz, M. 1986. "Catching Up, Forging Ahead and Falling Behind." *Journal of Economic History* 46: 385–406.

———. 1993. "The Search for the Sources of Growth: Areas of Ignorance—Old and New." *The Journal of Economic History* 53: 217–43.

Acemoglu, D., and S. Johnson. 2005. "Unbundling Institutions." *Journal of Political Economy* 113: 949–95.

Acemoglu, D., S. Johnson, J. A. Robinson, and Y. Thaicharoen. 2002. "Institutional Causes, Macroeconomic Symptoms: Volatility, Crisis and Growth." *Journal of Monetary Economics* 50: 49–123.

Aghion, P., D. Comin, and P. Howitt. 2006. "When Does Domestic Saving Matter for Economic Growth." NBER Working Paper 12275, National Bureau of Economic Research, Cambridge, MA.

Aghion, P., and S. N. Durlauf. eds. 2005. *Handbook of Economic Growth*, Vols. 1A and 1B. Amsterdam: Elsevier B.V.

Aghion, P., and P. Howitt. 1992. "A Model of Growth through Creative Destruction." *Econometrica* 60: 323–51.

Alesina, A., E. Spolaore, and R. Wacziarg. 2005. "Trade, Growth and the Size of Countries." In *Handbook of Economic Growth*, Vols. 1A and 1B, edited by P. Aghion and S. N. Durlauf. Amsterdam: Elsevier B.V.

Arrow, K. J. 1962. "The Economic Implications of Learning by Doing." *Review of Economic Studies* 29: 155–73.

Arthur, B. W. 1996. "Increasing Returns and New World of Business." *Harvard Business Review* July–August: 100–9.

Åslund, A. 2007. *How Capitalism Was Built: The Transformation of Central and Eastern Europe, Russia, and Central Asia*. New York: Cambridge University Press.

Aslund, A., and M. Dąbrowski. 2008. *Challenges of Globalization: Imbalances and Growth*. Washington, DC: Peterson Institute for International Economics.

Aziaradis, C., and J. Stachurski. 2005. "Poverty Traps." In *Handbook of Economic Growth*, Vols. 1A and 1B, edited by P. Aghion and S. N. Durlauf. Amsterdam: Elsevier B.V.

Baker, E. 2004. "Institutional Barriers to Technology Adoption in Rural Africa." Stanford University, Standford, CA.

Balcerowicz, L. 1989. Systemy gospodarcze. Elementy Analizy Porównawczej (Economic Systems. Elements of Comparative Analysis, in Polish) Warsaw School of Economics, Warsaw.

———. 1995. *Socialism, Capitalism, Transformation*. Budapest Central European University Press.

———. 2008. "Institutional Systems and Economic Growth." In *Challenges of Globalization: Imbalances and Growth*, edited by A. Aslund and M. Dąbrowski. Washington, DC: Peterson Institute for International Economics.

Barro, R., and X. Sala-i-Martin. 1997. "Technological Diffusion, Convergence, and Growth." *Journal of Economic Growth* 2: 1–27.

Barro, R. J. 1974. "Are Government Bonds Net Wealth?" *Journal of Political Economy* 82: 1095–17.

Basu, S., and D. Weil. 1998. "Appropriate Technology and Growth." *Quarterly Journal of Economics* 113: 1025–54.

Bauer, P. 1998. "The Disregard of Reality." In *The Revolution in Development Economics*, edited by, J. A. Dorn, S. H. Hanke, and A. A. Walters. Washington, DC: CATO Institute.

Baumol, W. J. 2002. *The Free-Market Innovation Machine. Analyzing the Growth Miracle of Capitalism.* Princeton, NJ: Princeton University Press.

Berger, H., and S. Danninger. 2005. "Labor and Product Deregulation: Partial, Sequential, or Simultaneous Reform?" IMF Working Paper, International Monetary Fund, Washington, DC.

Bindra, D., and J. Stewart. 1971. *Motivation.* Harmondsworth, England: Penguin.

Blanchard, O. J., and F. Giavazzi. 2002. "Current Account Deficits in the Euro Area. The End of the Feldstein Horioka Puzzle?" MIT Department of Economics Working Paper 03–05, Cambridge, MA.

Boldrin, M., and D. K. Levine. 2002. *Perfectly Competitive Innovation.* Federal Reserve Bank of Minneapolis Staff Report 303, Minneapolis.

Caselli, F. 2005. "Accounting for Cross-Country Income Differences." In *Handbook of Economic Growth*, Vols. 1A and 1B, edited by P. Aghion and S. N. Durlauf. Amsterdam: Elsevier B.V.

Collado, M. D., and I. Iturbe-Ormaetxe. 2006. "Public Transfers to the Poor: Is Really Europe More Generous than the United States?" Working Paper, Instituto Valenciano de Investigaciones Economicas, Valencia, Spain.

Crafts, N. 1998. "East Asian Growth Before and After the Crisis." IMF Working Paper, International Monetary Fund, Washington, DC, September.

Dowrick, S. 1992. "Technological Catch Up and Diverging Incomes: Patterns of Economic Growth 1960–88." *Economic Journal* 102: 600–10.

Durlauf, S. N., and P. A. Johnson. 1995. "Multiple Regimes and Cross-Country Growth Behavior." *Journal of Applied Econometrics* 10 (4): 365–84.

Easterly, W., and S. Fischer. 1994. "The Soviet Economic Decline: Historical and Republican Data." NBER Working Paper 4735, National Bureau of Economic Research, Cambridge, MA.

Easterly, W., and R. Levine. 2001. "It's Not Factor Accumulation. Stylized Facts and Growth Models." *World Bank Economic Review* 15: 177–219.

Eckhaus, R. 2004. "The Search for the Grail of Development." *The Journal of Economic Asymmetries* 1: 1–14.

Elmendorf, D. W., and G. Mankiw. 1998. "Public Debt." Paper prepared for the "Handbook of Macroeconomics."

Elster, J. 1989. "Social Norms and Economic Theory." *Journal of Economic Perspectives* 3(4): 99–117.

Festinger, L. 1957. *A Theory of Cognitive Dissonance.* Stanford, CA: Stanford University Press.

Frey, T. 2001. "Keeping Shop. The Value of the Rule of Law in Warsaw and in Moscow." In *Assessing the Value of the Law in Transition Economies*, edited by P. Murell. Ann Arbor, MI: The University of Michigan Press.

Gale, W. G., and P. R. Orszag. 2003. "The Economic Effects of Long-Term Fiscal Discipline." Discussion Paper 8, Urban-Brookings Tax Policy Centre, Urban Institute, Washington, DC, April.

Galor, O. 2005. "From Stagnation to Growth: Unified Growth Theory." In *Handbook of Economic Growth*, Vols. 1A and 1B, edited by P. Aghion and S. N. Durlauf. Amsterdam: Elsevier B.V.

Geenwood, J., Z. Hercowitz, and P. Krusell. 1997. "Long-Run Implications of Investment-Specific Technological Change." *American Economic Review* 87 (3): 342–62.

Gomułka, S. 1970, "Extensions of Golden Rule of Reseach of Phelps" in Review of Economic Studies 37 (1): 73–93.

Gomulka, S. 1990. *The Theory of Technical Change and Economic Growth.* London: Routledge.

Gonzalez, F. 2005. "Insecure Property Rights and Technical Backwardness." *The Economic Journal* 115: 703–21.

Greif, A. 2006. *Institutions and the Path to the Modern Economy. Lessons from Medieval Trade.* Cambridge, U.K.: Cambridge University Press.

Griffith, R., S. J. Redding, and J. M. Van Reenen. 2005. "Mapping the Two Faces of R and D: Productivity Growth in a Panel of OECD Industries." *The Review of Economics and Statistics* 86 (4): 883–95.

Grossman, H., and E. Helpman. 1991. "Quality Ladders in the Theory of Growth." *Review of Economic Studies* 68: 43–61.

Hausman, R., D. Rodrik, and A. Velasco. 2005. "Growth Diagnostics," NBER Working Paper No. 105666, Cambridge, MA: National Bureau of Economic Research.

Hebb, D. O. 1971. "Drives and the Conceptual Nervous System." In *Motivation*, ed. D. Bindra and J. Stewart, 118–36. Hammondsworth, Midx.: Penguin.

Hellman, J. S. 1998. "Winners Take All: The Politics of Partial Reform in Post-Communist Transition." *World Politics* 50 (2): 203–34.

Herrendorf, B., and A. Teixeira. 2003. "Monopoly Rights Can Reduce Income Big Time." Working Paper, University of Carlos III.

Jones, C. 1995. "R&D-Based Models of Economic Growth." *Journal of Political Economy* 102: 759–84.

———. 2005. "Growth and Ideas." In *Handbook of Economic Growth*, Vols. 1A and 1B, edited by P. Aghion and S.N. Durlauf. Amsterdam: Elsevier B.V.

Jones, C. I., and J. C. Williams. 1998. "Measuring the Social Return to R&D." *Quarterly Journal of Economics* 113 (4): 1119–35.

Jorgenson, D. W. 2005. "Accounting for Growth in the Information Age." In *Handbook of Economic Growth*, Vols. 1A and 1B, edited by P. Aghion and S. N. Durlauf. Amsterdam: Elsevier B.V.

Jovanovic, B., and P. L. Rousseau. 2005. "General Purpose Technologies." In *Handbook of Economic Growth*, Vols. 1A and 1B, edited by P. Aghion and S. N. Durlauf. Amsterdam: Elsevier B.V.

Keefer, P., and S. Knack. 1997. "Why Don't Poor Countries Catch Up? A Cross-National Test of an Institutional Explanation." *Economic Inquiry* 35 (3): 590–802.

Keller, W. 2004. "International Technology Diffusion." *Journal of Economic Literature* 42: 752–82.

Kuznets, S. 1971. "Economic Growth of Nations: Total Output and Production Structure." Cambridge, MA: Harvard University Press.

Leibenstein, H. 1957. *Economic Backwardness and Economic Growth*. New York: John Wiley and Sons.

Lewis, W. 2004. *The Power of Productivity: Wealth, Poverty, and the Threat to Global Stability*. Chicago: University of Chicago Press.

Li, W., and P. Sarte. 2001. "Growth Effects of Progressive Taxes." Federal Reserve Bank of Richmond Working Paper, Richmond.

Maddison, A. 1991. *Dynamic Forces in Capitalist Development: A Long-Run Comparative View*. Oxford, U.K.: Oxford University Press.

Maddison, A. 2001. *The World Economy: A Millennial Perspective*. Paris: Development Centre of OECD.

Madsen, K. B. 1968. *Modern Theories of Motivation*. Copenhagen: Munksgaard.

McClelland, C. D. 1961. *The Achieving Society*. Princeton, NJ: D. Van Nostrand Co.

Mokyr, J. 2005. "Long-Term Economic Growth and History of Technology." In *Handbook of Economic Growth*, Vols. 1A and 1B, edited by P. Aghion and S. N. Durlauf. Amsterdam: Elsevier B.V.

Mussa, M., and M. Goldstein. 1993. "The Integration of World Capital Markets." In *Changing Capital Markets: Implications for Monetary Policy*, Federal Reserve Bank of Kansas City, Kansas City.

Nelson, R. 1981. "Assessing Private Enterprise: An Exegesis of Tangled Doctrine." *Bell Journal of Economics* 12 (1): 93–111.

Nickell, S. J. 1996. "Competition and Corporate Performance." *Journal of Political Economy* 104 (4): 724–46.

North, D. C. 1990. *Institutions, Institutional Change and Economic Performance*. Cambridge, MA: Harvard University Press.

———. 1993. "The New Institutional Economics and Development." WUSTL Economics Working Paper Archive.

Nozick, R. 1974. *Anarchy, State, and Utopia*. Oxford, U.K.; Blackwell Publishers.

Parente, S. L., and E. C. Prescott. 2000. *Barriers to Riches*. Cambridge, MA: MIT Press.

Parente, S. L., and E. C. Prescott. 2005. "A Unified Theory of the Evolution of International Income Levels." In *Handbook of Economic Growth*, Vols. 1A and 1B, edited by P. Aghion and S. N. Durlauf. Amsterdam: Elsevier B.V.

Phelps, E. S. 2006. "The Genius of Capitalism." *The Wall Street Journal of Europe*, October 10, 12.

Prescott, Edward C., and Stephen L. Parente. 1999. "Monopoly Rights: A Barrier to Riches." *American Economic Review* 89 (5) (December): 1216–33. Published by the American Economic Association.

Rivera-Batiz, L. A., and P. Romer. 1991. "Economic Integration and Endogenous Growth." *Quarterly Journal of Economics* 106: 531–55.

Rodrik, D. 2006. "Goodbye Washington Consensus, Hello Washington Confusion? A Review of World Bank's Economic Growth in 1990's: Learning from a Decade of Reform." *Journal of Economic Literature* 44 (4): 973–87.

Rosenberg, N., and L. E. Birdzell Jr. 1986. *How the West Grew Rich*. Basic Books.

Rozelle, S., and J. F. M. Swinnen. 2004. "Success and Failure of Reform: Insights from the Transition of Agriculture." *Journal of Economic Literature* 42 (2): 404–56.

Rzońca, A. 2002. "Rachunek Wzrostu Na Przykładzie Gospodarki Irlandii W Latach Dziewięćdziesiątych." Warszawa.

———. 2007. Paraliżujący deficyt (The Paralyzing Deficit, in Polish). Zeszyt Edukacyjny FOR (Civil Development Forum Educational Paper). No. 1, Warsaw.

Sachs, J. D., and A. Warner. 1995. "Economic Reform and the Process of Global Integration." *Brookings Papers on Economic Activity* 1: 1–118.

Scarpetta, S., P. Hemmings, T. Tressel, and J. Woo. 2002. "The Role of Policy and Institutions for Productivity and Firm Dynamics: Evidence from Micro and Industry Data." OECD Working Paper 329, Organisation for Economic Co-operation and Development (OECD), Paris.

Schiff, E. 1971. *Industrialization without National Patent*. Princeton, NJ: Princeton University Press.

Schultz, T. W. 1980. "Nobel Lecture: The Economics of Being Poor." *The Journal of Political Economy* 88 (4): 639–51.

Schumpeter, J. A. 1962. *Capitalism, Socialism and Democracy*. New York: Harper Torchbooks [originally published in 1942 by Harper & Row].

Smith, A. 2007. *An Inquiry into the Nature and Causes of the Wealth of Nations*. Vols. 1 and 2. 2nd ed. [Original book published in 1776.] Warsaw: PWN.

Ventura, J. 2005. "A Global View of Economic Growth." In *Handbook of Economic Growth*, Vols. 1A and 1B, edited by P. Aghion and S. N. Durlauf. Amsterdam: Elsevier B.V.

Weede, E. 2006. "Economic Freedom and Development: New Calculations and Interpretations." *Cato Journal* 26 (3): 511–24.

Woo, W. T. 2006. "The Experimentalist-Convergence Debate in Interpreting China's Economic Growth." In *Living Standards and the Wealth of Nations: Successes and Failures in Real Convergence*, edited by L. Balcerowicz and S. Fisher. Cambridge, MA: MIT Press.

CHAPTER 3

How Did Australia Get Ahead of New Zealand?

Jakub Szeliga

The available literature has devoted little space to a qualitative, comparative analysis of the differences in the economic performance of Australia and New Zealand. Whenever the issue has been addressed, authors have tended to disregard the 1970s (see, among others, Briggs and Ballingall 2001; Buckle 2004), that is, the period when the growth rates of Australia and New Zealand diverged. Because of this oversight, the impact of the 1970s reforms—implemented by Australia but not by New Zealand—has not been accounted for. Ample attention has been given to the reforms initiated by New Zealand in 1984 (Boston 1997; Brasch 1996); yet the economic growth dip following the launch of those reforms—and lasting approximately into the early 1990s—is scarcely addressed. This chapter attempts to fill these gaps.

The size and growth of both countries' real per capita gross domestic product (GDP) between 1946 and (approximately) 1974 was similar (see figure 3.1). In the late 1970s, however, New Zealand's GDP per head slipped markedly behind that of Australia. Another decline in the country's output level, again relative to Australia, occurred in the second half of the 1980s (see figure 3.2 with highlighted periods of divergence).

Based on an analysis of per capita GDP level differentials between the two countries in 1970–2002, we have distinguished six subperiods characterized by distinct differences in growth rates. In 1971–74 average annual per capita GDP growth in New Zealand was well above that of Australia. Between 1975 and 1980 growth in New Zealand collapsed, while in Australia it remained almost unchanged. From 1981 to 1986 average annual per capita GDP in New Zealand accelerated enough for the country to get ahead of Australia again. Yet, in 1987–92 its economic growth fell back below zero, while Australia's average annual output continued to grow at a pace observed between 1981 and 1986. From 1993 to 2002 the discrepancy between the growth rates of the two analyzed countries gradually narrowed. In 1993–98 growth was 1.0 percentage

Figure 3.1 Average Annual Per Capita GDP: Australia and New Zealand, 1946–2002
1990 US$ thousands

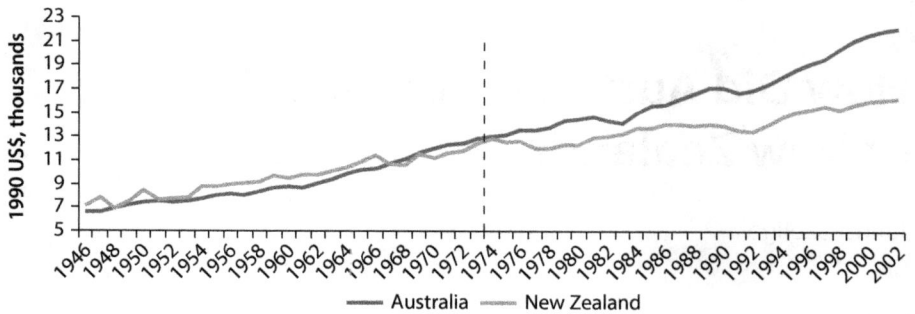

Source: World Bank 2004.

Figure 3.2 GDP Per Capita: Australia and New Zealand, 1970–2002
1990 US$ thousands

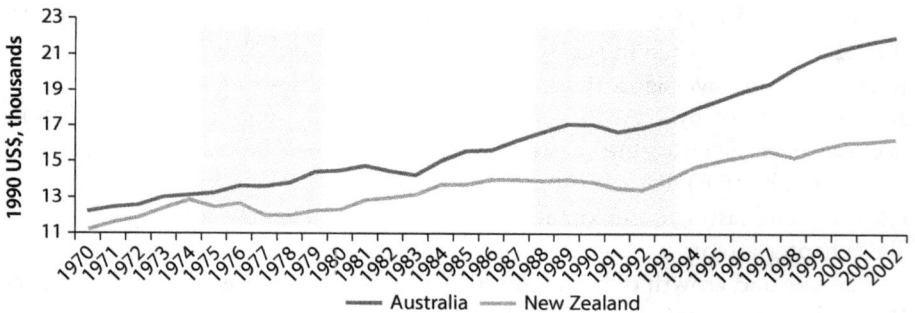

Source: World Bank 2004.
Note: Periods of significant divergence are shaded.

point higher in Australia than in New Zealand. In 1999–2002 the difference shrank to 0.5 percentage points (see table 3.1).

Throughout 1971–2002 Australia's expansion was markedly smoother than that of New Zealand. Economic collapses in New Zealand during the periods 1975–80 and 1987–92 were not echoed by parallel downturns in Australia. Had average annual GDP growth in New Zealand in 1975–80 and 1987–92 matched that of Australia in the entire 1997–2002 period, New Zealand would have expanded faster than Australia. The same would have happened if New Zealand had maintained a growth rate in the years 1975–80 and 1987–92 equal to that of the periods 1971–74 and 1981–86, respectively. Thus, the economic collapses of 1975–80 and 1987–92 more than account for the differences in the average economic growth rate between the two countries (see table 3.2).

Puzzles of Economic Growth · http://dx.doi.org/10.1596/978-1-4648-0325-3

Table 3.1 Average Annual Per Capita GDP Growth: Australia and New Zealand, 1971–2002

Percent

Years	Australia	New Zealand
1971–74	1.9	3.6
1975–80	1.8	−0.7
1981–86	1.4	2.1
1987–92	1.4	−0.7
1993–98	3.1	2.1
1999–2002	2.4	1.9
1971–2002	2.0	1.4

Source: Calculations based on World Bank 2004.

Table 3.2 Average Annual Per Capita GDP Growth in New Zealand, Excluding Collapses of 1971–74 and 1981–86

Percent

Country	Average annual GDP growth
Australia	2.0
New Zealand	1.4
New Zealand[a]	2.2
New Zealand[b]	2.6

Source: Calculations based on World Bank 2004.
a. Average annual per capita GDP growth in 1975–80 and 1987–92 substituted by Australia's average annual per capita GDP growth in the periods 1975–80 and 1987–92, respectively.
b. Average annual per capita GDP growth in 1975–80 and 1987–92 substituted by New Zealand's average annual per capita GDP growth in the periods 1971–74 and 1981–86, respectively.

Differences in Economic Performance: Factors and Causes

Between 1970 and 2002 two energy crises took place, affecting all countries that were net importers of crude oil and its derivative products. Oil prices rose sharply first in 1973, and then again in 1979–82.

New Zealand was a net oil importer, while Australia, considering the entire period under review, exported more oil and its derivatives than it imported (see table 3.3). As a result, the sudden hike in global oil prices in 1973 and in 1979–82 had an adverse effect on New Zealand, while actually benefiting Australia (apart from indirect effects such as a slowdown experienced by its major trading partners—which we will address further on).

The average share of oil and its derivatives in Australia's total exports, which amounted to approximately 6 percent in the years 1971–74, nearly doubled in 1975–80. A similar trend was observed in New Zealand's imports of this commodity and its derivatives, with the contribution to total imports standing at 8 percent and 16 percent in 1971–74 and 1975–80, respectively. In the years 1980–92 oil and its derivatives accounted for an average of 20 percent of Australia's total exports. In New Zealand, on the other hand, the share of oil in total imports shrank from 15 percent to approximately 7 percent on average in 1987–92 compared to 1980–86.

The contribution of net exports (that is, exports net of imports) of oil and its derivatives to Australia's GDP was just under 1 percent in 1975–80, a level not significantly different from that observed in 1971–74. Yet this figure rose gradually in the subsequent years, amounting to 5.2 percent in the period 1999–2002. In the case of New Zealand net oil exports amounted to –2.8 percent of GDP in 1971–74; in the wake of oil price hikes it slipped to –5.0 percent and stayed there for the next 11 years (–5.1 percent in 1971–75 and –5.3 percent in 1981–86). In subsequent years (1987–92), the negative net value of exports diminished to –1.9 percent of GDP. Thus, while the oil shock is helpful in explaining New Zealand's bust of 1975–80, it does not account for the 1987–92 collapse.

In 1971–2002 the average energy intensity—expressed as energy consumption (kilograms of oil equivalent) in relation to GDP—declined in Australia but rose in New Zealand. These adverse changes were observed during both the first and the second downturns of this period in New Zealand.

From New Zealand's perspective, adverse changes in the price of oil were not offset by changes in prices of other imports and exports (see table 3.4). Almost throughout the period under review, the country's terms of trade deteriorated,

Table 3.3 Oil Prices Changes and Their Importance for Foreign Trade of Australia and New Zealand, 1971–2002[a]

Years	Average annual ratio of exports to imports of oil and its derivatives		Average annual share of exports (imports) of oil and its derivatives in Australia's (New Zealand's) total exports (imports) (%)		Exports of oil and its derivatives (% of GDP)		Average energy intensity of the economy (ratio of kilogram of oil equivalent to GDP)	
	Australia	New Zealand	Australia	New Zealand	Australia	New Zealand	Australia	New Zealand
1971–74	1.43	0.09	6.8	8.3	0.06	−2.78	0.33	0.23
1975–80	1.34	0.06	12.7	16.0	0.08	−5.08	0.30	0.25
1981–86	2.27	0.05	21.8	14.8	2.45	−5.27	0.32	0.24
1987–92	3.57	0.35	20.2	6.8	4.44	−1.93	0.3	0.28
1993–98	3.28	0.36	19.8	6.2	5.46	−2.19	0.29	0.29
1999–2002	2.48	0.22	21.3	8.8	5.22	−4.10	0.27	0.29

Sources: IMF DOTS, World Bank 2004.
a. Adjusted for exchange rate.

Table 3.4 Rate of Changes to the Terms of Trade: Australia and New Zealand, 1971–2002

Percent

Years	Annual average rate of change to terms of trade	
	Australia	New Zealand
1971–74	6.43	0.68
1975–80	5.27	−1.83
1981–86	3.38	−2.60
1987–92	5.17	−0.62
1993–98	3.53	−0.23
1999–2002	8.30	0.30

Source: World Bank 2004.

while those of Australia improved steadily. During the first bust in New Zealand (that is, in 1975–80) terms of trade were deteriorating at an increasing pace, while during the second bust (that is, in 1987–92) the process eased down significantly. Thus, changes in the terms of trade may have contributed to New Zealand's weaker economic growth—against the background of Australia—in 1975–80, but they do not explain the slowdown of 1987–92.

Both downturn periods in New Zealand also differ with regard to the amount of demand from New Zealand and Australia's main trading partners (see table 3.5). The differences in external demand for the respective countries' exports explain—at least in part—New Zealand's weaker economic performance versus Australia's in 1975–80; yet, they do not explain the economic collapse seen between 1987 and 1992. In this second period the average annual economic growth of Australia's main trading partners remained roughly unchanged from its 1981–86 level, while New Zealand's partners saw expansion.

During the first analyzed bust in New Zealand (that is, 1975–80), the average annual GDP growth of most countries receiving goods from Australia and New Zealand fell. But the slowdown was more pronounced among countries importing goods from New Zealand. The country suffered the most from a slump in the United Kingdom—the destination of approximately 40 percent of New Zealand's exports in the 1970s. The United Kingdom's accession to the European Economic Community (EEC) in 1973 was another external trade-related shock to New Zealand. After joining the EEC, Britain was forced to withdraw the privileges New Zealand enjoyed in mutual trade. Thus, New Zealand lost its special status in its largest market at that time. In contrast, Australia had a far more diversified range of trading partners, making its exports less dependent on the economic conditions of any one of them.[1]

A relatively sharper economic growth decline among the countries importing goods from New Zealand was reflected in this country's export trends in 1975–80. Average annual exports growth in New Zealand, having sunk considerably from the previous period's level, was negative. On the other hand, Australia experienced a considerable rise in annual average exports growth in 1975–80 versus 1971–74 (though this was driven mainly by rising oil prices).

External shocks do not fully account for the differences in the growth rates of the two countries in the periods 1975–80 and 1987–92, respectively. This in particular—but not exclusively—concerns the second bust in New Zealand, as empirical research shows that the resilience of a given country to external shocks is to a great extent related to its institutions (see, among others, Rodrik 1991; Céspedes and others 2006).

The propelling institutions, with the exception of the taxation level, were similar in both countries in 1970–2000. Admittedly, the general government sector was more bloated in New Zealand than in Australia, but on the other hand, property rights were better protected (see table 3.6). Also, there were fewer barriers in place constraining, on the one hand, external trade, and on the other, domestic competition. Thus, institutions probably did not decide the differences in these two countries' economic performance, as the advantages

Table 3.5 Average Annual Real GDP Growth of Australia and New Zealand's Main Import and Export Partners, 1971–2002

Percent

			1971–74	1975–80	1981–86	1987–92	1993–98	1999–2002
Average annual real[a] GDP growth of main export partners[b]	Australia	China	6.3	6.1	10.3	8.1	11.5	7.7
		Japan	7.1	3.5	3.3	4.6	1.6	0.5
		Korea, Rep.	8.6	8.5	6.2	9.5	6.6	4.6
		New Zealand	5.6	0.1	2.8	0.3	3.7	3.2
		U.S.	5.0	3.0	2.6	2.6	3.4	3.0
		Average	6.5	4.2	5.0	5.0	5.4	3.8
	New Zealand	Australia	4.1	2.5	3.0	2.6	4.0	3.6
		Japan	7.1	3.5	3.3	4.6	1.6	0.5
		United States	5.0	3.0	2.6	2.6	3.4	3.0
		United Kingdom[c]	4.3	1.5	1.4	2.5	2.7	2.5
		Average	5.1	2.6	2.6	3.1	3.0	2.4
Average annual exports growth		Australia	−7.8	12.0	13.5	6.3	10.9	6.7
		New Zealand	11.7	−1.5	−6.8	6.7	7.0	4.2

Source: IMF DOTS, World Bank 2004.

a. Adjusted for inflation.

b. Main export partners are ones whose aggregate contribution to a country's total exports has exceeded 50 percent.

c. In the 1970s Britain was New Zealand's most important partner (comprised nearly 40 percent of its total exports).

Table 3.6 Selected Fraser Institute Subindices of Economic Freedom in Australia and New Zealand, 1970–2000 (Index Numbers from 0 to 10)

Year	Size of government[a]		Legal system and property rights[b]		Freedom to trade internationally[c]		Regulation[d]	
	Australia	New Zealand	Australia	New Zealand	Australia	New Zealand	Australia	New Zealand
1970	6.1	5.4	8.0	8.0	6.7	6.9	5.4	5.7
1975	5.2	4.4	5.1	5.1	6.3	6.9	5.8	5.7
1980	5.1	3.8	7.3	8.0	6.6	7.4	6.5	5.7
1985	4.9	3.5	7.9	7.9	7.2	7.2	6.6	5.8
1990	5.4	5.5	7.9	8.3	7.5	7.9	6.6	6.6
1995	5.7	7.5	9.0	9.2	7.5	8.1	7.3	8.8
2000	6.2	6.7	9.5	9.1	7.8	8.5	7.2	7.9
Average	5.5	5.3	7.8	7.9	7.1	7.6	6.5	6.6

Source: Based on www.freetheworld.com.

Note: 0 = complete lack of economic freedom in the area concerned; 10 = full economic freedom.

a. The size of the government index reflects the extent to which decisions on resource allocation are made by the market and to what extent by the state.

b. The index concerning the quality of the legal system and the security of property rights is based on survey data involving respondents' opinions on: the degree of judicial independence, the impartiality of the courts, the application of copyrights, military interference in the rule of law and politics, and the degree of integrity of the legal system.

c. The components include: data on the level of tariffs, survey-based assessment of nontariff barriers, size of trade flows relative to size calculated from regression equations, surplus of the black-market exchange rate over the official exchange rate, and the extent of capital flow control as per the International Monetary Fund classification.

d. The market regulation index describes regulation in the labor credit, and business markets.

of New Zealand in some areas were balanced by the advantages of Australia in other. Netting out of the impact of propelling institutions is plausible, because, the differences in the economic performance of the two countries are mainly due to New Zealand's short-term slumps in GDP growth.

In the following paragraphs, we present an analysis of the macroeconomic policy of both countries. Such policy reflects the strength (or weakness) of the stabilizing institutions that determine, among other things, the resilience of an economy to shocks. In New Zealand macroeconomic policy was on average less disciplined in the period under review than in Australia. This was especially true during New Zealand's first downturn and the period directly preceding its second.

After 1973 government expenditure in both countries rose considerably, even as output growth slowed. The speed of this rise varied, however. In 1977–82 Australia's government expenditure rose more slowly than that of New Zealand (and in 1975–80 Australia's expenditure was smaller than New Zealand's by 13 percent of GDP Then, as relative economic growth declined in New Zealand, *between 1987 and 1990* public expenditure increased by around 5 percent of GDP from the 1982–86 level. In the meantime, public expenditure in Australia fell by 4 percent of GDP. As a result, the difference in the general government expenditure level between New Zealand and Australia increased to over 18 percent of GDP in 1987–90. After 1990 and until 2002 government spending in New Zealand decreased steadily—from approximately 44 percent of GDP in 1990 to roughly 30 percent of in 2002. In Australia this expenditure was maintained at an average of 25 percent of GDP over the same period (see figure 3.3 with highlighted periods of significant increases of government expenditures in New Zealand).

The post-1973 rise in government expenditure in both countries led to higher tax burdens (see figure 3.4).[2]

In 1975–80 tax revenues in New Zealand were significantly above those of Australia; the difference amounted to approximately 10 percent of GDP (similar to the period 1970–74). Taxes, too, were higher than in the previous

Figure 3.3 Government Expenditure in Australia and New Zealand, 1970–2002

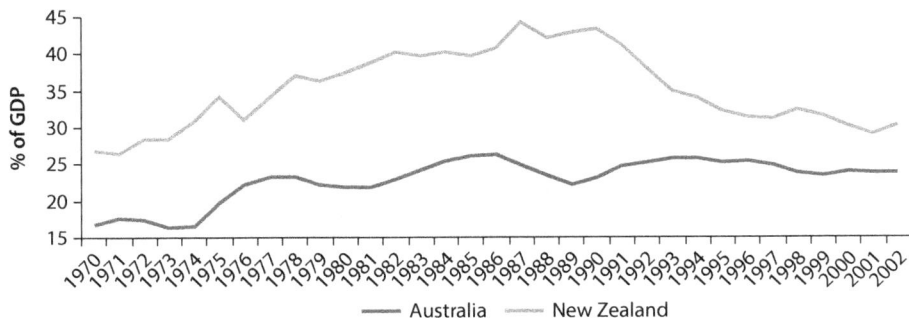

Source: World Bank 2004.
Note: Periods of significant increases are shaded.

period (note that the excess tax burden, as measured by pure deadweight loss, rises not in proportion to the level of taxes, but to its square—see, for example, Auerbach and Hines 2001). During the second clear downturn in New Zealand, tax expenditure[3] rose by approximately 5 percent of GDP in comparison to 1980–86, while remaining more or less the same in Australia. To finance all expenditure without boosting the public debt accumulated in the previous years, the government of New Zealand had to complement the shrinking tax base of its flagging economy with new taxes and the abolishment of tax reliefs. In 1987–90 the ratio of tax revenues to GDP was higher in New Zealand than in Australia by nearly 12 percentage points. From 1990 to 2002 New Zealand's fiscal burden eased off steadily. In the same period, the ratio of tax revenues to GDP remained at approximately 21 percent.

During the first downturn in New Zealand, the deficit of the overall government sector grew considerably (see figure 3.5). The deficit increased by an average of 6 percent of GDP in the 1970–73 period, while in Australia, following

Figure 3.4 Tax Revenues in Australia and New Zealand, 1970–2002

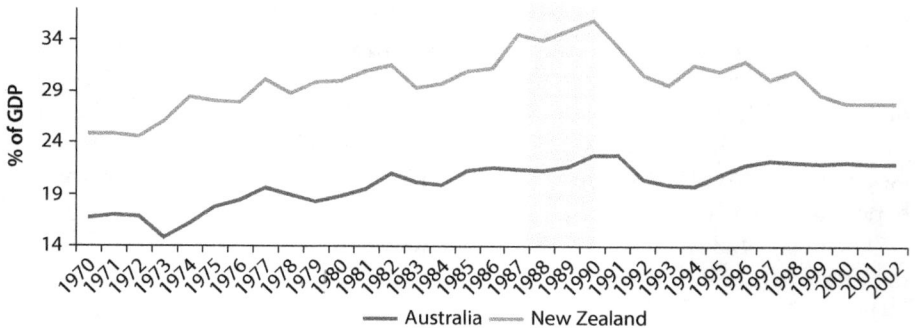

Source: World Bank 2004.
Note: Periods of significant divergence are shaded.

Figure 3.5 General Government Sector Deficit in Australia and New Zealand, 1970–2002

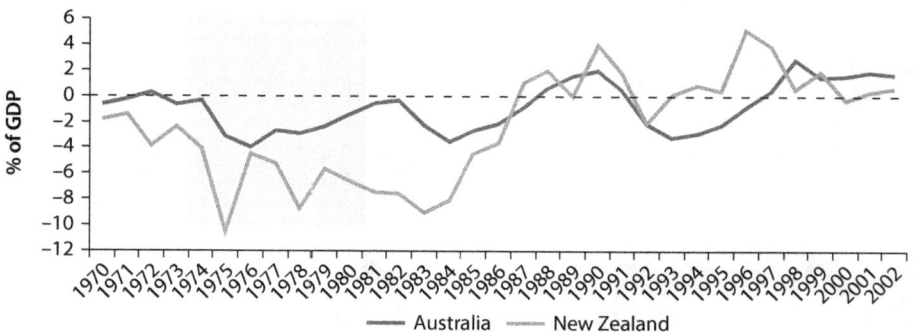

Source: World Bank 2004.
Note: Periods of significant divergence are shaded.

an initial rise, it was gradually contained in 1976–81. In 1982, for the first time in a decade, Australia's public sector was in balance, whereas in New Zealand the deficit reached 8 percent of GDP—that is, a level at which investors could reasonably voice concerns about the solvency, or at least the liquidity, of the sector. Furthermore, a deficit of this magnitude limited the potential to cushion possible shocks through fiscal expansion. In this context, the government could not allow automatic stabilizers to operate freely. After 1983 the balance of the government sector in New Zealand embarked on a clear upward trend, and by 1986 was on a par with Australia. Until 1992 the balance remained at a similar level in both countries, though more volatility observed in New Zealand. In 1992–98 New Zealand was characterized by a more balanced fiscal position than Australia. After 1998 and until 2002, both countries maintained a similar level of budget surplus.

The differing levels and trends of their basic fiscal magnitudes resulted from the different pace at which the two countries moved away from an extensive welfare-state system. This system—with its characteristically high and rising social expenditure, entailing high and rising taxes—was instituted in both countries after World War II. Yet, in Australia the welfare state was seriously limited in the 1970s, which improved the flexibility of its fiscal policy (Parham 2002) and mitigated the dwarfing impact of large social expenditure and related high taxes. After 1970 public consumption was gradually limited; by 1975 its share in total public spending decreased by roughly 10 percentage points. Social transfers also decreased steadily: by 1980 the contribution of transfers and subsidies to total government expenditure had shrunk by nearly 8 percentage points. In 1971 wage indexation in both the public and private sector was abolished, and in 1976 budget creation procedures were amended. The budgetary process started to take into account also future changes (within time span of over one year). Particular attention was paid to future changes in expenditures. At the same time, the Ministry of Finance was obliged to maintain long-term budget equilibrium. The privatization of publicly owned corporations was launched—although it did not take off until the mid-1980s, to be renewed after 1990. In 1974 the government banned involvement of other company's employees in strikes, and in 1977 tax relief for union members was abolished.

Meanwhile, New Zealand's extensive welfare system was preserved into the mid-1080s. This hampered fiscal policy, as the government was saddled with rigid obligations piling up in times of negative shocks. The government found itself unable to adjust fiscal policy to the environment in which it operated. This led to mounting imbalances in public finance (and further, in the entire economy). For example, in response to the first energy crisis, New Zealand's government increased subsidies for domestic exporters and for the energy industry (with a view to making it independent from oil imports, under the so-called Think Big project). The plan to release the energy industry from the constraints of oil imports was abandoned—or rather flopped—at the end of the 1970s. As farmers faced mounting challenges, government also increased subsidies for agriculture—the most heavily subsidized sector of New Zealand's economy.

Agricultural subsidies were the only category of government expenditure to rise substantially after 1973 (Leigh 2002).

Before the onset of the first oil crisis, indexation of wages in state institutions and public corporations was abolished in Australia. Consequently, during the first wave of hikes in the prices of oil and its derivatives in the early 1970s, the government was under no obligation to raise wages. New Zealand's reaction was in stark contrast—after 1973 the indexation of wages and pensions was introduced, additionally boosting government expenditure and fueling inflation.

To meet all its social obligations, during the first oil shock the government of New Zealand monetized part of the deficit. The Reserve Bank of Australia, in contrast to the Reserve Bank of New Zealand, was not forced to grant loans to the government (Macfarlane 1997; Skilling 2001; Spencer 2006).

After 1973 New Zealand saw inflation rise significantly (see figure 3.6). In Australia mounting inflation was curbed in 1974. In 1975–80, that is, during the first economic collapse in New Zealand, inflation was nearly 6 percentage points higher than in Australia (in 1970–74 the difference was approximately 1 percentage point in favor of New Zealand). Another sharp rise in inflation was observed in New Zealand in 1985–87, when it was roughly 8 percentage points above the level of Australia. The disinflation process launched in 1986 eliminated most of the differences by the early 1990s. In the period 1993–2002 average annual GDP deflator growth was running at 2.1 percent in Australia and 1.6 percent in New Zealand.

A rise in inflation in New Zealand in 1974–81 was fueled by the partial monetization of the government deficit. Its rise again in 1984–86 can be explained by the Reserve Bank's adoption of a monetary policy aimed at stabilizing the currency in terms of the U.S. dollar, whose real exchange rate in 1984–89 decreased markedly.[4] In the early 1980s the real U.S. dollar exchange rate gained approximately 70 percent, only to drop by nearly 30 percent in the period 1984–89.

Figure 3.6 Average Annual Change in the GDP Deflator in Australia and New Zealand, 1970–2002

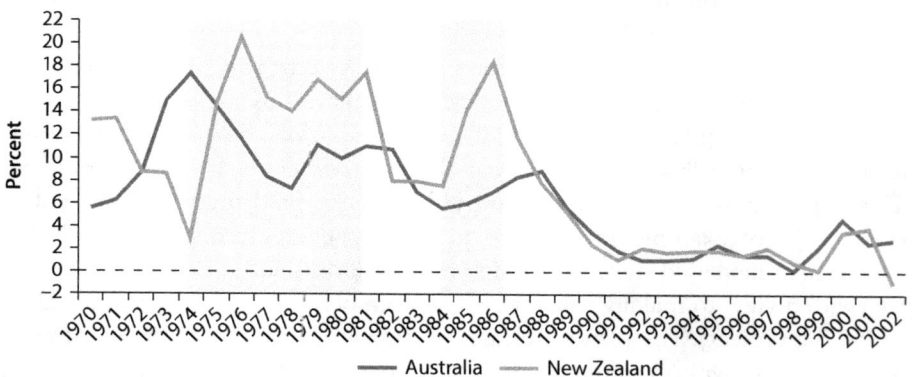

Source: World Bank 2004.
Note: Periods of significant divergence are shaded.

Low and stable inflation levels were only achieved when the independence of New Zealand's central bank was guaranteed, and when a direct inflation targeting strategy was adopted. When this strategy proved successful in New Zealand, Australia subsequently followed suit.[5]

New Zealand did not launch reforms to curb government interference in the economy until 1984 (Bell 1994; Buckle 2004; Scott 1996). From 1984 to 1990, 83 percent of agricultural subsidies and all industrial subsidies were abolished. Taxation of dividends was scrapped and trade unions' right to go on strike was curtailed (the number of days lost to strikes in 1984 was 331,000, while in 1994 it had sunk to 38,000). The tax system was streamlined, and 1986 saw the introduction of value added tax at 10 percent. At the same time, personal income tax was reduced and simplified—the number of tax brackets was reduced from five to three: 15 percent, 30 percent, and 48 percent. In 1988 it was further narrowed to 24 percent and 33 percent. The corporate income tax rate was cut back from 48 percent to 33 percent (in Australia the corresponding tax rates amounted to: personal income tax—15 percent, 30 percent, 40 percent, and 45 percent; corporate income tax—30 percent). Tax breaks were done away with, and unemployment benefits for 16- and 17-year-olds were abolished, as well as benefits for large families. The system of subsidies to dwelling construction, as well as to mortgage loans, was dismantled. Reimbursement of most drugs was discontinued. As a result of the 1986 commercialization, and subsequent privatization, state-owned banks, shipyards, industry, sea transport, railways, power plants, forestry, telecommunications, major lignite mines, air carriers, and courier and postal services were sold to private entities or wound up. In 1990 the central bank was granted a statutory guarantee of independence.

When comparing the institutional frameworks of the two countries between 1970 and 1992, one can say that the changes introduced by New Zealand in 1984–90 were similar to the Australian reforms of the 1970s (although, due to relatively worse economic conditions, the reform program was more radical than in Australia in the 1970s).

It was not only the fiscal magnitudes that were running at different levels in the two countries, but also the monetary ones.

Summary and Conclusions

In this chapter, we have sought to explain how significant differences in per capita national income arose between Australia and New Zealand in the period 1971–2002. Our analysis leads to the following conclusions:

- In 1971–2002 economic growth in New Zealand slumped twice, even as Australia's stayed more or less on course. The first relative dip in per capita GDP growth in New Zealand occurred in 1975–80; the second, in 1987–92. Both these developments account for the overall difference in per capita income between Australia and New Zealand.

- External shocks contributed to these economic slowdowns, especially to the first. In 1975–80 net exports of oil and its derivatives fell, negatively affecting New Zealand's GDP as the terms of trade deteriorated. Finally, exports to the United Kingdom, the country's main trading partner, plunged as UK domestic demand shrunk and the United Kingdom ascended to the EEC. Australia, being a net oil exporter, was not affected by the first oil shock in equal measure. As oil prices rose, terms of trade improved and the value of its exports was boosted—notwithstanding the slowdown seen by most of its key trading partners. Moreover, the Australian economy was characterized by lower energy intensity than that of New Zealand (this intensity continued to diminish over the entire period, in contrast to New Zealand's). Further, Australia's exports were more diversified.

  The extent of economic freedom—as determined by propelling institutions—evolved in a similar manner in both countries. The small differences in propelling institutions in both countries mostly netted out and as such cannot account for the differences in economic performance One exception was the fiscal position of the state—a rise in public expenditure after the first oil crisis entailed increased tax burdens in both countries. A particularly sharp rise in taxation in New Zealand (in comparison to Australia) occurred during the country's second downturn.

- New Zealand's slowdowns in GDP growth were in part due to the weakness of its stabilizing institutions. Macroeconomic policy, as shaped by these institutions, underwent far bigger changes in New Zealand than in Australia, causing additional shocks to the economy (besides external shocks). The biggest policy changes observed during the study period took place during the first bust in New Zealand and in the period directly before the second bust. Besides their immediate impact they also significantly reduced scope of available policy options in subsequent years.
  - In response to the first oil crisis, the general government deficit increased in both countries; yet, in New Zealand it increased more and for a longer time, reaching a peak in the period preceding the second collapse.
  - A rising government deficit was fueled by growing public spending. The upward trend in the sector's expenditure, as related to GDP, was reversed in Australia in 1986 and in New Zealand as late as 1990.
  - After the first oil crisis New Zealand experienced a significant jump in inflation, which persisted at an elevated level throughout the first downturn. In Australia, on the other hand, inflation was on the decline in the same years. New Zealand saw a rebound in inflation after 1984, which was successfully curbed only after 1990.
  - The shape of macroeconomic policy in New Zealand was determined by three factors. First, the absence of appropriate legal norms that would ensure discipline in public finance (inflationary financing of the government deficit was allowed) led to overspending. Second, the country's rigid expenditure was much higher than that of Australia, significantly

reducing policy space. Third, the choice of monetary policy strategy in the latter half of the 1980s was unfortunate—setting as an intermediate goal the stability of the exchange rate against the dollar, whose real exchange rate in that period dropped significantly, resulting in imported inflation.

Notes

1. In this period, no country contributed to Australia's imports by more than about 20 percent.

2. Due to incomplete data on, for example, marginal tax rates, the share of tax revenues in GDP was assumed as a measurement of fiscality.

3. Tax expenditure—assessment of the costs, in terms of forgone revenue, of various tax provisions that provide tax breaks for certain taxpayers and activities.

4. The real exchange rate is the nominal exchange rate adjusted for inflation differentials of consumer prices at home and abroad.

5. This paragraph is based on Scott (1996), Bell (1994), and Buckle (2004).

Bibliography

Auerbach, A. J., and J. R. Hines. 2001. "Taxation and Economic Efficiency." NBER Working Paper W8181, National Bureau of Economic Research, Cambridge, MA.

Bell, S. 1994. "State Strength and State Weakness: Manufacturing Industry and Post-War Australian State." In *State, Economy, and Public Policy in Australia*, edited by S. R. Bell and B. Head. Melbourne, Australia: Oxford University Press.

Boston, R. 1997. *Public Management the New Zealand Model*. Auckland, New Zealand: Oxford University Press.

Brasch, D. 1996. *New Zealand's Remarkable Reforms*. London: Institute of Economic Affairs.

Briggs, P., and J. Ballingall. 2001. *A Comparison of Australia's and New Zealand's Export Performance Using Shift Share Analyses*. Report of Treasury, NZ Institute of Economic Research, Wellington, July.

Buckle, B. 2004. "New Zealand Economic Growth: An Analysis of Policy and Performance." Treasury Paper, Wellington.

Céspedes, Luis Felipe, Ilan Goldfajn, Phil Lowe, and Rodrigo O. Valdés. 2006. "Policy Responses to External Shocks: The Experiences of Australia, Brazil, and Chile." In vol. 10 of *External Vulnerability and Preventive Policies*, edited by Ricardo Caballero, César Calderón, Luis Felipe Céspedes, Norman Loyaza, and Klaus Schmidt-Hebbel, chap. 5, 109–70. Central Banking, Analysis, and Economic Policies Book Series. Santiago: Central Bank of Chile.

Leigh, A. 2002. "Trade Liberalization and the Australian Labor Party." *Australian Journal of Politics and History* 48 (4): 487–508.

Macfarlane, I. 1997. "Monetary Policy Regimes: Past and Future." *Reserve Bank of Australia Bulletin*, October. http://www.rba.gov.au/publications/bulletin/1997/index.html.

Parham, D. 2002. "Productivity and Policy Reform in Australia." *International Productivity Monitor* 5: 53–63.

Rodrik, D. 1991. "Where Did All the Growth Go? External Shocks, Social Conflict, and Growth Collapses." NBER Working Paper W6350, National Bureau of Economic Research, Cambridge, MA.

Scott, G. 1996. "Government Reform in New Zealand." IMF Occasional Paper 140, International Monetary Fund, Washington, DC.

Skilling, D. 2001. "The Importance of Being Enormous: Towards an Understanding of the New Zealand Economy." *New Zealand Treasury*. New Zealand Treasury draft paper. http://www.treasury.govt.nz/et.

Spencer, G. 2006. "Modelling for Monetary Policy: The New Zealand Experience." *Reserve Bank of New Zealand Bulletin* 2 (June).

CHAPTER 4

How Did Austria (Nearly) Catch Up with Switzerland?

Marcin Hołda

Austria and Switzerland are "small" economies, and neighbors, characterized by a similar geographical location, total surface area, natural conditions, and population sizes.[1] They also share much in terms of language and culture.[2] In the period 1951–73 Austria and Switzerland both recorded impressive average growth rates, as measured in gross domestic product (GDP) per capita: 4.8 percent and 3.3 percent, respectively.[3] Although Switzerland entered that period with a level of GDP per capita much higher than that of many other small, developed European countries, it also grew faster than many of those countries. Switzerland's economic growth rate during that period was high enough for the absolute difference in GDP per capita between Austria and Switzerland to remain roughly stable at approximately $6,000–$8,000 (purchasing power parity [PPP] adjusted). The oil shock of 1973 marked the beginning of a period of slowdown in global economic growth. At the same time, in 1974 the gap between Austria and Switzerland in terms of absolute GDP per capita (measured in U.S. dollars) began to narrow: in 2003 Austria's GDP per capita amounted to $27,600, while Switzerland's was $28,800 (constant 2000 U.S. dollars, PPP adjusted).[4] That is why the present analysis focuses on the period between 1974 and 2003.

Taking into account that Switzerland's initial level of GDP per capita was high, the country's economic growth rate in 1951–73 was rapid in comparison with other small, developed European economies. In that period only Austria and Finland managed to significantly reduce the gap (expressed as a percentage of Swiss GDP per capita) that distanced them from Switzerland. The situation changed in 1974–2003 following a sharp decline in Switzerland's economic growth in the mid-1970s, and an atypical economic slowdown between 1991 and 2003 (see also figure 4.1). In 1991–2003 Austria was catching up with Switzerland at a rate similar to the average rate for other small, developed European economies (see the column "SD7" in table 4.1). Between 1977 and 1990, however, Austria made slow progress in terms of GDP per capita, while

Figure 4.1 GDP Per Capita in Austria and Switzerland, 1950–2003
2000 constant international dollars

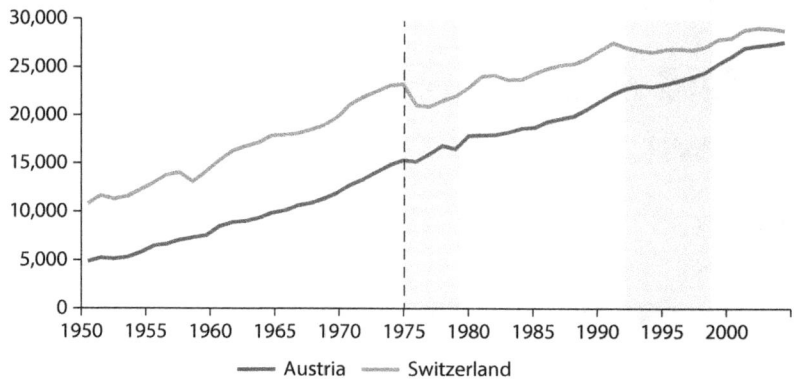

Austria ——— Switzerland

Source: Penn World Table 6.2 (Heston. Summers, and Aten 2006).
Note: Periods of significant divergence are shaded.

Table 4.1 GDP Per Capita in Seven Small, Developed European Countries as a Percentage of GDP Per Capita in Switzerland

GDP per capita in relation to Switzerland	AUT	BEL	NHL	DEN	FIN	NOR	SWE	SD7	CHE
1950	45	59	72	82	47	69	79	65	100
1973	64	62	71	79	59	65	71	67	100
1977	78	73	82	86	66	84	80	78	100
1990	81	75	76	81	73	87	79	79	100
2003	96	88	91	97	83	118	91	95	100

Source: Based on data from Penn World Table 6.2.
Note: AUT = Austria; BEL = Belgium; CHE = Switzerland; NHL = Netherlands; DEN = Denmark; FIN = Finland; NOR = Norway; SWE = Sweden; SD7 = the average for the seven countries. The comparison excludes Luxembourg which, being a city-state with strong links to its neighboring countries and home to a number of European Union institutions, must be considered as a case apart.

Switzerland was able to further increase its advantage over the Netherlands, Denmark, and, to a lesser extent, Sweden.

Given the changes in the growth rate of per capita GDP in Austria and Switzerland, the period between 1974 and 2003 can be divided into five subperiods:

- *1974–76.* An economic downturn took place in both countries, but was much more pronounced in Switzerland. In 1975 there was a mild recession (−0.7 percent decrease in GDP per capita) in Austria and a deep recession in Switzerland (−10.3 percent fall in GDP per capita in 1975; −0.6 percent in 1976).
- *1977–90.* There was fast and stable economic growth in both countries during these years. Both countries experienced an economic slowdown in the early 1980s: Austria in 1980–81 and Switzerland in 1981–83 (see figure 4.2), with the downturn in Switzerland being deeper and longer than in Austria. In 1977–90 both countries recorded one year of negative GDP per capita growth: Austria in 1978 (−2.0 percent) and Switzerland in 1982 (−2.1 percent).

Figure 4.2 Growth Rate as a Percentage of Per Capita GDP: Austria and Switzerland (International $ in 2000 Constant Prices), 1971–2003

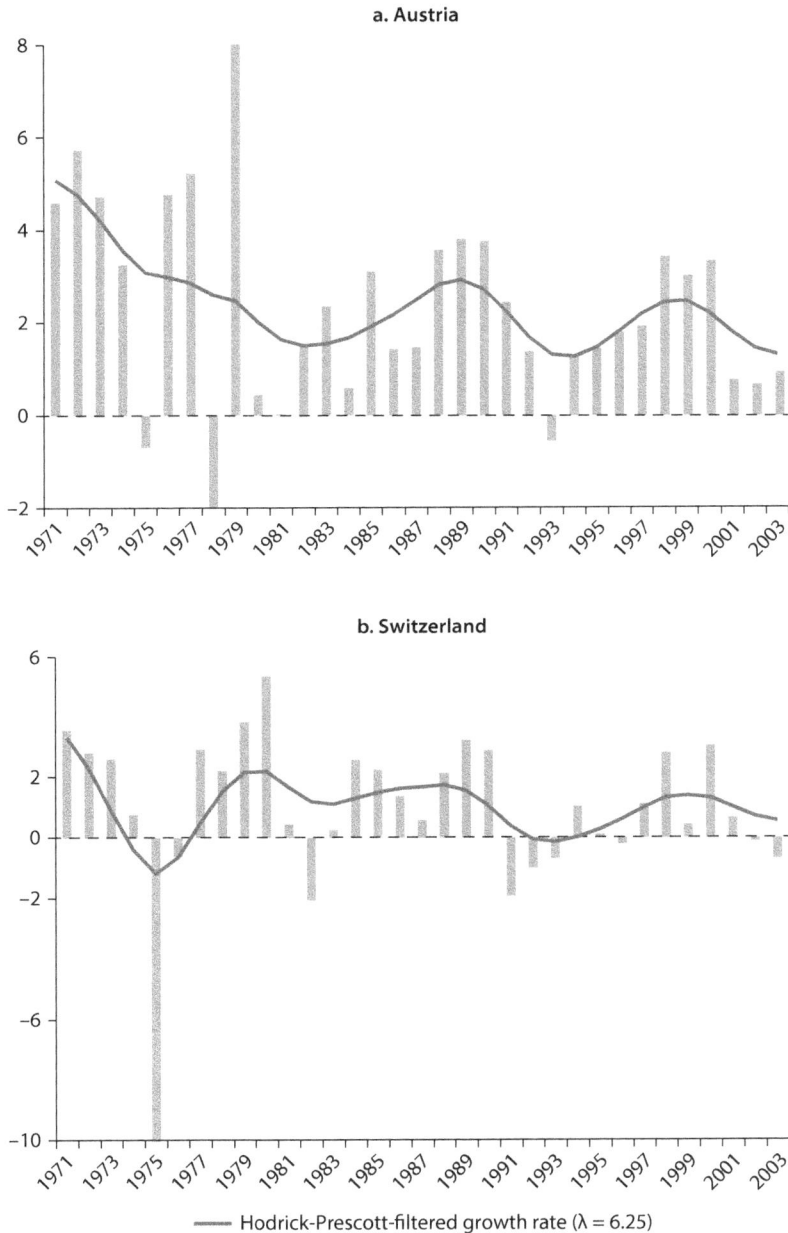

a. Austria

b. Switzerland

—— Hodrick-Prescott-filtered growth rate (λ = 6.25)

Source: Based on data from Penn World Table 6.2.

- *1991–96.* This was a period of slower economic growth in Austria and a prolonged recession in Switzerland, where negative growth of GDP per capita was recorded in four years: 1991 (–1.9 percent), 1992 (–1.0 percent), 1993 (–0.7 percent), and 1996 (–0.2 percent). By contrast, in Austria negative per capita GDP growth was observed only in 1993 (–0.5 percent). In 1995–96 Austria's economy recovered, while the Swiss economy remained stagnant.
- *1997–2000.* This was a period of economic recovery in both countries, with relatively slow economic growth in Switzerland as compared with Austria.
- *2001–03.* This was a time of economic slowdown in both countries, but more so in Switzerland, where the growth rate of GDP per capita was negative in 2002 (–0.1 percent) and 2003 (–0.7 percent).

To explain the causes of faster economic growth in Austria relative to Switzerland, it is crucial to identify the sources of the particularly deep recession that Switzerland experienced in 1975–76 and its prolonged recession of 1991–96, and to find reasons for the difference in economic growth rates between the two countries in the second half of the 1990s.[5]

Using data from 1960 to 2001 for a panel of 192 countries, Cerra and Saxena (2007) demonstrate that negative economic shocks generally result in slower economic growth in the long run. According to their results economic contractions are not offset by fast recoveries, implying that the momentum lost is not regained. Economic contractions had a particularly strong negative impact on the average growth rate of the Swiss economy over the period 1974–2003. But even if the Swiss economy had grown in 1974–76, 1982–83, 1991–96, and 2002–03 at the same pace as the Austrian economy, the average growth rate of GDP per capita in 1974–2003 would still have been lower than that of Austria, albeit by only 0.2 percentage points. Between 1974 and 1990 no difference would have been observed, but in 1991–2003 the difference would have amounted to as much as 0.4 percentage points.

As can be inferred from table 4.2, slower GDP growth in Switzerland in the period 1991–2003 was primarily due to slower total factor productivity (TFP) growth, or, according to another specification, lower labor efficiency.

An analysis of productivity growth and contributions to the gross value added of individual sectors of the Austrian and Swiss economies in 1991–2000[6] (table 4.3) leads to the following conclusions:

- In 1991–2000 economic growth was slower in Switzerland than Austria due to slower output growth in both the manufacturing and services sectors.
- In the services sector the largest discrepancies (in terms of contribution to value added) between Austria and Switzerland were observed in retail trade. Switzerland's slow economic growth resulted from the negative contributions of the "hotels and restaurants" segment and, to a lesser extent, the "transport and storage" segment.

Table 4.2 Decomposition of Economic Growth: Austria and Switzerland, 1991–2003

	First decomposition[a] (1991–2003)				Second decomposition[b] (1991–2003)				
	GDP per capita	Total factor productivity	Capital	Labor force	Potential output growth of the business sector	Capital stock	Trend labor efficiency	Trend hours	Potential employment
Austria	1.7	1.0	0.7	0.0	2.6	0.9	1.4	0.0	0.5
Switzerland	0.4	0.0	0.4	0.0	1.3	0.8	0.2	−0.1	0.4

Sources: Based on data from Penn World Table 6.2; OECD 2004.
a. Own calculations.
b. OECD's calculations.

Table 4.3 Contribution to GDP and Average Annual Labor Productivity Growth: Individual Sectors of the Austrian and Swiss Economies, 1991–2000

	ISIC code rev 3	Contribution to GDP growth		Labor productivity growth	
		Austria	Switzerland	Austria	Switzerland
Total	01–99	2.77	0.76	2.4	0.5
Agriculture, forestry, fishing	01, 02, 05	0.08	−0.05	4.4	−2.2
Mining and quarrying	10–14	−0.01	0.00	0.4	1.1
Manufacturing	15–37	1.20	0.35	7.3	3.6
Electricity, gas, and water supply	40–41	0.08	0.07	3.8	3.8
Construction	45	0.24	−0.21	2.1	−1.5
Total services	50–99	1.71	0.61	0.7	−0.2
Wholesale and retail trade	50–52	0.39	−0.22	2.1	−1.2
Hotels and restaurants	55	0.05	−0.09	−0.1	−2.3
Transport and storage	60–63	0.12	−0.02	1	−0.4
Post and telecommunications	64	0.09	0.11	4.2	2.3
Financial intermediation	65–67	0.12	0.25	2.2	1.9
Real estate activities	70	0.54	0.20	−2.0	4.0
Community, social, and personal services[a]	75–99	0.41	0.38	0.1	−0.3

Source: Based on 60 Industry Database (Groningen Growth and Development Centre).
Note: ISIC = International Standard Industrial Classification.
a. Public administration and defense; compulsory social security; education; health and social work; other community, social, and personal services; and private households with employed persons. The years analyzed were chosen because of the availability of comparable data.

- The contributions of "mining and quarrying"; "electricity, gas, and water supply"; "financial intermediation"; and "community, social, and personal services" to GDP growth were comparable in both countries.
- In most cases, those sectors of the Swiss economy whose contribution to GDP growth was negative or much lower than in Austria also recorded negative or slower labor productivity growth (again relative to Austria).

In the next section, we shall first explain the causes of economic downturns in Switzerland throughout the period 1974–2003, and, next, indicate reasons (other than negative economic shocks) for Switzerland's slower economic growth in the 1990s.

Differences in Economic Performance: Factors and Causes

The periods of economic contraction/downturn in Switzerland, during which economic growth slowed coincided with the global oil shocks:

- 1974–75: following the outbreak of the Arab-Israeli war in November 1973.
- 1980–81: following the outbreak of the Iraq-Iran war in October 1980.
- 1990–91: following the outbreak of the Gulf War in August 1990.
- 2001: following an energy crisis in California and increased tensions in the Middle East.

But oil price changes themselves should have affected the two countries to a similar extent; in 1971–2003 both Austria and Switzerland were net importers of oil, and the energy intensity of the Austrian economy was even slightly higher than that of Switzerland.[7] Changes in terms of trade were also not responsible for the recession in Switzerland in the mid-1970s and in 1991–96, and they were much more favorable than in Austria.

Austria and Switzerland are both small, open economies and their development depends to a large extent on exports to third countries. Exports, in turn, are related to the demand for Austrian and Swiss goods, which in turn is contingent on economic growth in trade partners. An analysis of export growth in Austria and Switzerland shows that during periods of recession/economic slowdown in Switzerland, the growth of Swiss exports slowed significantly as compared to Austria (table 4.4). Thus slower Swiss export growth could be one of the explanations why per capita GDP growth was slower in Switzerland than in Austria.

In the analyzed period slight differences in the geographical distribution of Austrian and Swiss exports could be observed. Generally speaking, Austrian

Table 4.4 Average Yearly Exports Growth: Austria and Switzerland (2000 $), 1971–2003

%, year on year

Years	Exports growth	
	Austria	Switzerland
1971–73	7.3	6.0
1974–76	6.5	1.3
1977–90	5.3	4.4
1991–96	3.1	1.5
1997–2000	9.0	8.4
2001–03	4.0	0.0

Source: Based on World Development Indicators 2006.

exports were geared more toward Germany and the Central and Eastern European Countries (CEEC), while Swiss exports were more often headed for the United States and developed Asian markets (table 4.5). It is quite likely that in 1974–75 faster export growth in Austria, as compared to Switzerland, was due to the fact that an increasing portion of Austria's exports was directed to developing countries, especially the CEEC (see figure 4.3). These countries were not as strongly affected by the oil shock of 1973. Although in the 1980s exports to the CEEC became less important to Austria—because of its policy aimed at integration with the European Union (EU) and the growing debt of the CEEC (Fenz and Schneider 2006)—after the fall of Communism the role of the CEEC in Austrian exports grew again, particularly in the mid-1990s (OECD 2003). The increase in Austrian exports to the CEEC was also driven by

Table 4.5 Major Trade Partners in Austria's and Switzerland's Exports, 1972 and 1989
Percent

Year	Country				Trade partner				
1972	Austria	GER	CHE	ITA	GBR	USA	SWE	*CEEC*	*Asia*	Rest of the world
		22.5	11.6	9.6	7.8	4.5	4.0	*14.8*	*1.7*	23.5
	Switzerland	GER	FRA	USA	ITA	GBR	AUT	*CEEC*	*Asia*[a]	Rest of the world
		15.0	8.9	8.8	8.3	7.8	5.9	*5.3*	*4.7*	35.3
1989	Austria	GER	ITA	CHE	FRA	GBR	USA	*CEEC*	*Asia*	Rest of the world
		34.5	10.5	7.2	4.7	4.5	3.5	*11.1*	*2.8*	21.2
	Switzerland	GER	FRA	ITA	USA	GBR	JAP	*CEEC*	*Asia*[a]	Rest of the world
		22.2	9.9	8.9	8	7.4	4.8	*4.0*	*8.2*	26.6

Source: Based on data from IMF DOTS.
Note: CEEC = Central and Eastern European Countries (the former Yugoslavia, Russian Federation, Czech Republic, Poland, Hungary, the German Democratic Republic, Romania, Bulgaria, and Albania); CHE = Switzerland; FRA = France; GBR = United Kingdom; GER = Germany; ITA = Italy; JAP = Japan; SWE = Sweden; USA = United States.
a. The majority of exports to Asia were directed to Japan and Hong Kong SAR, China.

Figure 4.3 Developing Countries' Share of Austria's and Switzerland's Total Exports, 1971–2003

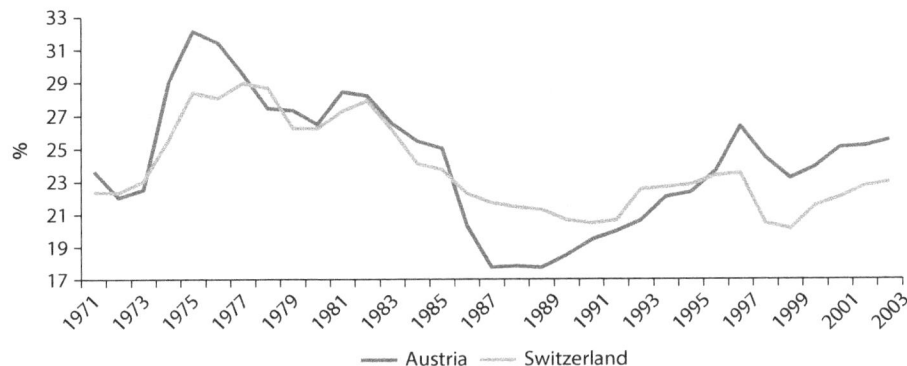

Source: Based on IMF DOTS data.

strong economic growth in these countries in 1997–2003. Breuss and Schebeck (1999) estimated that the opening up of these markets may have contributed to Austria's GDP being 3.3 percent larger in the 1990s (that is, Austrian GDP growth rose about 0.33 percentage points higher per year). As mentioned earlier, Swiss exports were to a greater extent directed toward Asian countries, mainly Japan and Hong Kong SAR, China.[8] Slower economic growth in these countries could have translated to weaker demand for Swiss goods, particularly in the period 2001–03. Nevertheless, weak external demand was neither the only nor a sufficient reason for differences in economic performance between Austria and Switzerland.

Exchange-rate fluctuations are another type of shock that may have had a negative impact on exports.

After the collapse of the Bretton-Woods system, both the Swiss franc and the Austrian schilling were subject to an appreciation trend, which was interrupted in the mid-1990s (figure 4.4). But while the real exchange rate in Austria experienced only slight deviations from the long-term trend, the Swiss franc's real exchange rate was much more volatile and appreciated during periods of economic downturns in Switzerland—especially in 1973–76, 1982, 1994–95, and 2001–02. The reasons for the sudden appreciation of the Swiss franc in the period 1971–2003 were mainly related to its traditional role as a "safe haven currency," which meant that international investors purchased the Swiss currency in times of increased uncertainty or risk aversion (Suess 1999; OECD 2004). Periods when the Swiss franc rapidly appreciated also coincided with weakening global economic conditions. The appreciation thus likely amplified the negative impact of weak external demand on Swiss exports. This was especially true for 1993 and 2001–03 (Doytchinov and Schmidbauer 2007).

Figure 4.4 The Real Effective Exchange Rate (2000 = 100) of the Austrian Currency and the Swiss Franc

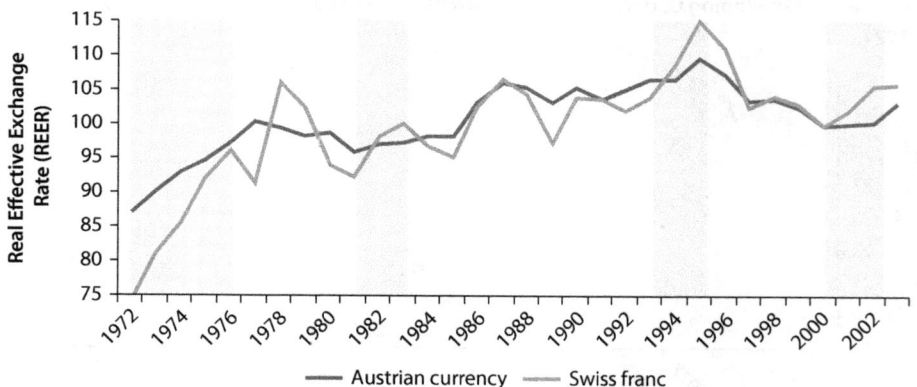

Source: OECD data.

Note: Austrian currency was Schilling in 1972–98, Euro in 1999–2003. Periods of significant appreciation of the Swiss franc REER coinciding with weak Swiss GDP growth performance are shaded.

The differences in economic performance between Austria and Switzerland cannot, however, be explained by external factors alone. Therefore, later in this chapter we shall analyze the possible domestic sources of these differences, including macroeconomic policy.

While the ratios of public spending, tax revenue, budget deficit, and public debt to GDP were generally lower in Switzerland than in Austria throughout the period 1974–2003, changes in these fiscal parameters during economic slowdowns could have had a more adverse impact in Switzerland. Fiscal policy in Switzerland was not adjusted to phases of the business cycle, which could have prolonged the period of recovery from recessions or economic slowdowns. According to the standard normative approach, fiscal policy should respond to the business cycle in a countercyclical manner, which means that the deficit should grow during a recession and change into a surplus during an economic boom (Alesina and Tabellini 2005; Mackiewicz 2006). Empirical studies indicate, however, that Swiss fiscal policy was carried out in a procyclical manner, while in Austria it was conducted in a neutral way (see, for example, Joumard and Giorno 2002; Lane 2003; Lampart 2005).

Among the reasons, mentioned in the economic literature, for the procyclicality of Swiss fiscal policy, one can list the long time lags (two to four years) between income accrual and income tax collection (Hviding 1998; Danninger 2002), the inadequate financing of the unemployment insurance system, (Danninger 2002), a high degree of decentralization and lack of fiscal coordination among the three levels of government (Danninger 2002), and Switzerland's political system of direct democracy (Lampart 2005). The last of these factors can be illustrated using the common pool resource model of Tornell and Lane (1999), in which various interest groups (different parties within the coalition or different ministers in the government, along with their supporting pressure groups) compete for access to tax revenues, which constitute a common resource. In a time of economic upturn, competition is intensified (voracity effect) among interest groups, because each knows that if it gives up its demand, the available resources will be granted to the competitors. The higher the number of potential decision makers, the fiercer the competition among them. Switzerland's system of direct democracy means that the number of potential decision makers is greater than in other countries.

The ratio of government expenditure to GDP in Austria and in Switzerland grew significantly in *1974–76*. In Switzerland consolidated central government expenditure increased by 5.5 percent[9] of GDP (an increase of 40 percent), and in Austria by 2.3 percent (an increase of 8 percent). In *1991–93* central government expenditure increased in both countries to a very similar extent: in Austria by 4.5 percentage points of GDP, and in Switzerland by 4.7 percentage points. In *1997–2000*—that is, when no adverse external shocks could account for the differences in economic growth between the two analyzed economies, even as economic recovery was observed in both—Austria reduced government expenditure by 4.1 percentage points of GDP (7 percent). In Switzerland in 1997–98 public spending increased by an additional 0.9 percentage points of GDP; but in 1999–2000 it declined by 1.3 percentage points of GDP (4 percent). Last, in *2001–03* the ratio of government expenditure to GDP in Austria remained roughly stable, while in Switzerland it rose by 2.8 percentage points (by 8 percent). According to research by Kirchgässner (2004a), the increase in the ratio of public spending to GDP in Switzerland in the mid-1970s and in the first half of the 1990s was primarily due to an increase in transfers. At the same time, the share of public investment in GDP decreased between 1972 and 2002. It needs to be said, however, that a drop in the share of public investment in GDP was also observed in Austria. Moreover, Schaltegger (2004), who estimates a panel model using data on public expenditure in 26 Swiss cantons in 1980–2001, achieves statistically significant results showing the negative impact of public spending on the growth of real per capita GDP in individual cantons. These results are confirmed by Kirchgässner (2004b), who uses the same data but applies more sophisticated methods. It could thus be argued that Switzerland's stronger growth in public spending may have contributed to the magnitude of its economic slowdown as compared with Austria's. It cannot be ruled out, however, that public spending growth in relation to GDP was a consequence rather than a cause of sluggish GDP growth.

Increased public spending led to an increased fiscal burden in both countries, although in Switzerland, spending increased relatively faster than in Austria. Switzerland experienced increased public spending in 1972–77 and in 1991–2000. These periods overlap with the two periods of economic recession in Switzerland, that is, 1974–76 and 1991–96. In 1972–76, income tax revenues increased in Switzerland by 6.4 percentage points of GDP[10] (which represented an increase of 33 percent), while in Austria they rose by 1.5 percentage points of GDP (around 6 percent). In 1991–2000, Swiss income tax revenue increased by 4.5 percentage points of GDP (around 17 percent), whereas in Austria it rose by 3.0 percentage points of GDP (around 8 percent).

The increase in the Swiss tax burden (as measured by income tax revenue to GDP) in 1972–76 may have contributed to the deepening of the recession in 1974–76. This measure is far from perfect, however, and similar to the public-spending-to-GDP ratio, its increase could owe more to changes in GDP than to changes in the actual tax burden. Moreover, it does not seem to be a convincing explanation why Switzerland's economic performance was worse than Austria's in the 1990s. An increase in public debt in that period may have had a far greater impact. In 1990–2003 public debt increased by 26 percentage points of GDP in Switzerland, and by 12.6 percentage points in Austria (figure 4.5).

In the 1990s a significant change in fiscal policy was observed in Austria, related to the country's integration with the EU. While in the mid-1970s to the mid-1980s, Austria pursued the so-called Austro-Keynesian policy[11]—which led to a sharp increase in public debt from 10 percent of GDP in 1974 to almost 50 percent of GDP in 1985 (Katterl and Köhler-Töglhofer 2005) and to serious structural problems—from 1987 until Austria's entry into the EU in 1995, important reforms in public finances were introduced (Katterl and Köhler-Töglhofer 2005; Solsten 1994). A program aimed at reducing the budget deficit to the target level of 2.5 percent of GDP (*Seidel formula*) was implemented. Whenever the

Figure 4.5 Public Debt, 1990–2003

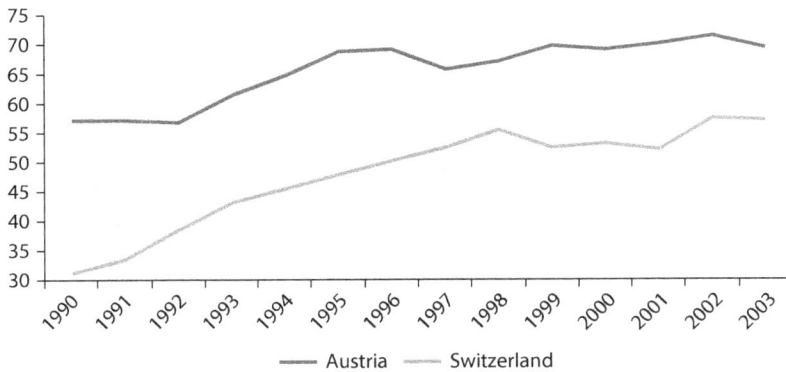

Source: Data from the OECD Economic Outlook 80 Database.
Note: Periods of significant increase in Swiss debt-to-GDP ratio are shaded.

budget deficit exceeded that threshold, consolidation packages were introduced to reduce the deficit in the ensuing years, along with reductions in public spending. A thorough fiscal reform was implemented in 1989–94. Personal income tax rates were reduced: the top rate from 62 percent to 50 percent and the bottom rate from 21 percent to 10 percent. At the same time, the tax base was expanded. Progressive corporate income tax was eliminated and replaced with a single-rate corporate income tax of 30 percent, which was the lowest rate of progressive corporate income tax compared to the former system (where the top rate was 55 percent). Finally, industrial and state enterprises were restructured and later privatized.[12] According to the Organisation for Economic Co-operation and Development (OECD 1994, 1995) these temporary tax cuts and investment incentives introduced in 1993–94 facilitated Austria's 1993 recovery from recession. In the late 1980s and in the early 1990s, the country also managed to reduce its budget deficit.

Following the easing of fiscal policy in 1993–95 and accession to the EU in 1995, a further phase of fiscal consolidation took place in Austria (figure 4.6). Fiscal policy was adapted to the country's intended entry into the euro zone and the requirements of the Maastricht criteria.[13] Consolidation efforts (expenditure cuts and additional revenue) amounted to a total of 4.5 percent of GDP in 1996–97, 1 percent of GDP in 1998, and 1.1 percent of GDP in 1999. The reduction of the deficit was due in two-thirds to spending cuts, and in one-third to measures aimed at increasing budget revenues. The following decisions were made as part of the reform effort (Keuschnigg and others 2000; Prammer 2004; Katterl and Köhler-Töglhofer 2005): public spending was reduced through redundancies in the public sector and freezing of nominal wages at the 1995 level; subsidies to state-owned enterprises and special funds were reduced; a pension reform was introduced in 1997 aimed at reducing the financial attractiveness of early retirement; family allowances (such as maternity leave, childbirth allowance, free transport to schools, and subsidies for the purchase of textbooks) were

Figure 4.6 Primary Government Balance, 1991–2003

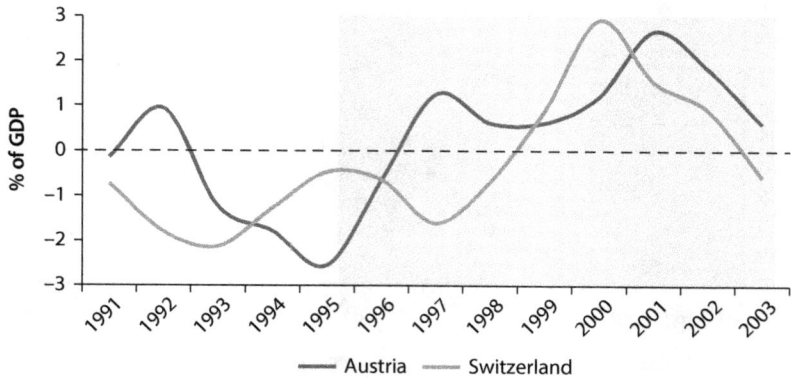

Source: Data from the OECD Economic Outlook 80 Database.
Note: Periods of significant divergence are shaded.

reduced; additional savings were generated (through the lowering of unemployment benefits, the introduction of stringent requirements for social allowance applications, and rigid controls to prevent potential abuses); and costs of nursing care were reduced. In 1996 a "stability pact" for local authorities was introduced to prevent the practice of "moving" the fiscal burden between different levels of the local government. On the revenue side, the definition of taxable income was broadened; tax rates, however, remained unchanged. Additional funding was generated through the sale of government stakes in several big companies.

Katterl and Köhler-Töglhofer (2005) suggest that the fiscal consolidation of 1996–97 may have yielded non-Keynesian effects; that is, it could have contributed to the acceleration of economic growth in Austria during that period. Thus, reducing spending and the fiscal deficit in 1996–2000 could be reasons for Austria's dynamic growth compared to that of Switzerland. Prammer (2004) questions, however, the possibility of non-Keynesian effects in Austria, because consolidation was partly based on measures aimed at increasing revenues, including one-off measures such as revenues from privatization.

As with fiscal policy, monetary policy may have a stabilizing or destabilizing effect on an economy. In 1973 Switzerland adopted a floating exchange-rate regime in response to large inflows of speculative capital dating from 1971. These inflows resulted in a double-digit growth of the money supply which, in turn, could have led to a sharp increase in inflation (Rich 2003). At the end of 1974 the Swiss National Bank (SNB) adopted a monetary policy strategy based on monetary targets. Under this strategy the SNB anticipated, on the basis of forecasts of GDP growth and inflation, changes in economic activity due to changes in the demand for money. It then compared the expected changes in demand with a benchmark for money growth, thus defining the desired money supply growth which the SNB recognized as consistent with price stability and potential GDP growth in Switzerland. In 1974–90 the SNB set annual monetary targets, whereas in 1990–99 medium-term (five-year) targets were applied.

But analytical difficulties on the one hand, together with communication issues on the other, eventually led the SNB to abandon monetary targeting at the end of 1999 and instead pursue inflation targeting.

The desire to prevent inflation and minimize its costs, which led to the floating of the Swiss franc, prompted Austria to adopt a fixed exchange-rate regime. In 1971 the exchange rate of the Austrian schilling was fixed against a currency basket, and from 1981 until the country's entry into the euro zone in 1999, the nominal exchange rate of the shilling remained unchanged against the German mark.

Austria and Switzerland had different monetary policy frameworks; inflation rates in both countries also differed. Although in 1973–2003 the average inflation rate (during both economic downturns and periods of economic stability) in Switzerland was lower than that in Austria, it was also characterized by greater fluctuation (figure 4.7). In particular, it was less stable in periods of economic slowdown, with a possible adverse impact on economic growth[14] through its negative impact on household consumption. The spikes in inflation in 1973–75, in the early 1980s, and early 1990s were mainly driven by oil shocks, but in the case of Switzerland some internal factors were also at play. These included the SNB's attempts to contain the excessive appreciation of the Swiss franc that led to excessive monetary expansion and difficulties estimating the demand for money in a policy framework based on monetary targets (Rich 2003). The SNB's task was further complicated by significant (three to four year) lags in the monetary transmission mechanism and the introduction of an electronic interbank clearing system (IMF 1999).

The macroeconomic policies of Austria and Switzerland together with the impact of external shocks provide a reasonable explanation of differences in their economic growth in the mid-1970s, the early 1980s, and in the first half of the 1990s. The Swiss economic downturns in those periods were a consequence of such factors as declining external demand, exchange-rate fluctuations, a procyclical fiscal policy, and, possibly, more volatile inflation. But as shown at

Figure 4.7 Inflation: Austria and Switzerland Consumer Price Index, 1971–2003

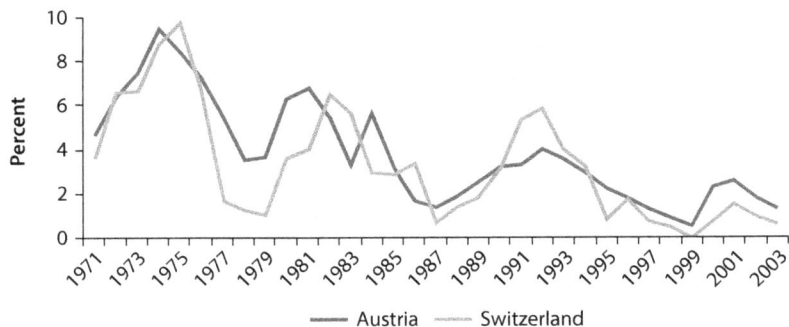

Source: IMF IFS data.
Note: Periods of significant divergence are shaded.

Puzzles of Economic Growth • http://dx.doi.org/10.1596/978-1-4648-0325-3

the beginning of the chapter, economic contraction in the early 1990s cannot account fully for Switzerland's slow economic growth in the entire decade.

Researchers who have studied Switzerland's weak economic performance in the 1990s typically attribute the country's slow growth in labor productivity in that period to low competition in the domestic product market (Hviding 1998; Lambelet and Mihailov 1999; EDV 2002; Gagales 2002; Kehoe and Ruhl 2003; Dreher and Sturm 2005). Those sectors of the Swiss economy where slow labor productivity growth was identified (that is, the construction, retail trade, postal services, and telecommunications sectors) were considered to be "sheltered" from competition, as opposed to the manufacturing sector, which was exposed to international competition (Hviding 1998; Dreher and Sturm 2005). Indeed, the Swiss manufacturing sector grew relatively faster in 1991–2000 than did other branches of the economy (table 4.3). Its growth was, however, slower than that of the manufacturing sector in Austria, which might have been due to the Swiss franc's exchange-rate fluctuations outlined earlier.

The level of competition can be assessed in two ways: by comparing the level of prices of goods and services[15] and by analyzing product market regulation indexes (such as those prepared by the OECD). A comparative analysis of price levels in Austria and in Switzerland (table 4.6) demonstrates that in 1995–2003, prices in Switzerland were much higher than the EU average—for almost all types of goods and services. "Machinery and equipment" was the only category of goods whose prices were close to the EU average. The relatively low price of machinery and equipment could be explained by the fact that the manufacturing

Table 4.6 A Comparison of Price Levels in Austria and Switzerland, 1995 and 2003

Sector	1995		2003	
	Austria	Switzerland	Austria	Switzerland
Government final consumption expenditure	114.8	178.3	100.5	143.3
Services	114.1	176.7	98.3	149.2
Food and nonalcoholic beverages	110.6	145.4	103.5	145.3
Alcoholic beverages	107.5	136.1	88.2	102.4
Tobacco	109.1	99.1	92.9	91.5
Clothing and footwear	109.1	116.3	107.6	117.4
Housing, water, electricity, gas, and other fuels	106.1	194.9	88.1	173.9
Household furnishings, equipment, and maintenance	115.3	129.4	101.6	120.0
Health	119.1	169.4	99.0	147.9
Transport	116.9	124.2	106.6	111.7
Communication	140.3	127.5	103.0	131.3
Recreation and culture	112.5	135.2	96.7	123.4
Education	122.5	194.9	107.2	151.2
Restaurants and hotels	112.4	145.3	97.6	125.3
Machinery and equipment	95.9	118.0	97.6	103.3
Construction	112.7	125.8	104.3	146.4

Source: Eurostat data.
Note: EU average = 100.

sector was exposed to strong international competition. In both 1995 and 2003 in Switzerland the highest prices were recorded in the following categories: food, housing and utilities, health, communication, education, and construction. Although most of the analyzed categories saw a decrease in the relative level of prices in Switzerland between 1995 and 2003 (which might have been due to the decreasing differences in the level of per capita income in Switzerland and the EU), the prices were still much above the EU average. At the same time food prices hardly changed since 1995, whereas prices in construction and communication increased even further. In 1995 the Austrian prices of most of the analyzed categories of goods and services were slightly higher than the EU average, but they reached that average by 2003. The most significant price reductions were observed in communication.[16]

Switzerland's high prices seem to confirm that the level of competition in the country's internal market was low in the period under consideration. At the same time, the decline in prices in Austria in 1995–2003 would support the hypothesis that competition in the Austrian product market increased between 1995 and 2003.

According to an indicator, designed by the OECD (Conway, Janod, and Nicoletti 2005: table 4.7), of product market regulation, the level of regulation in Switzerland was on the whole higher than that of Austria—both in 1998 and 2003. But the differences in indicator values were not large, and these values were close to the OECD average. Moreover, as the indicator values were available only for two years (1998 and 2003) within the period 1995–2003, one could not assess the dynamics of regulatory reforms before 1998, that is, in the period in which Austria changed its laws to prepare for entry into the EU common market.

But figure 4.8 sheds some light on the Swiss and Austrian product market regulations in seven nonmanufacturing sectors (electricity, gas, road transport, railways, airlines, postal services, and telecommunications), among which are

Table 4.7 Indicators of Product Market Regulation in Austria and Switzerland, 1998 and 2003 (Entire Economy)

Year	Overall product market regulation indicator			Constituent indicators								
				State control			Barriers to entrepreneurship			Barriers to trade and investment		
	A	S	OECD	A	S	OECD	A	S	OECD	A	S	OECD
1998	1.8	2.2	2.1	2.5	2.8	2.9	1.7	2.3	1.9	1.3	1.7	1.5
2003	1.4	1.7	1.5	1.9	2.2	2.1	1.6	1.9	1.5	0.7	1.0	1.0

Source: Conway, Janod, and Nicoletti 2005.
Note: A = Austria; OECD = Organisation for Economic Co-operation and Development; S = Switzerland. The indicators range from 0 (least restrictive) to 6 (most restrictive). They take into account the extent of public ownership, market access and competition issues, market structure and vertical relationships in utilities and other network industries, regulatory processes and capacities in public administration, administrative requirements for business start-ups, and regulations that may have an impact on (a) the accounting, legal services, engineering, and architectural professions; (b) access, business conduct, and the industry and market structure in road freight, railways, and passenger air travel; and (c) access and business conduct in the retail sector.

Figure 4.8 The Timing of Reforms in the Energy, Transport, and Communication Sectors: Austria and Switzerland, 1975–2003

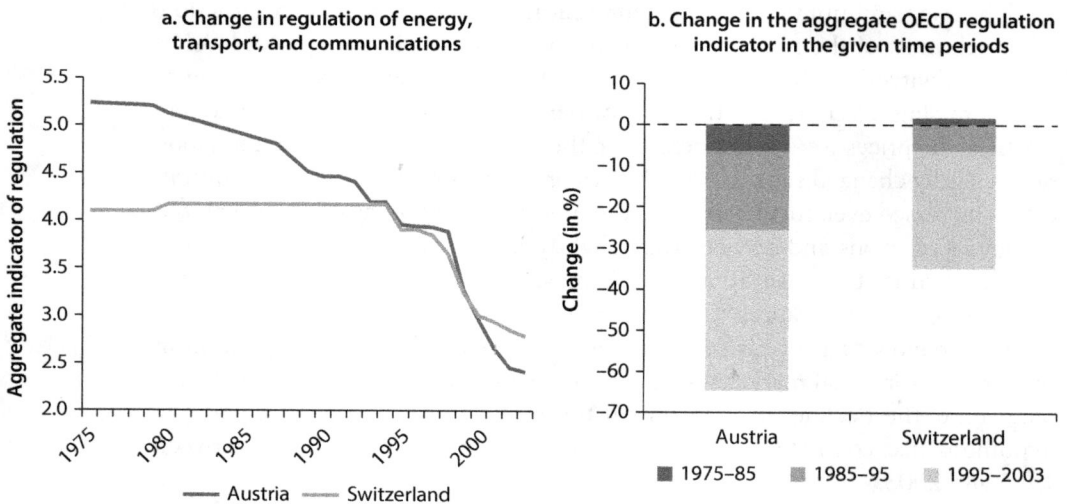

a. Change in regulation of energy, transport, and communications

b. Change in the aggregate OECD regulation indicator in the given time periods

■ 1975–85   ■ 1985–95   ▨ 1995–2003

Source: Data from the OECD International Regulation Database.

Note: Panel a: The aggregate indicator of regulation in seven nonmanufacturing sectors (electricity, gas, road transport, railways, airlines, postal services, and telecommunications), scale from 0 (least restrictive) to 6 (most restrictive).

sectors in which prices in Switzerland were much higher than in Austria and the EU as a whole (energy, telecommunications) and/or which had a negative contribution to Swiss GDP growth in 1991–2000 (transport).[17]

Figure 4.8 suggests that the process of deregulation in the seven sectors was deeper and started earlier in Austria than in Switzerland. As the majority of regulation reforms were implemented in Austria in the period between the late 1980s and 2003, it is quite likely that these reforms boosted economic growth in the 1990s.

Analysis of another OECD indicator, namely one reflecting the level of regulation in retail distribution and in professional services (for details, see Conway and Nicoletti 2006), suggests that (table 4.8) the level of regulation in the retail sector in Switzerland was not in itself the reason for the high prices and the sluggish growth of productivity in that sector relative to that of Austria. The level of retail regulation in Switzerland was relatively low, while in Austria it was relatively high and did not decline much between 1996 and 2003. On the other hand, the relatively large scale of deregulation in the professional services sector in Austria, as reflected by the decline in the relevant index down to approximately the OECD average by 2003 (table 4.8), may have contributed to price cuts and faster productivity growth in this sector.

Of course, such indicators as those presented earlier may be subject to large measurement errors and future revisions; one cannot draw firm conclusions from this type of analysis. Therefore, other factors that could have affected the level of competition in the product market as well as productivity growth in both countries need to be assessed. Among other things, the degree of competition

Table 4.8 Regulation Indicators in the Retail Sector and in Professional Services (Legal, Accounting, Engineering, and Architectural Services): Austria, Switzerland, and OECD Average, 1996–2003

Year	Retail distribution			Professional services		
	Austria	Switzerland	OECD	Austria	Switzerland	OECD
1998[a]/1996	4.1	1.2	2.7	4.2	1.8	2.4
2003	3.2	0.8	2.3	2.0	1.0	2.1

Source: Data from Conway and Nicoletti (2006).

Note: OECD = Organisation for Economic Co-operation and Development.

a. 1996 for professional services, 1998 for retail distribution. Indicator of regulation in retail distribution takes into account difficulties in setting up a business, license and permit requirements, restrictions regarding the store surface, protection of market incumbents against competition from new entrants, regulation of shop opening hours, and price controls. Indicator of regulation in professional services (legal, accounting, engineering, and architectural) takes into account licensing, education requirements, regulations on prices and fees, regulations on advertising, and restrictions on interprofessional cooperation.

in the product market can be increased through (EDV 2002; Giorno, Gugler, and Jimenez 2004) deregulation, the strengthening of competition laws and the elimination of administrative barriers, the reduction of state aid, and the opening of markets to international competition.

The faster pace and wider scope of reforms carried out by Austria from the mid-1980s to 2003 (in all of the aforementioned areas) could have played a decisive role in ensuring that the degree of market competition (as measured by the comparative price level and the product market regulation indicator) increased more and reached a higher level in Austria than in Switzerland. These factors could also have accounted for Austria's faster economic growth as compared to that of Switzerland in 1991–2003—even after controlling for Switzerland's lengthy recession in the first half of the 1990s. The most important reforms undertaken by Austria since the mid-1980s were the restructuring and privatization of state-owned enterprises and the opening of markets in connection with the country's accession into the EU.

In 1990–2001, the scale of privatization in Austria was much larger than that of Switzerland. The proceeds from privatization in Austria were more than twice as high as those in Switzerland in relation to GDP (according to Belke and others 2007, the revenue from privatization in 1990–2001 amounted to 5.9 percent of GDP in Austria versus 2.5 percent of GDP in Switzerland). One can think of several reasons why privatization could have boosted economic growth in Austria to a larger extent than in Switzerland in the 1990s. First, the potential for privatization itself was different in the two countries. Traditionally, Austria's economy was characterized by a high degree of state intervention (OECD 2003). An important part of Austrian industry, in particular the energy sector, was nationalized after World War II. The state's involvement in the telecommunications, transport, and banking sectors led to the creation of one of the largest public sectors in Western Europe (Aiginger 1999). At the end of the 1970s state-owned enterprises generated as much as 25 percent of GDP (Aiginger 1999). While state ownership of infrastructure was common to many European economies, state ownership of industry was, till the 1990s, a feature specific to Austria

(Aiginger 1999). By contrast, state ownership of industry hardly ever existed in Switzerland (Schedler and Keller 1998). Second, the privatization process in Austria covered, to a varying degree, nearly all sectors of the economy: industry, finance, telecommunications, public utilities, and transport. In Switzerland the privatization efforts undertaken in the 1990s resulted in a limited scope of privatization in the telecommunications sector (Bortolotti and Pinotti 2006; see, also, Belke and Schneider 2005). Third, privatization began in Austria a decade earlier than in Switzerland: the first phase took place in 1987–90 and after a pause in 1991, was continued. Switzerland, where the first major privatization transactions were conducted in 1998, was in the 1990s one of those developed countries that was the last to privatize the state-controlled sectors (Bortolotti and Pinotti 2006).

In Austria the inefficiency of industrial firms in the mid-1980s, together with preparations for EU membership, provided incentives for an early start of the privatization process (Belke and Schneider 2004). The sectors of the Austrian economy that were protected against international competition (mainly telecommunications, energy, and food) had to be integrated into the EU market, and therefore, prior to the entry of Austria into the EU, a restructuring program focused mainly on privatization and liberalization was launched.

The preparation and, later, the participation of Austria in the EU single market called for a series of changes to Austrian laws in the 1990s. Austria was one of five countries in the EU-15[18] that, in 1992–2001, recorded the most dynamic growth in the Internal Market Index—a rough measure of the effects of internal market policy as defined in the broadest terms by the free circulation of goods, services, capital, and workers within the EU (European Commission 2002). Austria's accession to the European Economic Area (EEA) and EU was a catalyst for regulation reforms and the extension of competition principles from the manufacturing sector (which had already been exposed to competition) to other sectors of the economy. As indicated by Janger (2005), Austria would have undertaken deregulation reforms and opened its markets even without its participation in the EEA and the EU, but this would probably have occurred later and to a lesser extent.

Swiss reforms aimed at the deregulation and liberalization of network industries were largely modeled on reforms carried out in the EU, for instance, in the electricity and gas sectors (Giorno, Gugler, and Jimenez 2004). But when compared to Austria, Switzerland's reforms were delayed and their extent limited. For example, while the liberalization of the telecommunications sector in Austria was completed in 1998 (Janger 2005), in Switzerland it only started in that year (Giorno, Gugler, and Jimenez 2004). In some cases, delays or failure to carry out reforms in Switzerland were a consequence of the system of direct democracy. This was, for example, the case of the liberalization of the electricity sector: even though the reform was approved by the parliament in 2000, it was rejected in a referendum in 2002.

Austria's EU integration was a also a driving force behind the growth of the country's exports, which in turn boosted the country's GDP growth, especially in 2001–03 and, to a lesser extent, in 1997–2000 (table 4.9).

Table 4.9 Contribution of Internal and External Demand to GDP Growth: Austria and Switzerland, 1991–2003

Years	GDP growth (%)		c+g+i (% points)		nx (% points)	
	A	S	A	S	A	S
1991–96	1.3	−0.4	1.5	−0.4	−0.2	0.0
1997–2000	2.4	1.3	1.6	1.1	0.6	0.3
2001–03	0.7	0.0	0.3	0.3	0.4	−0.4

Source: Calculations based on Penn World Table 6.2.

Note: A = Austria; c+g+i = consumption + government spending + investment; nx = net exports; S = Switzerland.

In this context it is interesting to observe that from their accession to the European Free Trade Association (EFTA) in 1960 until the early 1990s, Austria and Switzerland had the same integration and trade policies (Breuss 2006). In 1992 Switzerland applied for full membership in the EU, but entry into the EEA was rejected by the Swiss in a referendum held in the same year.[19] Austria became a member of the EEA in 1994 and of the EU in January 1995; in 1999 it adopted the euro. Austria's accession to the EEA in 1994 marked the introduction of the free movement of people, capital, and goods from the EU and EFTA countries (except Switzerland). To mitigate the adverse effects of remaining outside the EEA, Switzerland started negotiating a bilateral agreement covering seven sectors (individual transport, air traffic, ground traffic, agriculture, technical trade barriers, public procurement, and research) in 1994 with the EU. But the agreement (*Bilaterals I*), whose provisions encompassed the main areas on which the EEA is founded, did not enter into force until June 2002 (after a referendum). At the same time, in mid-2002 Switzerland started negotiations on the second package of agreements for the liberalization of trade in agricultural goods (*Bilaterals II*), which was completed in May 2004. As noted by Breuss (2006), however, both *Bilaterals I* and *Bilaterals II* included only parts of the EEA agreement and the internal market program regulations. Accession to the EU generated significant changes in Austria's trade policy. First, customs duties[20] were reduced by approximately 5 percent. Around 25 percent of Austria's imports from "third" countries (non-EU countries and countries that remained in the EFTA in 1995) were covered by more favorable customs regulations (Breuss 2006). Under the Common Agricultural Policy (CAP) all barriers to trade in agricultural goods were abolished. At the same time, average import tariffs on agricultural products in Switzerland amounted to 218 percent in 2000, and were therefore 3.6 times higher than in the EU (Giorno, Gugler, and Jimenez 2004). Tariffs on all consumer goods in Switzerland were 1.6 percentage points higher than in Austria—including tariffs on food products, which were 8.1 percentage points higher (BAK Basel Economics 2007). Austria imported around 77 percent of food products from the EU and did not impose any duties on them. In Switzerland the share of EU product imports among total imports was similar, but were subject to the highest customs duties.

Second, border controls were eliminated and, therefore, the cost of trade was reduced by about 2.5 percent (Breuss 2006). Meanwhile, the existence of the EU border generated four types of costs for an average Swiss company (Minsch and Moser 2006): (a) customs clearance, (b) waiting times at the border, (c) a certificate of origin to be able to import/export goods from/to the EU without additional costs, and (d) technical barriers to trade. According to the results of a survey (Minsch and Moser 2006), 18 percent of Swiss companies claimed that the trade costs they bore were high.[21] These costs accounted for an average of about 1.9 percent of the value of goods exported to the EU and 2.3 percent of the value of goods imported from the EU.

Third, the principle of national patent exhaustion was replaced by the principle of regional patent exhaustion in force in the EU. The principle of national patent exhaustion leads to a situation where direct parallel import of patented products is not allowed, since the patent holder can prevent their entry into the market where he owns their intellectual property rights. According to the OECD (2004), the prices of patented Swiss pharmaceutical products were up to 40 percent higher than the lowest possible prices abroad, whereas the wholesale prices of goods other than food were up to 30 percent higher. According to the results of two empirical studies commissioned by the Swiss government, the liberalization of parallel imports would cause the prices of consumer goods to fall by 4–8 percent and of drugs by 14–32 percent, and increase GDP by 0.1 percent (OECD 2004).

The effects of Austria's accession to the EU were threefold. First, a trade creation effect was observed. On the basis of a gravity model, Firdmuc (2005) estimated that Austria's trade with EU countries increased by 25 percent. At the same time, the variable controlling for EU entry was statistically significant at the 1 percent level. Second, trade diversion also occurred. In the case of retail trade, in 1994 the share of the EU-14[22] in Austrian imports was 56 percent, but in 1995 it rose to 76 percent. Nominal[23] Austrian imports from the EU increased in 1995 by more than 44 percent, while imports from other countries fell by almost 43 percent (BAK Basel Economics 2007). These effects were observed mainly in the food sector, where trade barriers against integration proved particularly significant. Third, integration with the EU internal market resulted in lower import prices in Austria (table 4.10).[24] In the case of Switzerland, high import prices (Grass 2007) accounted for 8 percentage points of the 15 percent difference in the level of retail trade prices in 2005 between Switzerland and the average for four EU countries (Austria, Germany, France, and Italy).

Austria's entry into the euro zone in 1999 also had a significant impact on the growth of Austrian exports. Micco, Stein, and Ordonez (2003) estimate that,

Table 4.10 A Comparison of Relative Import Price Levels: Austria and Switzerland, 2005[25]

Country	Total prices	Food products	Other products
Austria	84	73	86
Switzerland	100	100	100

Source: BAK Basel Economics 2007, 29.

following the introduction of the common currency, bilateral trade between the 12 countries of the euro area rose by 5–10 percent. According to Faruqee (2004), Austria—together with Spain, the Netherlands, and Belgium—achieved above-average trade gains from participation in the currency union.

Summary and Conclusions

The purpose of our analysis was to explain why Austria, whose GDP per capita in 1973 amounted to 64 percent of Switzerland's GDP per capita, had by 2003 nearly caught up with Switzerland. The following conclusions can be drawn:

- In 1974–2003 Switzerland suffered from two periods of significant (relative to Austria) economic contraction (in 1974–76 and 1991–96). The economic slump in the first half of the 1990s, however, cannot fully account for Switzerland's bad economic performance in the 1990s as a whole.

- The different average economic growth rates in Austria and Switzerland in 1974–2003 were largely due to *external shocks* that affected the Swiss economy more deeply than Austria:
  - A significant part of Austria's exports in 1974–76 was directed toward the (then Communist) countries of Central and Eastern Europe, which were less negatively affected by the first oil shock than Switzerland's export partners. Later demand from these countries, supported by strong economic growth due to their transition to a market economy, as well as their preparations for accession to the EU (which took place in May 2004), stimulated the growth of Austrian exports in the 1990s and in the early 2000s. The stable exchange rate of the Austrian schilling also created a favorable environment for Austrian export growth.
  - During periods of global economic slowdown and turmoil in the financial markets, the Swiss franc appreciated strongly and rapidly, due to the currency's traditional role of a "safe haven." These episodes of sudden appreciation led to a large deterioration in the competitiveness of Swiss exports, which only exacerbated the problems connected with the already-weak external demand due to the global economic downturn.

- The negative impact of external shocks on Switzerland's economic growth might have been strengthened by Swiss macroeconomic policy:
  - Fiscal policy in Switzerland was procyclical (that is, it contributed to wider fluctuations), which in turn could have resulted in deeper and longer recessions than in Austria, where fiscal policy was broadly neutral. During economic slumps in Switzerland (1974–76 and 1991–96), public spending in relation to GDP increased in both countries, and although the increase in Swiss public spending was relatively higher than in Austria, it resulted mainly from an increase in transfers, that is, the least-"productive" expenditure category.

– The average inflation rate in 1974–2003 was lower in Switzerland than in Austria, but inflation was on average more volatile in the former. Swiss inflation increased particularly strongly, relative to inflation in Austria, in the early 1990s.

• Austria's faster economic growth in 1991–2003 may have been the result of bolder institutional reforms, as compared to those conducted in Switzerland:
  – In 1996–2000 Austria made significant cuts in public spending and reduced the budget deficit in preparation for the country's entry into the euro zone. During the same period, the share of public spending in Swiss GDP did not change. Fiscal consolidation in Austria in the second half of the 1990s might have triggered non-Keynesian effects, which led to faster economic growth.
  – Preparations for Austria's accession and the country's actual membership in the EEA since 1994 made the opening of markets and the implementation of reforms deregulating the product market a necessity. This resulted in an increase of competitive pressure on many Austrian companies, and a drop in prices and faster growth of labor productivity in several sectors of the Austrian economy.
  – Following its rejection of the EEA membership in 1992, Switzerland participated in the common European market only partially, and its product market regulation reforms were also relatively more timid. The relatively low level of competition in the Swiss product market resulted in relatively high prices and low productivity growth in many sectors of the economy.
  – Austria's accession to the EU and, consequently, the reduction of barriers to trade, also led to an increase in the country's international trade. The introduction of the euro also contributed to trade growth.
  – The relatively larger scale of privatization in Austria was also conducive to faster productivity growth in that country, as compared to Switzerland in the 1990s.

Notes

1. In 1950 the population of Austria was 6.9 million and the population of Switzerland, 4.7 million. In 2003 the population of the two countries was 8.2 million and 7.5 million, respectively (Total Economy Database, Groningen Growth and Development Centre).
2. German speakers account for approximately two-thirds of the population of Switzerland (http://www.swissworld.org).
3. Calculations based on data from the Penn World Table 6.2 (Heston, Summers, and Aten 2006).
4. Data from the Penn World Table 6.2.
5. The results of the growth comparison remain essentially unchanged if instead of GDP, we analyze changes in the gross national product (GNP). Despite the fact that in 1970–2003, the Swiss GNP was several percentage points higher than the Swiss GDP, the GNP growth rate was on average only 0.1 percentage points higher than the

GDP growth rate in the period 1980–2002, and approximately 0.2 percentage points higher in 1990–2002 (OECD 2004). Thus, on average, Swiss GNP growth would still have been slower than Austrian GDP growth. Moreover, in the periods of recession in the mid-1970s and 1991–96, the ratio of GNP/GDP remained stable in Switzerland; a sharp upsurge in Swiss net factor income from abroad could only be observed in 1997–2000.

6. The period choice was dictated by the availability of comparable data for both economies.

7. In 1975–76 Austria's energy intensity (measured as the ratio of GDP per kilogram of oil equivalent) amounted to $6 at constant 2000 prices (PPP), whereas that of the Swiss economy amounted to $8. In 1991–96 the average energy intensity level of the Austrian economy amounted to $7, whereas in Switzerland it remained at $8—which means that it had fallen in Austria and remained constant in Switzerland as compared to the 1970s.

8. In 1972 exports to China accounted for only 0.3 percent, and in 1989 for only 0.7 percent of Switzerland's total exports (author's own calculations based on IMF DOTS).

9. The figures in this paragraph are the author's own calculations based on the International Monetary Fund's (IMF's) Government Finance Statistics. Consolidated central budget expenditure is used because of a lack of comparable government data.

10. The figures in this paragraph are the author's own calculations based on the *OECD Revenue Statistics 1965–2005 (2006 Edition)*.

11. For details, see Marterbauer (1998).

12. Privatization will be discussed further in this chapter.

13. The euro convergence criteria which European Union member states are required to meet to adopt the euro as their currency. These criteria concern the level of HICP inflation, the size of the government budget deficit and the government debt-to-GDP ratio, the exchange rate and long-term interest rates.

14. The negative impact of inflation volatility on economic growth has been discussed, for example, by Judson and Orphanides (1999); Fountas, Karanasos, and Kim (2001); and Grier and others (2004).

15. Although international price comparisons are an easy method of assessing the intensity of competition in the product market, they should be interpreted with caution. Price differences are only an indirect indicator of the degree of competition. High prices in a given sector do not necessarily indicate low competition, but could be caused by high prices in other sectors of the economy. Moreover, the level of prices in those sectors that produce goods not subject to international trade is the higher, the higher the productivity in the tradable goods sector (and the related overall level of economic development). Finally, price comparisons between countries are also imprecise because of differences in indirect taxes (in the period 1995–2003 they were lower in Switzerland than in Austria).

16. Communication prices in Austria were being reduced even before 1995.

17. While the indicator in figure 4.8 misses important aspects of economywide regulation, it includes some of the sectors in which anti-competitive regulation is concentrated in the OECD countries, given that the manufacturing sectors are typically lightly regulated and open to international competition. In addition, this indicator is highly correlated with the cross-section indicator of economywide product market regulation in

the years in which they overlap, suggesting that the former is a reasonable proxy for the latter (Conway and others 2006, 6).

18. Together with Finland, Spain, Sweden, and Italy.

19. It is worth noting that the three other EFTA countries—Norway, Iceland, and Liechtenstein—joined the European Economic Area.

20. Although the direct relevance of tariffs is not as significant as is often assumed, tariffs generate indirect costs. First, high tariffs on agricultural products result in higher producer prices in the agricultural sector, and thus higher consumer prices in retail trade. Second, tariffs lead to suboptimal allocation of resources, which means that the tariff protection of domestic producers hampers or prevents necessary structural changes (BAK Basel Economics 2007).

21. Swiss entrepreneurs declared that the two major cost-generating barriers to trade were the requirement to obtain separate permits for the entry of Swiss products into the EU market and a longer waiting time, as compared to their EU competitors, for the approval of Swiss products to enter the EU market.

22. The EU-12 and Sweden and Finland.

23. The trade creation effect was also found when analyzing data expressed in constant prices (see BAK Basel Economics 2007).

24. But globalization also had a significant impact on lowering import prices in the *nonfood* sector.

25. Although our study period ends in 2003, presenting data for 2005 does not influence our conclusions, given that an uninterrupted, clear downward trend in import prices was observed between 1995 and 2005 (see BAK Basel Economics 2007, 39).

Bibliography

Aiginger, K. 1999. "The Privatization Experiment in Austria." Reprint from *Austrian Economic Quarterly* 4: 261–70. http://www.wifo.ac.at/Karl.Aiginger/abstracts/privat3 .html.

Alesina, A., and G. Tabellini. 2005. "Why Is Fiscal Policy Often Procyclical?" NBER Working Paper 11600, National Bureau of Economic Research, Cambridge, MA.

BAK Basel Economics. 2007. *Auswirkungen einer Liberalisierung des internationalen Warenhandels auf den Schweizer Detailhandel.* Studie im Auftrag des SECO, Basel, Switzerland. http://www.bakbasel.ch/downloads/services/reports_studies /2007/200702_liberalisierung_warenhandel_study.pdf.

Belke, A., F. Baumgärtner, F. Schneider, and R. Setzer. 2007. "The Different Extent of Privatisation Proceeds in OECD Countries: A Preliminary Explanation Using a Public Choice Approach." *Public Finance Analysis* 63 (2): 211–43.

Belke, A., and F. Schneider. 2004. "Privatization in Austria: Some Theoretical Reasons and Performance Measures." Working Paper 0404, University of Linz, Austria.

———. 2005. *Privatisation in Austria: Response to Internal and External Pressures.* CESifo DICE Report, Center for Economic Studies, Munich.

Bortolotti, B., and P. Pinotti. 2006. "Delayed Privatization." http://web.econ.unito.it /bortolotti/bb/delayedpriva.pdf.

Breuss, F. 2006. "Austria and Switzerland—Experiences with and without EU Membership." *Austrian Economic Quarterly* 1: 13–39.

Breuss, F., and F. Schebeck. 1999. "Costs and Benefits of EU Eastern Enlargement for Austria." *Austrian Economic Quarterly* 1: 43–53.

Cerra, V., and S. Saxena. 2007. "Growth Dynamics: The Myth of Economic Recovery." BIS Working Papers 226, Bank for International Settlements (BIS), Basel.

Conway, P., V. Janod, and G. Nicoletti. 2005. "Product Market Regulation in OECD Countries: 1998 to 2003." Economics Department Working Papers 419, Organisation for Economic Co-operation and Development Paris, April.

Conway, P., and G. Nicoletti. 2006. "Product Market Regulation in the Non-Manufacturing Sectors of OECD Countries: Measurement and Highlights." Economics Department Working Papers 530, Organisation for Economic Co-operation and Development Paris.

Conway, P., D. de Rosa, G. Nicoletti, and F. Steiner. 2006. "Regulation, Competition and Productivity Convergence." Economics Department Working Papers 509, Organisation for Economic Co-operation and Development, Paris.

Danninger, S. 2002. "A New Rule: The Swiss Debt Brake." IMF Working Paper WP/02/18, International Monetary Fund, Washington, DC.

Doytchinov, S., and F. Schmidbauer. 2007. "Schweizer Warenexporte im Hoch—eine Ursachenanalyse." *Die Volkswirtschaft* 7/8: 38–41.

Dreher, A., and J. A. Sturm. 2005. *Wachstumsschwäche Schweiz: Ein Vergleich mit anderen (kleinen) europäischen Staaten.* Kreuzlingen, Switzerland: Thurgauer Wirtschaftsinstitut.

EDV (Eidgenössisches Volkswirtschaftsdepartement). 2002. *Der Wachstumsbericht. Determinanten des Schweizer Wirtschaftswachstums und Ansatzpunkte für eine wachstumsorientierte Wirtschaftspolitik* Bern: Switzerland Department of Economic Affairs.

European Commission. 2002. *Internal Market Scoreboard, No. 11.* Special Edition, November 2002.

Faruqee, H. 2004. "Measuring the Trade Effects of EMU." IMF Working Paper WP/04/154, International Monetary Fund, August.

Fenz, M., and M. Schneider. 2006. "Output Fluctuations in Germany and Austria: Comovement and Shock Transmission." Österreichische National Bank, Vienna, Austria.

Firdmuc, J. 2005. "Austria's EU Accession and Trade." *Monetary Policy and the Economy* Q2/05 (August): 170–77.

Fountas, S., M. Karanasos, and J. Kim. 2001. "Uncertainty and Their Relationship with Inflation and Output Growth." *Economics Letters* 75: 293–301.

Gagales, A. 2002. "Growth in Switzerland: Can Better Performance Be Sustained?" IMF Working Paper WP/02/153, International Monetary Fund, Washington, DC.

Giorno, C., P. Gugler, and M. Jimenez. 2004. "Product Market Competition and Economic Performance in Switzerland." OECD Economics Department Working Paper 383, Organisation for Economic Co-operation and Development, Paris.

Grass, M. 2007. "Retail Trade Effects from Liberalisation of Goods Trade." Presentation given at the Reform Works symposium, February 19. http://www.bakbasel.ch/downloads/services/reports_studies/2007/200702_liberalisierung_warenhandel_pres.pdf.

Grier, K., O. Henry, N. Olekalns, and K. Shields. 2004. "The Asymmetric Effects of Uncertainty on Inflation and Output Growth." *Journal of Applied Econometrics* 19: 551–65.

Heston, Alan, Robert Summers, and Bettina Aten. 2006. "Penn World Table Version 6.2." Center for International Comparisons of Production, Income and Prices at the University of Pennsylvania, September.

Hviding, K. 1998. "Switzerland's Long-Run Growth Slowdown." In *Switzerland: Selected Issues and Statistical Appendix*, IMF Staff Country Report 98/43, International Monetary Fund, Washington, DC.

IMF (International Monetary Fund). 1999. *Switzerland: Selected Issues and Statistical Appendix*. IMF Staff Country Report 99/30, April, IMF, Washington, DC.

Janger, J. 2005. "Sectoral Regulation in Austria Before and After EU Accession—The Network Industries as a Case in Point." *Monetary Policy and the Economy* Q2/05: 178–95.

Joumard, I., and C. Giorno. 2002. "Enhancing the Effectiveness of Public Spending in Switzerland." OECD Economics Department Working Paper 332, Organisation for Economic Co-operation and Development, Paris.

Judson, R., and A. Orphanides. 1999. "Inflation, Volatility, and Growth." *International Finance* 2 (1): 117–38.

Katterl, A., and W. Köhler-Töglhofer. 2005. "The Impact of EU Accession on Austria's Budget Policy." *Monetary Policy and the Economy* 2: 101–16.

Kehoe, T. J., and K. J. Ruhl. 2003. "Recent Great Depressions: Aggregate Growth in New Zealand and Switzerland." *New Zealand Economic Papers* 37 (1): 5–40.

Keuschnigg, C., M. Keuschnigg, R. Koman, E. Lüth, and B. Raffelhüschen. 2000. "Public Debt and Generational Balance in Austria." Economics Series 80, Institute for Advanced Studies (IHS), Vienna.

Kirchgässner, G. 2004a. "Die langfristige Entwicklung der Bundesfinanzen, 1960– 2002." Universität St. Gallen, Switzerland. http://www.kfk.admin.ch/pdf%20d/3 .Kirchg%C3%A4ssner04.pdf.

———. 2004b. "Zum Zusammenhang zwischen staatlicher Aktivität und wirtschaftlicher Entwicklung." Department of Economics Discussion Paper 2004–16, University of St. Gallen, Switzerland. http://www.alexandria.unisg.ch/publications/person/K /Gebhard_Kirchgaessner/31590.

Lambelet, J.-C., and A. Mihailov. 1999. "A Note on Switzerland's Economy. Did the Swiss Economy Really Stagnate in the 1990's, and Is Switzerland Really All that Rich?" http://www.hec.unil.ch/jlambelet/RichSwitzerland.PDF.

Lampart, D. 2005. "Die konjunkturelle Ausrichtung der Schweizer Finanzpolitik im internationalen Vergleich. Ex-ante vs. Ex-post Betrachtung." Working Papers 109, KOF (Swiss Institute for Business Cycle Research), September.

Lane, P. 2003. "The Cyclical Behaviour of Fiscal Policy: Evidence from the OECD." *Journal of Public Economics* 87: 2661–75.

Mackiewicz, M. 2006. *Reakcje polityki fiskalnej na wahania koniunkturalne—przyczyny zróżnicowania*. Bank i Kredyt, październik: 3–16.

Marterbauer, M. 1998. "Post-Keynesian Economic Policy in Austria and Sweden: The Employment Record in a Changing International Environment." Presentation at the European Association for Evolutionary Political Economy Conference, Lisbon, Portugal, WIFO (Austrian Institute of Research), November 5–8.

Micco, A., E. Stein, and G. Ordonez. 2003. *The Currency Union Effect on Trade: Early Evidence from EMU*. Washington, DC: Inter-American Development Bank. http:// faculty.haas.berkeley.edu/arose/MSOIADBEMU.pdf.

Minsch, R., and P. Moser. 2006. "Volkswirtschaftliche Kosten der Zollschranken: Ergebnisse einer Unternehmensumfrage." *Die Volkswirtschaft*, 79 (3): 51–54.

OECD (Organisation for Economic Co-operation and Development). 1994. "Economic Outlook—Austria." http://findarticles.com/p/articles/mi_m4456/is_n56/ai_16565395.

———. 1995. "Economic Outlook—Austria." http://findarticles.com/p/articles/mi_m4456/is_n57/ai_17335644.

———. 2003. *Economic Surveys 2002–2003: Austria*. Paris: OECD.

———. 2004. *Economic Surveys 2003–2004: Switzerland*. Paris: OECD.

Prammer, D. 2004. "Expansionary Fiscal Consolidations? An Appraisal of the Literature on Non-Keynesian Effects of Fiscal Policy and a Case Study for Austria." *Monetary Policy and the Economy*, 2004/Q3: 34–52.

Ravn, M. O., and H. Uhlig. 2001. "On Adjusting the HP-Filter for the Frequency of Observations." CESifo Working Paper 479, Center for Economic Studies and Ifo Institute for Economic Research, Munich.

Rich, G. 2003. "Swiss Monetary Targeting 1974–1996: The Role of Internal Policy Analysis." Working Paper 236, European Central Bank, Frankfurt am Main, Germany.

Schaltegger, C. 2004. "Ist die Höhe der Staatsquote schuld an der Schweizer Wachstumsschwäche?" *Die Volkswirtschaft* 1/2 (2005): 55–8.

Schedler, K., and F. Keller. 1998. "Reforming Public Enterprises—Case Studies: Switzerland." http://www.oecd.org/dataoecd/19/59/1901744.pdf.

Solsten, E. 1994. *Austria: A Country Study*. Washington, DC: GPO for the Library of Congress. http://countrystudies.us/austria/.

Suess, F. R. 1999. "The Swiss Franc—Still a Safe Haven Currency in the New Millennium?" BFI Consulting AG, Walnut Creek, CA. http://www.bfi-consulting.com/files/pdfs/reports/swiss_franc_after_2000.pdf.

Tornell, A., and P. R. Lane. 1999. "The Voracity Effect." *American Economic Review* 89 (1): 22–46.

Websites

Penn World Table, Center for International Comparisons at the University of Pennsylvania: http://pwt.econ.upenn.edu.

Switzerland's Official Information Portal: http://www.swissworld.org.

Total Economy Database, Groningen Growth and Development Centre: http://www.ggdc.net.

CHAPTER 5

Why Did the Economic Growth Paths of Estonia and Slovenia Diverge?

Paweł Cwalina

This chapter seeks to explain differences in the economic performance of Estonia and Slovenia in the period 1990–2004, as both transitioned from being centrally planned economies to members of the European Union.

The two countries are relatively small, both in terms of land area and population (1.3 million in Estonia and 2.0 million in Slovenia). Both underwent the socialist experiment,[1] which—although the degree of central planning differed—generated similar effects. Both regained independence in 1991. Today, their economies—notwithstanding their differences—rank among the fastest-growing among post-socialist nations.

The relationship of per capita gross domestic product (GDP) in Estonia to per capita GDP in Slovenia, after holding stable for a fairly long time, tumbled in the years 1990–94. This was followed by a steady upward trend in 1995–2004, interrupted by only a small dip in 1999. In 1990–94 both countries experienced a decline in per capita GDP that affected Estonia to a much greater degree. This period of economic contraction was followed by a rapid recovery—especially in Estonia, where growth gathered momentum in 2000 (figure 5.1 and table 5.1).

Had the 1990–94 collapse in Estonia been as deep as in Slovenia, the average annual per capita GDP growth in this country would have been somewhere around 2.1 percentage points (according to Penn World Table, PWT, 6.2 data) or 2.8 percentage points (according to Economic Research Service, ERS, data) higher than actually observed (table 5.2). The 1998 Russian crisis[2] took a further 0.2 percentage points (according to the PWT 6.2 data) or 0.4 percentage points (according to the ERS data) off that growth.

The Russian crisis had more severe consequences for Estonia than for Slovenia, primarily due to Estonia's closer trade relations with the Russian Federation (but also due to its greater reliance on international trade). Despite the consistent redirection of trade transactions toward the European Union (EU) after 1991,

Figure 5.1 Estimated GDP Per Capita in Slovenia and Estonia, 1971–2007

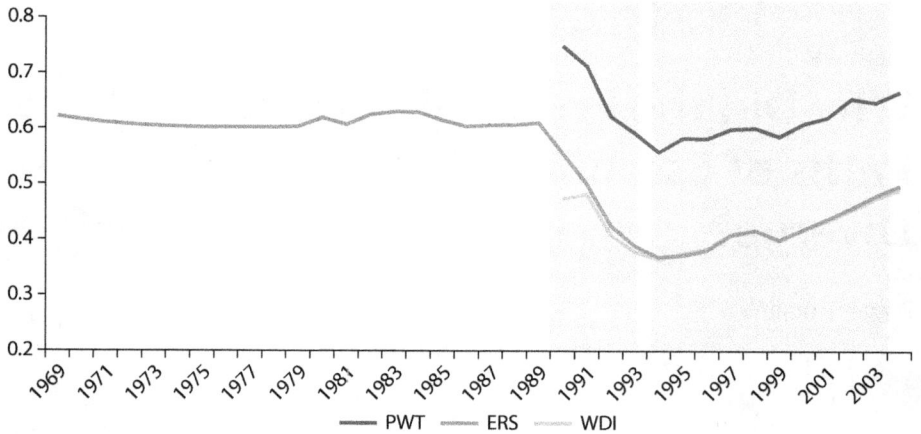

Sources: Based on data from the World Development Indicators (WDI) 2006 and Penn World Table (PWT) 6.2 databases, as well as data compiled by the Economic Research Service (ERS, United States Department of Agriculture).
Note: Periods of significant divergence are shaded.

Table 5.1 Per Capita GDP Growth in Slovenia and Estonia, 1990–2004
Percent

	1990–2004	1990–94	1995–2004
World Development Indicators 2006			
Estonia	**2.30**	−6.33	6.25
Slovenia	**2.06**	−1.29	3.41
Penn World Tables 6.2			
Estonia	**1.28**	−6.94	4.72
Slovenia	**2.07**	−1.28	3.31
Economic Research Service			
Estonia	**1.96**	−6.98	6.20
Slovenia	**2.85**	0.99	3.36

Sources: Based on data from the World Development Indicators 2006 and Penn World Table 6.2 databases, as well as data compiled by the Economic Research Service.
Note: Because of the large contribution of foreign enterprises to GDP growth in Estonia, gross national product (GNP) growth in that country was on average 0.47 percentage points lower than GDP growth. In the case of Estonia, the difference between GNP and GDP growth was marginal. Figures for the total per capita GDP growth in the entire analyzed period are bolded.

Russia's share of Estonia's total exports amounted to nearly 19 percent in 1997 (that is, the year preceding the crisis). The corresponding figure for imports exceeded 14 percent. In Slovenia those figures were much lower—at 4 percent and 3 percent, respectively (table 5.3).

Table 5.4 indicates that the primary driver of per capita GDP growth in Estonia in 1995–2004[3] (accounting for the 95.1 percent increase during this period) was rising total factor productivity (TFP). Higher capital outlays made a considerably smaller contribution to growth (5.7 percent), while the impact of change in

Table 5.2 Average Annual Per Capita GDP Growth in Slovenia and Estonia, 1990–2004

Country	Average annual growth in per capita GDP (%)		
	WDI	PWT	ERS
Slovenia	2.3019	2.0659	2.8460
Estonia	2.0557	1.2831	1.9631
Estonia[a]	4.1954	3.3839	4.8489
Estonia[b]	4.4921	3.4714	5.2149

Sources: Based on data from the World Development Indicators 2006 and Penn World Table 6.2 databases, as well as data compiled by the Economic Research Bureau of the U.S. Department of Agriculture.
a. Average annual per capita GDP growth in 1990–94 was substituted with average annual GDP per capita growth of Slovenia in this period.
b. Average annual 1990–94 GDP per capita growth was substituted with the corresponding figure recorded in Slovenia in this period, whereas average annual GDP per capita growth in 1999 was replaced with the corresponding figure for 1998.

Table 5.3 Russia's Share of Total Exports and Imports: Slovenia and Estonia, 1994–98

Percent

Country	1994	1995	1996	1997	1998
Exports					
Slovenia	3.9	3.7	3.6	3.9	2.6
Estonia	23.1	17.7	16.5	18.8	13.4
Imports					
Slovenia	2.0	2.5	2.2	2.7	1.8
Estonia	16.8	16.1	13.6	14.4	11.1

Sources: Statistical Yearbook of Slovenia 1997, Statistical Yearbook of Slovenia 1999, and Statistical Office of Estonia.

Table 5.4 Contributions to GDP Growth in Slovenia and Estonia, 1995–2004[3]

		Average growth rate (%)	Contributions to growth	
			Percentage points	%
Estonia	Per capita GDP	4.73	4.73	
	Total factor productivity	4.50	4.50	95.11
	Capital outlays per capita	0.98	0.27	5.65
	n	−0.05	−0.04	−0.76
Slovenia	Per capita GDP	3.31	3.31	
	Total factor productivity	1.67	1.67	50.47
	Capital outlays per capita	4.15	1.24	37.57
	n	0.57	0.04	11.96

Sources: Based on the Penn World Table 6.2, Statistical Yearbook of Slovenia 1997, Statistical Office of Estonia, and the International Labour Organization (ILO) database.
Note: n = number of persons working in relation to population.

labor input was marginal (−0.8 percent). Slovenia's economic expansion was also chiefly driven by rising TFP, yet its contribution to GDP growth in the analyzed period was much smaller than in Estonia (at 50.5 percent). At the same time, growth in capital outlays in Slovenia was of substantially greater significance to growth than in Estonia (37.6 percent).[4]

The key source of Estonia's productivity boost was the more efficient use of production factors, which suggests, on the one hand, considerable waste in the preceding period and its swift elimination on the other. In contrast, changes in Slovenia's productivity were supported, above all, by technological modernization (Badunenko, Henderson, and Zelenyuk 2005).

The faster TFP growth in Estonia than in Slovenia was not driven by research and development (R&D) activity in that country—R&D expenditure per inhabitant in Estonia was, on average, half the amount recorded in Slovenia, and the number of patents several times lower.[5] Much more considerable contribution to growth was made by technology transfers (as is the case in any small open economy, especially one that is both small and rather isolated from the cutting edge of technology). Knowledge of how to use such transfers effectively occurs, among others, through the inflow of foreign direct investment (FDI) and international trade (mainly imports) (Vahter 2004). In Estonia both FDI and external trade played a greater role than in Slovenia.

In 1991 FDI was of marginal importance in both analyzed countries, yet the FDI to GDP ratio was higher in Slovenia and amounted to approximately 5 percent. But as early as 1992, this ratio grew more in Estonia than in Slovenia and, after staying 20 percent in 1994–96 embarked on a steady upward trend, to reach 85.1 percent in 2004.[6] In the corresponding period, this ratio ranged between 6.7 percent and 18.7 percent in the Slovenian economy, reaching 15.1 percent in 2004 (figure 5.2).

Figure 5.2 Aggregate FDI-to-GDP Ratio, Estonia and Slovenia, 1990–2004

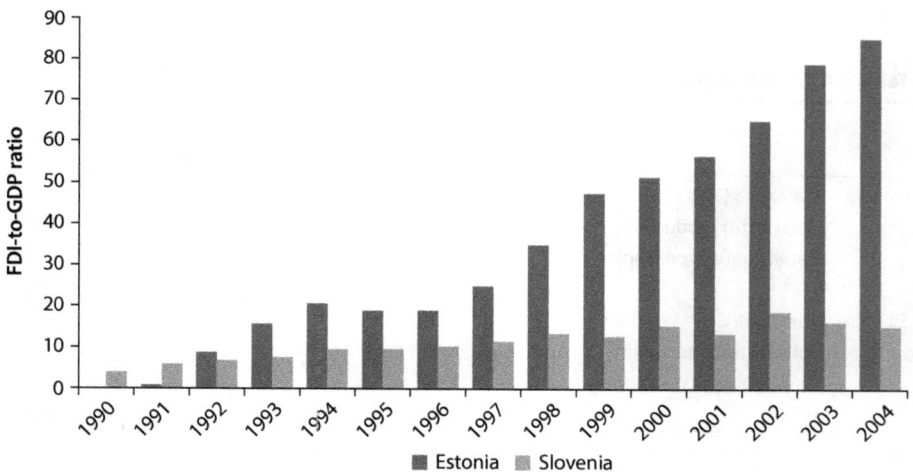

Sources: Based on the United Nations Conference on Trade and Development (UNCTAD) statistics.
Note: FDI = foreign direct investment.

Figure 5.3 Imports-to-GDP Ratio, Estonia and Slovenia, 1992–2004

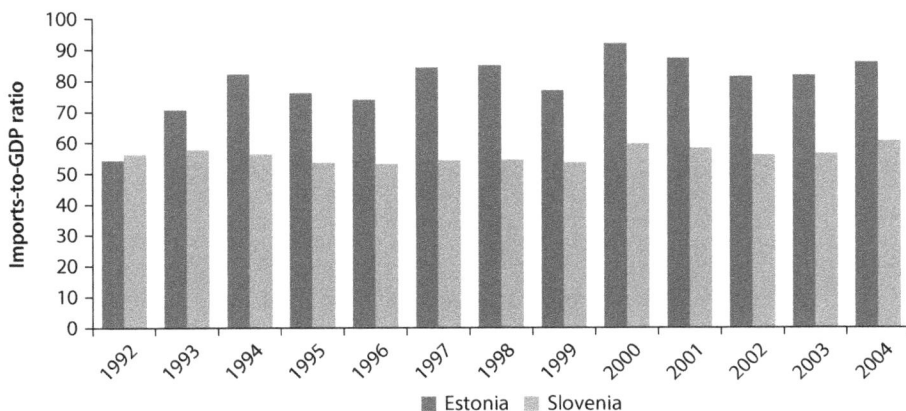

Source: Based on World Development Indicators 2006.

In Slovenia, the ratio of imports and exports to GDP was higher than in Estonia only until 1992. In subsequent years, it fluctuated within the range of 50–60 percent of GDP. In Estonia, a rising trend in this ratio did not level off until 2000. In subsequent years, it ranged between 80 percent and 90 percent of GDP (figure 5.3).

Differences in Economic Performance: Factors and Causes

The Years 1990–94

Differences in Estonia's and Slovenia's growth rates between 1990 and 1994 can be explained by the countries' different conditions at the outset, in particular:

- Estonia's greater reliance—as compared with Slovenia—on shrinking external markets
- The more distorted structure of the Estonian economy (which became evident upon the release of prices)

In the 1980s, only 2–3 percent of Estonia's exports were sold outside the USSR. By comparison, 75 percent of Slovenian exports had destinations beyond the remaining republics of the former Yugoslavia (Buchen 2005). Also, Estonia's economy was far more reliant on imports from the former Soviet republics—in 1989 approximately 82 percent of its imports originated there. The ratio of Estonia's exports to other post-Soviet republics to Estonia's GDP was 51 percent, and that of imports, 62 percent.[7]

Estonia's greater dependence on markets that more or less simultaneously started to suffer from the inefficiencies of centrally planned economies—and whose subsequent economic collapse hampered both exports and imports—made its slump far worse than that of Slovenia (figure 5.4).

Figure 5.4 Index of the Value Added by Industry: Slovenia and Estonia, 1990–2004

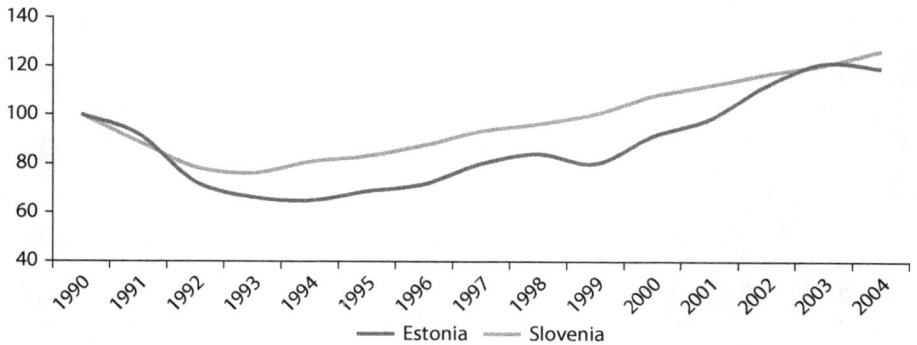

Source: Based on the United Nations Children's Fund (UNICEF) database statistics.
Note: In 1990, index = 100.

Figure 5.5 Index of the Value Added by Agriculture: Four Once-Socialist Republics in Transition, 1990–2004

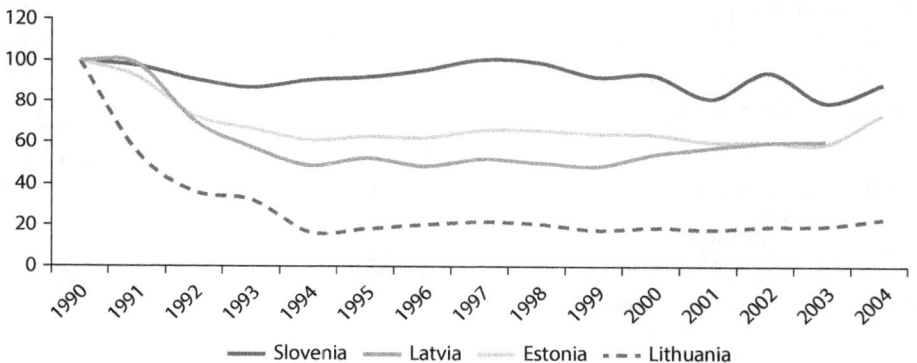

Source: Based on the UNICEF database statistics.
Note: In 1990, index = 100.

The collapse observed in Estonia affected not only industry but also agriculture. Until the transition, agriculture had been an important sector of the country's economy. As part of the USSR, Estonia had been a net exporter of dairy and meat products to other republics. Yet at the end of the 1980s, when the supply of cereals from Russia had been substantially reduced, Estonia had not yet established itself as a credible partner to the non-Soviet countries. Meanwhile, it was impossible to import cereal from other former Soviet republics; these, too, were experiencing a precipitous decline in agricultural output (figure 5.5).

Meanwhile, Estonia's specialization in food production was not underpinned by any competitive advantage in this area, but was only due to the role assigned under the centrally planned Soviet system. After Estonia regained independence, it turned out that the production structure of its economy was out of line with free market requirements; Estonian products were not competitive in foreign markets because of their poor quality and high production costs (Kaufman and Hardt 1993; Norgaard and others 1999).

That the distortion of the Slovenian and Estonian economies differed in its degree was because of systemic differences observed in those countries in the years preceding their transition. Economic activity in Slovenia had not been suppressed as strongly as in other socialist countries: 83 percent of arable land was owned by private farms, while the corresponding figure in Estonia was only 4 percent (Macours and Swinnen 2002).[8] In 1991 over 6,000 small, privately owned businesses operated in Slovenia, employing approximately 3.8 percent of the total workforce. Over 33,000 craft work-shops had a staff accounting for approximately 14 percent of the total work-force.[9] The prevailing type of enterprise was, as in other parts of Yugoslavia, technically owned by the local government (Balcerowicz 1997). Although privately owned enterprises were closely controlled by the party apparatus, they enjoyed far more freedom of operation than state-owned enterprises in the Soviet Bloc. In Slovenia there was limited competition and no capital market. Meanwhile, the restrictive entrepreneurial regime in Estonia, while it was part of the USSR, prevented the establishment of even quasi-private enterprises. Slovenia's GDP structure in 1990 was close to that of Western European countries. Approximately 51 percent of its GDP was generated in the services sector, with agriculture accounting for a mere 5 percent. In Estonia, on the other hand, industry accounted for the highest share of GDP (44 percent) in 1989, while the services sector accounted for 36 percent and agriculture for 20 percent.

The release of prices exposed the extent of inefficiency in both economies—it turned out that in a market economy, many enterprises generated large losses. But since the price structure in Estonia was far more distorted, both the scale of the shock and the ensuing adjustments in the economy were much more severe here than in Slovenia. Moreover, price liberalization progressed much faster in Estonia. It started as early as late 1989, when businesses were allowed to freely set the prices of furniture, vegetables, and stationery products. Price liberaliza-tion gathered speed in 1991—at the end of that year, the state was in control of 10 percent of consumer good prices, and could further affect 30 percent of prices through administrative decisions (Bauc 1995). The process was finalized in 1992. At that point, only rents and energy prices were still controlled by the state. In Slovenia, as late as 2004, the scope of price control was wider than in developed countries.

In both countries, relation of prices of agricultural products to the prices of goods used in agriculture notably decreased (i.e., terms of trade for agricultural producers deteriorated); yet, in Estonia the decline was much deeper—mainly due to the previous and severe underpricing of fuel.[10] Falling margins on agricul-tural produce had an adverse effect on output volume (with agriculture contrib-uting to GDP four times more than in Slovenia).

In the short term, agricultural output was also adversely affected by privatization. Given the greater state involvement in agricultural production in

Estonia, the process was far more intensive here than in Slovenia. Privatization boosted incentives for more effective allocation of production factors, yet this effect was cancelled by cuts in subsidies to self-financing private farms. The initial productivity drop was also precipitated by the fact that assets and technology, previously held by collective farms, were dispersed (Macours and Swinnen 2002). Yet, as late as in 1992 the efficiency of Estonian agriculture started improving.

When prices of commodities and semiprocessed products were released in Estonia, making them more realistic, it had an equally dire effect on added value in industry as in agriculture. Output decline, especially in the food industry, was aggravated by the economy's opening to external trade. Estonian enterprises fell short of the challenge posed by foreign competition. Their already difficult position deteriorated further during a 1992–94 slump in domestic demand. The problems Slovenian enterprises faced were much less serious. On the one hand, since the country's price structure was less distorted, so was the production structure (and hence, less realignment was required after prices had been released). Moreover, enterprises were already experienced in competing in the Western European markets.

The differences in starting conditions, which explain the different degrees of the initial GDP drop as both countries embarked on their transition, also affected the direction and pace of their systemic transformation. In Estonia officials in charge of economic policy had far stronger incentives to launch reforms than in Slovenia (Gelb and others 1997). Since the starting conditions impacted decisions about the extent of systemic changes, they also affected performance levels at a later stage; yet the influence worked in the opposite direction to that observed at the beginning of the transition period (i.e., worse conditions at the outset leading to radical restructuring of the economic system laid a solid foundation for a comparatively higher pace of economic growth in the years following a deeper slump).

The Years 1995–2004

Estonia extended the scope of economic freedom much faster and more radically than Slovenia.[11] This concerned, in particular, the degree of freedom in external trade and in capital flows:

- By 1992, Estonia had abolished most tariffs, subsidies, and other barriers to free trade in both industrial and agricultural goods (Ratso 2005). Only tariffs on tobacco products (40–60 percent), spirit (50–300 percent), other alcohol (20–100 percent),[12] fur coats (16 percent), and motor vehicles (10 percent) were maintained. In 1993 the tariffs were replaced with an excise tax that was also imposed on fuel (Laar 2006; Taaler 1994). The undervalued currency acted as an instrument of (limited) protection against foreign competition (which generated a side effect in the form of protracted disinflation; in spite of the kron being pegged to the German mark in mid-1992, inflation did not sink to single-digit figures until 1998).[13] Duty protection was given up with a view to making the public sector less reliant on customs revenues, which would result in growing resistance to customs abolishment. Besides, the reduction of tariffs and other trade barriers was believed to fuel the development of subcontracting, which was, in turn, was supposed to help enterprises restructure (Laar 2006). These expectations were fulfilled when Estonia's economy was observed to have a high reexport level (Sobańska 2006). Such extensive trade liberalization meant that when Estonia sought to enter the EU it had to, paradoxically, raise its trade barriers. In 2000 tariffs were imposed on certain agricultural products imported from countries with which Estonia had not concluded any free trade agreements—countries that notably included the United States, Canada, and Russia. The main objective of this move was to demonstrate the country's administrative capacity to introduce a common customs tariff after EU accession. Other tariffs were imposed upon the country's entry to the EU, and bilateral free trade agreements with non-EU countries were terminated.[14] Slovenia was much slower (as well as less consistent) in eliminating protectionism. The average tariff rate was running at over 10 percent just before the country joined EU; that is, it was three times higher than the common tariff introduced upon accession.[15]

- To attract foreign investment, firms with foreign capital in Estonia were wholly or half exempted from corporate tax for a period of two to three years (depending on the share of foreign capital). Almost from the beginning of the transition period,[16] foreign businesses were granted the same rights as those enjoyed by domestic entrepreneurs. There were exceptions to this general rule with regard to, mainly, the purchase and use of land as well as the excavation of raw materials (as of 1993, foreign citizens were allowed to purchase land with permission of province governors; see, for example, OECD 2000). Additional restrictions were imposed in 1993. According to an Estonian government decree of April 6, 1992 (that specified a list of sectors in which foreign capital entities required a license), foreign investors were obliged to obtain special licenses when planning to operate in sectors such as telecommunications, ports, railways, power industry, and mining. These were specific foreign investment licenses required for the establishment of a foreign capital company.[17] The stability of legal acts relating to investors was safeguarded by bilateral agreements on promotion and investment protection, bilateral taxation, and relevant references to international conventions. Moreover, duty-free zones were created.[18]

Second, the pace and extent of privatization processes was different in both countries:

- In Estonia, domestic investors enjoyed privileges only during the first stage of privatization (a so-called small-scale privatization in which foreign investors were not allowed to participate at all). In the next privatization stage, all investors were treated alike. The only privilege retained by domestic investors was the ability to spread payment for a purchased enterprise over a 10-year period. The government organized three large international tenders: in 1992 for 38 enterprises, in May 1993 for 52 enterprises, and in the autumn of 1993, for 40 enterprises (IMF 1999). By mid-1996, approximately 430 out of the 450 large, state-owned enterprises had been privatized. Altogether, foreign investors had purchased 25 percent of all assets intended for privatization. Foreign capital companies had—among other things—much higher labor productivity, as well as better capacity to compete in the international markets than other enterprises (see, for example, Mygind 2000). The state preserved control of the ports, railways, telecommunications, and power industry. These monopolies were privatized, except for the energy sector, in 1999–2001. The first stage of privatization involved small, state-owned companies, which were, in many cases, taken over by their employees. In the second stage, privatization was supposed to ensure concentration of ownership of privatized companies. On average, the largest shareholders held stakes of approximately 56.2 percent of total shares, with the second-largest shareholdings holding 9 percent and third-largest ones holding 4 percent. Ownership concentration combined with the fast pace of privatization helped to achieve a swift and full economic reversal. This process was also supported by a rigorously enforced bankruptcy law—modeled after the German solutions[19]—as well as radical cuts in subsidies to state-owned enterprises at the initial stage of transition. The substantial reduction in subsidies to state-owned enterprises in Estonia was reflected in the changed structure of public expenditure. While in the mid-1980s total subsidies accounted for roughly 60–65 percent of the republic's budget expenditure, the figure was down to approximately 25 percent in 1991 (Kaufman and Hardt 1993).

- In Slovenia, a mass privatization scheme was launched (Mygind 2000). Under the scheme, privatization was conducted through the issue of so-called ownership vouchers. Forty percent of the equity in each privatized enterprise was transferred to three state-controlled funds and 20 percent to its employees; the remaining 40 percent was sold either to the employees or publicly traded. In most cases, the sale of 40 percent of vouchers to employees was standard.[20] To maintain control of voucher transactions, privatization investment funds were established. Foreign entities were allowed to participate in privatization based only on sale of the so-called ownership certificates. When privatization was completed, Slovenia's ownership structure was much more dispersed than Estonia's. Therefore, state-controlled bodies continued to play an important role in enterprises. In some of them, instead of privatization, a restructuring program was launched, supervised by the government, but its effectiveness was rather low. The improvement in factor productivity in these enterprises was substantially smaller than in companies covered by the mass privatization program (Simoneti and others 2002). In 2004 state ownership continued to prevail, among others, in the power, steel, rail, transport, and insurance sectors. The state also owned two of the largest Slovenian banks (OECD 2002).

The pace and extent of privatization was constrained by the slow implementation of bankruptcy proceedings against unprofitable enterprises.

- A mass privatization program was also implemented in Estonia. Equity vouchers were distributed among citizens proportionate to their years of service or as compensation for requisitioned property if restitution in kind was impossible. Yet, such vouchers were mostly used to purchase buyer-occupied homes. Their significance for the privatization of enterprises was initially curtailed by a ban on their sale and purchase and, subsequently, by the bankruptcy (in 1995) of the largest investment fund in charge of their purchase. After privatization was virtually completed in 1995, the only use they could be put to was purchase of real property.

The differences in the characteristics of the privatization processes translated into a different significance of the private sector in the economies (tables 5.5 and 5.6).

Third, both countries were substantially different in terms of labor market rigidity. Estonia's greater flexibility in this area was reflected in a much higher labor turnover than in Slovenia (figure 5.6).

The difference in labor market rigidity between the two countries resulted mainly from the method of mitigating social tensions arising during economic restructuring, as adopted in Slovenia. Such tensions were reduced by impeding lay-offs, maintaining a high minimum wage, and granting generous benefits to the unemployed and high pensions to labor market leavers.[21]

- In Estonia, employee dismissal required a minimum of two months' notice and a severance pay equivalent to two to four months' salary.[22] In Slovenia redundancies involved much higher employer costs. As well as paying six months'

Table 5.5 Contribution of the Private Sector to GDP: Estonia and Slovenia, 1995–2004
Percent

Country	1995	1996	1997	1998	1999	2000	2001	2002	2003	2004
Estonia	65.0	70.0	70.0	70.0	75.0	75.0	75.0	80.0	80.0	80.0
Slovenia	50.0	55.0	60.0	60.0	60.0	65.0	65.0	65.0	65.0	65.0

Source: European Bank for Reconstruction and Development (EBRD) data contained in the Transition Report 2008.

Table 5.6 Private Sector Employment Related to Total Employment, 1995–2004
Percent

Country	1995	1996	1997	1998	1999	2000	2001	2002	2003	2004
Estonia	60.5	62.6	67.5	68.6	68.4	70.7	70.8	73.3	73.7	74.5
Slovenia	48.0	—	—	—	65.0	70.0	70.0	70.0	69.0	69.0

Source: EBRD data contained in the Transition Report 2008.
Note: — = not available.

Figure 5.6 Basic Indicators of Labor Market Flows in Selected Countries

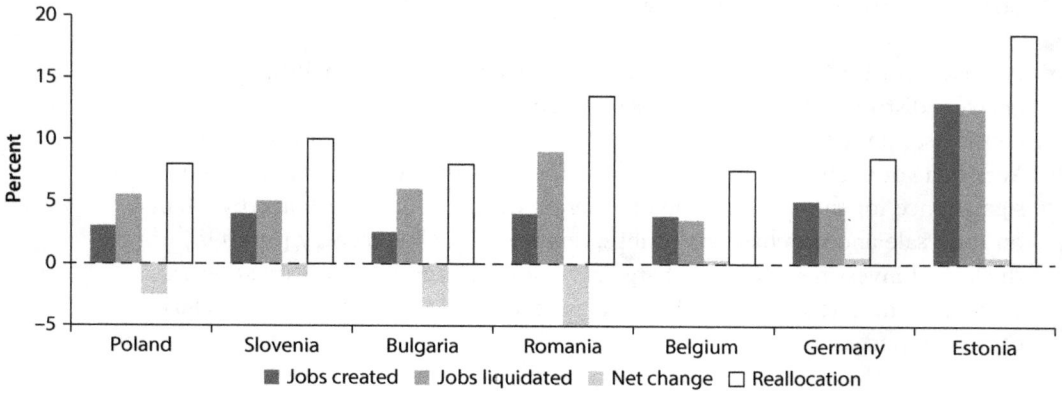

Source: Based on Masso, Eamets, and Philips 2004.
Note: The values of the indices for Slovenia, Poland, and Bulgaria refer to the period 1994–97; for Belgium, 1989–95; for Germany, 1988–95; and for Estonia, 1995–2001.

Figure 5.7 The Share of Fixed-Time Contracts in Total Employment Contracts: Slovenia and Estonia, 1989–98

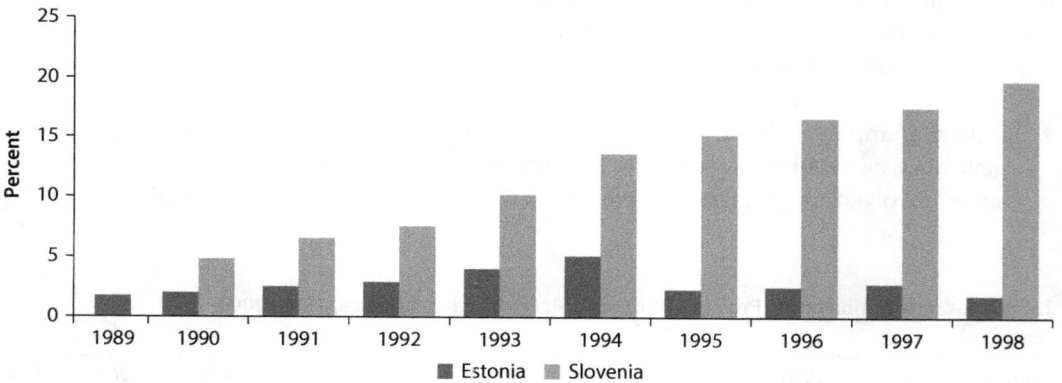

Source: NBP calculations based on Vodopivec.

salary, companies were obliged to provide appropriate training to the employees being made redundant. If they were not capable of meeting these requirements, the employees were entitled to a money benefit equivalent to one month's salary for each year they had served at the company.[23] Such punitive redundancy costs hampered company restructuring. Newly established companies tried to circumvent the restrictions by employing their staff on fixed-time contracts (figure 5.7).

- In Estonia, the minimum-to-average wage ratio remained below 35 percent and ranked among the lowest in Europe.[24] In Slovenia it fluctuated around 45 percent and was among the highest on the continent, making it difficult for people with the lowest qualifications to find employment.

- From 1994, unemployment benefits were phased down in Estonia—from 60 percent of the minimum wage in 1994 to 29 percent in 2000 (Kluve, Leetmaa, and Schmidt 2002, 31). The benefit eligibility period did not exceed six months, during which the unemployed were obliged to meet certain requirements (among other things, they had to report at the employment office every 15 days and participate in public works for at least 10 days during the year). After six months, the jobless were offered an opportunity to participate, free of charge, in retraining courses. In Slovenia, unemployment benefits amounted to up to 70 percent of the previous remuneration and could be drawn for up to 24 months. Thus, the system provided no incentive for the unemployed person to seek a job (Vodopivec 2002).

- In Slovenia, pensions were indexed in fact with average wage increases in the economy. At the same time, over the period under review the average pension amounted to 75 percent of the average wage. Thus, the system involved incentives for employees on lower incomes to take early retirement.[25]

The different level of labor market rigidities involved different labor costs in the two countries; as a result, the two attracted investment to a different degree. A pool of cheap and well-qualified labor is a key factor determining the location of FDI (Bevan and Estrin 2000). Among the countries joining the EU in 2004, Estonia posted among the lowest labor costs. The average hourly employee rate in this country was half the amount paid in Slovenia (amid a much smaller difference in average labor productivity).

Fourth, both countries opted for a different tax structure. Owing to much lower social expenditure, the tax burden in Estonia was much smaller than in Slovenia, and continued to fall, while in Slovenia it remained unchanged (table 5.7).

Estonia's tax burden was reduced thanks to falling public expenditure in relation to GDP. In Slovenia this ratio followed an upward trend in the period analyzed (table 5.8).

Table 5.7 Public Sector Revenue (Including Social Security Contributions) in Slovenia and Estonia, 1995–2004

% GDP

Country	1995	1996	1997	1998	1999	2000	2001	2002	2003	2004
Estonia	37.9	35.6	35.9	34.9	34.6	31.3	30.2	31.1	31.5	31.4
Slovenia	40.2	39.1	38.0	38.8	39.2	38.6	38.9	39.3	39.5	39.6

Source: European Commission 2009.

Table 5.8 Public Expenditure in Slovenia and Estonia, 1995–2004
% GDP

	1995	1996	1997	1998	1999	2000	2001	2002	2003	2004
Estonia	39.4	40.2	37.8	38.2	40.6	36.2	34.9	35.5	35.0	37.1
Slovenia	39.8	39.1	39.9	40.7	41.2	41.4	42.3	41.8	42.2	42.7

Source: IMF 1999.

In Estonia, taxes were not only lower than in Slovenia, but also had a smaller distortionary impact on incentives to work, increase qualifications, invest, and innovate.

- Estonia inherited a specific structure of company taxes from the previous economic system. The following taxes were in place at that time:
  - Turnover tax at different rates for different product groups, which made it possible to control the structure of output and, consequently, consumption.
  - Corporate profit tax (at a rate approximating 100 percent).
  - Income tax (at 6 percent).

  After Estonia's independence was restored in 1991, a tax system was formed that was a conglomerate of solutions operating under the previous system and of concepts applied in Western Europe. Before the fundamental tax reform was launched with the introduction of a uniform corporate income tax (CIT) rate in 1992, corporate income was taxed at three different rates:
  - Fifteen percent on taxable income of up to 500 thousand rubles.
  - Twenty-three percent on taxable income of over 500 thousand rubles.
  - Thirty percent on taxable income of over 1 million rubles (Laar 2006; Stepanyan 2003).

- In 1991 value added tax (VAT) was introduced; from 1992 it was raised to 18 percent.[26] Initially, health, education, financial, and postal services as well as medicine and certain kinds of energy were VAT exempt, yet the list of exemptions was gradually reduced and a reduced VAT rate was imposed on some of the goods previously enjoying exemption. This was applicable to a limited number of items—books, medicine, and certain kinds of energy— which also limited the scale of distortion in the consumption structure (and, in effect, production) caused by inconsistent taxation. From the beginning, VAT was the largest contributor to public sector revenues. Along with excise tax, it accounted, on average, for almost 39 percent of government revenues in the period under analysis. At the end of 1993 the Income Tax Act was adopted, providing for the replacement of a progressive personal income tax (PIT) with three rates—16 percent, 24 percent, and 33 percent with a flat tax of 26 percent (in 2004 this was reduced by 2 percentage points)[27]— and the abolishment of most tax breaks previously in place. Additionally, the tax-exempt amount was raised, giving the PIT a progressive character without complicating its structure. In 1992 a single tax rate was introduced for company tax (which initially amounted to 33 percent and was reduced to 26 percent at the end of 1993) and capital gains tax. At the same time, a 40 percent depreciation rate for machinery was set, as well as an 8 percent rate for buildings. Reinvested profits were exempted from tax (after this solution was implemented, these profits started to account for a large proportion of investment). In 2000 companies were exempted from tax on retained profit (regardless of whether it was reinvested) and capital gains tax.[28] Before that—in February 1999—a parliamentary act was passed, pursuant to which any fixed asset purchases made by enterprises operating out of Tallin between January 1, 1998, and December 31, 2007, could be in their entirety deducted as expenses within a year (any loss could be spread over seven years). Throughout the analyzed period, the effective tax on company profits in Estonia was the lowest in the EU.[29]

- In Slovenia, similar to Estonia, most public sector revenue was derived from indirect taxes, which had a smaller distortionary impact on economic agents' decisions than most other taxes. In the discussed period, they accounted for 42 percent of public revenue. The basic VAT rate was set at 20 percent, while the reduced rate—a single one as in Estonia—was set at 8.5 percent. Company profits were moderately taxed, as in Estonia. In 1996 the CIT rate was raised from 25 percent to 30 percent, but was later brought back to its previous level (after 2006 another round of cuts was launched, bringing it down to the target level of 20 percent in 2010). Companies operating in special economic zones paid a much lower tax (10 percent in 2010). A progressive PIT, combined with very high social security contributions,[30] resulted in a labor taxation level among the highest in Europe. The tax wedge on gross earnings of an average employee in production amounted to 48.2 percent in 2002 as against the EU-15 average of 40.5 percent.[31]

Fifth, the two countries differed in terms of their administrative efficiency and the number of bureaucratic burdens imposed upon entrepreneurs (table 5.9 and figure 5.8):

- In Estonia, the efficiency of the administration and bureaucratic procedures did not discourage agents, including foreign investors, from launching and developing business activity. A prospective investor in the Estonian market needed relatively few permits and little time to launch business operations (Masso, Eamets, and Philips 2004).

- Slovenia was different:[32] despite the many reforms introduced in the analyzed period—affecting the tax structure, customs, company registration procedures, and reporting requirements relating to transactions involving foreign capital to facilitate business activity—administrative procedures continued to constrain the growth of entrepreneurship (OECD 2002).

Table 5.9 The Impact of Administration on New Enterprise Establishment: A Comparison

	Entry into the local market[a]		Administrative procedures for enterprise establishment[b]		Permission to establish an enterprise		Number of days necessary to launch business operations	
	Value	Ranking[c]	Value	Ranking[c]	Value	Ranking[c]	Value	Ranking[c]
Slovenia					5	35	60	54
Estonia	5.6	12	5.8	5	3	5	30	34
EU average	5.5	23.6	4.8	27.3	4.8	26.8	41.4	38.2
OECD average	5.4	27.5	4.8	28.8	4.8	27.2	38.3	36.8

Sources: Based on the *Global Competitiveness Report 2001–02* and *World Competitiveness Yearbook 2001.*
Note: EU = European Union; OECD = Organisation for Economic Co-operation and Development.
a. How often new competitors appear on the local market (1–7 scale).
b. Scale: 1 (it is not difficult to set up a new enterprise) to 7 (it is complicated to set up a new enterprise).
c. A ranking of 75 countries.

Figure 5.8 The Value of the Respective Dimensions of the Fraser Index: Slovenia and Estonia in 1995, 2000, and 2004

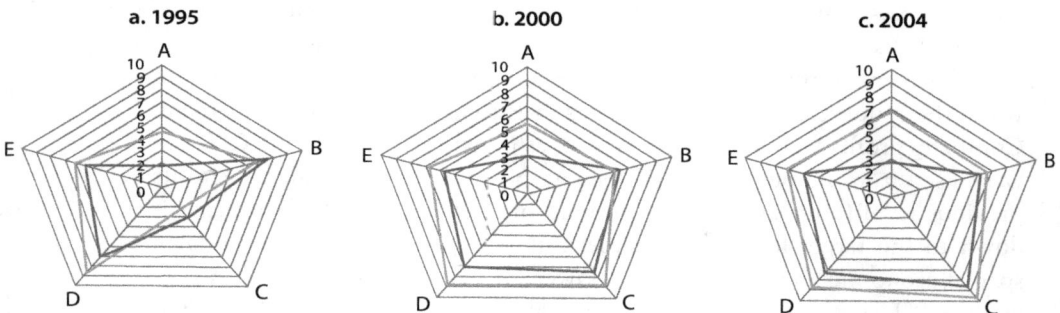

Source: Based on Fraser Institute data.
Note: A = size of government; B = legal system and property rights; C = sound money; D = freedom to trade internationally; and E = regulation. Blue line, Slovenia; orange line, Estonia.

The better efficiency of the Estonian administration stemmed from its deeper restructuring at the start of its transition. Also, it is sometimes attributed to the generational shift among those in power. In line with the election slogan of the party to win the first free elections in this country—"to clean house," which epitomized the task of clearing Estonian politics and the economy of Soviet influences—Estonia's central government offices, political institutions, and economic principles were fundamentally restructured. In particular administrative staff were replaced and the structures of ministries and local administrations simplified. The government employed mostly young people, who were less influenced by the past (Laar 2006; Norgaard and others 1999).

The differences in the pace and extent of structural reforms were reflected in the position of the two countries in indexes of economic freedom. For example, according to the Fraser Institute's economic freedom index,[33] in 1995 Estonia ranked 75th among countries arranged from the highest to lowest degree of economic freedom, in 2000 the 32nd, and in 2004 the 12th.[34] In the same years,

Slovenia occupied the 93th, 80th, and 74th position. Its inferior position resulted from a lower assessment of the quality of institutions determining the freedom of international trade and capital flows and more state involvement in the economy.

Summary and Conclusions

In 1990–94, both Estonia and Slovenia saw a drop in per capita GDP, yet this drop was much deeper in Estonia. Thereafter, in 1995–2004, both countries' per capita GDP rose, and at a much faster pace in Estonia.

Estonia's steeper drop in per capita GDP in the initial period was due its much less favorable starting conditions, including far greater dependence on its main market (the former USSR) and a more pronounced distortion of its economic structure; price liberalization exposed the unprofitability of many enterprises and farms.

The source of faster economic growth in Estonia versus Slovenia in the second period was higher TFP growth. This resulted primarily from improved efficiency in production factor utilization. This improvement reflected the massive scale of wastefulness before the transition. Meanwhile, Estonia's faster productivity growth was also driven by a wider and more intensive transfer of technology— along with knowledge of how to use it. The basic source of this transfer was (a) a much larger inflow of FDI to Estonia and (b) that nation's much wider opening to international trade, including a markedly higher share of imports in its GDP.

The difference in the pace and extent of restructuring between the two countries, the magnitude of FDI inflows, and the size of international trade was not influenced, in the period under review, by differences in their stabilizing institutions; a greater role was played by differences in propelling institutions. Estonia differed from Slovenia in the following respects:

- A complete lack of duty protection in the domestic market and, in effect, more intensive competition.
- The uniform treatment of domestic and foreign investors by the state; the privatization process resulted in a material participation of foreign investors and a concentration of ownership that was conducive to the fast and radical turnaround of productivity.
- A substantially smaller number of labor market rigidities that could hamper the restructuring process and inflate labor costs, thus reducing the profitability of investment in the country.
- A lower and declining tax burden, owing to smaller social expenditure (also supported by the structure of the tax system, which had a less distortionary impact on economic decisions).
- Efficient administration (highly appreciated by foreign investors) and insignificant bureaucratic barriers to entrepreneurship.

After 2004, when domestic demand started burgeoning beyond control, the weaknesses of Estonia's stabilizing institutions were exposed.

Puzzles of Economic Growth • http://dx.doi.org/10.1596/978-1-4648-0325-3

In 1992, the country introduced the currency board system. Initially, this was not perceived as fully credible. Only as late as 2000 did an inflow of foreign capital help bring lending interest rates below 10 percent. In subsequent years, as euro area interest rates declined, it fell further to 5 percent on an annual basis. Private sector credit growth exceeded 50 percent in 2005–06, providing a strong stimulus for domestic demand. In 2004–07 it grew at the rate of 9.6 percent, causing the positive output gap to widen from 1.6 percent to 10.4 percent of potential GDP (European Commission 2009).

Such a big imbalance of demand in the economy and its productive capacity shows that growth would have decelerated sharply even if the global financial crisis had not occurred. The signs of a slowdown appeared in 2007. As companies tried to outbid each other for employees, labor cost growth sped up to 20 percent. A hike in labor costs of this magnitude undermined the competitiveness of Estonian firms in the international markets (exports growth in 2007 fell to nought) and their capacity to invest.

The central bank was not in the position to curb lending growth—in line with the adopted institutional model, its role was limited to the purchase (and sale) of currencies on demand at previously set fixed rates. This growth should have been curbed with fiscal policy measures. In 1997 a Stabilisation Reserve Fund was created, whose objectives included siphoning off liquidity from the banking sector through transfer of public savings abroad, to impede fast credit growth (IMF 1999).[35] Yet, or more broadly the fiscal policy, was never successful in achieving this objective. In spite of the budget surplus reaching 2.9 percent of GDP in 2006, the structural balance deteriorated by 1.7 percent of GDP between 2004 and 2007. Fiscal policy, instead of cooling the economy, stimulated it further. At the same time, banking supervision activities aimed at limiting credit expansion through tighter macroprudential requirements also proved ineffective amid free capital flows.[36]

Estonia's recent problems show how important it is for a country with a fast pace of economic growth, and, consequently, a high natural interest rate, to create an effective mechanism to constrain credit growth after relinquishing an independent monetary policy.

Meanwhile, Slovenia's economic problems, which became apparent amid the collapse of its foreign markets, pay testimony to the deep structural problems of that country's economy. In particular, incomplete transformation of a corporate ownership structure is the reason behind the low elasticity of the production structure and strong pressure from trade unions on further wage growth, even in the face of a mounting recession.

Notes

1. Estonia was a socialist economy for five years longer than Slovenia (Estonia, 51 years; Slovenia, 46 years).
2. The financial crisis in Russia of 1998 was a combined effect of the multiple factors, including: (a) declining productivity, (b) overvalued real exchange rate,

(c) unsustainable fiscal position, (d) lowered demand (and prices) for crude oil and nonferrous metals, and increased uncertainties among investors due to the Asian crisis, (e) economic cost of the first war in Chechnya (Chiodo and Owyang 2002; Feridun 2004; Henry and Nixon 1998). As a result, in 1999, GDP per capita of Russia (at current prices in U.S. dollars) amounted to 35 percent of the level of 1991 and reached its lowest level in the history of modern Russia (own calculations based on UN Data). Russian crisis was transmitted into other economies of the former Soviet Union by different channels with the major role of direct and indirect trade links and reduced external capital flows due to increased uncertainties in the countries of the region (Pastor and Damjanovic 2001). The sharp depreciation of the ruble and an increase in international oil prices helped the Russian economy to recover rather quickly in the next years.

3. In our growth accounting, we disregard the period 1990–94, when the economies of both Slovenia and Estonia experienced a deep slump resulting from the fundamental restructuring of their economic systems. As the countries went into the process of rapid economic transition, the reasons behind differences in the pace of economic growth in that period should be laid in other aspects than the different pace of change in production factor inputs or their productivity. In particular, while attempting to account for the different extent of the collapse, one should look at factors related to shocks.

4. Qualitatively similar factors—albeit ones referring to slightly different periods—can be found in Padilla and Mayer (2003) and Pellenyi (2005).

5. Data from Eurostat.

6. When entering the Estonian market, foreign investors contributed to the newly established or acquired companies by offering know-how related to marketing (74 percent of the surveyed enterprises) and management (77 percent of the surveyed enterprises). There was also a substantial transfer of unpatented technological solutions (68 percent) as well as products and technological processes (62 percent). There was less transfer of patented technological solutions (Varblane 2001).

7. Based on information from Estonian Institute [http://www.einst.ee].

8. In Estonia, individual farms were allowed to operate as late as in 1989 following adoption of the Law on Peasant Farming, which recognized the principle of private farming with very limited rights to the land allotted by the state (Lane and others 2013).

9. *Slovenia: Country Study for GDN Project*, http://www.cerge-ei.cz/.

10. In May 1992 the government stopped subsidizing, on the one hand, purchases of dairy products, and on the other, energy (see, for example, Tang and Nilgo 1994).

11. This point focuses on propelling institutions. In 1995–2004 the differences in stabilizing institutions generated no major differences in the economic performance in the countries under review. They started playing a bigger role after 2004—in particular to the depth of the current recession. That is why stabilizing institutions have not been included in the present section. We focus on them more in the last section—summary and conclusions.

12. According to the Estonian Duty Act "spirit" means a product which is classified as other alcohol obtained by synthesis or by the distillation or rectification of fermented mash; according to the Estonian Alcohol Act—"Spirit" means a liquid which is obtained by the fermentation and subsequent processing of raw materials of agricultural origin with an ethanol content of at least 96 percent by volume.

13. The disinflation process was additionally hampered by the initially low credibility of the currency board system in Estonia. The central bank initially had no foreign exchange reserves sufficient to cover all the cash in circulation. In 1992 the shortage of reserves on its balance sheet was complemented with a forest worth $150 million—the bank could cut down and sell the timber should the reserves run out (Sorg and Kallas 1994).

14. Information posted on the Estonian Ministry of Foreign Affairs Web site: http://www .vm.ee/.

15. The figure was retrieved from the data used to compute the Fraser Index number.

16. Although the decrees adopted in Estonia as early as 1988 and 1989 abolished most of the Soviet government's restrictive decisions relating to foreign investors, it is the Act on Foreign Investment adopted by the Estonian government on September 10, 1991, that is perceived as the turning point in equalizing the rights and obligations of domestic and foreign capital enterprises (Sobańska 2007).

17. The procedure for seeking foreign investor licenses was laid down in the Estonian Republic's Foreign Investment Act, which came into effect on September 27, 1991 (Campbell 2006).

18. Three free zones were created in Estonia: Munga, located close to Tallin; Sillamae in the northwestern part of Estonia; and Valga, close to the Latvian border. The first of them was established on July 1, 1997. Its formation was justified with the need to increase the competitiveness of the Estonian transportation services market, by putting in place more flexible customs procedures for businesses providing transit transport. In particular, goods stored within the bounds of the zone and declared as goods in transit were not subject to duty, excise tax, or value added tax (VAT). They were allowed to remain in the zone for up to three years, unless the period was reasonably extended by the competent authorities (Reuvid and Terterov 2005).

19. The first Estonian Bankruptcy Act was adopted in 1992 and aimed mainly at a protection of the creditors' interests rather than debtors' interests. In 1996, major amendments in the Act were implemented as a result of the conclusion that the protection of the debtor's and creditor's rights should be more balanced (Varul 1999).

20. This mixed privatization method resulted from a conflict in the Slovenian parliament. Left-wing parties demanded that shares in enterprises be sold to their employees with an option to sell in public trading, while right-wing parties opted for a voucher system.

21. Furthermore, unprofitable enterprises were subsidized and bankruptcies were made difficult to keep their number in check (see Vodopivec 2002).

22. The amount of severance pay depended on the employee's length of service (Vodopivec 2002).

23. Prior to 1991, the employer was obliged to observe a notice period as long as 24 months (Vodopivec 2002).

24. But in an agreement concluded with the EU, Estonia undertook to gradually raise the minimum wage to 41 percent of the average wage.

25. See Vodopivec (2002); the trend toward early exits from labor resources observed in Slovenia made—as late as 2004—the effective retirement age in this country one of the lowest among 25 EU countries (see, for example, World Bank 2005).

26. Initially, the basic VAT rate amounted to 10 percent. In 1992 it was raised to 18 percent as part of a stabilization program aimed at, among others, balancing the state budget. Also, the CIT rate was made uniform at that time at the lowest level

(33 percent), while the top rate for PIT was increased from 33 percent to 50 percent (Taaler 1994).

27. It was further reduced in subsequent years, and the tax-exempt amount was raised. In 2009 the tax rate was 21 percent, and the tax exempt amount was EEK 27,000 (€1,726) (Estonian Ministry of Finance).

28. Capital gains are understood here as profit realized on the sale of assets previously purchased at a lower price. The most frequent source of this income is the disposal of shares, bonds, precious metals, and real property. Pursuant to the Income Tax Act of 2000, capital gains were not subject to tax, as long as they were earned by an Estonian enterprise with a legal personality and were not divided. If earned by an individual, a 26 percent tax rate applied—that is, the income was treated in the same manner as regular income.

29. Among those EU countries for which the European Commission publishes relevant estimates.

30. Public sector revenues resulting from social security contributions were among the highest in Europe throughout the period analyzed. In 2004 they were higher in only three EU countries.

31. For the EU-15 the average value of this index amounted to 40.5 percent (Dolenc and Vodopivec 2005).

32. Poor efficiency of the administration and excessive bureaucratic burdens were indicated among the key causes of slower GDP growth in Slovenia than in Estonia by, among others, Slovenia's prime minister, Janez Jansa.

33. This index, similar to its particular subindices, may acquire values from 1 to 10. The higher the index value, the higher the assessment of the extent of economic freedom in the country concerned. The value of the index at the level of 10 denotes full economic freedom, while the lowest value of the index means complete lack of economic freedom.

34. The Fraser Institute index in 1995 and 2000 comprised 123 countries and in 2004, 130 countries.

35. The main objective of the fund was to accumulate budget surpluses and privatization proceeds that could be used to mitigate severe shocks or finance reforms that would provide benefits in the long term (for example, pension reform).

36. Estonia's banking supervision took measures to limit credit expansion by (a) increasing risk weights used for all loans secured with a mortgage on real property with the capital adequacy calculation methodology, (b) increasing of the base for the calculation of the required reserves with 50 percent of the total amount of loans secured with a mortgage on residential property, and (c) introducing other higher requirements with regard to the level of reserved held (Sirtaine and Skamnelosm 2007).

Bibliography

Badunenko, O., D. J. Henderson, and V. Zelenyuk. 2005. "Technological Change and Transition: Relative Contributions to Worldwide Growth During the 1990's." Discussion Paper 0509, Institute of Statistics, University Catholique de Louvain, Belgium.

Balcerowicz, L. 1997. *Socjalizm, kapitalizm, transformacja: szkice z przełomu epok.* Warsaw, Poland: PWN.

Bauc, J. 1995. *Estonian Way to Liberal Economic System*. Warsaw, Poland: CASE.

Bevan, A., and S. Estrin. 2000. "The Determinants of Foreign Direct Investment in Transition Economies." Discussion Paper 2638, Centre for Economic Policy Research, London, December.

Buchen, C. 2005. "East European Antipodes: Varieties of Capitalism in Estonia and Slovenia." Paper presented at the conference on Varieties of Capitalism in Post-Communist Countries, Paysley University, U.K., September 23–24.

Campbell, C. 2006. "Republic of Estonia Foreign Investment Act." In *Legal Aspects of Doing Business in Europe 2006*, vol. 1, 408. Yorkhill Law Publishing. http://www.legaltext.ee/et/andmebaas/tekst.asp?dok=X1036K1&keel=en.

Chiodo, A., and M. T. Owyang. 2002. "A Case Study of a Currency Crisis: The Russian Default of 1998." *Federal Reserve Bank of St. Louis Review* 84 (6): 7–18.

Dolenc, P, and M. Vodopivec. 2005. "The Tax Wedge in Slovenia: International Comparison and Policy Recommendations." *Financial Theory and Practice* 29, Institute of Public Finance, 229–43.

European Commission. 2009. "Economic Forecast Spring 2009." *European Economy* 3/2009. Luxembourg: Office for Official Publications of the European Communities, vi–165.

Feridun, M. 2004. "Russian Financial Crisis of 1998: An Economic Investigation." *International Journal of Applied Econometrics and Quantitative Studies* 1 (4), Euro-American Association of Economic Development, 113–22.

Gelb, A., S. Tenev, M. de Melo, and C. Denizer. 1997. *Circumstance and Choice: The Role of Initial Conditions and Policies in Transition Economies*. Washington, DC: World Bank.

Henry, B., and J. Nixon. 1998. 'The Crisis in Russia: Some Initial Observations." *Economic Outlook* 23: 22–9.

IMF (International Monetary Fund). 1999. *Republic of Estonia: Selected Issues and Statistical Appendix*. IMF Staff Country Report 99/74, International Monetary Fund, Washington, DC.

Kaufman, R. F., and J. P. Hardt. 1993. *The Former Soviet Union in Transition*. Publication for the Joint Economic Committee, Congress of the United States, New York: M. E. Sharpe.

Kluve, J., R. Leetmaa, and C. Schmidt. 2002. "Labour Force Status Dynamics in the Estonian Labour Market." Paper presented at the 2nd WDI-IZA International Conference on "Labor Market Dynamics in Emerging Market Economies" in Costa Rica, April.

Laar, M. 2006. *Estoński cud*. Warsaw, Poland: Wydawnictwo Arwil.

Lane, T., A. Pabriks, A. Purs, and D. J. Smith. 2013. *The Baltic States: Estonia, Latvia and Lithuania*. New York: Routledge.

Macours, K., and J. Swinnen. 2002. "Patterns of Agrarian Transition." In *Economic Development and Cultural Change* 50 (2): 365–394.

Masso, J., R. Eamets, and K. Philips. 2004. "Job Creation and Job Destruction in Estonia: Labor Reallocation and Structural Changes." Working Paper Series 39, Centre for the Study of Economic and Social Change in Europe, School of Slavonic and East European Studies, University College London.

Mygind, N. 2000. *Privatization, Governance and Restructuring of Enterprises in the Baltics.* Working Paper, CCNM/BALT (2000) 6, Organisation for Economic Co-operation and Development, Paris.

Norgaard, O., L. Johannsen, M. Skak, and R. H. Sorensen. 1999. *The Baltic States after Independence.* London: Edward Elgar Publishing.

OECD (Organisation for Economic Co-operation and Development). 2000. *Economic Surveys: Baltic States—A Regional Economic Assessment.* Paris: OECD.

———. 2002. *Foreign Direct Investment in Slovenia: Trends and Prospects.* Paris: OECD.

Padilla, S. B., and H. P. Mayer. 2003. *Sources of Growth in Selected Central and Eastern European Countries.* Research Paper, Ljubljana, Slovenia: BP&Mayer Consultants, Ultd and IMAD.

Pastor, G., and T. Damjanovic. 2001. "The Russian Financial Crisis and Its Consequences for Central Asia." IMF Working Paper 01/169, 1–42, International Monetary Fund, Washington, DC.

Pellenyi, G. 2005. "Wages and Competitiveness in the Central European New Member States." ICEG EC Opinion 7, International Center for Economic Growth. Presentation for the joint conference of MGYOSZ-ICEG, Brussels, November 18.

Ratso, S. 2005. "Miracle of Estonia: Entrepreneurship and Competitiveness Policy in Estonia." Research Paper prepared for Trade, Industry and Enterprise Development Week, United Nations Economic Commission for Europe, Geneva, May 24–25.

Reuvid, J., and M. Terterov. 2005. *Doing Business with Estonia.* London: GMB Publishing.

Simoneti, M., J. P. Damijan, M. Rojec, and B. Majcen. 2002. *Efficiency of Mass Privatization and Government-Led Restructuring: Owner vs. Seller Effects on Performance of Companies in Slovenia.* Ljubljana, Slovenia: Global Development Network.

Sirtaine, S., and I. Skamnelosm. 2007. "Credit Growth in Emerging Europe. A Cause for Stability Concerns?" Policy Research Working Paper 4281, World Bank, Washington, DC.

Sobańska, M. A. 2006. "Bezpośrednie inwestycje zagraniczne w Estonii." Master's thesis in Szkoła Główna Handlowa, Warsaw.

———. 2007. "Bezpośrednie inwestycje zagraniczne w Estonii." *Gospodarka Narodowa* 9.

Sorg, M., and S. Kallas. 1994. "Currency Reform in Estonia." Working Paper 9, Estonian Academy of Sciences, Reform Round Table, Tallinn.

Stepanyan, V. 2003. "Reforming Tax Systems: Experience of Baltics, Russia and Other Countries of the Former Soviet Union." IMF Working Paper 03/173, International Monetary Fund, Washington, DC.

Taaler, J. 1994. "Currency Reform in Estonia." Working Paper 6, Estonian Academy of Sciences, Reform Round Table, Tallinn.

Tang, P., and N. Nilgo. 1994. "Budget Reform in Estonia." Working Paper 7, Estonian Academy of Sciences, Reform Round Table, Tallinn.

Vahter, P. 2004. *The Effect of Foreign Direct Investment on Labor Productivity. Evidence from Estonia and Slovenia.* Tartu, Estonia: Tartu University Press.

Varblane, U. 2001. *Foreign Direct Investments in the Estonian Economy.* Tartu, Estonia: Tartu University Press.

Varul, P. 1999. "On the Development of Bankruptcy Law in Estonia." *Jurisdica International* 4: 172–78.

Vodopivec, M. 2002. "Worker Reallocation during Estonia's Transition to Market." *International Journal of Manpower* 23 (1): 77–97.

World Bank. 2005. *Special Topic: Sustainability of Pension Systems in the EU-8.* World Bank EU8 Quarterly Economic Report, World Bank, Washington, DC, October.

Websites

http://www.stat.si (Eesti Statistika)

http://www.einst.ee (Estonian Institute)

http://www.stat.ee (Statisticni Urad Republike Slovenije)

http://epp.eurostat.cec.eu.int (Eurostat)

http://www.investinestonia.com (Estonian Investment Agency)

http://www.unece.org (United Nations Economic Commission for Europe)

http://www.unece.org (United Nations Economic Commission for Europe)

http://laborsta.ilo.org (International Labour Organization)

http://www.vlada.si/en (Government of Slovenia)

http://www.stat.si (Eesti Statistika)

http://www.icegec.hu (ICEG European Center)

http://www.unece.org (United Nations Economic Commission for Europe)

http://www.bsi.si (Banka Slovenije)

http://www.worldbank.org (World Bank)

http://www.imf.org (International Monetary Fund)

CHAPTER 6

Why Is Mexico Poorer Than Spain?

Anna Kurowska

Mexico, which was a Spanish colony from its conquest in the 16th century until 1810 (and formally until 1821),[1] inherited many features of its hegemon's legal and institutional system.[2] In the mid-19th century both Mexico and Spain underwent important changes: (a) the church was stripped of its monopoly to possess and manage land—the main factor of production at that time; and (b) a half-authoritarian system was set up, comprising a parliament, albeit not an entirely autonomous one (*Porfiriato* in Mexico and *Restauración* in Spain) (Coatsworth and Casares 2002). From the end of World War I (WWI) until the 1950s, both countries experienced revolutions and civil wars (the civil war of 1931–39 in Spain, leading to the installation of the Franco regime; and the Mexican Revolution of 1911–40 and its aftermath).[3]

Until the middle of the 20th century, the two countries displayed many similarities, not only in politics and institutions, but also—and not unexpectedly, in light of the previously described parallel historical developments—in their social and economic profiles. As late as 1960, the two posted a similar gross domestic product (GDP) per capita (in fact, Spain's was even somewhat lower), a comparable participation of agriculture and industry in GDP generation (accounting for 21 percent of Spain's GDP each and for 15 percent and 24 percent of Mexico's output, respectively), a similar percentage of urban population (56.7 percent in Spain and 50.8 percent in Mexico), and a comparable total population (approximately 31 million in Spain against approximately 37 million in Mexico) whose age structure was also similar.

Differences began to materialize after 1961, when Spain's economy took off (figure 6.1). Between 1961 and 2000, per capita growth averaged 3.8 percent in Spain, compared to Mexico's 2 percent.

Figure 6.1 Differential in GDP Per Capita between Mexico and Spain, 1960–2001

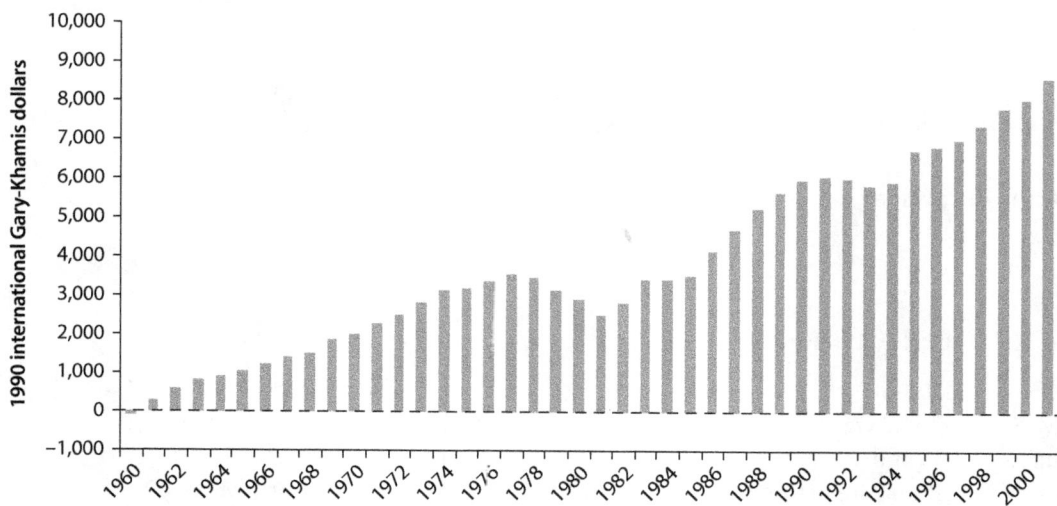

Source: Based on Maddison 2006.

Throughout the period 1961–2001, differences in the growth rates between the two countries varied; to analyze the causes underpinning these differences, it is best to divide the period into specific subperiods:

- *Between 1961 and 1977, neither country experienced economic collapse. This enables us to use growth accounting to pin down the causes of the different growth rates (see table 6.1).*
  - During this period, Spain enjoyed considerably higher per capita GDP growth due to faster capital accumulation. It also boasted a materially higher factor productivity growth.
  - Historians describe the 1960s in Spain as the Spanish Industrial Revolution (see Tortella 2000). The force driving growth in the entire economy was industry, a sector with high capital needs. In the 10 years between 1961 and 1971 industrial output expanded by 10.4 percent per year, a pace well above overall GDP growth. The share of industry in GDP generation jumped from 26 percent in 1964 to 34 percent in 1974.

- *Between 1978 and 2001, on the other hand, growth fluctuated considerably in both countries.*
  - In 1978–81 Spain experienced a slowdown (including occasional GDP drops), while Mexico saw a substantial rise in growth.
  - During 1982–88 Spain initially expanded at a slow pace, to gradually gain momentum in 1986 (upon accession to the European Community);[4] at the same time, Mexico suffered an economic collapse.

Table 6.1 GDP Growth Breakdown: Spain and Mexico, 1961–77
Percent

Country	Growth 1961–77				Contributions to growth (in percentage points)		
	y	A	k	n	A	k	n
Spain	5.51	1.42	7.19	−0.55	1.42	4.31	−0.22
Mexico	3.00	0.82	3.49	0.22	0.82	2.09	0.09

Source: Own compilation.
Note: y = per capita GDP; A = total factor productivity; k = capital outlays per capita; n = number of persons working in relation to population.

- In 1989–95 Spain's rapid growth gradually weakened, hitting a trough in 1993, when GDP slumped for the second time since the World War II. Yet, in 1994 growth returned to an upward path. In Mexico, on the other hand, activity picked up at the beginning of the period; until 1994 the country enjoyed a positive—if slowing—growth. In 1995 Mexico experienced a dramatic collapse.
- The period 1996–01 is one of sustained and fairly robust growth for Spain, while Mexico, following the meltdown of 1995, took the next five years to return to a path of uneven but positive growth. In some of these years, growth accelerated, only to collapse again in 2001.

- GDP per capita growth in Mexico[5] averaged 1.24 percent in 1978–01, while in Spain it averaged 2.41 percent. If Mexico's negative growth rates are replaced with the rates recorded in Spain in the corresponding years, average annual GDP per capita growth in Mexico becomes 2.96 percent, thus exceeding Spain's rate. The same result would apply if GDP drops were substituted with the average growth rates seen in the 10-year periods preceding the downturns (in that case, the average annual GDP per capita growth in Mexico would have worked out at 2.88 percent). Thus, the collapses in Mexico's growth more than account for the widening gap in the per capita incomes of Spain and Mexico in 1978–2001. For this reason, when explaining the causes of the divergence in the average growth between Mexico and Spain in the 1978–2001 period, we focus on the causes of the Mexican downturns.

Differences in Economic Performance: Factors and Causes

The Years 1961–77

Considering that in every year of the analyzed period both countries registered positive economic growth and collapses did not occur,[6] the differences in GDP growth between them should be traced back to the evolution of their *propelling institutions*.

The sixties and seventies were the final years of General Franco's rule in Spain. This period was quite different from the previous ones in that the country opened to external trade. Until the late 1950s Spain had adhered to a policy

Puzzles of Economic Growth • http://dx.doi.org/10.1596/978-1-4648-0325-3

of protectionism and attempts at an autarky. As of 1959 these policies were
being reversed. In effect, industrial exports, following a decade of stagnation due
to trade restrictions, soared by 14.2 percent a year throughout the 1960s. This
boost was possible owing to trade liberalization implemented amid a worldwide
economic boom.[7]

Spain's opening to external trade triggered drivers of growth such as competition
and technology imports.[8] As a consequence, expansion was observed in not only
those industries where external trade played a major role in generating revenue,
but also those catering chiefly to the domestic market—such as the automotive
sector (which, incidentally, saw the fastest expansion—of more than 20 percent a
year) and the metallurgical, steel, and oil-refining industries (Tortella 2000).

It was industry, and in particular its most dynamically growing sectors, that
captured the bulk of foreign direct investment (FDI) flows (76 percent in
1960–75). These flows were the key drivers of investment expansion in the
period under review (Molero 2001). The influx was supported by the law prevailing in 1963–73, which allowed investment in 18 key industry sectors without
any government restrictions whatsoever.[9]

While Spain was opening to international trade, Mexico raised protectionist barriers, stifling competition and the import of technology.[10] Between 1956
and 1962 tariffs were increased on four occasions. But qualitative restrictions
on imports were even more hurting. Mexico remained outside the General
Agreement on Tariffs and Trade (GATT) until 1986 and was able set up nontariff protectionist barriers on an almost limitless scale. In 1973, 80 percent of
import items were subject to licensing, as compared with 33 percent in 1956.
The number of individual import items subject to import controls rose from
1,376 in 1956 to 12,800 in 1973 (Maddison 1992). More than 30 government
committees were busy issuing approximately 3,000 individual import licenses
per week. No auditing institution existed to monitor this entire import control
system, so the potential for inefficiency, corruption, and smuggling was enormous
(Maddison 1992). The authorities procrastinated taking any steps toward import
liberalization until 1977.[11]

The economic openness index, which is the sum of exports and imports
related to GDP, was higher in Mexico than in Spain as late as 1960 and 1961.
In 1962 the value of the index for both countries equalized, and in the next five
years Spain gained a substantial edge over Mexico, which it maintained until
almost the end of the 1980s (see figure 6.2).

Spain's advantage was supported by, apart from the greater openness of the
economy, better property rights protection and a higher quality of the legal system.
This is indicated by the "legal system and property rights protection" index computed by the Fraser Institute. In 1970—that is, approximately at the midpoint of
the analyzed period—it stood at 7.1 points for Spain and 4.7 points for Mexico.[12]

The Years 1978–2001

Because Mexico's economic collapses between 1978 and 2001 more than account
for the different growth rates of the two analyzed countries in this period,

Figure 6.2 Index of Economic Openness in Spain and Mexico, 1960–2002

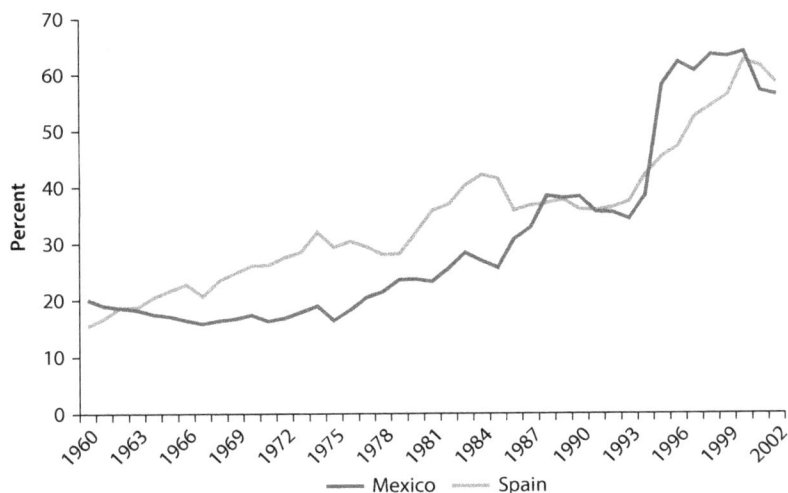

Source: Based on World Development Indicators 2004 data.

there is reason to look into the causes of these collapses. Why did they hit Mexico but spare Spain?

The first of the major shocks to Mexico's economy in the examined period took place in 1982 and was of a domestic nature (while being compounded by developments in the country's external environment). The shock involved a dramatic drop (nearly 50 percent) in the peso's exchange rate.

The discovery of vast oil deposits in Mexico in 1972–73 and a sharp rise in the global price of this commodity enabled Mexico to achieve an exceptionally high growth rate toward the end of that decade. This encouraged the Mexican government to incur external debt against future proceeds from oil exports (Maddison 1992; De Seguin 2004). Mexico lacked regulations limiting the government's spending (due to a lack of stabilizing institutions). New and costly programs were launched.[13] Government budgets were constructed on the overoptimistic expectation of an endless economic boom (long-term investment plans assumed annual GDP to grow at 8 percent). In reality, the boom rested exclusively on the sudden hike in the prices of oil, a commodity exported by Mexico in large quantities since the discovery of new deposits in 1972–73. To finance the high government deficit, not only were funds borrowed abroad, but banks were tapped for private savings as well. Taking advantage of the dependent position of the central bank, the government kept raising the ratio of the reserves that banks were obliged to hold in treasury bonds; these bore interest below the inflation rate (for example, while in 1956 the ratio was 3 percent of deposits, in 1979 it had jumped to 46 percent). The private sector, whose access to credit was thus restricted, was encouraged to finance expansion by borrowing abroad (Maddison 1992). Foreign loans boosted domestic demand—investment grew by an annual average of 16.8 percent in 1978–80, while consumption rose by 8.3 percent a year (Maddison 1992). Expanding demand, in turn, fueled inflation and stimulated imports growth, which amounted to 14.1 percent a year in 1978–80. In spite of high revenues from oil exports, the value of exports fell below that of exports. To finance the resulting trade deficit, increasingly more foreign loans were incurred, as interest rates were conveniently, if temporarily, negative. Warnings of a possible decline in global oil prices passed unheeded. In 1982 the fiscal deficit reached 15 percent of GDP (Li, Philippopoulos, and Tzavalis 2000). Ultimately, in1982 the peso could no longer withstand the pace of inflation (59 percent) (Li, Philippopoulos, and Tzavalis 2000, 89) and the pressure of the mounting trade deficit. A massive outflow of capital ensued, and the currency tumbled by 50 percent. Mexico defaulted on its external debt, which had risen by 140 percent in 1978–82, amounting to 53 percent of its GDP (Bergoeing and others 2001). This was preceded by a sharp increase in its debt service cost, as the developed countries had tightened their monetary policies. In addition, most private banks' profitability was eroded by high inflation. In August 1982 the government converted dollar-denominated bank deposits into peso-denominated ones at the official exchange rate (that is, half the black market rate) and nationalized the banks.[14] Nationalization of the banking system put the government in control—directly or indirectly—of 60–80 percent of GDP (Lusting 2001).

Two key factors had triggered the crisis, both resulting from the reckless macroeconomic policy inspired by flaws in Mexico's stabilizing institutions: mounting sovereign debt and soaring inflation that enhanced the real overvaluation of the peso.

Mexico's fiscal policy lacked an institutional harness that might force authorities to use the economic windfall to strengthen public finance. Mexico's budget deficit, with the exception of the years 1978 and 1980, was higher than Spain's— even though the former thrived on the 1970s oil price hike while the latter suffered from it. The practice of forcing domestic banks into financing the deficit, increasingly widespread throughout the 1970s, made the financial market much shallower (loans to private corporations fell from 36 percent of GDP in 1969 to 10 percent of GDP in 1974).[15] As a consequence, it became impossible to finance the deficit other than through external debt or monetization (figure 6.3). In contrast to Mexico, Spain liberalized and deregulated its banking system in 1974–85.[16] This included, among other things, the removal of territorial barriers for bank expansion—and conversely, the opening of the national system to foreign competition. Between 1978 and 1983, the sector experienced a serious crisis (due to the oil shocks, irregularities in company boards, and lack of adequate supervision from the Bank of Spain). Yet, it was not one capable of upsetting the economy. Domestic credit, ranging between 85 percent and 95 percent of the GDP, was second in size only to Japan (Plizga 2003).

Since Mexico lacked an independent central bank, the country had no authority to keep inflation in check. As a consequence, Mexico once again fell prey to rampant inflation (see figure 6.4). Spain, despite being an oil importer and not having an independent central bank—a feature it shared with Mexico—succeeded

Figure 6.3 Central Government Debt as a Percentage of GDP in Spain and Mexico, 1972–97

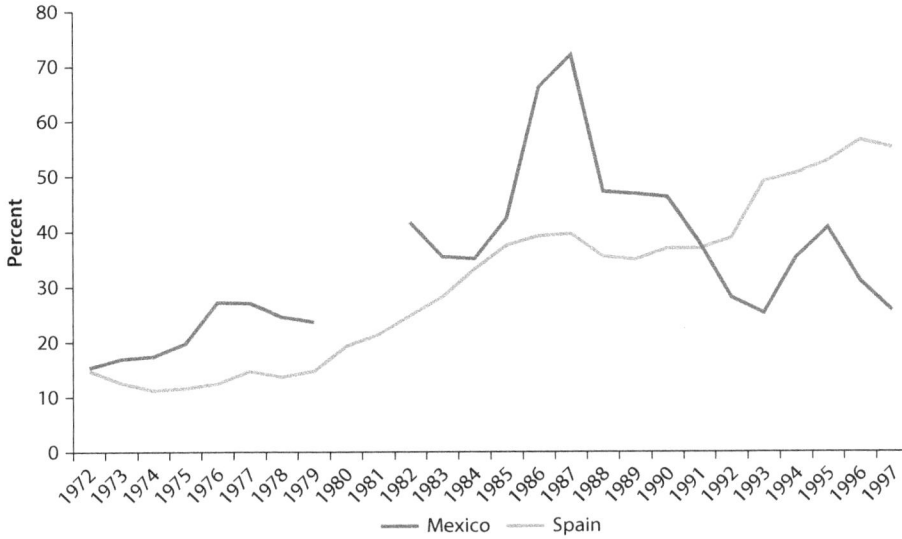

Sources: Based on World Development Indicators 2004 data. No earlier data available for either country. Also, 1980 and 1981 data are missing for Mexico.

Figure 6.4 GDP Deflator in Mexico and Spain, 1961–2002

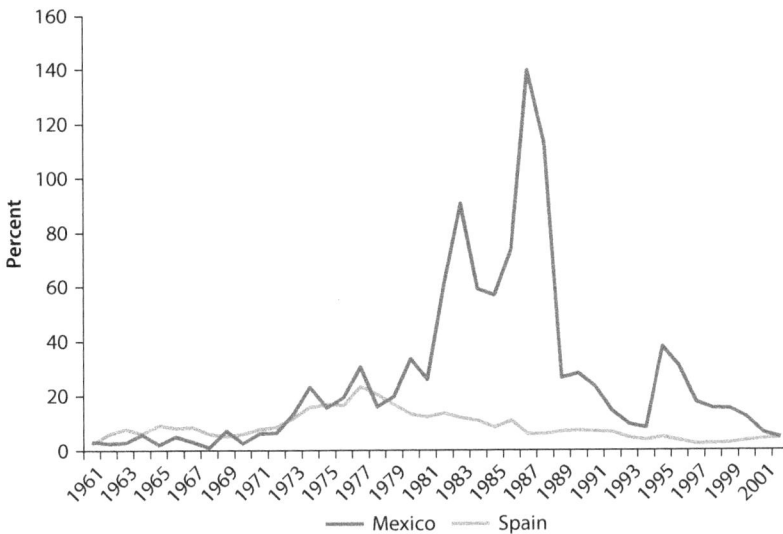

Sources: Based on World Development Indicators 2004 data; graph based on consumer inflation.

in keeping inflation below 20 percent. In contrast to Mexico, the ruling center-right party in Spain had struck, back in 1977, an accord with the left-wing opposition and the Communist Party to curb inflation as the new government's key objective. Detailed tasks aimed at reducing inflation were laid down in the so-called Moncloa Pacts (1977). The agreed objective was upheld when Felipe Gonzalez's Socialist government took over in 1982.

Mexico's monetary policy makers made a mistake of not responding to the real appreciation of the Mexican currency. In the period concerned, the country's exchange rate regime was the managed or "dirty" floating system. Such a regime aims at eliminating the main shortcoming of the fully fledged floating regime—that is, high volatility. Yet, it may prove dangerous if the rate becomes too tightly pegged and the central bank—as was the case in Mexico—fails to secure low inflation levels (Sławiński 1975; Lutkowski 1998).

Directly after the 1982 crisis, when the Mexican economy had not yet scrambled out of recession for good, further shocks ensued: (a) domestic, following an earthquake in 1985, and (b) external, linked to a dramatic drop in the prices of oil, the country's key export commodity.

In 1982 Mexico's new president, Miguel de la Madrid, launched a reform package under the Immediate Economic Reorganization Program, adopted in consultation with the International Monetary Fund (IMF) (De Seguin 2004). Yet, the extent of the initial imbalance caused by the economic policies of the 1970s was too large, and the pace of changes too slow, to build up the economy's resilience to shocks. Inflation was higher in 1984 than in 1982, the fiscal deficit exceeded 8 percent, state-owned banks granted loans on a discretionary basis to enterprises indicated by the government (Bergoeing and others 2001), and privatization was practically put on hold until 1998. Following a precipitous drop in revenue, the deficit of the general government sector jumped to 13 percent of GDP in 1986. Since the only way to finance the deficit was monetization, the already high inflation was further boosted, up to 86 percent. GDP per capita contracted by almost another 4 percent in 1984–86 (see table 6.2).

Meanwhile, in Spain a welfare state was being formed in 1976–84 (Castro, González-Páramo, and Hernández de Cos 2001). Rising government expenditure, exceeding 30 percent of GDP in 1984, fueled the budget deficit. The deficit peaked in 1984 at an all-time high of 8 percent of the GDP. Furthermore, marginal income tax and social security contribution rates, already high, were increased substantially (this was reflected in the slipping tax index published by the Fraser Institute—from 4 points in 1974 to 1 point in 1980–85). The burgeoning fiscal position of the state was not offset by shifts in the banking sector (Plizga 2003), where government interference in the operations of banking institutions was further curbed, access to the banking services market was deregulated, and laws governing the operations of foreign banks were relaxed (due to the adoption of European Union [EU] solutions). Slow GDP growth in the first half of the decade, following a drop in 1981 due to a dramatic surge in oil prices, enhanced the adverse effect of labor market rigidities. In 1985 years of relentless growth took the unemployment rate up to 21 percent, the highest level in Europe.

Table 6.2 GDP Growth, Inflation, and Fiscal Deficit in Mexico, 1982–88

Year	Economic growth (%)	Inflation (%)	Public deficit (% GDP)
1982	–0.5	54	16.9
1983	–4.2	102	8.6
1984	3.6	65	8.5
1985	2.6	57	9
1986	–3.8	86	16
1987	1.9	132	16
1988	1.3	114	12.5

Source: De Seguin 2004.
Note: The levels of the indicators listed are different than those presented elsewhere in the chapter as they derive from different sources. But this is of no consequence to the assessment of the period under examination.

Fixed-term contracts[17] and employee dismissal[18] were particularly constrained by restrictions. Another key rigidity was the generous unemployment benefit system (see Garcia-Rubiales 2004).

In Mexico the turn of the 1980s saw president Carlos Salinas de Gotami launch a program of stabilization, liberalization, and privatization adopted in consultation with the IMF.

- Through a number of measures, inflation was gradually reduced (down to 7 percent in 1994): a temporary freeze on wages was negotiated with trade unions and employer representatives, high interest rates were maintained, and a fixed exchange rate with a target band was introduced. Also, a redenomination of the peso was carried out (new peso = 1,000 old pesos). There were dramatic cuts to public spending,[19] which fell (in percentage of GDP terms) from 30 percent in 1987 to 15 percent in 1991. At the beginning of the 1990s the government balance saw a surplus for the first time since the 1950s. The debt-to-GDP ratio had been substantially reduced. By comparison, Spain's public expenditure in this period exceeded 35 percent of GDP (in 1995 it reached a record level of 35 percent of GDP), the government deficit remained at the level of a few percent of GDP (in 1994 it reached as much as 7 percent of GDP), and public debt was on an upward trend (figure 6.3).

- The inflow of FDI was fully liberated. In 1992 Mexico signed the North American Free Trade Agreement (NAFTA) treaty, which took effect in 1994 (in the same year, Mexico became a member of the Organisation for Economic Co-operation and Development [OECD], and in 1987 a member of GATT) (De Seguin 2004).

- Furthermore, hundreds of state-owned enterprises were privatized with the participation of foreign capital (for example, in 1991–92 as many as 18 banks were privatized; Cyper 1996). According to estimates by Chong and Lopez-de-Silanes (2004), in the years 1983–88, nominal privatization proceeds accounted for 0.4 percent of the 2003 GDP (in 1989–93 it was 4.2 percent and in 1994–03, 0.73 percent; in the entire period 1983–2003 it was 5.32 percent).

Between 1991 and 1994 Mexico developed markedly faster than Spain. Independent forecasts for the subsequent years anticipated the Mexican economy to expand at an average annual rate of 3.8 percent (Espinosa and Russell 1996). Yet, in 1995 it collapsed again: 40 percent of the peso's value was wiped out, inflation soared to 52 percent, interest rates to 100 percent, and GDP slipped by more than 6 percent. This meltdown shows how costly a single economic policy mistake can be amidst adverse circumstances and the weakness of certain stabilizing institutions—even though some other institutions might have been strengthened.

What primarily fueled the crisis was an inappropriate exchange rate policy (Dornbusch and Werner 1994; Sachs, Tornell, and Velasco 1995) In spite of the crawling devaluation, the peso appreciated steadily in real terms (that is, when inflation at home and abroad was taken into account).[20] This was accompanied by a quantum leap in the current account deficit—from $14.6 billion in 1991 to $28.8 billion in 1994 (which accounted for 8 percent of GDP in that year). The deficit was financed—to a great extent—with portfolio investment flows rather than FDI.

The share of portfolio flows in the overall capital inflow in the examined period amounted to 84 percent (Sidaoui 2005). The expanding current account deficit could suggest a change in the valuation of the peso (Witt 1996), which generated expectations of its devaluation (see figure 6.5). These expectations were all the stronger since the mounting deficit resulted from lower savings

Figure 6.5 Current Account Balance as a Percentage of GDP in Spain and Mexico, 1978–2002

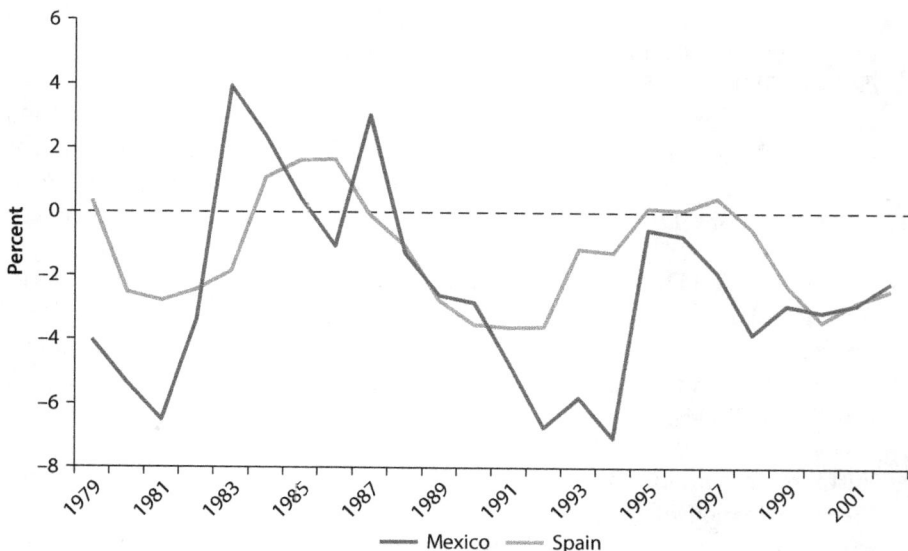

Sources: Based on World Development Indicators 2004 data. No data available for earlier years.

rather than higher investment; the latter could have enhanced Mexico's future capacity to pay off its external debt, incurred to finance the trade deficit. The share of domestic investment in GDP rose from 20 percent in 1988 to 23 percent in 1992, while private savings rate fell from 18 percent to 9 percent of GDP (Espinosa and Russell 1996). Yet, the peso exchange rate adjustment was postponed, adding to the strain on the financial markets. This was reflected in the ever-shorter maturities at which investors were willing to lend to the government. In 1992 the average maturity of government bonds was slightly more than 400 days; in 1993 it had shrunk to 300 days; and in the autumn of 1994 to a mere 200 days. Tensions in the financial markets were compounded by turmoil in the political arena (see box 6.1). Each subsequent political shock undermined investors' confidence in Mexico even more, raising the financial market's sensitivity to further alarming signals. The central bank's response to the speculative attacks was to intervene in the currency market; interest rates, already very high, were not raised (they were markedly above GDP growth). Yet, interest rate increases could have curbed domestic demand expansion, in effect

---

Box 6.1 Speculative Attacks on the Peso in 1993–94 Preceding Devaluation: Political Context

The first speculative attack on the peso occurred in November 1993, when a stormy debate broke out in the U.S. Congress over Mexico's accession to the NAFTA—which investors had considered a foregone conclusion. Even though ultimately the debate leaned in favor of Mexico, the peso brushed the upper limit of its target band.

The second speculative attack took place in 1994, after a spate of incidents triggering political turmoil. On January 1, 1994, Ejercito Zapatista de Liberacion Nacional declared war on the president in office, Carlos Salinas. Nine days of armed struggle followed and several towns were seized by rebel forces. In the subsequent weeks, despite a ceasefire, bomb attacks were mounted in some towns and cities. On March 23, Lus Donaldo Colosio—the presidential candidate for the ruling Partido Revolucionario Institucional (PRI party), considered a sure-fire winner of the 1994 election—was assassinated. The turmoil at home was boosted by an unpropitious situation abroad: interest rates in the United States rose, triggering considerable capital outflows from Mexico's financial markets.

The third attack on the peso in 1994 occurred after subsequent political disturbances following the resignation of the Minister of the Interior, Jorge Carpizo, and the abduction of a prominent Mexican businessman, Alfredo Harp.

The fourth attack on the peso ensued in the autumn of 1994 (after a government change over and the installation of Ernesto Zedillo as the new president). This time, the trigger was another assassination—that of Jose Francisco Ruiz Massieu, head of the PRI parliamentary caucus. It mounted when public accusation of the murder itself and obstruction of justice were directed at the victim's brother, the prosecutor general. The speculative attack was preceded by the announcement that the Mexican authorities did not intend to extend the corridor for peso fluctuations.

Puzzles of Economic Growth • http://dx.doi.org/10.1596/978-1-4648-0325-3

reducing the trade deficit and stopping capital outflow. In 1994, following an intervention in defense of the peso, Mexico's foreign exchange reserves fell from $30 billion in March to $6 billion in December.[21] Faced with almost completely exhausted foreign exchange reserves, on December 22 the government floated the exchange rate. The peso lost almost 50 percent of its value, tumbling from 4 pesos to 7.2 pesos to the dollar within as little as a week.

Spain's response to tensions in the financial markets was different from Mexico's. The late 1980s and early 1990s were a period of rapid development in the country, largely in the wake of its accession to the European Community in 1986. In 1989 Spain joined the European Exchange Rate Mechanism, introducing a fixed exchange-rate system with a ±2.25 percent fluctuation band. As Spain's interest rates were relatively high,[22] the country experienced considerable inflows of foreign capital, which, amid a fixed exchange rate regime and only partial sterilization, entailed expanding money supply (although it should be noted that capital inflows to Spain—in contrast to Mexico—consisted largely of FDI, which is far more difficult to reverse than portfolio investment (see figure 6.6). Rising inflation and wages eroded the price competitiveness of Spanish goods in the international markets, leading to a sizeable current account deficit (if smaller than Mexico's). After interest rates were raised in Germany in response to the inflation hike spurred by that country's unification, the Spanish currency faced downward pressures.[23] Initially, the bank defended the peseta exchange rate by drawing on currency reserves, and simultaneously increasing interest rates

Figure 6.6 Total Net FDI Flows as a Percentage of GDP in Spain and Mexico, 1975–2002

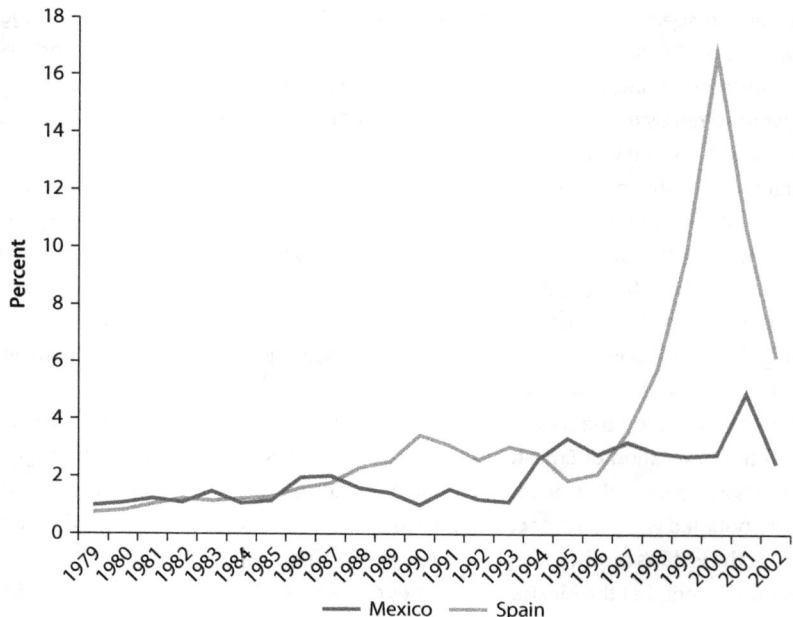

Source: Based on World Development Indicators 2004 data.

even higher (Bacchetta 1997; Juselius and Ordóñez 2005). But after the first speculative attack in September 1992, Spanish authorities decided to devalue the currency (Juselius and Ordóñez 2005): by 5 percent in September 1992, another 6 percent in November 1992, 8 percent in May 1993, and, finally, by 7 percent in March 1995. Spain's GDP contracted by a mere 1 percent, which is even more noteworthy in the light of the economic problems experienced by its main trading partners.

The drop in Mexico's GDP following the 1995 currency crisis was enhanced by the banking crisis. This resulted from the absence of efficient banking supervision and the banks' poor risk management capacity (no foreign banks had been allowed to participate in their privatization; restrictions in the access by foreign competition to Mexico's banking sector were also included in the treaty establishing the NAFTA) (Haber 2005). Following deregulation, fierce competition between banks resulted in lending expansion—credit growth reached 24 percent annually. Private bank owners strove to promptly recover the amounts invested in the acquisition (on the one hand, purchase prices were on average more than three times the book value of the banks; on the other, investors could not be certain whether a change of president would mean a return to statist economic policies) (Haber 2005). Thus, loans were often granted without due analysis of the borrowers' capacity to repay them. Consequently, the share of bad debts rose from 3 percent in 1991 to almost 10 percent in 1994, and as much as 17 percent in September 1995 (while the share of bad debts, at only 4 percent, is deemed to be a sign of the poor condition of the banking system; see Cyper 1996). Bad debts exceeded the banks' equity by two-thirds (Cyper 1996; Haber 2005).

The liberalization of the banking system in Spain took a more controlled course than in Mexico (despite the sector being almost immediately opened to foreign competition). As in Mexico, but much earlier (between 1978 and 1983), the system had undergone a crisis in consequence of which 52 out the existing 116 banks were closed down or taken over. Against this backdrop, the Bank of Spain had already tightened banking supervision by the late 1970s. In the mid-1980s, stricter regulations of banks' solvency were introduced, as well as principles for financial accounting (including appropriate classification of loans).[24] Owing to a sound banking system, the 1992–93 turmoil in the currency market bore no grave consequences for the Spanish economy.

After the 1995 crisis, Mexico returned to the path of fast economic growth, which was to last several years (and average 5.4 percent annually) (Lusting 1998). The reforms started in the early 1980s were continued (albeit with a lag) and systemic flaws that had led to the economic crisis were gradually eliminated:

- Inflation was decreased slowly but steadily. In 1999 the central bank adopted as its mid-term target a reduction of inflation down to 3 percent (by 2003)—that is, to a level observed in Mexico's main trading partners (OECD 2002a). A tax reform was launched, aimed at simplifying the tax system. Low government spending (15 percent of GDP) (OECD 2002a) and a deficit (between 0.75 and 1.25 percent of GDP)[25] were maintained. Public debt declined from nearly 40 percent of GDP at the end of 1995, to 23 percent at the end of 2001. Its average maturity increased by two years.

- In 1998–99 a broad package of reforms to the financial system was adopted—abolishing, among other things, restrictions in foreign investors' access to sale of equity in banks. As a result, the share of banks controlled by foreign capital rose to 77.1 percent from 6.2 percent in 1995 (OECD 2002b). In April 2000 a new bankruptcy law was introduced, clearly specifying procedures for recovering bad debts. Banking supervision was strengthened and accounting principles, modeled on international standards, were introduced. The share of bad debts fell to less than 6 percent at the beginning of 2001.

These reforms and an appropriate economic policy strengthened Mexico to a sufficient degree to survive both the Asian and Russian crisis in 1997–98, the oil price drop in 1998 (Lusting 1998), and the Argentine financial crisis in 1999 (OECD 2002a).

Over the 1990s the dependence of Mexico on the economic conditions in the United States deepened significantly. The share of Mexican exports destined for the United States rose to almost 90 percent (see figure 6.7).[26] At the same time, exports came to play a more prominent role in the Mexican economy.[27] Also, the overwhelming majority of FDI originated in the United States.

These ties, amid strong business conditions prevailing in the United States, sped up Mexico's return to a steeply rising path of economic growth after the

Figure 6.7 Share of the United States, Emerging Countries, and the European Union in Mexican Exports, 1980–2005

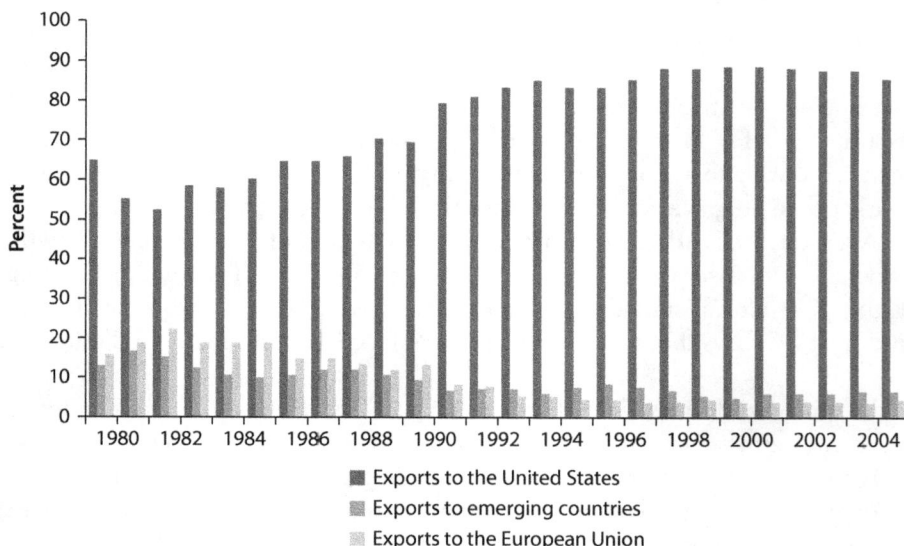

Source: Data based on the IMF Balance of Payments Database, available through Université Libre de Bruxelles.

1995 crisis. But in 2001, when output growth in the United States almost came to a stop, Mexico experienced a shock that led to a decline in its GDP.[28]

The 2001 recession, unlike the previous downturns, was not very grave and did not entail serious disturbances either in the financial or the currency market (OECD 2005). The level of portfolio and FDI, and, consequently, the exchange rate, remained stable, while inflation continued along a downward path.

Summary and Conclusions

This chapter has aimed to explain why Mexico posts lower per capita income than Spain. Until the mid-19th century, these two countries had many features in common in terms of politics, institutions, culture, as well as the economy. They generated almost identical GDP per capita and grew at a similar pace. In the 1960s the paths of the two countries diverged. In 1960–2001 average annual growth stood at 3.8 percent in Spain and at only 2 percent in Mexico.

- Between 1961 and 1977 both countries developed at a stable pace. Higher GDP growth in Spain resulted from much faster capital growth (than in Mexico) and a slightly stronger factor productivity growth. The more robust capital formation was the effect of rapidly expanding industry. Owing to the liberalization of foreign trade, launched during a global boom, Spain enjoyed inflows of foreign capital that was invested mostly in industry. Lifting restrictions on imports opened the gate to technology transfer from abroad, which in turn triggered productivity growth. In the same period Mexico stepped up protectionist policies, both through higher tariffs and nontariff barriers.

- In 1978–2001 Mexico experienced several GDP declines—in 1982, 1986, 1995, and 2001. Barring those growth collapses, Mexico would have expanded at a pace even slightly higher, on average, than that of Spain.
  - The cause of Mexico's growth collapses in 1982 and 1986—as well as their severity—was the weakness of Mexico's stabilizing institutions: an absence of restrictions to rein in reckless fiscal policy, no independent central bank, and a banking sector exposed to state interference. These frailties were reflected in a steadily rising public deficit and inflation, a falling ratio of private sector credit to GDP, as well as the slipping profitability of banks.
  - After the crises of the 1980s, Mexican authorities implemented several reforms to strengthen both the driving and stabilizing institutions. But the reforms were late and incomplete, especially with respect to the banking system. In particular, a properly functioning regulatory framework was missing (among others, the accounting system used by Mexican banks did not comply with international standards), as was adequate supervision. A banking crisis spurred by ballooning bad debts exacerbated the GDP drop of 1995. The drop followed a currency meltdown that had been unleashed after devaluation had been postponed too long—amid a mounting current account deficit, waning investor confidence, and political disturbances.

In contrast to Mexico, the reform of the financial system was implemented much earlier in Spain (in the late 1970s and early 1980s) and on a larger scale. A new and more efficient banking supervision system was introduced, including strict regulations concerning banks' solvency and their accounting principles (along with an appropriate classification of loans).

– The last GDP drop at was observed in Mexico in 2001 resulted, above all, from a collapse in demand from the United States, which was Mexico's main trading partner (accounting for 90 percent of its exports). Owing to the completion of the reforms initiated at the turn of the 1980s, the 2001 recession was shallow and short lived.

Notes

1. Spain did not officially recognize Mexico's independence until 1821.

2. The foundations of the legal system were formed in Castile and later spread over the whole of Spain and its colonies (Coatsworth and Casares 2002).

3. Coatsworth and Casares (2002) observe that the civil war in Spain had a far more damaging effect on the country's economy than the Mexican Revolution had on the Mexican economy.

4. Predecessor to the European Economic Community (EEC) and the European Union (EU).

5. Calculations are based on Angus Maddison's database figures to remain consistent with the data used in the figure 6.1.

6. Even though neither country experienced economic collapses, both were exposed to shocks. Spain was hit by a negative external shock in 1974 due to a sudden hike in oil prices, while the same shock was positive for Mexico since the country was—and still is—an oil exporter. Mexico experienced a negative shock in 1976, after the collapse of the peso. But these shocks contribute little to an understanding of the differences in the growth rates of Mexico and Spain.

7. In the 1960s both Western Europe (Spain's main trading partner) and the United States (Mexico's main trading partner) developed at a robust pace. Western Europe grew at an average annual rate of 4.8 percent (taking 29 countries into account; 4.5 percent per year when considering only the 12 major ones), while the United States expanded at 4.6 percent per year (author's own calculations based on Angus Maddison, 2006, *The World Economy: Historical Statistics*).

8. More on the imports of new technology in Molero (2001). The second important source of capital accumulation was investment financed from corporate profits.

9. Molero (2001) writes that in the period referred to, investment in the aforementioned 18 key industries did not, by way of "exception" require the consent of the Spanish government (in the remaining industries, the restrictions still applied). But it is worth pointing out that the 18 key sectors represented a considerable chunk of the Spanish industry, and one recording the strongest growth.

10. Andre de Seguin (2004) describes the period of Adolfo Lopez Mateosa's rule (1958–64) as one of "pronounced nationalism, protectionism and state interventionism."

11. Maddison 1992, 156. According to Andre de Seguin (2004), Mexico owed its development, which took place in spite of the increasing protectionism and mounting

import restrictions, to the Alliance for Progress program launched by John F. Kennedy, addressed at Latin American countries. Between 1962 and 1967, the United States pumped $1.4 billion a year into the countries covered by the program; with new investment included in the calculation, the amount rises to $3.3 billion. In the first two years of program operation alone, Mexico received over $700 million (accounting for 5.5 percent of Mexico's GDP at that time).

12. The index ranges from 0 to 10; the higher the score, the better protection of property rights and legal system.

13. At issue was mostly public investment under the five-year plan initiated in 1978, which included electrification of the entire country, construction of tourist compounds, and development of public housing. Another notable program was that of agricultural development, launched by the Mexican government in 1980 with a view to securing the country's self-sufficiency in food. The program envisaged, among other things, vast subsidies to agriculture (Maddison 1992; De Seguin 2004).

14. More on the nationalization of the banking system in, among others, McKinley and Alacorn (1993) and Maxfield (1992).

15. It is worth noting at this point that the weaknesses of Mexico's banking system could be arguably traced back to the mid-1800s. This possibility is discussed in detail in Haber (2005).

16. A description of the reforms is given in Plizga (2003).

17. No substantial change in this respect took place until 1984. Pursuant to the new law, fixed-time contracts could be signed in any area of professional activity for a period of at least six months (from 1992, at least a year), and the total term could not exceed three years (four years from 1992 on). More on this issue in Teixeira (2001).

18. Some of these restrictions were not abolished until 1994. More on the issue in Teixeira (2001).

19. Between 1982 and 1988 it is estimated that the social expenditure was reduced by 50 percent. The biggest cuts were made under the headings of "regional development" and "rural development" (Randall 2006).

20. In the 1990s inflation in Mexico exceeded the sum of consumer price index (CPI) inflation in the United States and the crawling devaluation of the peso.

21. Under a fixed exchange regime, there is no mechanism to restore the equilibrium in the balance of payments. Hence, a country's monetary authorities have to take good care of their foreign exchange reserves, which they need for currency interventions to defend the exchange rate.

22. High interest rates resulted from the restrictive monetary policy implemented in the preceding years, aimed at reducing inflation rate differentials between Spain and the remaining EC countries, notably Germany (see Bacchetta 1997).

23. The ERM crisis is discussed in more detail in, among others, Beeby, Hall, and Marcet (2001) and Sevilla (1995).

24. For more on the background to the Spanish banking system crisis of 1978–83 and description of changes in banking regulations, see De Juan (1993).

25. See OECD 2002a: "Government revenue is closely dependent on oil export revenue, and hence on global oil prices, which entails considerable uncertainty in determining the future budget position. To at least tackle the problem partly, a Stabilisation Fund was established in 2000, where part of oil export proceeds are stored in periods of high prices, to be later drawn on to cover government spending when oil prices flag."

26. By comparison, the share of Mexico's exports to the United States amounted to a little over 50 percent; in 1992 it exceeded 80 percent and in 2000 reached 90 percent.

27. It is worth noticing that the Mexican export-to-GDP ratio in the 1996–2000 period for the first time in the history exceeded the export-to-GDP ratio in Spain, and in 2000 this ratio equalized for both countries.

28. Another reason behind the output drop in 2001 was, according to the authors of the OECD Economic Survey, falling public investment in that year (OECD 2002b).

Bibliography

Bacchetta, P. 1997. "Exchange Rate Policy and Disinflation: The Spanish Experience in the ERM." *World Economy* 20 (2): 221–39.

Beeby, M., S. Hall, and A. Marcet. 2001. "Expectation Formation and the 1990s ERM Crisis." https://www2.le.ac.uk/departments/economics/people/shall/online-papers/expectations-formation.

Bergoeing, R., P. J. Koheoe, T. J. Koheoe, and R. Soto. 2001. "A Decade Lost and Fund: Mexico and Chile In the 1980s." NBER Working Paper 8520, National Bureau of Economic Research, Cambridge, MA.

Castro, F., J. M. González-Páramo, and P. Hernández de Cos. 2001. "Evaluating the Dynamics of Fiscal Policy in Spain: Patterns of Interdependence and Consistency of Public Expenditure and Revenues." Banco de España, Servicio de Estudios, Documento de Trabajo, 0103.

Chong, A., and F. Lopez-de-Silanes. 2004. "Privatization in Mexico." Inter-American Development Bank (IADB) Working Paper 5/3, IADB, Washington, DC.

Coatsworth, J. H., and G. T. Casares. 2002. "Institutions and Long-Run Economic Performance in Mexico and Spain, 1800–00." Article written for the 13th Congress of the International Economic History Association in Buenos Aires, June.

Cyper, J. M. 1996. "Mexico: Financial Fragility or Structural Crisis?" *Journal of Economic Issues* XXX (2): 451–61.

De Juan, A. 1993. "Dealing with Problem Banks: The Case of Spain (1978–84)." In *Transformation of the Banking System: Portfolio Restructuring, Privatization and the Payment System*, edited by H. J. Blommestein and J. R. Lange. Paris: Organisation for Economic Co-operation and Development.

De Seguin, A. 2004. *Le Mexique dans la nouvelle ekonomie mundiale.* Paris: Presses Universitaires de France.

Dornbusch, R., and A. Werner. 1994. "Mexico: Stabilization, Reform and No Growth." World Economy Laboratory Working Paper 94–08, Massachusetts Institute of Technology, Cambridge, MA.

Espinosa, M., and S. Russell. 1996. "The Mexican Crisis: Alternative Views." *Federal Reserve Bank of Atlanta Economic Review* 81 (1): 21–44.

Garcia-Rubiales, V. 2004. "Unemployment in Spain: An Analysis of Labor Mobility and Young Adult Unemployment." Stanford University, Stanford, CA. http://www-econ.stanford.edu/academics/Honors_Theses/Theses_2004/Garcia-Rubiales.pdf.

Haber, S. 2005. "Banking With and Without Deposit Insurance: Mexico's Banking Experiments 1884–04." SCID Working Paper No. 266, p. 23, Stanford Institute of

Economic Policy Research, Stanford, CA. http://www.stanford.edu/~haber/papers/Haber-Deposit%20Insurance%20in%20Mexico.pdf.

IMF (International Monetary Fund) Balance of Payments Database. https://www.imf.org/external/data.htm.

Juselius, K., and J. Ordóñez. 2005. "The Balassa-Samuelsom Effect and the Wage Price and Unemployment Dynamics in Spain." http://www.cide.info/conf/papers/j1.pdf.

Li, C. A., A. Philippopoulos, and E. Tzavalis. 2000. "Inflation and Exchange Regimes in Mexico." *Review of Development Economics* 4 (1): 87–100.

Lusting, N. 1998. *Mexico: The Remaking of an Economy*. 2nd ed. Washington, DC: Brookings Institution.

———. 2001. "Life Is Not Easy: Mexico's Quest for Stability and Growth." *Journal of Economic Perspectives* 15 (1): 85–106.

Lutkowski, K. 1998. *Międzynarodowy System Walutowy, SGH*. Warsaw, Poland: Studia Finansowo-Bankowe.

Maddison, A. 1992. *Brazil and Mexico: The Political Economy of Poverty, Equity and Growth*. A World Bank comparative study. New York: Oxford University Press.

Maddison, A. 2006. *The World Economy: Historical Statistics*. Vol. 2. Paris: OECD.

Maxfield, S. 1992. "The International Political Economy of Bank Nationalization: Mexico in Comparative Perspective." *Latin American Research Review* 27 (1): 75–103.

McKinley, T., and D. Alacorn. 1993. "Mexican Bank Nationalization." *Latin American Perspectives* 20 (3).

Molero, J. 2001. "Industrialisation and Internationalisation in the Spanish Economy." ESRC "One Europe or Several" Programme Working Paper 28/01, 54, Economic ad Social Research Council, Swindon, U.K.

OECD (Organisation for Economic Co-operation and Development). 2002a. *Mexico: Macroeconomic Policies and Issues*. OECD Economic Survey, OECD, Paris.

———. 2002b. *Mexico: Recent Developments and Prospects*. OECD Economic Survey, OECD, Paris.

———. 2005. *Mexico 2005*. OECD Economic Survey, OECD, Paris.

Plizga, P. 2003. "System bankowy w Hiszpanii w latach 1974–00." Zarys Ewolucji, National Bank of Poland, Department of Macroeconomic and Structural Analysis, Materials and Studies Volume 160, Warsaw, Poland.

Randall, L. 2006. *Changing Structure of Mexico. Political, Social and Economic Prospects*. New York: M.E Sharpe.

Sachs, J., A. Tornell, and A. Velasco. 1995. "The Collapse of The Mexican Peso: What Have We Learned?" NBER Working Paper 5142, National Bureau of Economic Research, Cambridge, MA.

Sevilla, C. R. 1995. "Explaining the September 1992 ERM Crisis: The Maastricht Bargain and Domestic Politics in Germany, France, and Britain." Text presented at the European Community Studies Association, Fourth Biennial International Conference, Charleston, May 11–14. http://aei.pitt.edu/7014/01/sevilla_christina.pdf.

Sidaoui, J. 2005. "The Mexican Financial System: Reforms and Evolution 1995–00." https://www.bis.org/publ/bppdf/bispap28s.pdf.

Sławiński, A., ed. 1975. "Teoria i polityka stabilizacji koniunktury." Selection of Texts, PWE, Warsaw, Poland.

Teixeira, P. 2001. "Labour Market Transition in Portugal, Spain, and Poland." http://gemf
.fe.uc.pt/workingpapers/pdf/2001/gemf01_05_newversion.pdf.

Tortella, G. 2000. *The Development of Modern Spain. An Economic History of the Nineteenth
and Twentieth Centuries*. Cambridge, MA: Harvard University Press.

Witt, J. A., Jr. 1996. "The Mexican Peso Crisis." *Federal Reserve Bank of Atlanta Economic
Review* 81 (1).

CHAPTER 7

Why Has República Bolivariana de Venezuela's Economy Stagnated and Chile's Flourished?

Agnieszka Łyniewska

Chile and República Bolivariana de Venezuela are South American countries of similar size and population. They were both conquered by Spain and made dependent on their colonizer, and therefore share a similar history, cultural heritage and comparable social structures based on a system of large farms (Bulmer-Thomas 2003). In both countries, raw materials greatly influenced the process of economic development. From the 1930s until the present day, copper and crude oil have been the main source of export revenues for Chile and República Bolivariana de Venezuela, respectively (see figures 7.1 and 7.2; Hofman 2000).

This analysis covers the period 1971–2003, when a major difference in per capita income became apparent in the two countries. In 1971, they recorded a similar level of per capita income, that is, $6,603 (chained dollars with a base year of 2000[1]) in Chile and $7,231 in República Bolivariana de Venezuela. In 2003, this value was nearly twice as high in Chile ($12,140) as in República Bolivariana de Venezuela ($6,253).

In the analyzed period, both countries experienced economic downturns (see figure 7.3). In República Bolivariana de Venezuela, the pace of growth slowed down particularly in 1978–83, 1989, and 2002–03, which, cumulatively, cost the national economy 21 percent, 11 percent, and 14 percent of its gross domestic product (GDP).[2] Chile was not immune to economic downturn; growth in GDP fell cumulatively by 22 percent in 1972–75 and by 20 percent in 1982–83. Despite these two periods of inferior economic performance, the country has entered a sustainable high-growth path, since 1985. Consequently, Chile became a stellar economic growth example in the region and has been outperforming República Bolivariana de Venezuela ever since. The ratio of GDP per capita in Chile and in República Bolivariana de Venezuela changed from 0.75 in 1983 to 1.94 in 2003.

Figure 7.1 Share of Copper and Crude Oil Exports among Total National Exports: Chile and República Bolivariana de Venezuela, 1980–2004

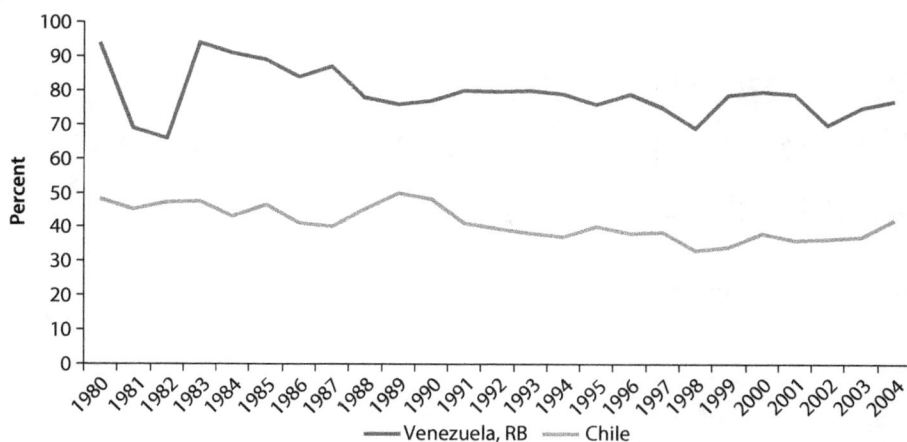

Source: Data based on Databases and Statistical Publications of the Economic Commission for Latin America: http://estadisticas.cepal.org/cepalstat.

Figure 7.2 The Ratio of Copper and Crude Oil Exports to GDP: Chile and República Bolivariana de Venezuela, 1980–2004

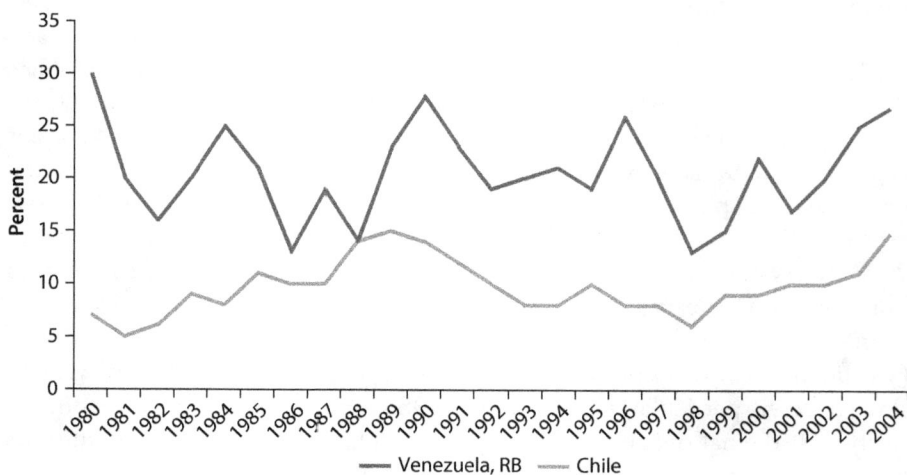

Source: Data based on Databases and Statistical Publications of the Economic Commission for Latin America: http://estadisticas.cepal.org/cepalstat.

In the analyzed period of 1971–2003, two subperiods have been distinguished: 1971–83 and 1984–2003. These periods are characterized by different growth patterns and hence will be analyzed using different research methods.

In 1971–83, the economic growth of both countries was characterized by significant downturns in production growth. The rates of GDP change were subject to great fluctuations (see table 7.1).

Figure 7.3 Per Capita GDP: Chile and República Bolivariana de Venezuela, 1971–2003

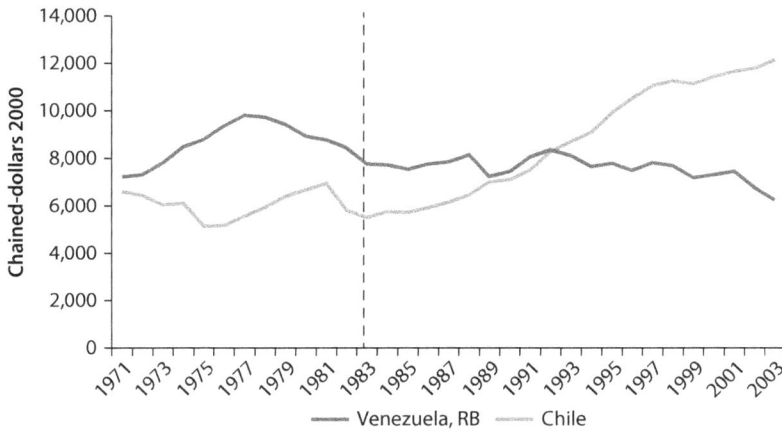

Source: Penn World Table 6.2.

Table 7.1 The Dynamics of GDP Per Capita in Chile and República Bolivariana de Venezuela, 1971–1983

	Chile—average growth rate: −1.5 percent	República Bolivariana de Venezuela—average growth rate: 0.6 percent
1971	A period of very uneven and mostly negative economic growth—the average change in GDP per capita amounted to −3.22 percent. The largest decline was observed in 1973 (−6.38 percent), which was the consequence of the policy pursued earlier by Allende—the nationalization of the economy and a fiscal expansion.	A period of relatively high growth of GDP per capita (3.13 percent on average) was a consequence of the oil shocks and improved terms of trade. After a slowdown in economic growth in 1971 when GDP per capita fell by nearly 10 percent, the growth rate of República Bolivariana de Venezuela was positive over the remaining period.
1972		
1973		
1974	An initial decline in GDP per capita (by around 15.93 percent in 1975), followed by a period of positive growth (5.18 percent on average in 1976–81) was associated with reforms that enhanced the economic freedom in the country.	
1975		
1976		
1977		
1978		A period of severe recession, with a significant fall in GDP per capita, particularly in 1980 and 1983 (average annual change in GDP per capita: −2.58 percent).
1979		
1980		
1981		
1982	Economic downturn as a result of a debt crisis. In 1982 alone, GDP per capita fell by 16.34 percent.	
1983		

The period between 1984 and 2003 was characterized by a stable and relatively high per capita GDP growth in Chile. Over that time, República Bolivariana de Venezuela's GDP per capita did not change (its slight decrease began in the mid-1990s).

- The differences in Chile's and República Bolivariana de Venezuela's per capita GDP growth in the second considered period (1984–2003) can be explained

Puzzles of Economic Growth • http://dx.doi.org/10.1596/978-1-4648-0325-3

Table 7.2 A Growth Analysis: Chile and República Bolivariana de Venezuela, 1984–2003
Percent

Country	Growth rate 1984–2003				Contribution to growth		
	y	*A*	*k*	*n*	*A*	*k*	*n*
Chile	4.06	2.35	3.73	0.85	2.35	1.12	0.59
Venezuela, RB	−0.95	−1	−1.95	0.92	−1	−0.58	0.64

Source: Based on Penn World Table 6.2.
Note: y = per capita GDP; A = total factor productivity; k = capital outlays per capita; n = number of persons working in relation to population.

mostly by differences in the productivity factor growth rate (see table 7.2). Negative growth in República Bolivariana de Venezuela reflected decreased efficiency in the use of production factors (the result of their insufficient use, blocking their flow toward more efficient sectors/companies).

- Another factor differentiating the economic performance of the two countries was the rate of real capital accumulation. In 1984, this index was negative both in Chile and República Bolivariana de Venezuela. But in the following years, it increased significantly in Chile, reaching nearly 10 percent in 1995, while it remained negative in República Bolivariana de Venezuela (except for 1992, 1997, and 1998). The share of investment in Chilean GDP increased from 13 percent in 1987 to nearly 25 percent in 1995, while in República Bolivariana de Venezuela it ranged between 10 percent and 15 percent. The key factor that triggered the increase in the rate of capital accumulation in Chile was foreign direct investment (FDI) (Hurtado 2007), accounting for more than 60 percent of the total increase in investment. FDI inflows amounted to 0.7 percent of GDP by 1990, 1.4 percent of GDP in 1990–91, and 7.5 percent of GDP in 1997–99 (Hurtado 2007). Throughout period (with the exception of 1991 and 1997), they were higher than in República Bolivariana de Venezuela. They also contributed to the improvement of productivity factors, among other things, through technology transfers.

- Differences in terms of the labor productivity were insignificant—their level was similar in both countries, with a positive contribution to the growth of GDP per capita.[3]

Differences in Economic Performance: Factors and Causes

The Years 1971–83
At the start of the 1970s, Chile and República Bolivariana de Venezuela both pursued a strategy of economic development that supported industrialization. This was to guarantee the state's independence from external conditions and factors by replacing imports with domestic production.

- In Chile, after the nationalization of the majority of industries in the early 1970s, the public sector was expanded by nearly 500 small and medium enterprises, which joined the largest companies operating in the sector of raw materials. The state became the largest employer. Foreign trade was controlled through a diversified system of tariffs (from 0 percent for capital imports to 750 percent for imported luxury goods, with an average fee of 90 percent of the value of a particular good). In addition, each import transaction required a permission granted by the relevant authorities. A system of multiple exchange rates was introduced.[4] In 1973, the ratio between the two extreme official exchange rates was 52 to 1.

• In 1973, República Bolivariana de Venezuela adopted a legal act according to which all oil used by foreign entities (the most important among them being Shell and Exxon) and several small Venezuelan companies were to be controlled by the Venezuelan State (Mommer 1998). Before the nationalization, multinational companies' share in oil production exceeded 80 percent (Mommer 1998). Petroleos de Venezuela S.A. (PdVSA), established by the government, became the country's largest employer, accounting for one-third of total GDP, 50 percent of budget revenues, and 80 percent of export revenues (Gelb and others 1988). In addition, as part of the La Gran Venezuela project whose implementation started after the first oil shock, a number of new state-owned enterprises were established in the aluminum, iron, steel, bauxite, petrochemical, oil refinery, and hydroelectric power generation sectors. In 1975, the steel industry (thus far owned by American companies) was nationalized and a state enterprise, Ferrominera Orinoco, was established (Cole and others 2004).

Chile and República Bolivariana de Venezuela were deeply affected by the first oil shock of 1973–74; its impact was, however, different for their respective economies: it contributed to a deterioration in the terms of trade and exacerbated tensions in the Chilean economy,[5] whereas it led to huge oil profit windfalls and initiated the economic boom of República Bolivariana de Venezuela—the budget benefited from an influx that exceeded the expected amount by $10 billion (about 5 percent of GDP). The fiscal income per barrel of exported oil increased from $1.65 to $9.68, that is, by 587 percent (Karl 1997).

In Chile, the external shock proved less dramatic than an internal blow. The policy of wage increase and government spending, initiated in 1970, resulted in a sharp increase in the fiscal deficit and inflation. The imbalance was exacerbated by the decline in world prices of copper (by 40 percent in 1971–73), the sales of which accounted for a quarter of budget revenues, and by progressive inefficiency in the public sector. In 1973, the deficit reached the level of 22 percent of GDP and the inflation rate exceeded 800 percent.

In República Bolivariana de Venezuela, stable economic growth was upheld in the period between 1971 and 1973, mainly because of a single, fixed exchange rate and fiscal discipline. It was only in 1973, during the first oil price shock, that fiscal policy was significantly eased.

The economic developments contributed to differences between the two countries not only in the early 1970s but also in the subsequent years.

Chile entered the 1970s as a very weak country with a closed economy. In the first half of that decade it underwent a turbulent period of transformations: from an attempt to introduce socialism by the Allende administration and the crisis of his policy, to a military coup and the beginning of a large-scale economic liberalization. Reforms introduced from 1973 by the Pinochet administration covered a number of areas:

- A stabilization program drastically reduced state subsidies with a view to restoring equilibrium in public finances. The reduction of the budget deficit (from 23 percent to 0 percent of GDP in 1977, Edwards 1996) was accompanied by severe monetary discipline (the procedure of financing budget expenditure by printing more money was discontinued). In addition, prices were no longer subject to state control.

- Following a fiscal reform, value added tax (VAT) was introduced to replace sales tax limiting specialization. Over the following years, the new VAT[6] became the main source of budget financing (Corbo 2002). The rates of personal income tax and corporate income tax were consolidated.

- In 1975–79 all nontariff restrictions on international trade were eliminated, and a uniform tariff rate of 10 percent was established (as compared to an average of 94 percent in 1973, Corbo 2002). A single exchange rate for all foreign transactions was also introduced.

- The social security system was reformed, and thus a transition from the PAYG[7] system to a funded pension took place. The process commenced in 1974 by reducing fees and simplifying the system of employee benefits. In 1980 a funded pension system was introduced. The positive effects of the reform were first observed in the second half of the 1980s. The reform established a direct link between individual contributions to the system and a return on them. As the development of financial markets accelerated, and the efficiency of resource allocation improved, a positive effect on domestic savings and capital accumulation was observed.

- Financial sector reforms started with the privatization of many state-owned banks and the entry of foreign capital into the sector (Gallego and Loayza 2000). Interest rate controls and lending restrictions were eliminated. The required bank reserves were drastically reduced. By the mid-1980s, the banking supervision system had not been, however, sufficiently strengthened.

- The labor market reforms introduced in 1981 abolished the privileges that had been exploited by trade unions. Changes were made to wage policy, severance pay and redundancy regulations, trade union activities, and the right to strike (Edwards 1996).

- The privatization program was developed over two phases. In 1974–79, almost all the companies taken over by the Allende administration were returned to their owners. Many banks were privatized as a result of opening the sector to foreign investment. This phase came to an end after the debt crisis of 1982, when a number of financial institutions were renationalized.[8] The privatization process restarted in 1984; the percentage of companies owned by the state in 1973 and that became privatized by 1996 amounted to 96 percent. The copper company Codelco was an exception (Edwards 1996).

- The reform of the health-care system led to the establishment of general insurance and free basic health care for the most disadvantaged social groups. Local government authorities were entrusted with the management of educational institutions following an education reform at the beginning of the 1980s. The provision of higher education services was opened to the private sector (Corbo 2002).

Reforms began to bring about a positive growth rate in the second half of the 1970s. The period of economic growth was interrupted by the debt crisis of 1982–83. In 1982, the Chilean foreign debt was estimated at $17.2 billion (70 percent of the country's GDP), that is, one of the world's highest foreign debt rates per capita (Edwards 1996). Foreign debt was incurred mainly by the private sector, whereas the public sector accounted for 35.6 percent of total debt (this figure also takes into account the debt secured with state guarantees; see Bergoeing and others 2001).

The crisis was generated by two erroneous economic policy decisions.

- In 1979, the *tablita* system (rolling devaluation set below the current inflation rate) was replaced with a fixed exchange rate of 39 pesos to the dollar. It was supposed to reduce inflation, which, despite drastic spending cuts aimed at restoring budget and public finance equilibrium, remained at a two-digit level until 1979. The system of full wage indexation generated, however, a slight reduction of inflation levels that (combined with a fixed nominal exchange rate) led to a significant overvaluation of the real exchange rate of the peso (Corbo 2002). The decreased price competitiveness of Chilean goods in international markets resulted in the increase of the current account deficit. In 1981, it reached 14.5 percent of GDP (Bergoeing and others 2001). The deficit was financed with loans incurred abroad by the private sector (given the high inflation rate, interest rates on loans in the national currency were much higher than those of loans in foreign currencies).

- The second mistake was the liberalization of the financial system without an adequate strengthening of banking supervision. Banks were unable to estimate credit risk. At the same time, the increasing competition in the sector required them to ease the standards of granting loans (Kalter and others 2004).

The growing current account deficit undermined the confidence of foreign investors, who began to withdraw their capital from the Chilean economy. In June 1982, the peso was devalued by 19 percent. One year later, foreign debt reached 130 percent of GDP and the budget deficit, as a result of the collapse of revenues, soared to nearly 9 percent of GDP. In 1982–85 the government intervened in the activities of 21 financial institutions, 14 of which were eventually liquidated (Gallego and Loayza 2000).

The crisis was very deep—in 1983–84, GDP per capita decreased by 16.34 and 5.04 percent, respectively, forcing the economy out of its growth path for a brief period of time.

In the second half of the 1970s, República Bolivariana de Venezuela became one of the weakest countries in the region in terms of economic performance. Since the positive growth trend was reversed in 1977, its GDP per capita was falling almost continuously until the end of the 20th century. Back in the early 1970s, República Bolivariana de Venezuela seemed to be one of the leaders in the region, capable of maintaining high growth rates. In 1974–85, the country's budget benefited from an extraordinary influx of oil revenues. It maintained a relatively high level of investment until the mid-1970s and the country was one of the most stable democracies in Latin America. In 1950–80, República Bolivariana de Venezuela boasted the lowest inflation rate among all the countries listed in the International Financial Statistics of the International Monetary Fund (IMF). In 1978, its creditworthiness was rated as AAA (Hausmann 1997).

It soon transpired that the oil shock had led to significant disruptions in the governance system and national economy of República Bolivariana de Venezuela in the period between 1973 and 1983. Large oil profit windfalls generated a number of inefficient undertakings and provided an incentive for rent-seeking.[9] As a result, the quality of the policy deteriorated significantly. Fiscal discipline was eased and government spending in the period between 1973 and 1978 increased by 68 percent (Clemente and Puenete 2001). In 1976 budget deficit reached 14 percent of GDP.

The economy was particularly adversely affected by such a policy upon the downturn of the oil market after 1982. Given the significant drop in oil prices, the country was no longer able to pay back its foreign debt. But the economy had began to shrink long before the collapse of oil prices.

The main reason was the sharp decline in private investment (Hausmann 1997), which in 1976–77 had grown quickly due to the inflow of foreign capital. Some investments were, however, unsuccessful. Following the adoption of Decision No. 24 of the Andean Pact,[10] at the time of Venezuela's accession to the organization in 1973, companies could only invest in certain types of activities. The pact provided for the distribution of different industrial branches among the member states (Astorga 2000). As a result, private investment focused on the following sectors: textiles, automotive, and construction (Melcher 1992). A sudden surge of production capacity in these sectors led to problems with the supply of raw materials and semi-finished products, which made full use of production capacity impossible and diminished overall profitability. In addition, the strong appreciation of the bolivar in República Bolivariana de Venezuela reduced the price competitiveness of local goods in relation to that of imported goods (Hausmann 1997).

The decrease in production was a result of inefficiencies in the economy's nationalized sectors and the fact that, at the time, these shortcomings were becoming more apparent. After the nationalization of the oil sector—accompanied by increased employment in the sector and rising overall operational costs—production volumes were in decline until 1985. A decrease was observed in budget revenues generated by the oil sector, as table 7.3 indicates (Clemente and Puente 2001). A similar decline in productivity was observed in the nationalized steel industry (Cole and others 2004).

The crisis broke out in 1983, after a collapse in oil export revenues. As agreed by the Organization of the Petroleum Exporting Countries (OPEC), the production volume was reduced, but failed to prevent a significant fall in prices. A large current account deficit and tensions in public finances followed. Fiscal deficit was monetized. As a result of capital outflows, foreign exchange reserves declined by over $10 billion (13 percent of GDP; Hausmann 1997).

Additional import restrictions and the system of multiple exchange rates (foreign currencies were sold on preferential terms to importers of basic consumer goods, raw materials, and companies paying back foreign debt; Mommer 1998) were introduced. A surge of inflation followed, and the national currency lost over 50 percent of its value.

Chile's and República Bolivariana de Venezuela's differing growth rates in 1971–83 can be explained primarily by the different extent and effectiveness of the institutional changes carried out in this period. Chile benefited from the liberalization of its economy. In República Bolivariana de Venezuela changes were conducted in the opposite direction, that is, toward restricting economic freedom.

Several indicators are used to compare the extent of economic freedom among the countries of Latin America.[11] The author of this analysis uses the indicator of structural reforms published by Morley, Machado, and Pettinato (1999), which is the only one to cover the entire period and outline the extent of economic freedom in each year (see figure 7.4).[12]

Chile made significant progress in implementing reforms in all the analyzed areas, whereas República Bolivariana de Venezuela did not make any major

Table 7.3 Importance of the Oil Sector in República Bolivariana de Venezuela, 1970–99

Indices in %	1970–79	1980–89	1990–99
Budget revenues from the oil sector/GDP	15.1	13.2	11.4
Budget revenues from the oil sector/budget revenue	70.1	60.7	59
Oil export/total exports	87.4	82.2	71.1
Oil export/GDP	23.0	21.2	20.5
Contribution of the oil sector to GDP	31.3	20	24.5

Source: Clemente and Puente 2001.
Note: GDP = gross domestic product.

Figure 7.4 Reform Indices of Chile and República Bolivariana de Venezuela, 1971 and 1983

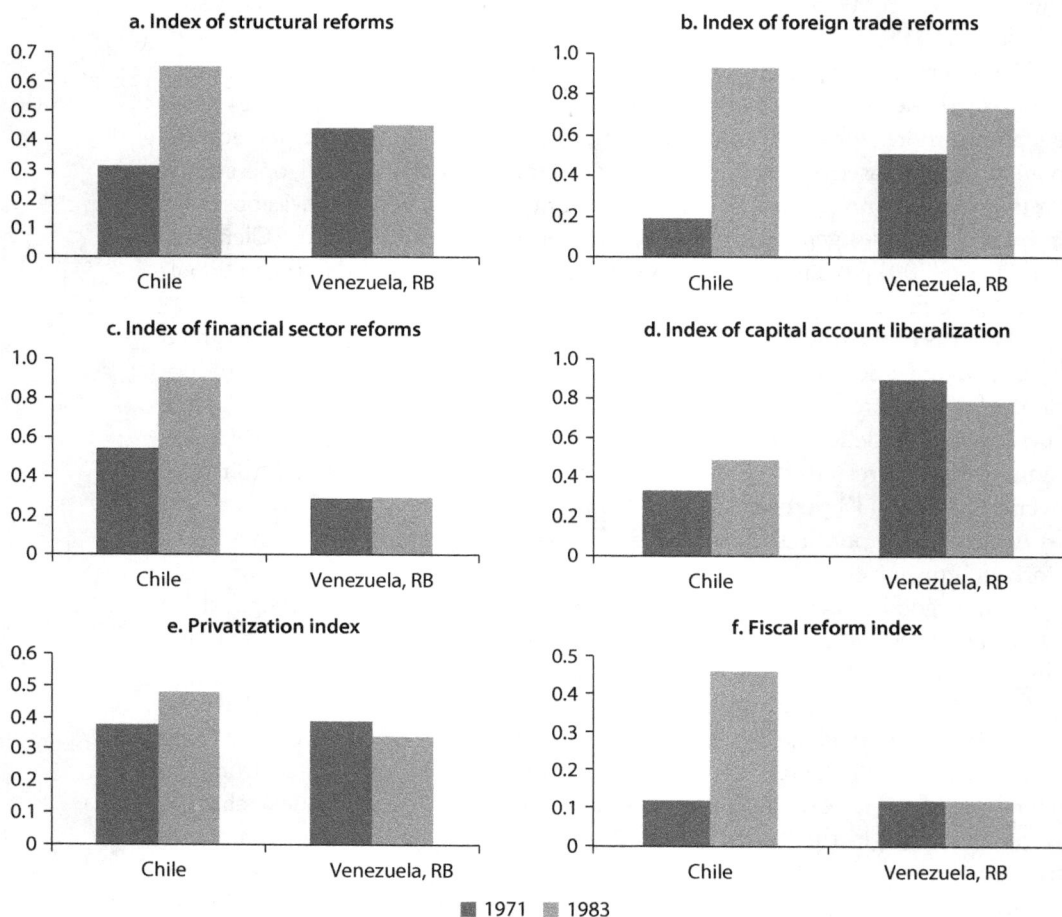

a. Index of structural reforms

b. Index of foreign trade reforms

c. Index of financial sector reforms

d. Index of capital account liberalization

e. Privatization index

f. Fiscal reform index

■ 1971 ▨ 1983

Source: Based on Morley, Machado, and Pettinato 1999.

positive changes and even regressed in certain aspects. The main areas of change in Chile were the tax system and the system of trade restrictions.

- When we compare the two countries in the period between 1971 and 1983, the greatest change is observed in relation to privatization, fiscal reform, and financial system reform.
- In the early 1970s, the private sector contributed to República Bolivariana de Venezuela's GDP more than it did to Chile's GDP. But in subsequent years, the state extended its control over the business sector (the nationalization of the two most important sectors of the economy, namely the steel industry in 1975 and petrochemicals a year later, was of particular importance). Although Chile had maintained the status of Codelco (a company engaged in copper mining) as a state-owned company, most other sectors of the economy were

privatized. Foreign investors were granted access to the mining sector and the processing of copper. In 1974–79, during the first phase of the Chilean privatization program, the number of state-owned enterprises fell from 596 to 48, and the share of GDP generated by the public sector decreased by 15 percentage points. (Bergoeing and others 2001).

- In addition, República Bolivariana de Venezuela maintained its tax system unchanged. The first significant fiscal reform took place in 1985 and was aimed at improving the process of income tax collection; VAT was not introduced until 1993 (Arreaza and Dorta 2004).

- The low rate of capital account liberalization in Chile (the only indicator pursuant to which Chile rated lower than República Bolivariana de Venezuela in 1983) was due to the introduction of temporary restrictions on capital flows after the debt crisis of 1982.

Key economic reforms started in Chile in 1973 and led to a period of rapid growth beginning in 1976. In the early 1980s both countries operated in similar external circumstances. Both were surprised by the negative shock caused by a sudden increase in global interest rates, the falling prices of their main export items, and the fact that they were cut off from foreign loans. Between 1980 and 1982 the price of oil fell by 21 percent, and the price of copper by about 39 percent (Bergoeing and others 2001). The crisis of the banking sectors in both countries was addressed by the governments through nationalization.

During the crisis, Chilean authorities did not reverse the program of reforms expanding the scope of economic freedom, apart from temporarily raising the level of trade tariffs. Instead, they managed to single out those elements of policy that contributed to the crisis and to change them. One of the first decisions made in 1984 and aimed at bringing the economy back onto a path of steady growth was, on the one hand, fiscal adjustment (including reduced government spending and increased taxation) and, on the other, the suspension of wage indexation and the introduction of a managed floating exchange rate (changed to a floating exchange rate in 1999; Corbo 2002). In addition, appropriate prudential regulations were introduced into the banking sector (Loayza, Fajnzylber, and Calderon 2005).

Meanwhile, the economic situation in República Bolivariana de Venezuela began to deteriorate even before the country was shaken by the effects of the plummeting oil prices in 1983. GDP started to drop in 1977 as a result of public sector expansion and the scope of regulations and restrictions imposed on private companies. Expansionary fiscal and monetary policies increased the economy's vulnerability to external shocks.

The Years 1984–2003

The difference in the rate of economic growth between the two countries in 1984–2003 was affected by the differences in the strength of the propelling institutions.[13] In Chile, following the reforms initiated in the mid-1970s, these institutions were significantly stronger than in República Bolivariana de Venezuela. In addition, after the crisis of the early 1980s, they were consistently strengthened. With the exception of one event at the beginning of the 1990s,[14] these institutions continued to be weakened in República Bolivariana de Venezuela as the scope of the public sector continuously expanded and the intensity of competition between suppliers was diminished.

Far fewer barriers obstructed international trade in Chile as compared to República Bolivariana de Venezuela:

- From 1979, Chile's economy was characterized by the lowest level of tariff restrictions in all of Latin America (10 percent) and a lack of nontariff barriers (with the exception of the period immediately following the debt crisis in 1982). The effective customs rate was systematically lowered following agreements signed by Chile and providing for the free exchange of goods (Corbo 2002).
- República Bolivariana de Venezuela increased its trade restrictions to force consumers to purchase goods produced by the nationalized industries. Until the late 1980s, average tariffs stood at 60 percent for consumer goods, 30 percent for intermediate goods, and 27 percent for capital goods. In 1989 the maximum amount of tariffs was reduced from 135 percent to 80 percent for consumer goods and to 50 percent for raw materials. Two years later, further reductions in customs duties were made (down to 40 percent) and some quantitative trade restrictions were eliminated. But after Hugo Chávez's failed military coup of 1992, the government withdrew from many of the initiated changes; after the new government took over in 1994, free-market reforms were completely blocked.[15]

The two countries differed also in terms of ownership structure in the main sectors of the economy.

- From 1971 Chile's largest copper mines, accounting for 85 percent of raw material production, were in the hands of the state-owned Codelco company. The copper industry was exposed to minor domestic or foreign competition. In the 1980s Pinochet's government attempted to introduce certain reforms with a view to increasing private sector participation in the market.[16] After 1990, the sector benefited from large foreign investments. Despite the decline in Codelco's production volume, the total production and productivity in the sector rocketed. In the 1990s, the average annual growth rate rose to 14 percent, as compared to 3.5 percent before the opening of the sector to competition (Cole and others 2004).

- In República Bolivariana de Venezuela, an attempt to open the fuel sector to private investment was undertaken in 1989 (Mommer 1998). Following the adoption of overly strict regulations (as well as, among other things, an inadequate level of property rights protection), the sector did not benefit from any significant influx of foreign investment.

In 1984–2003, entry barriers in other sectors of the economy were significantly lower in Chile than in República Bolivariana de Venezuela.[17] This is particularly

Table 7.4 The Number of Procedures and the Time Necessary to Register a New Company in Chile and República Bolivariana de Venezuela, 1999

Country	Number of procedures	Time (working days)
Chile	10	28
Venezuela, RB	14	104

Source: Djankov and others 2002.

apparent when one considers the different amount of time required to start a business. In addition, entrepreneurs in Chile faced fewer bureaucratic barriers impeding the functioning of individual markets (see table 7.4).

Another difference was the structure of the tax system in the two countries.

- In Chile VAT was the main source of government revenue. VAT does not affect price relations between current and future consumption, or the profitability of work as compared to benefits generated by transfers. The tax reform of 1984 introduced tax incentives in relation to various forms of private financial savings and profits generated through them. The reform of 1991 provided for a single tax rate of 15 percent on company profits (even though this meant an increase in the tax rate of retained earnings from 0 percent to 15 percent, but reduced the barriers to capital movement toward the most efficient forms of its use). The reform of 1994 slightly eased fiscal progression—the maximum income tax rate for individuals was reduced from 50 percent to 45 percent.
- In República Bolivariana de Venezuela VAT was not introduced until 1993. Only minor changes had been carried out until then. In 1985 the income tax legislation was modified to speed up and streamline the process of tax collection. In 1991 and 1992 corporate income tax was reduced from 45 percent in 1990 to 40 percent and 35 percent, respectively (Rodriguez 2001).

Last but not least, while Chilean authorities strengthened the protection of intellectual property, this was minimized in República Bolivariana de Venezuela. The high risk of investing in República Bolivariana de Venezuela was reflected by the cost of capital. In the mid-1990s República Bolivariana de Venezuela showed certain features of a failed state.[18] The lack of an effective system of property rights protection and a well-functioning legal system resulted in an explosion of corruption. In 1995 the Corruption Perceptions Index, elaborated by Transparency International,[19] indicated 2.66 points for República Bolivariana de Venezuela and 7.94 points for Chile. Only 4 out of 41 surveyed countries had perceived corruption levels that exceeded those of República Bolivariana de Venezuela. Chile, on the other hand, was classified among the 14 countries with the least corruption. Comparative indicators elaborated by The Fraser Institute are listed in table 7.5 (with marked differences for 1995).

GDP growth in 1984–2003 was influenced not only by institutional differences, but also by external shocks. While these turbulences encouraged Chile to rapidly combat the debt crisis of the early 1980s, they hampered the process

Table 7.5 Selected Indexes of Economic Freedom in Chile and República Bolivariana de Venezuela, 1980–2000

Year	Legal system and property rights protection		Scope of market regulation	
	Chile	Venezuela, RB	Chile	Venezuela, RB
1980	6.4	6.2	5.7	5.0
1985	5.0	5.3	5.7	5.4
1990	6.2	5.7	5.8	4.6
1995	**6.8**	**3.8**	**7.1**	**4.0**
2000	6.5	3.7	7.0	5.2
Average	6.18	4.94	6.26	4.84

Source: Compilation based on data provided by the Fraser Institute: http://www.freetheworld.co.
Note: Bold values signify marked differences in values between Chile and Venezuela, RB.

in the case of República Bolivariana de Venezuela. Their negative effects in República Bolivariana de Venezuela were compounded by macroeconomic policies and triggered internal shocks, which further aggravated the economic situation. In Chile the economic policy did not give rise to disturbances. The serious political change that took place in 1989—namely, the end of Pinochet's rule and the takeover of power by the first democratically elected government—proceeded without conflicts [Hurtado 2007).[20]

In the second half of the 1980s, the terms of trade in Chile improved greatly. From 1986 to 1990 copper prices increased by more than 50 percent and remained at a relatively high level over the following seven years.

Meanwhile, oil prices had been declining steadily since the mid-1980s, with one interlude—1990–91—which was the consequence of the Gulf War. The significant drop in oil prices provided a strong shock to the Venezuelan economy, as it was not prepared for such a development. In 1980–89 per capita earnings from oil exports fell by 66.4 percent (this amount corresponded to 17.7 percent of GDP in 1980) (Hausmann 1997). The decline in oil prices was preceded by the government's decision to increase public investment to reduce the unemployment rate (12.1 percent at the time).

The program of economy stabilization in 1983–84 triggered a budget surplus and reduced the inflation rate to 9.1 percent (Rodriguez 2001) in República Bolivariana de Venezuela. The government was convinced that additional public spending could accelerate the growth of GDP, as it would increase the use of the available production capacity. But the decision concerning fiscal expansion was taken when a sudden drop in oil prices occurred in 1986. The government's failure to adapt public spending to the reduced revenues from oil exports deepened the budget deficit and led investors to abandon the domestic currency, which was additionally amplified by devaluation expectations. Following the observed shrinking of foreign reserves, the government decided to devalue the bolivar by 93 percent in December 1986 (Hausmann 1997). In 1987 and 1988 fiscal policy remained expansionary. The rising public finance deficit resulted in further capital outflows, which forced the government to devalue the currency even further. The surge in the inflation rate was hampered by administrative price controls.

Consequently, the official price did not even suffice to cover the technical costs[21] of production (Mommer 1998). This led to a drop in supply. At the same time, abandoning the national currency—as an increasing mass of money was issued to cover the fiscal deficit—triggered increased demand. Consequently, Venezuelan society suffered from a shortage of basic goods. In 1989 the government doubled domestic fuel prices under a stabilization program. In response to this growth, public transport operators raised their prices without the government issuing a formal announcement relating to ticket prices. The increase in prices sparked mass protests of workers whose real wages had been falling for 10 years. Over 2,000 people died in the Caracazo[22] riots that erupted in all major cities.

In 1990–91, the Gulf War brought an unexpected increase in government revenue. The income generated in this manner was used to finance additional public spending, which, in turn, boosted the country's economic activity. The economic recovery did not, however, last long. In 1992–94, production in all other sectors of the economy dropped significantly. The situation was worsened by the financial crisis in 1994, which led to a complete collapse of financial intermediation. It cost 13 percent of GDP in 1994 and 4 percent of GDP in the next year (Rodriguez 2001). Dramatic production fluctuations occurred repeatedly over the following years.

Economic downturns were accompanied by political destabilization. Two failed coups took place in 1992 alone. In 1993, the president was removed from office on charges of corruption. In 1994, the new president first triggered (by introducing restrictions on currency conversion) and then exacerbated a banking crisis, eventually resulting in the closing of the country's biggest bank—Banco Latino (owned by a group associated with the previous administration). Public discontent boosted the popularity ratings of a populist politician, Hugo Chávez, who took over in 1998. In 2002 PDVSA strikes and the fuel shortages they generated (due to a production downtime of 2 months) stirred up social discontent. Chávez was temporarily removed from office. In the following two years, the country was ruled by two interim presidents, until a referendum was held in August 2004. This was won by Chávez, who became the country's president.

Social conflicts in República Bolivariana de Venezuela were stirred up by changes in income distribution in the period between 1989 and 1998, and by the resulting growth of income disparities (see table 7.6). Macroeconomic instability increased both the risk of investment and the cost of capital (Hausmann 1997). This in turn led to an increased share of wages in total income, at the expense of the share of labor remuneration.

The stabilization of the macroeconomic situation after the debt crisis and the country's political stability enabled Chile to quickly regain the confidence of investors, including foreign investors. At the same time, continuous macroeconomic instability and growing social conflicts (that were the result thereof) discouraged potential investors, including the country's national enterprises, from undertaking any activities in República Bolivariana de Venezuela. In terms of macroeconomic stability, the differences between the two countries were due to

Table 7.6 Distribution of National Income in República Bolivariana de Venezuela, 1950–98
Percent

Years	The share of wages and salaries in the national income (annual average)	The share of corporate profits, dividends, and loan interest repayments in the national income (annual average)
1950–60	47	53
1960–70	46	54
1970–80	49	51
1980–88	46	54
1989–98	36	64

Source: Di John 2005.

the different external shocks that affected them, and their respective macroeconomic policies. But the ability to overcome these shock—and the nature of their macroeconomic policy—were determined by their fiscal and monetary policies, which in turn depended on the strength of their stabilizing institutions.

Both countries attempted to reduce the vulnerability of their economies to fluctuations in commodity export prices, through the creation of stabilization funds. But this process started much earlier in Chile than in República Bolivariana de Venezuela. In addition, only Chile would consistently abide by the established rules (which were soon relaxed in República Bolivariana de Venezuela).

- The Copper Stabilization Fund (Fondo de Compensación del Cobre) was established in Chile in 1985 (it started operations two years later). Its task was to stabilize, on the one hand, tax revenues, and on the other to accumulate foreign exchange reserves (with a view to maintaining the desired foreign exchange rate). But even before the institution started its operations, when copper prices were higher than the limit established on the basis of the six previous years' average, the immense profits generated through the sale of copper were not used to finance additional public expenditure, but were earmarked to repay public debt (Jimenez and Tromben 2006). The fund fulfilled its functions, reducing the fluctuations caused by changes in copper prices. When in the early 1990s, copper prices were high, the fund accumulated resources. When prices fell sharply in 1998, the government used its assets to finance part of the planned expenditure (Spilimbergo 1999). The fund was also used by the government to repay the debt incurred with the central bank and corresponding to the private foreign debt, taken over by the government after the 1982 crisis.

- The Venezuelan Macroeconomic Stabilization Fund (Fondo de Inversión para la Estabilización Macroeconómica), designed to protect the budget and the economy from fluctuations in world oil prices, was only created in 1998. Initially, certain amounts could be paid out only after having been approved by congress, if in a given year oil gains were lower than the set level, or if the fund's resources exceeded 80 percent of the average annual income for the previous five years (in the latter case, they could only be spent on debt repayment and capital expenditure of regional government authorities). Nevertheless, back in 1999, reference prices were significantly reduced and the president was given the right to make independent decisions about the use of the fund for social purposes and investments, or the repayment of debt. It was also decided that the fund would only receive every other dollar once prices increased over the set limit (Jimenez and Tromben 2006).

Only the Chilean fiscal policy was conducted with strict discipline. It was strengthened by public sector borrowing limits specified in the legal provisions.

- In Chile, budget deficit periods were offset by periods of surplus when the rapid growth of the economy helped significantly reduce the ratio of public debt to GDP. Regional authorities were no longer allowed to incur debts and monetize deficit. In 2000, the new government adopted the rule of maintaining a surplus in public finances amounting to 1 percent of GDP over each economic cycle. The size of the recurring adjustments necessary to meet the fixed goal was determined by independent experts, which increased the target's credibility. The previous government also maintained a surplus—the only exception was the period of the Asian financial crisis in 1997–98, which brought a significant drop in the price of copper (at the time, an important source of budget revenue).
- Venezuelan fiscal policy was procyclical, and therefore fluctuations in economic activity were magnified. Any additional income from oil exports was immediately spent. At the same time, no rules limiting the growth of spending had been established. The increase in spending often continued despite significant income reductions (for instance, in 1981–83 and 1986).

The two countries also differed in terms of the central bank's institutional legitimacy, which had an impact on the manner in which monetary policy was conducted.

- After the surge of inflation in the early 1970s, Chile pursued a consistent monetary policy focused on ensuring price stability (although the process of disinflation was extended by the crisis of the early 1980s), which was the consequence of maintaining (for a long time and in conditions of full inflation indexation of wages) a fixed exchange rate, which was supposed to ensure the credibility of the central bank of Chile. In 1989 the central bank was granted autonomy. In the early 1990s it adopted an inflation targeting regime, which helped reduce inflation to a low level, and later—in 1999–2003—maintain it at an average rate of 2.6 percent (World Development Indicators 2004).

- In República Bolivariana de Venezuela, inflation in 1984–2003 increased significantly in comparison with the previous period (see table 7.7). Until the crisis of 1982–83, the bolivar was a stable currency. It was later repeatedly devalued.

Table 7.7 Average Annual Changes in Inflation: Chile and República Bolivariana de Venezuela, 1960–2002

Percent

Country	1960–70	1970–80	1980–90	1990–98	1998–2002
Chile	26.6	174.6	21.4	12.7	3.5
Venezuela, RB	1.0	6.6	23.0	50.1	23.4

Source: Di John 2005.

In the early 1990s, the central bank was granted a certain degree of autonomy, but began to gradually lose it from 1998 onwards (Di John 2005). Relative prices in República Bolivariana de Venezuela were subject to disruptions not only through a high inflation rate, but also as a result of administrative controls.

After the banking crisis of the early 1980s, only Chile introduced a modern system of supervision and withdrew from banking activities.

- In 1986 the Bank and Financial Institution Surveillance Authority (SBIF) in Chile was endowed with new powers, which were supposed to limit the risks taken by banks. Restrictions were introduced to limit banks' dealings with affiliated clients, systems assessing the quality of banking investment were developed, and the banks were obligated to abide by the requirements set forth in the Basel Convention;[23] the rules of bank insolvency and bankruptcy were clearly defined. Banks that had been nationalized in the aftermath of the crisis of the early 1980s were soon privatized. Only one bank is now entirely owned by the state—BancoEstado, which holds 14 percent of the sector's total assets. The sector benefited from foreign capital inflows—assets held under its control account for 44 percent of the sector's total assets (as of 2002; Kalter and others 2004). The development of financial institutions was enhanced by the privatization of the pension system and by macroeconomic stability.

- In República Bolivariana de Venezuela the first attempt at reforming the banking system was made in 1993—the new law was to strengthen prudential regulations, increase capital requirements, and open the sector to foreign competition. But these changes were introduced too late to prevent another banking crisis. Despite the opening of the sector to limited foreign investment, their inflow remained low. The crisis of 1994–95 led to a large-scale capital outflow from República Bolivariana de Venezuela. Foreign exchange reserves decreased by 28 percent (Blavy 2006). The ratio of domestic loans to GDP fell from over 30 percent of GDP before the crisis to 19 percent of GDP in 1996 (Rodriguez 2001). The state's large share in the banking sector was further increased. The state intervened in the operations of 17 financial institutions, including 9 banks that were nationalized and 7 (including 1 financial group) that were wound up. The privatization of institutions taken over during the crisis started in 1996. Nevertheless, the state maintained its prevailing share in the sector.[24]

After the currency crisis of the early 1980s, Chile carefully monitored portfolio capital flows to prevent large fluctuations. When in the early 1990s, the inflow of portfolio capital to developing countries increased, the so-called *encaje* was introduced, which was a requirement for investors to deposit 20 percent of their funds for one year in a non–interest-bearing account with the central bank (this percentage was subsequently increased to 30 percent). These limitations remained in force until 1998. While restrictions on capital inflows were imposed, the outflows were gradually liberalized (a consequence of reinforced intellectual property protection). Despite a certain degree of liberalization of the Venezuelan financial markets in 1993, the level of development of capital markets remained low throughout the 1990s (Rodriguez 2001).

The difference in per capita GDP growth in 1984–2003 between Chile and República Bolivariana de Venezuela stemmed from the strength of their propelling institutions, the number and nature of the shocks experienced, their respective macroeconomic policies, and the situation of the stabilizing institutions that determined them. The Chilean institutions—both propelling and stabilizing—were far stronger than those of República Bolivariana de Venezuela. Moreover, unlike República Bolivariana de Venezuela, Chile systematically reinforced them. It is true that Chile experienced fewer external shocks than República Bolivariana de Venezuela, but it was also able to deal with them in a more effective manner due to its disciplined macroeconomic policies. In República Bolivariana de Venezuela the macroeconomic policy enhanced the destabilizing economic effects of external shocks. The scale of these negative effects resulted in internal shocks, which Chile managed to avoid.

Summary and Conclusions

The purpose of this chapter was to identify the sources of profound differences in economic performance between Chile and República Bolivariana de Venezuela in 1971–2003. In the early 1970s the two countries had a similar per capita income, they shared a common history and elements of political and social legacy, also exports of raw materials were key to both national economies.

In 1971–2003, both Chile and República Bolivariana de Venezuela experienced periods of growing statism in their economic policy. In Chile, however, it was only a short episode (Allende's socialist experiment in 1971–73), while in República Bolivariana de Venezuela this policy direction was maintained nearly for the entire period covered by the analysis (with its culmination being Chávez's populist administration elected in 1998). During these periods, state-owned enterprises grew in both countries; market mechanisms were additionally disturbed by administrative price controls and restrictions imposed on freedom of entry into the market—and constrained business activity in many sectors of the economy, especially in the sector of raw materials: copper in Chile and oil in República Bolivariana de Venezuela. Furthermore, severe restrictions on foreign trade and capital flows were imposed.

In Chile, the statist experiment was interrupted after three years—once it had driven the economy into a state of profound imbalance with a giant deficit and unchecked inflation. A radical program of economic stabilization and reforms broadening the scope of economic freedom was initiated. This dramatic change in economic orientation produced positive results. From the second half of the 1980s until the end of the analyzed period (2003), Chile was the fastest-growing country in South America. In the 1970s, the pace of economic growth had accelerated, but was interrupted by the crisis. It took place in the early 1980s following a number of errors in the economic policy: maintaining a fixed foreign exchange rate with a full indexation of wages for inflation, the weakness of certain stabilizing institutions (lack of proper supervision of the banking sector), and external shocks (a sharp decline in copper prices that reduced export revenues, and an increase in interest rates that raised the cost of foreign debt servicing). But this did not lead to the reversal of free-market reforms. The sources of the crisis were quickly removed: a managed floating exchange rate was introduced, the price indexation of wages was abandoned, and a modern system of banking supervision was introduced. An increase in copper prices also facilitated the country's return to a path of rapid growth. It was used to repay public debt (including amounts due to the central bank and incurred in the process of banking sector nationalization). Privatization was resumed and the state withdrew almost entirely from the banking sector. The copper sector was opened to competition, including the influx of foreign capital, which resulted in a significant increase in the sector's productivity. The inflow of FDI explained the acceleration of capital accumulation in the economy in 1984–2003 as compared to 1971–83. It also contributed to significant improvements in factor productivity growth.

In República Bolivariana de Venezuela not only the propelling institutions, but also those that were supposed to stabilize the economy remained weak—which diminished the effectiveness of any pro-development incentives, while adding to the economy's vulnerability to shocks. The increasing scope of state economic intervention was accompanied by the weakening of macroeconomic policy discipline, which was not protected by any institutional restrictions. Until the 1970s public finances remained balanced. Despite the lack of a formally independent central bank, the bolivar remained one of the world's most stable currencies. But the large windfalls from oil exports led to an explosion of public spending in the 1970s and compounded the phenomenon of rent-seeking. Large budget deficits were recorded even before the fall in oil prices. These activities increased the vulnerability of the Venezuelan economy to fluctuations in the global oil markets. When oil prices dropped in the early 1980s, the state finances collapsed, which in turn resulted in the flight of capital from República Bolivariana de Venezuela (a scenario that was to reoccur on several later occasions). The government, unable to find a source of financing the huge deficit, had to monetize it. This practice, together with repeated devaluation, led to a long-lasting, high rate of inflation. Crises and inconsistent attempts to stabilize the economy stirred up social conflicts. These were fueled by the growing income gap, which was also the result of macroeconomic instability increasing the cost of capital and—in effect—the share of capital in total income. The deteriorating standard of living, particularly among the poorest strata of society, prompted the victory of a populist party. The election of Hugo Chávez in 1998 gave rise to a further increase in state intervention in the Venezuelan economy.

The comparison of economic performance in Chile and República Bolivariana de Venezuela allows to demonstrate how important are the propelling and stabilizing institutions in the context of resource abundant economies where both the high rents flowing into the economy as well as their excessive volatility are a common scenario.

Notes

1. Chain-weighted indexes offer significantly improved accuracy of GDP estimation versus real dollar numbers. They offer a method of adjustment of real dollar amounts for inflation over time so as to allow comparison of figures from different years. In this case, chained dollars reflect dollar figures computed with 2000 as the base year.

2. Less important decreases, amounting to approximately 9 percent of GDP, were observed in 1993–94 and 1998–99.

3. Results of the growth analysis carried out for the purposes of this chapter resemble those obtained in other, earlier studies (see, for example, Astorga 2000; Loayza, Fajnzylber, and Calderon, 2005; Solimano and Soto 2005).

4. There were separate exchange rate ratios, for instance, for copper sale transactions, consumer goods, and capital goods.

5. Following an increase in the price of copper in 1974, a drastic decline took place in 1975, while the price of oil rose in 1973–75 by over 400 percent.

6. Although originally a single rate of 20 percent was to be applied, in practice, there was a number of exceptions (agricultural products, except for highly processed foods, were exempt from the tax and higher taxes were imposed on some luxury consumer goods, such as soft drinks and alcohol, whereas tax rates for specific goods differed; with a few exceptions, services were also subject to tax).

7. Pay-as-you-go Social Security System means that today's workers pay Social Security into the program and money flows back out as monthly income to beneficiaries.

8. In 1982–85, the government intervened in the activities of 21 financial institutions, 14 of which were eventually liquidated; the remaining were rehabilitated following the Central Bank's purchase of their long-term debt (Gallego and Loayza 2000).

9. The attempts made by individuals, companies, and other organizations to obtain material benefits by influencing the economic environment or the legal situation.

10. The Andean Pact, Andean Common Market—Latin American Integration group established in 1969 by Bolivia and Chile (which withdrew from the organization in 1976), and which include Ecuador, Colombia, Peru, and (since 1973) República Bolivariana de Venezuela.

11. See, for example, Index of Economic Measure (1995–2005, annual rates, the Heritage Foundation); Economic Freedom of the World (1970–2003, data published every five years until 2000 and annually thereafter, Fraser Institute); Morley, Machado, and Pettinato (1999); and Country Policy and Institutional Assessment (1977–2004, data published every year, the World Bank).

12. The overall rate of structural reforms consists of five components relating to: trade reform, domestic and international financial liberalization, tax reform, and privatization. Each component contains a number of items selected to reflect the degree of government control, or in the case of taxes and tariffs, the degree of neutrality of the tax system. The trade reform index consists of two components: it measures the average level of tariffs and their diversity in a given country. The domestic financial reforms index assesses three components: the reserve requirement, interest rates on bank loans, and commercial loans. The degree of financial liberalization is an average of four components: sectoral foreign investment controls, restrictions on transfer of profits and taxes, control of foreign borrowing by domestic entities, and the outflow of capital. The tax reform index measures the maximum marginal tax rate on company and personal profits, the VAT rate, and efficiency. The privatization index estimates the importance of added value generated by the public sector. In each category, the indexes are based on a value between 0 and 1, where 1 represents the state of the economy free from any state intervention (Morley, Machado, and Pettinato 1999).

13. Propelling institutions determine the strength of the systematic forces of growth, while stabilizing institutions influence the frequency and severity of domestic shocks and the capacity of the economy to deal with external shocks (Balcerowicz 2007).

14. Promarket reforms introduced by the administration of President Carlos Andres Perez (president in 1989–93) until the coup of Hugo Chávez in 1992.

15. The first decision of the new Caldera administration (1994–98) was the introduction of price and foreign exchange control, which led to a banking crisis in the second half of the year (Ortega Alvarez 2003). In 1989–92, labor productivity increased, but by 1996 it was fully offset by the growing limitations and state control of the economy.

16. In 1982 the Constitutional Mining Law was adopted; it provided for foreign investor protection in the event of future seizures. Yet, the act was criticized by the political opposition and, as a result, did not generate any major investment in the sector.

17. For example, allowing private investment in infrastructure (such as a program of roads privatization) led to a significant increase in investment in Chile (De Gregorio 2004).

18. A failed state is characterized by an inadequate level of property rights protection. It is usually accompanied by a very low level of institutional transparency and, consequently, a high level of corruption.

19. Data available at: http://www.transparency.org. The scale of the indicator includes values between 0 (meaning that public life is perceived as totally corrupt) and 10 (meaning that the government is perceived as totally transparent).

20. Pinochet stepped down after losing a referendum and a new president was elected in the democratic elections.

21. Technical production cost = materials + wages.

22. Caracazo is the generally accepted term referring to riots that took place in República Bolivariana de Venezuela on February 27, 1989. The protests against the rise of public transport ticket prices in Guarenas spread over all the cities in the country. The violent suppression of protests by the government of President Carlos Andreas Perez resulted in hundreds of deaths.

23. The Basel Convention (1988) was the first international document regarding complex capital requirements.

24. In 2003, there were 51 financial intermediaries, including nine units owned by the state (Blavy 2006).

Bibliography

Arreaza, A., and M. Dorta. 2004. *Sources of Macroeconomic Fluctuations in Venezuela.* Banco Central de Venezuela.

Astorga, P. 2000. "Industrialization in Venezuela 1936–83." In *An Economic History of Twentieth-Century Latin America, Vol. 3: Industrialization and the State in Latin America, The Post War Years,* edited by E. Cardenas, J. A. Ocampio, and R. Thorp. Houndmills, U.K.: Palgrave.

Balcerowicz, L. 2007. "Institutions and Convergence." Studies and Analyses CASE 342, Center for Social and Economic Research, Warsaw.

Bergoeing, R., J. P. Kehoe, J. T. Kehoe, and R. Soto. 2001. "A Decade Lost and Found: Mexico and Chile in the 1980s." NBER Working Paper 8520, Cambridge, MA.

Blavy, R. 2006. "Assessing Banking Sector Soundness in a Long-Term Framework: The Case of Venezuela." IMF Working Paper 225, International Monetary Fund, Washington, DC.

Bulmer-Thomas, V. 2003. *The Economic History of Latin America since Independence.* Cambridge, U.K.: Cambridge University Press.

Clemente, L., and A. Puente. 2001. Choques externos y Volatilidad en Venezuela. Proyecto Andino de Competividad.

Cole, H. L., L. E. Ohanian, A. Riascos, and J. A. Schmitz. 2004. "Latin America in the Review Mirror." Research Department Staff Report 351, Federal Reserve Bank of Minneapolis.

Corbo, V. 2002. Reformy gospodarcze w Ameryce Łacińskiej. Warsaw: Zeszyty Bre Bank—CASE.

De Gregorio, J. 2004. *Economic Growth in Chile: Evidence, Sources and Prospects.* Santiago de Chile: Banco Central de Chile.

Di John, J. 2005. "The Political Economy of Antipolitics and Social Polarisation in Venezuela 1998–2004." Working Paper 76, Crisis States Research Centre, London School of Economics.

Djankov, S., R. La Porta, F. Lopez-De-Silanes, and A. Schlaifer. 2002. "The Regulation of Entry." *The Quarterly Journal of Economics* 117 (1): 1–37.

Edwards, S. 1996. "The Tale of Two Crises: Chile and Mexico." NBER Working Paper 5794, National Bureau of Economic Research, Cambridge, MA.

Gallego, F., and N. Loayza 2000. "Financial Structure in Chile: Macroeconomic Developments and Microeconomic Effects." Working Paper 75, Central Bank of Chile, Santiago.

Gelb, A., and Associates. 1988. *Oil Windfalls: Blessing or Curse?* New York: Oxford University Press.

Hausmann, R. 1997. "Dealing with Negative Oil Shocks: The Venezuelan Experience in the Eighties." Working Paper Series 307, Inter-American Development Bank, Washington, DC.

Hofman, A. 2000. *The Economic Development of Latin America in the Twentieth Century.* Cheltenham: Edward Elgar.

Hurtado, A. G. 2007. "Development in Chile 1990–2005: Lessons from a Positive Experience." In *Advancing Development: Core Themes in Global Economics,* edited by G. Morrotas and A. Shorrocks. Houndmills, U.K.: Palgrave Macmillan.

Jimenez, J. P., and V. Tromben. 2006. *Politica fiscal en paises especializados en productos no renovables en America Latina*. Santiago de Chile: Economic Commission for Latin America and the Caribbean.

Kalter, E., S. Philips, M. A. Espinosa-Vega, R. Luzio, M. Villafuerte, and M. Singh, 2004. "Chile Institutions and Policies Underpinning Stability and Growth." Occasional Paper 231, International Monetary Fund, Washington, DC.

Karl, L. T. 1997. *The Paradox of Plenty: Oil Booms and Petro States*. Oakland, CA: University of California Press.

Loayza, N., P. Fajnzylber, and C. Calderon. 2005. *Economic Growth in Latin America and the Caribbean; Stylized Facts, Explanations, and Forecasts*. Washington, DC: World Bank.

Melcher, D. 1992. *Estado y movimiento obrero en Venezuela: Represión e integración hasta 1948*. Caracas: Academia Nacional de la Historia and Universidad de Los Andes.

Mommer, B. 1998. "The New Governance of Venezuelan Oil." The Oxford Institute for Energy Studies, Oxford, U.K.

Morley, A. S., R. Machado, and S. Pettinato. 1999. "Indexes of Structural Reforms in Latin America." *Serie Reformas Economicas* 12, Economics Development Division, Economic Commission for Latin America and the Caribbean.

Ortega Alvarez, D. E. 2003. *Attempting Export-Led Growth in Venezuela*. Caracas: Universidad Central de Venezuela.

Rodriguez, F. C. 2001. *Factor Shares and Resource Booms: Accounting for the Evolution of Venezuelan Inequality*. Helsinki, Finland: WIDER.

Solimano, A., and R. Soto. 2005. *Economic Growth in Latin America in the Late 20th Century: Evidence and Interpretation*. Santiago de Chile: CEPAL ONZ.

Spilimbergo, A. 1999. *Copper and the Chilean Economy 1960–98*. IMF Working Paper 99/57, International Monetary Fund, Washington, DC.

CHAPTER 8

Why Is Costa Rica Lagging Behind Puerto Rico?

Kamil Czop

Back in 1960, Costa Rica and Puerto Rico had roughly the same income per capita, and a similar population size and structure. Both had a democratic political system, and neither of them incurred outlays for an army. Despite these and other similarities, by 2003[1] Costa Rica's gross domestic product (GDP) per capita was only 67 percent of Puerto Rico's gross national product (GNP) per capita (figure 8.1).[2]

The economy of Puerto Rico, which is a dependent territory of the United States, has been studied mainly by U.S. researchers. Comparative studies focused primarily on the reasons behind the lack of convergence between Puerto Rico and the United States. Economic literature presents Costa Rica, in turn, as a positive example in the context of the economic disaster faced by other Central American economies. The reasons for Costa Rica's low economic growth (in global terms) in the second half of the 20th century—and reaching beyond the debt crisis of the early 1980s—have not been analyzed in depth.

Between 1961 and 2003, the average annual GNP growth per capita in Puerto Rico (2.26 percent) was almost 1 percentage point higher than GDP growth per capita in Costa Rica (1.29 percent). The two subperiods when Puerto Rico developed at a much faster pace than Costa Rica were 1961–73 and 1982–91. In the years 1974–81 gross national income (GNI) per capita increased faster in Costa Rica than in Puerto Rico. In the years 1991–2003 Costa Rica developed slightly faster. The following should be noted:

- In the years 1961–73, when the Puerto Rican economy developed at a faster pace than the Costa Rican, neither experienced any negative economic shocks.

- Both later experienced economic growth slumps (table 8.1). In the case of Puerto Rico there were two such slumps—in 1974 and 1979—which coincided with oil crises. As a result of the shocks, GDP per capita in 1981 was lower than in 1974. At that time, Costa Rica faced growth deceleration and

Figure 8.1 Annual Average GNP and GDP Per Capita: Puerto Rico and Costa Rica, 1961–2003

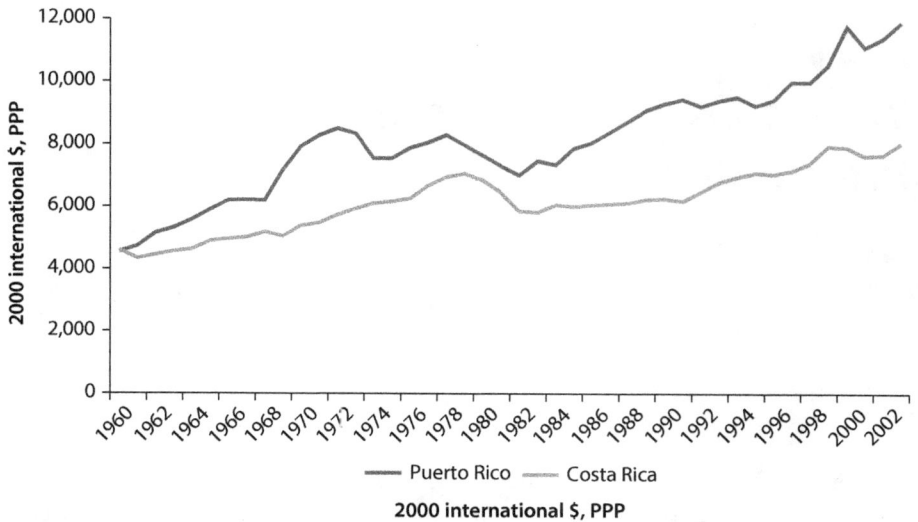

Puerto Rico ——— Costa Rica

2000 international $, PPP

Source: Based on Penn World Table 6.2.
Note: PPP = purchasing power parity.

Table 8.1 Annual Average GNP and GDP Growth Rate Per Capita: Puerto Rico and Costa Rica Divided into Four Subperiods, 1961–2003

Period	Puerto Rico (%)	Costa Rica (%)	Absolute difference (pp)	Ratio of GDP/cap of Costa Rica to GNP/cap of Puerto Rico in threshold years (%)	
1961–2003	2.26	1.29	0.96	1960	101.21
1961–73	4.74	1.95	2.79	1973	71.27
1974–81	−1.63	1.06	2.69	1981	88.42
1982–91	2.58	−0.44	3.01	1991	65.62
1992–2003	1.97	2.19	0.22	2003	67.34

Source: Based on Penn World Table 6.2.

experienced a breakdown between 1982 and 1991 as a result of a foreign debt crisis. Even if we leave out 1982 and 1983 from the calculation, when Costa Rica's growth slumped, in the remaining years of the 1980s the country's economy still grew at a much slower pace than that of Puerto Rico.

- Puerto Rico's average annual economic growth rate (excluding the breakdown period) had been slower from decade to decade, while Costa Rica's rate in the 1990s (after a period of slowdown in the 1970s and the crisis in the 1980s) developed at a pace much higher than the average for 1961–2003. In 1961–2003 labor productivity[3] in Puerto Rico increased on average at 1.8 percentage points a year faster than in Costa Rica. As a result, by the end of the period, an employee in Costa Rica was more than 60 percent less productive than an employee in Puerto Rico (table 8.2).

- In 1961–2003, the relation of working-age population to the total population increased by an annual average of 0.43 percent both in Puerto Rico and Costa Rica, which means that children below 15 and pensioners were maintained by a potentially increasing number of people of working age (depending on the labor force participation rate).

- Puerto Rico had a very low labor force participation rate among people of working age (47 percent in 1961, 53 percent in 2003)—well below the level in the United States (75 percent in 2005; see OECD 2006). In Costa Rica, the rate was higher throughout the 1961–2003 period (57 percent in 1961, 64 percent in 2003).

- The increase in GDP per citizen active on the labor market was the dominating factor behind the increase in income per capita in both Puerto Rico and Costa Rica.

- The Puerto Rican sector of the economy that registered the highest increase in labor productivity was industry (in 1961–2003 the sector attracted about 80 percent of foreign direct investments (FDIs) in Puerto Rico; see Bosworth, Collins, and Soto-Class 2006)—in 2003 a worker in the production sectors generated value added three times higher than such a worker in Costa Rica

Table 8.2 Decomposition of GNP and GDP Per Capita in Puerto Rico and Costa Rica, Average Annual Changes in Individual Subperiods, 1961–2003

Percent

Period	GDP/L	Demographic effect	Labor force participation rate	GNP/GDP	GNP/cap
Puerto Rico					
1961–73	5.01	0.53	−0.05	−0.73	**4.74**
1974–81	−0.13	0.49	0.02	−2.01	**−1.63**
1982–91	1.99	0.49	0.90	−0.80	**2.58**
1991–2003	1.85	0.25	0.33	−0.46	**1.97**
1961–2003	2.45	0.43	0.29	−0.91	**2.26**
Costa Rica					
1961–73	1.66	0.11	0.18	NA	**1.95**
1974–81	−0.12	0.90	0.29	NA	**1.06**
1982–91	−1.31	0.24	0.64	NA	**−0.44**
1991–2003	1.60	0.62	−0.04	NA	**2.19**
1961–2003	0.61	0.43	0.24	NA	**1.29**

Sources: Based on Penn World Table 6.2, United Nations Population Division, United Nations Department of Economic and Social Affairs.
Note: GDP/L—labor productivity defined as GDP per one employee. NA = not applicable.

and two-thirds higher than a worker in the Puerto Rican services sector. In 1961–2003, the Costa Rican services sector—dominated by public monopolies[4]—registered a negative labor productivity growth (annual average of –0.18 percent; table 8.3).[5]

- In the period 1961–2003, the most dynamic increase in labor productivity posted by the Puerto Rican and Costa Rican economies took place in the years 1961–73. The labor productivity of a resident of Costa Rica employed in industry increased by an annual average similar to that of a Puerto Rican resident (by 3.88 percent and 4.26 percent, respectively), but the growth rate of labor productivity in the Costa Rican economy as a whole was 3.35 percentage points lower (annual average of 1.66 percent as compared to 5.01 percent in Puerto Rico). This was primarily due to a much slower pace of changes in labor productivity in the Costa Rican services sector (annual average of –0.12 percent as compared to 4.4 percent in Puerto Rico).

- In the last subperiod under analysis (1992–2003), when, as in 1961–73, the economies of Puerto Rico and Costa Rica did not experience any sudden slumps in economic growth, labor productivity per capita in Costa Rica increased by an annual average of 1.6 percent, or at the pace similar to that of 1961–73 (1.66 percent). At the same time the growth rate of the labor productivity of an average Puerto Rican was 3.16 percentage points lower than in 1961–73 (1.85 percent against 5.01 percent).

- Almost the entire advantage of Puerto Rico over Costa Rica in terms of labor productivity growth over 1961–2003 is due to differences in the dynamics of technological progress (a) and human capital accumulation (h) (table 8.4).

Table 8.3 Labor Productivity (Annual Average Changes) and GDP of Employees in Individual Sectors, Puerto Rico and Costa Rica, 1961–2003

	Labor productivity (%)				GDP of employees (2000 $, PPP)		
	Industry	Services	Agriculture		Industry	Services	Agriculture
Puerto Rico							
1961–73	4.26	4.40	2.69	1960	22,108	20,274	7,591
1974–81	1.89	−1.76	5.62	1973	38,037	35,501	10,720
1982–91	2.44	1.83	0.88	1981	44,182	30,811	16,605
1991–2003	2.57	1.75	1.10	1991	56,222	36,949	18,118
1961–2003	2.92	1.90	2.36	2003	76,200	45,522	20,660
Costa Rica							
1961–73	3.88	−0.12	0.61	1960	15,987	21,109	10,642
1974–81	−0.62	−3.11	5.21	1973	26,235	20,794	11,514
1982–91	−3.05	1.70	−6.92	1981	24,953	16,143	17,289
1991–2003	2.68	0.20	2.41	1991	18,313	19,108	8,441
1961–2003	1.06	−0.18	0.12	2003	25,142	19,564	11,227

Sources: Based on Penn World Table 6.2 and World Development Indicators 2006.

Although the years that saw the greatest slumps in growth caused by external shocks have been excluded[6] (1974–75 for Puerto Rico and 1980–83 for Costa Rica), the results of the growth calculation for the entire period should be interpreted with a degree of caution. The growth calculation for the years 1961–73, that is, for the period without any shocks in the analyzed country and territory, produces more reliable results.

• Technological progress (a) accounted for half the labor productivity growth in Puerto Rico over 1961–73. The contribution of human capital (h) and physical capital equipment of the labor force (k/l) to labor productivity growth rate was similar.[7] In the case of Costa Rica, the main factor behind the increase in labor productivity in the subperiod under analysis was improvement in the physical capital equipment of the labor force (k/l).

Differences in Economic Performance: Factors and Causes

The Years 1961–73

Costa Rica had a much higher degree of economy monopolization by state-owned enterprises than Puerto Rico. From the end of the 1940s, state enterprises in Costa Rica had a formal monopoly over, for example, rendering insurance, telecommunications, and health-care services; and supplying electricity. The Costa Rican banking system, nationalized in 1948, held a monopoly over accepting deposits, granting loans, and exchanging currency. Private banks were only allowed to incur foreign liabilities in 1964; nonbanking financial institutions first appeared on the market in 1972 (see Goss and Pacheco 1999). In Puerto Rico the state monopoly concerned primarily the energy sector, water supply systems, and water economy.

Table 8.4 Growth of Puerto Rico and Costa Rica over 1961–2003 and in the Subperiod, 1961–73
Percent

	1961—2003[a]				Contribution to growth		
	y/l	a	k/l	h	a	k/l	h
Puerto Rico	**3.07**	1.70	0.40	0.97	55.34	12.96	31.70
Costa Rica	**1.32**	0.47	0.57	0.31	35.31	41.20	23.49
	1961—2003[a]				Contribution to growth		
	y/l	a	k/l	h	a	k/l	h
Puerto Rico	**5.01**	2.65	1.17	1.20	52.76	23.26	23.98
Costa Rica	**1.66**	0.59	0.93	0.14	35.51	56.04	8.45

Sources: Based on Penn World Table 6.2 and International Data on Educational Attainment.
Note: y/l = labor productivity; a = technological progress; h = human capital; k/l = physical capital available of the labor force. Bolded numbers indicate total growth that is further divided into key factors. Shading indicates key growth drivers for Puerto Rico and Costa Rica during those periods.
a. This excludes the years 1974–75 for Puerto Rico and 1980–83 for Costa Rica (these years saw serious slumps of economic growth in both, due to external shocks).

Puzzles of Economic Growth • http://dx.doi.org/10.1596/978-1-4648-0325-3

Costa Rica was also much less open to international trade than Puerto Rico (figure 8.2). In the years 1961–73, Puerto Rico's total exports and imports exceeded 140 percent of GDP (in 1968, the record year, this figure was 165 percent of GDP). In the same period, Costa Rica's economy openness indicator ranged between 28 percent (1960) and 43 percent (1973).

In addition, Puerto Rican entrepreneurs enjoyed a higher level of property rights protection. The Puerto Rican legal system is based on American law (with the exception of the civil code, based on Spanish tradition). Moreover, the verdicts of Puerto Rican courts can be appealed in the American federal court competent for Puerto Rico (that is, after the verdict of the Puerto Rican Supreme Court is issued)—therefore, the degree of property rights protection is similar to that in the United States.

In the years 1961–73, the state's fiscal position increased in both Puerto Rico and Costa Rica. Public spending in Puerto Rico increased from 35.3 percent to 44.2 percent of GDP, and in Costa Rica from 28.7 percent to 39 percent of GDP (figure 8.3). The increase in public spending in Puerto Rico was, to a much lesser extent than in Costa Rica, the result of social spending expansion. Forty percent of the public spending increase in Puerto Rico was attributed to the increase in spending of state-owned enterprises (from 19.5 percent to 22.7 percent of GDP; see Bosworth, Collins, and Soto-Class 2006). In Costa Rica, 75 percent of the increase was due to social spending, which rose from 8.7 percent of GDP in 1958 to 16.4 percent of GDP in 1971 (see Sanchez-Acochea 2006).

The conclusion is that propelling institutions in Puerto Rico in the years 1961–73 were much stronger than in Costa Rica. Stabilizing institutions, too—or at least those shaping monetary policy—evolved in a more positive direction in Puerto Rico during this period.

Figure 8.2 Economy Openness Indicator of Puerto Rico and Costa Rica, 1960–73

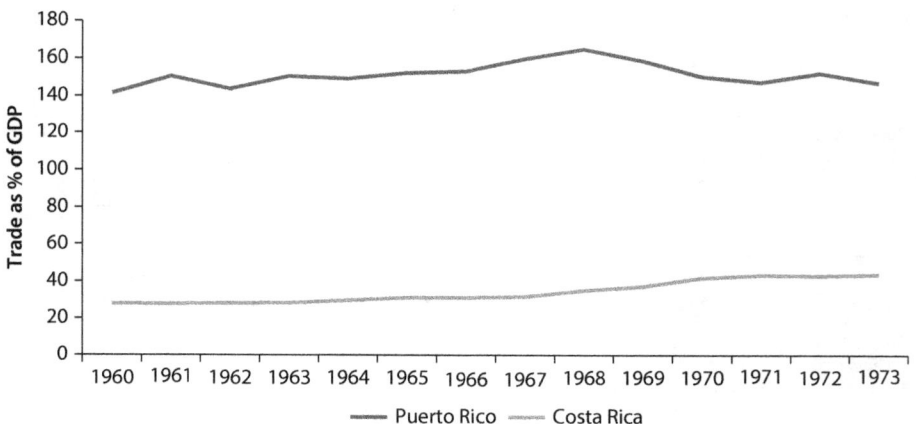

Source: Based on Penn World Table 6.2.

Figure 8.3 Public Sector Spending in Puerto Rico and Costa Rica, 1961–73

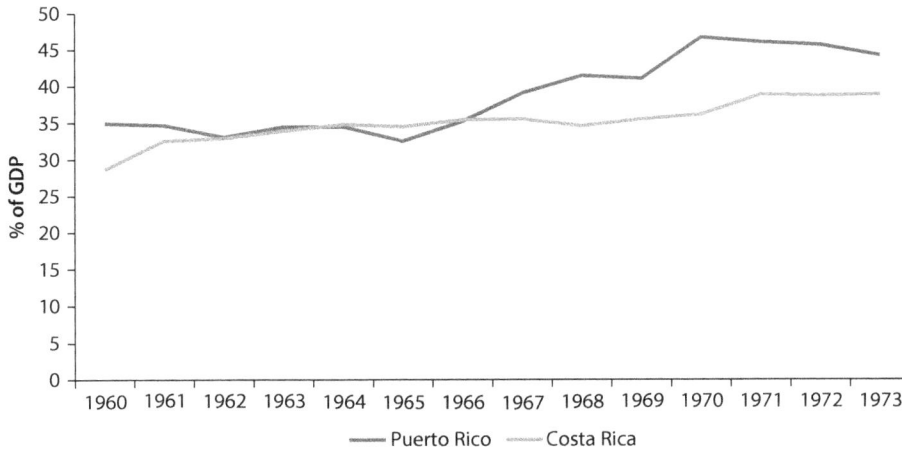

Sources: Based on data from the Central Bank of Costa Rica and Bosworth, Collins, and Soto-Class 2006.

The U.S. Federal Reserve Bank is in charge of Puerto Rico's monetary policy. Costa Rica's Central Bank is not actually independent of the executive and legislative authorities. The absence of its actual independence is proven by the executive's ability to dismiss the bank's governor and the fact that the governor's term in office is linked with the term of Costa Rica's president, that the five members of the board of directors have terms lasting only 1.5 years, and that the finance minister sits on the board. The main purpose of the bank, provided for in its statutes, is to "support the correct development of Costa Rica's economy so as to achieve full employment of the country's resources, while attempting to prevent or mitigate inflation and deflation trends."[8] In addition, a prohibition on the central bank formally providing credit facilities to the Costa Rican government and public institutions was only introduced in the late 1980s and early 1990s.

Inflation rates in both Puerto Rico and Costa Rica rose between 1960 and 1972 (in the United States from 1.4 percent to 4.3 percent, and in Costa Rica from 0.9 percent to 4.5 percent). In 1973 there was a sharp rise in inflation in Costa Rica, where it reached 15.25 percent (figure 8.4).

Although the institutions governing monetary policy were stronger in Puerto Rico than in Costa Rica, institutional constraints on public debt expansion were inadequate in both. In Costa Rica, there were none. The Puerto Rican constitution stipulates that in a given budget year the value of bonds issued by the Puerto Rican administration may not exceed 15 percent of average budget revenues from the two preceding years, but state enterprises are not covered by the constitutional debt issue constraint. In 1965–74 Costa Rica's public sector debt increased from 21.7 percent of GDP to 29.4 percent of GDP,[9] while Puerto Rico's debt-to-GDP ratio increased from 31.6 percent to 38.4 percent.[10]

Puzzles of Economic Growth • http://dx.doi.org/10.1596/978-1-4648-0325-3

Figure 8.4 Inflation Rate in Puerto Rico (U.S. GDP Deflator) and in Costa Rica (CPI), 1960–73

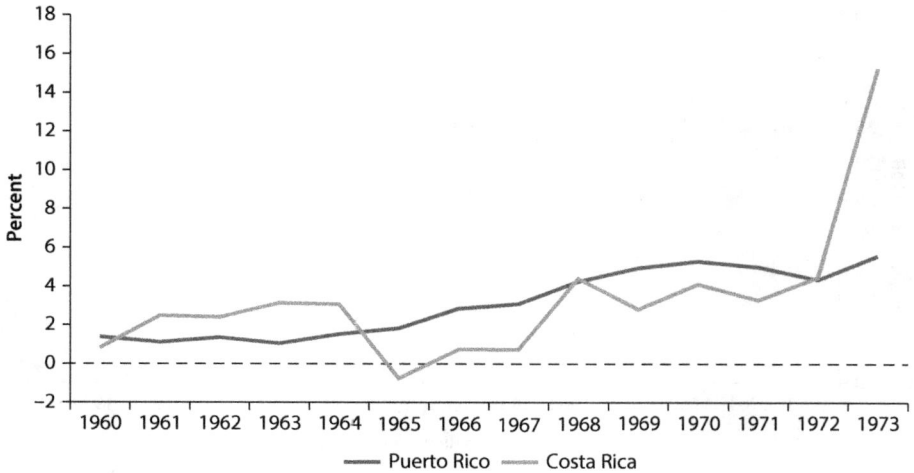

Sources: Based on data from the Bureau of Economic Analysis, U.S. Department of Commerce; Oxford Latin American Economic History Database.
Note: CPI = consumer price index.

It should also be noted that bonds issued by state enterprises to finance their operations accounted for 77 percent of Puerto Rico's public debt in that period. (see Caban 1989, 577). In Costa Rica, the increase in public debt was primarily due to budget imbalance: in the years 1961–73 the budget deficit was on average 3.2 percent of GDP (Rodríguez-Clare, Saenz, and Trejos 2003).

There were no significant internal and external shocks experienced in Puerto Rico and Costa Rica in the years 1961–73, and so it may be concluded that these were propelling, rather than stabilizing, institutions that determined the course of business activity during the period. Different economic development strategies were introduced in each: Puerto Rico focused on attracting foreign investments, while Costa Rica focused on industrialization in the framework of protectionism and state expansion.

The development strategy of Puerto Rico adopted in 1948[11] (right after the first general election for Puerto Rico governor) provided for industrialization on the basis of foreign (primarily U.S.) investments in labor-intensive branches of industry: textiles, apparel, textile industry (a similar strategy was pursued, among others, by Singapore; see Huang 2003). The development of industry— and of exporting goods involving high labor intensity—was supposed to bring about fast national income growth and a reduction in the agrarian unemployment rate (that had exceeded 20 percent at the end of the 1940s; U.S. Census Bureau). Puerto Rico's investment attractiveness was to come from: cheap labor, no tariff barriers in trade with the United States (with an external U.S. tariff barrier for import of industrial goods of about 12 percent in 1960;

see Irwin 2005), and a package of facilitations offered to foreign companies by the local administration. From 1948 on companies investing capital in the island were exempt from all local taxes (corporate income tax [CIT], real estate tax, license fees, excise, taxes imposed by local governments) for a period ranging from 10 to 30 years (depending on the region where production was located; see Dietz 1976). In addition, in 1954 the U.S. Congress adopted an amendment to the U.S. tax law, Section 931, which exempted profits transferred by American corporations operating in Puerto Rico from federal tax (see Rivera-Batiz 1998; the exemption was granted only when liquidating operations on the island).

In 1963, Costa Rica joined the regional integration group: the Central American Common Market (CACM). Economic integration was to facilitate industrialization in protectionist conditions. In the framework of the CACM, there was a single tariff for industrial goods imported from third countries (the average duty rate for imported industrial goods was 53 percent between 1963 and 1985) (see Bertelsmann Stiftung 2006), which applied to 90 percent of goods traded in the region and protected primarily food processing from external competition.

Good protection of property rights in Puerto Rico, openness to international trade, and tax relief for foreign investors attracted U.S. capital to the island. Initially, capital was mainly invested in the apparel sector, and from the mid-1960s in the petrochemical sector.

In 1961–73, foreign direct investment (FDI) generated close to 90 percent of the capital input of Puerto Rico's private sector (against 12.5 percent in Costa Rica) (Dietz 1982; Rodríguez-Clare, Saenz, and Trejos 2003) and the state's share in investments was two times lower than in Costa Rica (11 percent against 22 percent). The difference in the structure of capital inputs explains why technological progress in the Puerto Rican economy was much faster than in Costa Rica (its average contribution to labor productivity growth was 2.65 percentage points in Puerto Rico against 0.6 percentage points in Costa Rica).

The public sector invested a lot in education, both in Puerto Rico and in Costa Rica. In Puerto Rico, by the end of the 1960s and the beginning of the 1970s, input into education amounted to an average of 5.2 percent of GDP (see Rodríguez-Clare, and Soto-Class 2006), while in Costa Rica it was 4.9 percent of GDP (1958) and 6.1 percent of GDP (in 1971) (see Sanchez-Acochea 2006). Yet, while the educational system in Costa Rica was entirely state run, 11.5 percent of primary and secondary school pupils and 32.5 percent of university students in Puerto Rico in 1970 attended private educational establishments (see Bosworth, Collins, and Soto-Class 2006). Significant input into education in Puerto Rico from the 1940s—and permission for the private sector to render educational services (as compared to an entirely nationalized educational system in Costa Rica)—resulted in faster accumulation of human capital in the country (average annual contribution of human capital input to labor productivity [defined as GDP per employee] was 1.2 percentage points and 0.14 percentage points, respectively).

As a result of adopting different development strategies (opening the economy and industrializing with the help of foreign investors in Puerto Rico; protectionism and industrialization based on state-owned enterprises in Costa Rica), a considerable gap emerged in income levels per capita between Puerto Rico and Costa Rica in slightly more than a decade. In 1973 GDP per capita in Costa Rica was only 71.3 percent of Puerto Rico's level, against 101.2 percent in 1960.

The Years 1974–81

Puerto Rico's slump in economic growth in the years 1974–81 was the consequence of two oil crises (1973 and 1979).

A sudden increase in global oil prices hit the Puerto Rican economy hard as its energy intensity was several times higher in the 1970s than was Costa Rica's (table 8.5). The high energy intensity of the Puerto Rican economy was the effect of developing the petrochemical industry based on higher oil contingents[12] and tax reliefs in the mid-1960s. In 1974 Puerto Rico was the source of 40 percent of p-Xylene, 30 percent of cyclohexane, 26 percent of benzene, 24 percent of xylene, and 12 percent of vinyl chloride used in the United States (see Garcia 1984). The crisis started when República Bolivariana de Venezuela, the main supplier of oil to the island, reduced production in accord with Organization of the Petroleum Exporting Countries (OPEC) arrangements. At the same time, President Nixon decided to eliminate contingents for imported oil, and replaced them with a license fee on every batch of imported oil. In effect, the profitability of oil enterprises operating in Puerto Rico declined considerably—the profitability of the sector's assets declined from 25.8 percent in 1973 to 6.9 percent three years later. The chemical sector was affected to a lesser extent, although its profitability also slumped—from 34.1 percent to 17.6 percent (see Garcia 1984). The largest Puerto Rican enterprise, CORCO (Commonwealth Oil and Refining Company), went bankrupt, and 155 petrochemical companies wound up their operations on the island (see Caban 1989).

The recession in Puerto Rico was deepened by a slowdown in exports to the United States that resulted from problems in the U.S. economy (table 8.6).

Table 8.5 Energy Intensity of Puerto Rican and Costa Rican Economies, 1980

Oil Consumption and import			
Oil barrels/day (thousands)		Oil import % GDP	
Puerto Rico	Costa Rica	Puerto Rico	Costa Rica
200	16	6.62	2.35
Energy consumption for economic purposes			
Thousand tonnes of oil equivalent		Translated into $ thousand GDP	
Puerto Rico	Costa Rica	Puerto Rico	Costa Rica
8,042	949	0.25	0.06

Sources: Basis on World Development Indicators 1998, International Energy Annual 2004, and Oxford Latin American Economic History Data Base.
Note: 1980 was adopted as the reference year as data for earlier years were not available.

It was calculated that during 1975–2003 a 1 percentage point change (decrease or increase) in the rate of U.S. economic growth led to a change (with the same sign) in Puerto Rican exports growth by an average of 2 percentage points (see Bosworth, Collins, and Soto-Class 2006).

The slump was mitigated by tax changes in the United States. When after the surge in oil prices in 1973 U.S. oil companies wound up their operations in Puerto Rico, the U.S. Congress introduced an amendment to the tax law in 1976—Section 931 was replaced by Section 936. It eased the existing restrictions on the transfer of federal tax-exempt profit generated in Puerto Rico. Previously, the tax exemption was only due upon liquidation of operations on the island. After the change, the condition for tax exemption was to deposit funds in Puerto Rican financial institutions for at least six months prior to their transfer to the United States. This was conducive to the development of Puerto Rico's financial sector—the average value of the so-called "Section 936 deposits" in the 1980s amounted to approximately $12 billion (see Rivera-Batiz 1998) (in $2000), that is, an average of 30 percent of GDP (40 percent of all bank deposits). Another consequence of changes in the U.S. tax law was the decision of international corporations from highly profitable sectors such as the pharmaceutical, chemical (see table 8.7), and electronic industries to increase their presence in Puerto

Table 8.6 Average Annual Economic Growth of Major Trade Partners and the Export Growth Rate: Puerto Rico and Costa Rica, 1961–2003
Percent

	Average annual growth or real GDP of major export partners				Average annual export partners	
	Puerto Rico	Costa Rica				
Years	United States	United States	CACM[a]	EU/EEA[b]	Puerto Rico	Costa Rica
1961–73	4.45	4.45	5.58	5.31	7.92	10.39
1974–81	2.43	2.43	3.10	−1.79	2.01	4.82
1982–91	3.01	3.01	0.95	2.62	5.38	6.25
1992–2003	3.33	3.33	3.34	2.04	3.65	8.71

Source: Based on Penn World Table 6.2.
Note: CACM = Central American Common Market; EEA = European Economic Area; EU = European Union; GDP = gross domestic product.
a. Average annual GDP change rate for Nicaragua, El Salvador, Honduras, and Guatemala.
b. Average annual GDP change rate for 12 countries making up the EEA (after the accession of Spain and Greece in 1986).

Table 8.7 Profitability of Chemical and Pharmaceutical Enterprises in Puerto Rico and the United States, 1997
Percent

	Sector			
	Chemical		Pharmaceutical	
	Puerto Rico	United States	Puerto Rico	United States
Asset profitability	42.0	7.3	43.8	9.7
Own capital profitability	47.8	15.5	111.8	25.4

Source: Based on Bosworth, Collins, and Soto-Class 2006.

Rico—between 1973 and 1978 the total value of U.S. direct investment increased from $24.5 billion to $35.3 billion (in $2000; UNECLAC 2004). High spending research and development expenses were recorded in the United States, where taxes on profits were high, and most of the profits from sales were recorded in Puerto Rico, where they were almost entirely tax exempt.

The first oil shock oil was not accompanied by a deterioration in the commodity terms of trade in Costa Rica—to a large extent, their negative impact was offset by the "coffee boom" of 1975–79. In 1974, the index of commodity terms of trade stood at 85, while in 1978 it reached 130, and at the end of the subperiod under analysis it stabilized at 105 (UNECLAC 2004, 43). But due to the economic slowdown faced by major trade partners and the collapse of the CACM, Costa Rican export growth suffered a decline similar to that experienced in Puerto Rico. Yet, it should be noted that exports were much less significant to Costa Rica than to Puerto Rico.

In the 1970s, both Puerto Rico and Costa Rica saw an increase in the number of state-owned monopolies in the economy. In 1974, the government of Puerto Rico decided to buy a controlling stake in a local telecommunications company from IT, a U.S. company, and to create a public sea transport company. Both entities were in fact monopolies in their sectors. The public sector in Costa Rica expanded its dominance in the petrochemical sector and in fertilizer manufacturing. It was also active on the domestic market for cement, transport, sugar, and cotton. The expansion took place via the Costa Rican Development Corporation (CODESA), established in 1972. The corporation made new investments and purchased controlling stakes in existing private companies. As the corporation was exempted from certain provisions of the constitution of Costa Rica, it could consolidate the decentralized public sector—it was officially registered as a private company whose shareholders were the president and the ministers (see Bertelsmann Stiftung 2006). It was also granted unlimited credit with the Central Bank of Costa Rica.

As a result of the aforementioned purchase of shares in the local telecommunications monopoly and the creation of the maritime transport public enterprise, in 1974 the ratio of public expenditure to GDP in Puerto Rico increased from 44.3 percent in 1973 to 51.9 percent of GDP. In 1975, investors on the New York bond market demanded a higher interest on the island's debt securities, and then refused to continue financing the increasing public spending of the territory. As a result of the fiscal crisis, subsequent years saw a reduction in public spending (from 51.9 percent of GDP in 1974 to 41.6 percent in 1982).

In the second half of the 1970s, there was an explosion of social expenditure financed from the federal budget of the United States. In 1971 (and in practice since 1974), the "war against poverty" program initiated by the administration of President Johnson in 1964 was extended to include Puerto Rico. In 1980 food stamps (as part of the program) were distributed to 60 percent of Puerto Rican households (see Bosworth, Collins, and Soto-Class 2006). Federal transfers were increased in response to an increase in the unemployment rate after the first oil crisis (from 11.6 percent in 1973 to 19.5 percent in 1976; Bureau of Statistics,

ILO 2006). The transfers increased from $567 million in 1965 to $3.3 billion in 1976 (in $2000; see Caban 1989). By 1982 the share of funds from welfare programs (80 percent financed from the central budget of the United States) increased to 30 percent of the disposable income of an average Puerto Rican (figure 8.5). This resulted in a consolidation of low labor force participation of the island population—high benefits were not an incentive to work. In 1981, 53.3 percent of the working-age population were unemployed; at the same time, in Costa Rica the ratio stood at 40 percent.

In addition, in the 1970s Puerto Rico was affected by an abrupt increase in the minimum wage in 1974, when it was covered by the U.S. minimum wage law (Fair Labor Standards Act of 1938) for the first time. At the request of Democratic congressman Gillespie Montgomery, representing the state of Mississippi (home to small textile companies competing with Puerto Rico), the U.S. Congress equaled the minimum wage in Puerto Rico with the federal level (in 1974, $1.68 and $2.00 per hour, respectively). The entry into force of the new law was spread over the years 1977–81. The increase in the minimum wage in certain sectors of the economy of Puerto Rico, where in 1973 it was more than 10 cents below the U.S. level (mainly in apparel and footwear manufacturing), resulted in a decline in employment by as much as 32 percent (see Freeman and Freeman 1991) in the years 1974–83. This contributed to an increase in the unemployment rate from 17.0 percent in 1979 to 23.4 percent in 1983 (Bureau of Statistics, ILO 2006) (at the same time, open unemployment rate in Costa Rica increased from 5.0 percent to 9.4 percent).

Figure 8.5 Share of Federal (U.S. Budget) and Local Social Transfers in Income Per Capita in Puerto Rico, 1965–82

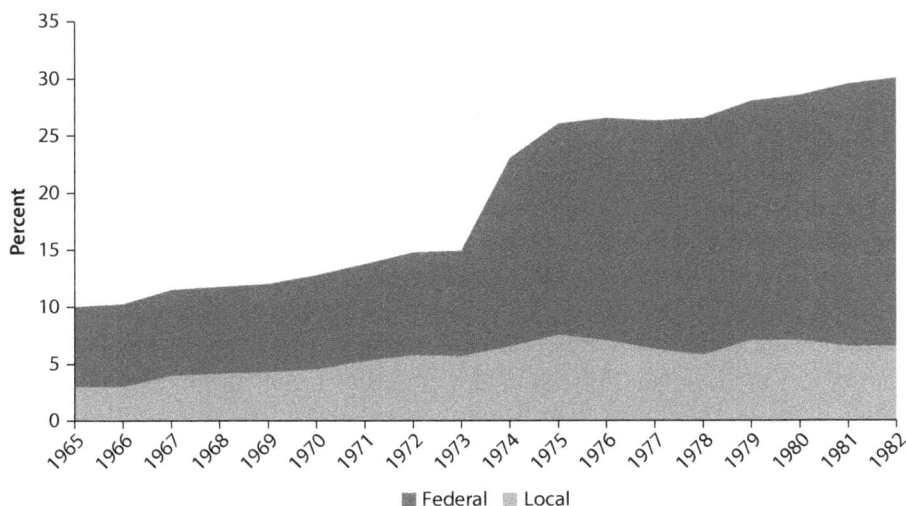

Source: Based on Bosworth, Collins, and Soto-Class 2006.

Figure 8.6 Public Sector Spending in Puerto Rico and in Costa Rica, 1970–82

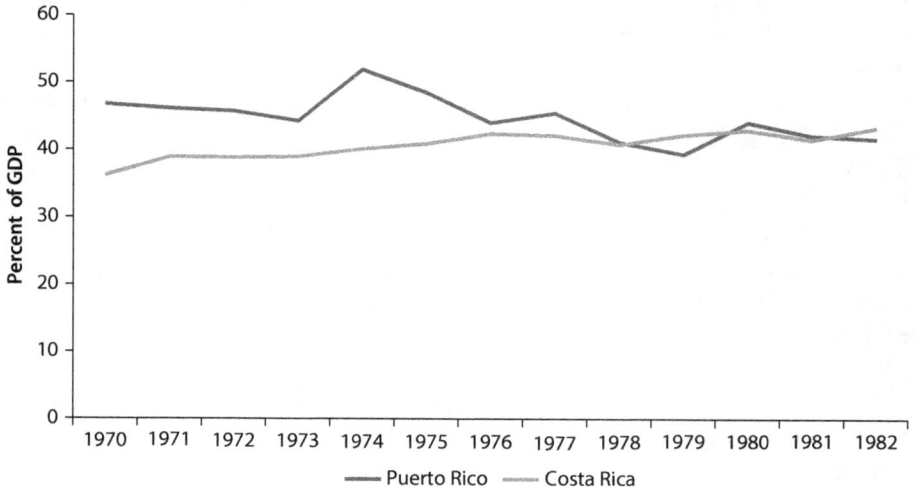

Sources: Based on the data from the Central Bank of Costa Rica (http://www.bccr.fi.cr/indicadores_economicos_) and Bosworth, Collins, and Soto-Class 2006.
Note: GDP = gross domestic product. In the case of Puerto Rico, public sector spending includes the spending of the island's central administration, local governments, and state enterprises.

In Costa Rica, public spending increased from 36.2 percent in 1970 to 43.3 percent of GDP in 1982 (figure 8.6). The increase in the country's fiscal position also resulted from an increase in the government's social spending (from 16.4 percent of GDP in 1971 to 23.6 percent of GDP in 1980; Sanchez-Acochea 2006) and the spending of state enterprises. The authorities spent all the windfall income from the tax on coffee exports, which between 1976 and 1977 increased their total revenues by almost 30 percent (Sanchez-Acochea 2006).

Both Puerto Rico and Costa Rica pursued macroeconomic policies that destabilized their economies due to the weakness of stabilizing institutions. In Puerto Rico they did not cushion the negative effects of external shocks to the growth of the economy, while in Costa Rica they strengthened the imbalances triggered by the shocks.

The expansive monetary policy connected with the central bank's dependence on the state in Costa Rica resulted in a sharp increase in inflation, already stimulated by external shocks. In the years 1974–81, the inflation rate ranged between 3.5 percent and 37 percent compared to 5–10 percent in Puerto Rico (figure 8.7). While the central bank managed to reduce the Costa Rican inflation rate following the first oil crisis, it did not manage to counteract the inflation at the end of the 1970s and the beginning of the 1980s. This was due, among other things, to the fact that state-owned enterprises in Costa Rica could borrow from the central bank with no restrictions whatsoever.

Neither Puerto Rico nor Costa Rica strengthened its institutional debt constraints. In Puerto Rico fiscal discipline was imposed by the market. American investors' refusal to invest in the island's new debt securities in 1975 forced the

Figure 8.7 Inflation Rate in Puerto Rico (U.S. GDP Deflator) and in Costa Rica (CPI), 1972–81

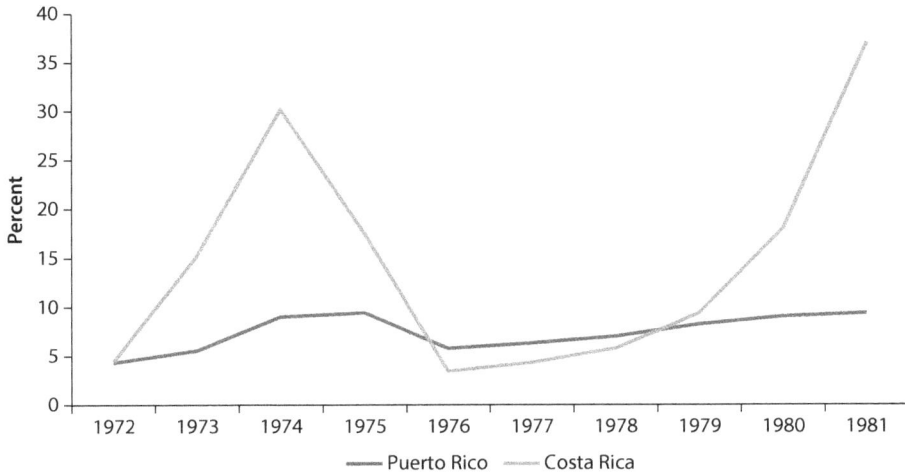

Sources: Based on data from the Bureau of Economic Analysis, U.S. Department of Commerce; Oxford Latin American Economic History Database.
Note: CPI = consumer price index; GDP = gross domestic product.

government to reduce public spending and increase taxes (a new 5 percent excise tax was introduced). The result was a decline, despite a shrinking economy, in the ratio of public debt to GDP, from 42.3 percent in 1976 to 40.4 percent in 1981. In the period under analysis, Costa Rican public debt increased from 25.7 to 51.8 percent of GDP. The increase was the result of maintaining high deficits. In the years 1974–81 the budget deficit amounted, on average, to 5.6 percent of GDP (compared to 3.2 percent of GDP in the previous decade). What is worse, despite increased tax revenues during the "coffee boom," the deficit was increasing from year to year (in 1975 it amounted to 2.2 percent of GDP, in 1979 to 4.9 percent, and in 1981 to 14.3 percent of GDP; see, for example, Clark 1997; Rodríguez-Clare 2001; Sanchez-Acochea 2006). The growing budget gap was financed with foreign loans. The first oil shock created favorable conditions for developing countries to obtain financing in international financial markets. In view of the high inflation in highly developed countries and the inflow of dollar deposits from oil-exporting countries, the real interest rate in the global market was negative. In addition, because of the economic slowdown in Western Europe and the United States, less developed countries that had not been affected by the oil shocks, such as Costa Rica, became a group of potentially interesting customers for large banking corporations. Growing foreign debt led to a crisis in the early 1980s.

The Years 1982–91
Differences in the growth rate trends observed in Puerto Rico and Costa Rica between 1982 and 1991 were due to two groups of factors.

The first group includes the debt crisis in Costa Rica and the disclosure of that country's economy structural problems—a policy of import substitution had led to low labor productivity and the inability of local companies to cope with global competition, while intensive state investment resulted in the creation of a number of inefficient public enterprises and an increase in the country's debt.

The first of the shocks that triggered the debt crisis was the collapse of global coffee prices. This coincided with the second oil crisis in 1979 and a twofold increase in oil prices, resulting in the significant deterioration of Costa Rica's terms of trade. In addition, in the same year, the new head of the U.S. central bank, Paul Volker, initiated an anti-inflation policy that was adopted by many developed countries, following in the footsteps of the United States. Interest rates increased abruptly in international financial markets. At the same time, the government of Costa Rica decided to reduce import duties on luxury goods (see Seligson and Muller 1987; Clark 1997).

In the light of a dramatic increase in imports and foreign-debt-servicing costs and an outflow of foreign capital, Paul Volker also decided to maintain a rigid exchange rate against the U.S. dollar. But because of resistance from trade unions, he did not reduce public sector spending, which could hamper imports and reduce demand for foreign capital. Eventually, Costa Rican foreign exchange reserves were exhausted in December 1980. Foreign investors started to become aware of the increasing problems of Costa Rica related to the repayment of debt and, taking into account the increased risk of the entire region after the outbreak of the civil war in Nicaragua in 1979, refused to grant further loans to Costa Rica. The delayed decision to release the home currency exchange rate was considered unconstitutional by the country's Supreme Court (see Seligson and Muller 1987) in July 1981 (colón devaluation took place only in 1982). An unofficial colón exchange market emerged, and a high degree of uncertainty led to significant exchange rate fluctuations (in the period from July to December 1981, amid large fluctuations, the currency weakened from 8.6 to more than 60 colones per $1). In 1982, the inflation rate reached 90 percent, compared with 37 percent in 1981 and 9.3 percent in 1979. In 1982 Costa Rica announced indefinite suspension of foreign debt servicing.

The second group of factors behind Costa Rica's "lost" decade was the slow pace of reforms (a very slow deregulation of the financial sector and privatization). The reforms began to yield visible effects only in the 1990s. Chile can serve as a reference point to determine the cost of putting off or abandoning reforms, since Chile's GDP per capita in the early 1980s was at a level similar to that of Costa Rica. In the following years, due to radical free-market reforms, Chile became the most dynamic economy in Latin America—in 2001 it outpaced Argentina, which had been the wealthiest country in the region in terms of income per capita (figure 8.8).

In Costa Rica, the greatest reform-related success was the sale and liquidation of the loss-making state conglomerate CODESA and the opening of the economy to foreign trade (see, for example, Rodríguez-Clare 2001; Gindling and

Figure 8.8 GDP Per Capita in Selected Latin American Countries, 1960–2003

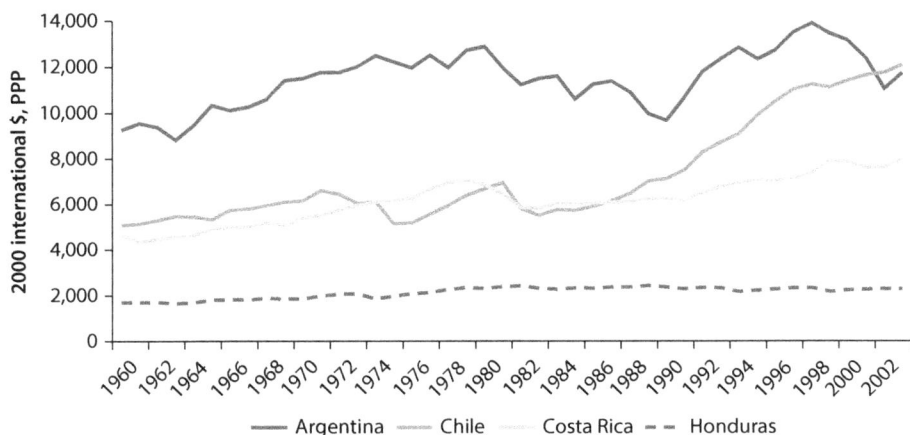

Source: Based on Heston, Summers, and Aten 2006.
Note: GDP = gross domestic product; PPP = purchasing power parity.

Trejos 2002). In 1983 special export zones were established, where companies were exempt from duty on imported components and machines and also enjoyed a 12-year tax holiday—full for the first eight years and 50 percent for the next four. Export duties were abolished in 1994; import duties on finished products were gradually reduced and quantitative restrictions on imports were lifted—the average tariff on imported industrial goods declined from 53 percent in 1983 to an average of 26 percent in the second half of the 1980s (Wilson 1994). Also, a number of regional bilateral free trade agreements were signed with other Central American countries (including the revitalization of the CACM) and Mexico. After Costa Rica joined the General Agreement on Tariffs and Trade (GATT) in 1990, exports grew at a rate of 6.25 percent per year and their ratio to GDP increased from 17.9 to 27.8 percent of in 1982–91.[13] The financial sector was liberalized at a very slow pace. No reforms were carried out in many areas: for example the state monopoly was preserved in the sectors of energy, telecommunications, education,[14] health care, and insurance.

Luckily enough, and contrary to many other countries affected by the crisis, Costa Rica did not postpone stabilizing its economy. The colón exchange rate was released, wages in the public sector were frozen, and taxes were raised,[15] which reduced the budget deficit by 3.4 percent of GDP in 1983 (against 14.3 percent of GDP in 1982; see Clark 1997). Throughout the years 1982–91 it amounted to an average of 2.45 percent of GDP (compared to 5.6 percent of GDP in the years 1974–81).[16] The increasing nominal GDP made it possible to reduce and stabilize the ratio of public debt to GDP—and the ratio declined from almost 120 percent in 1982 to about 60 percent at the beginning of the 1990s.

Foreign aid, especially from the United States, played a significant role in the stabilization of the economy. The Caribbean Basin Initiative established in 1982 by the Cabinet of President Reagan on the one hand, provided for the abolition of customs duties on imports of nontraditional agricultural products and low-processed goods from the countries in the region (this did not concern coffee, bananas, and beef), and on the other hand, stipulated significant financial aid provided by the U.S. Agency for International Development (USAID). Funds from the United States and aid from the International Monetary Fund (IMF) allowed Costa Rican authorities to stabilize the balance of payments in late 1982 and early 1983 (and the conditional nature of the aid created incentives for reforms). Overall, in the years 1981–95 foreign transfers to Costa Rica amounted to a total of $2.93 billion (in 2000 $), of which 64 percent was nonrefundable aid from the United States (in the same period, the total value of all FDI in Costa Rica was $2.33 billion [in $2000]; CINDE 2006).

In the same period, due to an inflow of foreign high-tech investment—and an economic revival in the United States—Puerto Rico's economy recovered from the recession caused by the oil crises of the 1970s.

Prompted by the new system of investment incentives introduced after 1976, the world's largest pharmaceutical companies (such as Pfizer, Johnson & Johnson, GlaxoSmithKline, Warner Chilcott, Clariant, and Procter & Gamble) set up their plants in Puerto Rico in the 1980s.[17] In addition to the pharmaceutical sector, manufacturers of medical equipment (such as Baxter, Medtronic, B. Braun, Unilever, and Roche) and electronics (including Siemens, General Electric, Hewlett-Packard, Microsoft, and Storage Technology) were major investors on the island.

Because of foreign capital, the rate of investments that collapsed in the late 1970s increased to 15.9 percent in 1990. Yet, this was about 12 percentage points lower than in the record year of 1971 (28.2 percent). In the years 1982–91 private investment accounted for 90 percent of total capital input in the island (in Costa Rica it represented 75 percent of total investment).

In the 1980s the fiscal position of the state was reduced in both Costa Rica and Puerto Rico. In Costa Rica public spending was reduced from 43.3 percent of GDP in 1982 to 33.4 percent of GDP in 1991, and in Puerto Rico from 41.6 to 38.7 percent of GDP (figure 8.9). This was the result of reducing inputs contributed by state-owned enterprises by 70 percent and 100 percent, respectively.[18]

Despite a lower ratio of public expenditure to GDP (than in Puerto Rico), in the years 1982–91 the state influence on the economy in Costa Rica remained higher than in Puerto Rico. Property rights continued to be protected inadequately (as indicated by a quality measure of the system for securing property rights and the rule of law published by the Fraser Institute) (see table 8.8).

Its stabilizing institutions and, as a result, its monetary policy also remained weak—the inflation rate in Costa Rica remained in double digits, while the monetary policy of the U.S. Federal Reserve Bank sheltered Puerto Rico from sudden price increases (figure 8.10).

At the same time, however, it should be noted that the extensive welfare state system—financed mainly from the U.S. federal budget—discouraged Puerto Rican citizens from work. Although when the scale of social transfers was limited in the years 1982–91 (from 30 percent to 25.6 percent of the disposable

Figure 8.9 Public Sector Spending in Puerto Rico and Costa Rica, 1980–93

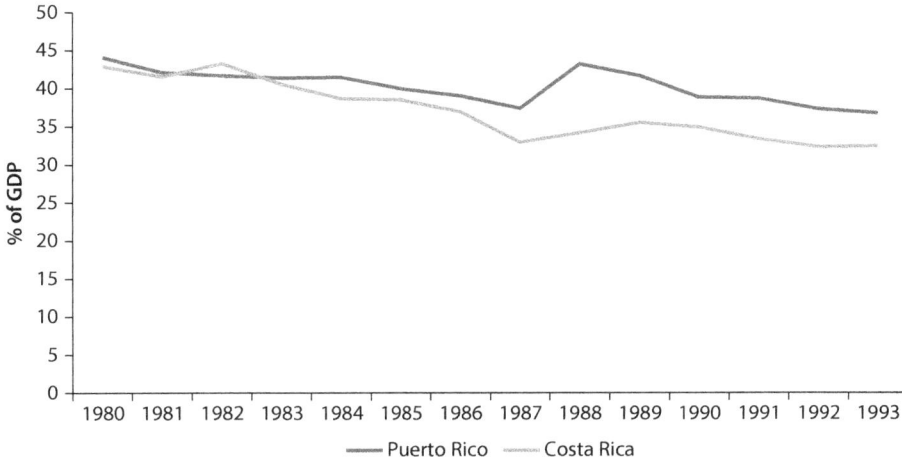

Puerto Rico   Costa Rica

Sources: Based on the data from the Central Bank of Costa Rica (http://www.bccr.fi.cr/indicadores_economicos_) and Bosworth, Collins, and Soto-Class 2006.
Note: GDP = gross domestic product. In the case of Puerto Rico, public sector spending includes the spending of the island's central administration, local governments, and state enterprises.

Table 8.8 Legal Structure and Security of Property Rights: The United States and Costa Rica, 1980–90

Year	United States	Costa Rica
1980	8.35	5.21
1985	8.35	5.25
1990	8.35	5.46

Source: Based on Fraser Institute 2006, http://www.freetheworld.com.
Note: The United States is used for comparison because separate data on Puerto Rico are not available. Values are based on an Economic Freedom Index compiled by the Fraser Institute on a scale from 0 (lowest possible score) to 10 (highest possible score).

income of a Puerto Rican), the labor force participation rate increased from 47 percent (1981) to 51 percent (1991), but stood well below the respective level of Costa Rica (64 percent) and the United States (69 percent). At the same time, Puerto Rico saw an increase in the percentage of men of working age who declared they were disabled or unable to work (16.4 percent in 1990 against 12 percent in 1972). Taking into account the fact that the size of the informal economy of the island was estimated at 20-30 percent of GDP in the 1980s (see Bosworth, Collins, and Soto-Class 2006), there was a strong moral hazard for welfare program beneficiaries—people officially registered as "unemployed" or "disabled" could derive additional profits from work in informal areas of the economy. As a result, although economic growth in the years 1982–91 was on average 3 percentage points higher in Puerto Rico than in Costa Rica, in 1991 the official unemployment rate exceeded the level of Costa Rica almost three times (16 percent vs. 5.5 percent; Bureau of Statistics, ILO 2006).

Puzzles of Economic Growth • http://dx.doi.org/10.1596/978-1-4648-0325-3

Figure 8.10 Inflation Rate in Puerto Rico (U.S. GDP Deflator) and Costa Rica (CPI), 1979–92

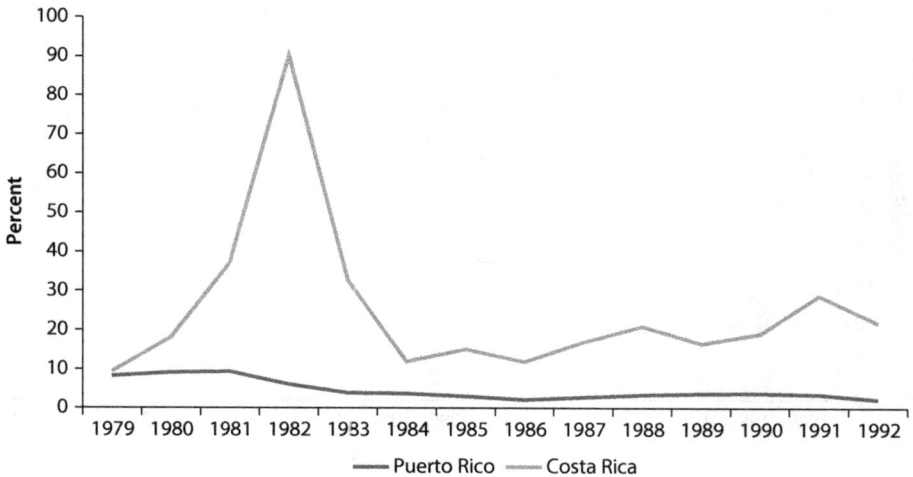

Sources: Based on data from the Bureau of Economic Analysis, U.S. Department of Commerce; and the Oxford Latin American Economic History Database.

The Years 1992–2003

In the years 1992–2003 Costa Rica developed slightly faster than Puerto Rico for the first time, which led to an improvement in the ratio of national income per capita in Costa Rica to GNP per capita in Puerto Rico from 65.7 percent to 67.3 percent.

The rapid opening of the Costa Rican economy to international trade accelerated the country's economic growth. An indicator of the economy's openness[19] increased from 63 percent of GDP in 1991 to 94 percent of GDP in 2003 (figure 8.11). The was due to a Costa Rican government policy, launched in the 1980s, the envisaged implementing the provisions of regional free trade agreements and resulted in the average tariff rate being reduced to 3.3 percent in 1999 (Bureau of Statistics, ILO 2006). A positive role was also played by the bottom-up initiative of local business. Through the Costa Rican Investment Board, local businesses promoted exports and successfully attracted foreign investors to the country. As a result, in the 1990s Costa Rica managed to attract FDI in high-technology sectors, crowned by the construction of Intel's microprocessor plant—the first in Latin America (the investment's value exceeded $1 billion). The share of high-tech products in exports reached 43 percent in 2000, mainly as a result of the "Intel effect."

Yet, there were no significant changes that could boost Costa Rica's economic growth:

- An attempt to privatize the state monopolist, the power and telecommunications conglomerate the Costa Rican Electricity Institute (ICE), was paralyzed by mass trade union rallies in 2000.

Puzzles of Economic Growth • http://dx.doi.org/10.1596/978-1-4648-0325-3

Figure 8.11 Indicator of Economic Openness: Puerto Rico and Costa Rica, 1991–2003

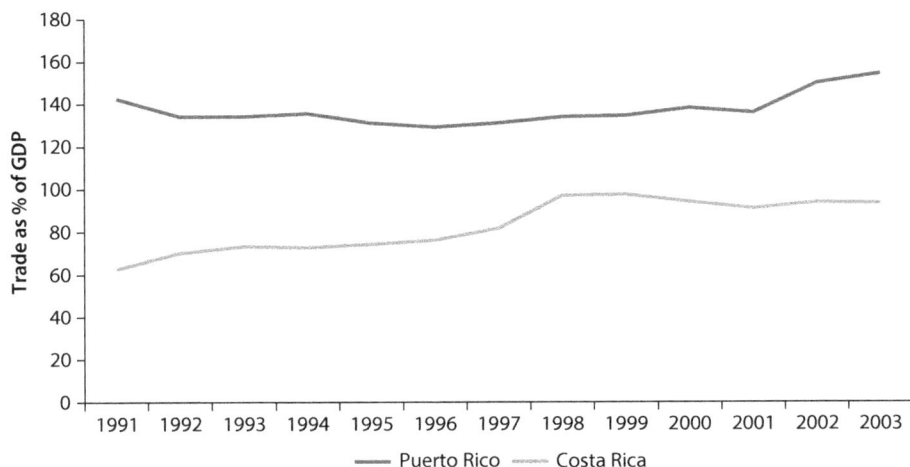

Source: Based on Penn World Table 6.2.
Note: GDP = gross domestic product.

- In the early 2000s, the fiscal position of the state increased again (figure 8.12). In 2003 public spending reached 37.3 percent of GDP, after a decrease from 32.3 percent of GDP in 1992 to 30 percent of GDP in 1999. The increase was entirely due to the increased spending of state-owned companies—mainly the inefficient telecommunications and energy monopolist ICE (central budget expenditure decreased from 19 percent of GDP in 1992 to 14.7 percent in 2003).[20]

- The budget deficit increased. In the years 1992–2003 it was on average 3.1 percent of GDP compared to 2.4 percent of GDP in 1982–91. This, combined with higher spending of state-owned companies in the second half of the 1990s, resulted in an increase of the ratio of public debt to GDP from 47.4 percent in 1998 to 58.1 percent in 2003 (figure 8.13). In 2003 its servicing costs consumed about one-third of government spending (see Bertelsmann Stiftung 2006) (in the mid-1990s the state budget and public enterprises were banned from borrowing from the central bank).

On the other hand, the dynamics of Puerto Rico's GDP decreased as the territory was affected by changes in U.S. economic policy.

- As a result of the U.S. tax law amendment in 1996, the provision exempting U.S. companies operating in Puerto Rico from federal tax on the transfer of profits generated on the island expired.[21] From its introduction in 1976 until the mid-1990s, the provision (Section 936) allowed U.S. pharmaceutical and chemical concerns to generate tax savings for the federal budget whose total amount was $70 billion (see Hexner and Jenkins 1998).

Puzzles of Economic Growth · http://dx.doi.org/10.1596/978-1-4648-0325-3

Figure 8.12 Public Sector Spending, Puerto Rico and Costa Rica, 1991–2003

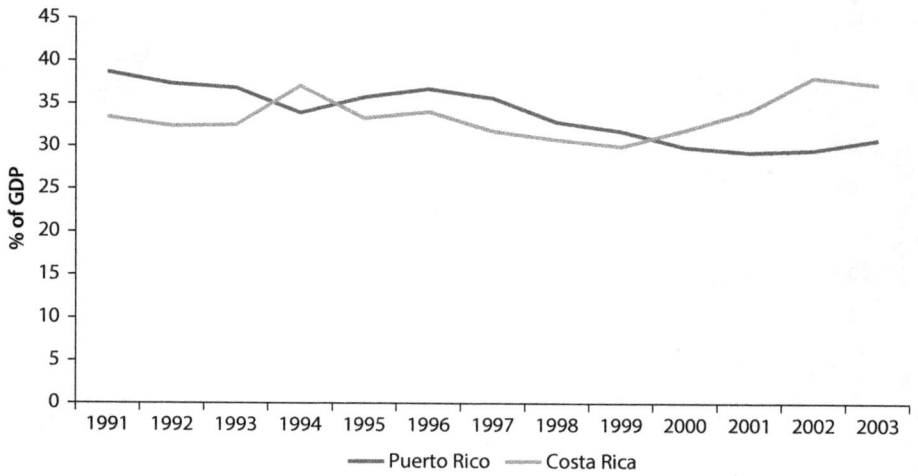

Sources: Based on the data from the Central Bank of Costa Rica (http://www.bccr.fi.cr/indicadores_economicos_) and Bosworth, Collins, and Soto-Class 2006.
Note: GDP = gross domestic product. In the case of Puerto Rico, public sector spending includes the spending of the island's central administration, local governments, and state enterprises.

Figure 8.13 Public Debt of Puerto Rico and Costa Rica, 1991–2003

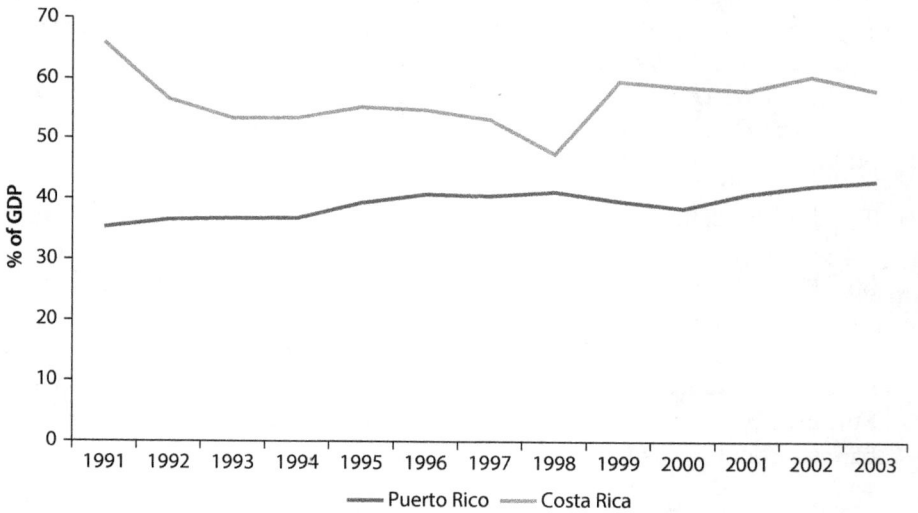

Sources: Based on Obando 2006; Bosworth, Collins, and Soto-Class 2006.

- At the same time, the U.S. Congress also decided to increase the minimum wage in the United States (and therefore in Puerto Rico)—in real terms from $4.93 in 1995 to $5.53 in 1997 (in 2000 $).
- The establishment of the North American Free Trade Agreement (NAFTA) made Mexico a major competitor of Puerto Rico, both in lobbying for U.S. FDI and in the segment of labor-intensive production (in 1997 it employed 14.5 percent of all employees of the Puerto Rican industry; see Bosworth, Collins, and Soto-Class 2006).

The adverse impact of those changes on the economic growth of Puerto Rico was not offset by another, positive congressional decision. In 1996 the U.S. Congress passed a bill allowing U.S. banks operating in line with the rules of the Eurodollar area (IBF—International Banking Facilities) to open branches in Puerto Rico. This was the response of the U.S. authorities to the decreasing competitiveness of the U.S. banks in the international market in the context of a dynamic development of Eurodollar markets in Europe and Asia. IBFs, which were exempt from the Federal Reserve System reserve requirements, could offer equally favorable interest rates on dollar deposits and loans as London or Asian banks (see, for example, Edwards 1981; Bosworth, Collins, and Soto-Class 2006). As a result of the decision, financial services became the most dynamically developing segment of the Puerto Rican economy. The assets of the financial sector in Puerto Rico grew from $78.2 billion in 1995 (153 percent of GDP) to $196 billion in 2003, that is, 243 percent of GDP (in $2000; see Bosworth, Collins, and Soto-Class 2006).

In response to adverse developments in the external environment, in 1998 the authorities of the island adopted a new package of investment incentives (see UNECLAC 2004) that included a preferential CIT rate of 4 percent for all enterprises in the apparel, shoe, and food-processing sectors; complete income tax exemption for strategic investments in the pharmaceutical, biotechnology, and electronics sectors; lifting of the local tax (10 percent) on the transfer of profits by branches of foreign corporations; and a possibility to classify all expenditure for employee training and for research and development as tax-deductible costs to encourage pharmaceutical companies operating in Puerto Rico to open biotechnology laboratories on the island (between 1999 and 2003 investments in this segment amounted to $1.6 billion[22]).

In the same year, a decision was made to privatize the state monopoly in fixed telephony, that is, the Puerto Rico Telephone Company. The total value of the transaction (GTE was the buyer) amounted to $1.88 billion.

Earlier, that is, after 1993, the administration of the island had reformed the health-care system. From the main supplier of medical services (previously health-care services had been almost wholly managed by the state), the state had become only an insurer that negotiated health insurance contracts with private hospitals and outpatient clinics. However, despite the aforementioned reform, Puerto Rican administration still covered health insurance contributions of significant percentage of the island population (for example, in 2004 the health insurance contributions of 41 percent of residents were financed by the state budget and value of these state-financed contributions was the equivalent of 20 percent of Puerto Rico's tax revenues; (see Bosworth, Collins, and Soto-Class 2006).

Public spending in Puerto Rico decreased from 37.3 percent of GDP to 30.8 percent of GDP in the years 1992–2003. (Reduction of state enterprises' spending represented 83 percent of the total public spending decline.)

A decline in the rate of investment was avoided. In the analyzed period, the rate ranged between 15 percent of GDP (1992) and 20 percent of GDP (1999), but was on average lower than in Costa Rica (16.9 percent compared to 20.8 percent).

Male labor force participation had gradually declined (from 60 percent in 1991 to 57 percent in 2001; see Bosworth, Collins, and Soto-Class 2006). The percentage of men of working age who declared themselves to be disabled or unable to work totaled 25.6 percent in 2000 (compared to 16.4 percent in 1990; see Bosworth, Collins, and Soto-Class 2006). As a result, despite the growth (as in other areas) of female labor force participation, in 2003 only 53.1 percent of the island population of working age participated in the labor force (the figures for Costa Rica and the United States were 63.8 percent and 71.2 percent, respectively).

The existing propelling institutions in Puerto Rico were not strong enough to compensate for the negative impact that external factors had on the economic growth rate. In the years 1992–2003 the economic growth rate (1.97 percent) was lower than between 1982 and 1991 (2.58 percent), not to mention the years 1961–73 (4.74 percent).

- Despite a decrease in state-owned enterprises' spending in the years 1992–2003, their debt grew from $8.7 billion (23.8 percent of GDP) in 1990 to $23 billion (31.3 percent of GDP) in 2003 (in $2000; see Bosworth, Collins, and Soto-Class 2006)—which accounted for almost the entire increase in the Puerto Rican public debt in that period (from 33.9 percent of GDP to 43 percent of GDP). Three companies with the largest debt included the state energy monopoly, Puerto Rico Electric Power Authority; a road infrastructure construction company, Puerto Rico Highways and Transportation Authority; and a company responsible for state construction, Puerto Rico Public Buildings Authority—accounting for $2.9 billion. The neglected infrastructure of Puerto Rico is often described as the "bottleneck" hampering economic growth (see Bosworth, Collins, and Soto-Class 2006).

- As in the previous decade, social transfers in the years 1992–2003 accounted for approximately one-fourth of average income. The role of local administration in financing social assistance schemes increased in the analyzed period, with 27 percent coming from the budget of Puerto Rico (in the years 1982–91, it was 20.6 percent). The share of transfers in the budget of the island increased from 23.9 percent in 1992 to 36.4 percent in 2003.

- One-off sources of income (such as the privatization of the telecommunications monopoly, worth approximately $1.8 billion) were used to finance the current budget deficit.[23]

- According to the analyses of the World Bank under the Doing Business project, conducting business activity in Puerto Rico, although much easier than in Costa Rica, was more costly and time consuming than in the United States.

Summary and Conclusions

The aim of this chapter was to explain why Costa Rica lags behind Puerto Rico in terms of income per capita. The most significant differences in their GDP growth rates were recorded in the years 1961–73, 1974–81, and 1982–91. Those years were decisive for the difference in the wealth of both in 2003.

- The most important element of Puerto Rico's advantage over Costa Rica in the first of the aforementioned periods was the fact that the island was institutionally and economically integrated with the United States. The inflow of FDI (mainly American) to Puerto Rico in the 1960s was significantly higher than to Costa Rica. In addition, Puerto Rico's propelling institutions were stronger than Costa Rica's; there was less state control of the economy, more openness to foreign trade, and better property rights protection. It also had more efficient stabilizing institutions in the area of monetary policy—as conducted by the U.S. Federal Reserve Bank. In the same period, Costa Rica decided to focus on industrialization of the sectors (primarily food processing) competing with imports and became involved in building the CACM. In consequence, new technologies reached Puerto Rico much faster. Meanwhile, that territory's investment in education, which began a decade earlier than in Costa Rica, resulted in a faster accumulation of human capital.

- The collapse of economic growth in Puerto Rico between 1974 and 1981 and in Costa Rica between 1982 and 1991 was caused by negative external shocks. In the case of Puerto Rico these included two oil crises. The problems experienced by Costa Rica resulted from a sudden surge in the costs of foreign debt servicing. External shocks exposed the structural problems of both economies and their destabilizing fiscal policies.

Table 8.9 The Ease of Doing Business: Ranks 175 of Puerto Rico, Costa Rica, and the United States, 2007

	General rank	Starting a business	Dealing with licenses	Paying taxes	Enforcing contracts
Puerto Rico	19	8	99	26	127
Costa Rica	105	99	57	160	114
United States	3	3	22	62	6

Source: Based on World Bank 2007.

– The difficulties faced by Puerto Rico between 1974 and 1981 were caused by the high energy intensity of the economy. The economic growth slump was the effect of the withdrawal of petrochemical sector investors from the island. The crisis was made more severe by decrease in export growth as a result of the economic slowdown in the United States (the destination of 90 percent of Puerto Rican exports). An additional shock, in particular for employment, came as minimum wages were raised to the same level as that of the United States, which severely undercut Puerto Rico's ability to compete with countries producing labor-intensive goods (such as apparel). Combined with a dramatic increase in social transfers financed from the federal budget, which discouraged employment, this led to persistent low labor force participation.

– Costa Rica's debt at the beginning of the 1980s was the result of public investment expansion and huge social spending in the 1970s. Increased budgetary revenues resulting from the "coffee boom" in 1975-79 were allocated for consumption or the creation of state-owned enterprises, which proved to be extremely inefficient. The severity of the crisis was due to the weak stabilizing institutions in Costa Rica, especially the central bank, which had no real independence and was ineffective in curbing inflation.

• Both the government of Costa Rica and the administration of Puerto Rico decided to change their development strategy after the economic slump they had experienced.

– The administration of Puerto Rico, in cooperation with the U.S. Congress, introduced tax reliefs at the local and federal level, respectively, to attract American investors from high-tech sectors (mainly from pharmaceutical and chemical industries, and starting from the 1990s also from the biotechnology sector). In 2003 highly processed goods accounted for 90 percent of Puerto Rican exports with a total value of $59 billion.

– After the debt crisis of 1982, the government of Costa Rica, along with the CINDE Investment Promotion Agency representing the private sector, developed and introduced a strategy for abandoning protectionism, opening the economy to foreign trade, and promoting exports. In the 1980s the strategy relied on the export of apparel and nontraditional agricultural products (pineapples, melons). Moreover, in the 1990s CINDE managed to persuade foreign investors, mainly from the electronics sector, to invest their capital in Costa Rica. The crowning achievement of this bottom-up private sector initiative was the opening of Latin America's only microprocessor factory in Costa Rica by Intel.

• The economies of Puerto Rico and Costa Rica are still burdened by significant structural problems that undermine their future growth prospects.

– In Costa Rica those problems include ineffective state monopolies in such segments of the economy as commercial insurance, telecommunications, energy production, health care, social care, and education. All attempts to privatize or deregulate those sectors are opposed by trade unions. The lack of independence of the central bank, and the high inflation rate (which has ranged between 10 percent and 25 percent during the period 1995–2003 are Costa Rica's other serious problems.

- A growth-inhibiting factor in Puerto Rico is the extensive system of social assistance and social transfers, 70 percent of them financed by the U.S. budget. This is why labor force participation in Puerto Rico is almost 20 percentage points lower than in the United States (53 percent compared to 72 percent).

- Although at the beginning of the analyzed period Puerto Rico and Costa Rica did not vary in terms of income per capita, in 2003 GDP per capita in Costa Rica constituted only 67 percent of GNP per capita in Puerto Rico. It must, however, be remembered that in the four decades of the study period, the average level of income per capita in the United States did not converge with Puerto Rico's. Between 1961 and 2003 Puerto Rico managed to make up just for 7.5 percent of the development gap, that is 50% less than the poorest state of the United States, that is, Mississippi.

Notes

1. The year 2003 was selected as the final one of the analysis because, at the time of this writing, it was the last available for both nations in the time series of PWT 6.2.

2. For the purpose of this study, GNP is a more reliable measure of Puerto Rico's economic growth. The visible deteriorating trend of Puerto Rico's GNP-to-GDP ratio is the result of special U.S. tax regulations (mainly Section 936, which entered into force in 1976) that exempt profit generated by U.S. companies operating in Puerto Rico from all or some federal taxes.

3. Defined as GDP per employee.

4. In Costa Rica there were "autonomous institutions" established in 1948—monopolies that operated like public enterprises. These included the Costa Rican Social Security Institute (CCSS), responsible for the health-care system, pensions (for the entire population), and the purchasing and distributing of medicines and medical equipment; the Costa Rican Electricity Institute (ICE), a monopolist in the electricity and telecommunication market; and the National Insurance Institute, a monopolist in the commercial insurance market. The 1948 constitution provided these and many of close to 200 smaller "autonomous institutions" (for example, national airlines) with transfers from the state budget with a fixed rate against total government spending and the possibility to collect fees for their services (Wilson 1994).

5. The negative growth of labor productivity in the Costa Rican services sector is also proven by studies by other authors that are based on data series other than Penn World Table 6.2 (see Rodríguez-Clare, Saenz, and Trejos 2003).

6. If the shock periods were not excluded, the contribution of technological progress would seem much lower—in the case of Costa Rica it would be negative for the entire 1961–2000 period (see, for example, Rodríguez-Clare, Saenz, and Trejos 2003).

7. Recent publications on Puerto Rico (growth calculation based on data series other than PWT 6.2) suggest the dominating role of physical capital accumulation per employee in productivity growth in the 1960s and in the entire period under analysis of 1961–2003 (see Bosworth, Collins, and Soto-Class 2006).

8. See Article 2 of Costa Rica's Central Bank statutes.

9. Estimates by the author based on Obando (2006).

10. Estimates by the author based on Caban (1989).

11. The reason behind adopting the new strategy was that the earlier anti-import strategy failed to yield satisfactory results (the strategy did not concern imports from the United States—from the beginning of the 20th century the United States and Puerto Rico formed a single tariff area).

12. A directive of the U.S. president of December 10, 1963, increased the limits for oil imports to Puerto Rico; oil processed in Puerto Rican refineries was to be transported to the United States.

13. Values in international dollars (as of 2000) according to purchasing power parity (PPP) after PWT 6.2.

14. In Puerto Rico in the years 1982–91, the process of bottom-up privatization of educational services continued. Between 1980 and 1990, the share of nonpublic educational establishments among primary and secondary schools increased from 12.1 percent to 18.7 percent, and among universities from 58.7 percent to 63.9 percent (Bosworth, Collins, and Soto-Class 2006).

15. In the second half of the 1980s, tax rates were reduced again and unified—the personal income tax (PIT) rate ranged between 12 percent and 14 percent, while in 1988 linear corporate income tax (CIT) was introduced of 30 percent. It was possible thanks to reducing public spending.

16. Central Bank of Costa Rica.

17. Pharmaceutical Industry Association of Puerto Rico (http://www.piapr.com).

18. Author's estimates based on data from the Central Bank of Costa Rica.

19. Economy openness index understood as = trade (imports + exports) / GDP.

20. Central Bank of Costa Rica.

21. The expiry of Section 936 was spread over 10 years (it ultimately expired in 2006).

22. Pharmaceutical Industry Association of Puerto Rico (http://www.piapr.com).

23. In May 2005 this practice led to the reduction of the rating of Puerto Rican debt securities by Moody's and Standard and Poor's to Baa2 and BBB rating, respectively.

Bibliography

Bertelsmann Stiftung. 2006. *Country Report: Costa Rica.* http://www.bertelsmann-stiftung.de/cps/rde/xbcr/SID-943CD756-34CEA538/bst_engl/CostaRica.pdf.

Bosworth, B. P., S. M. Collins, and M. A. Soto-Class. 2006. *The Economy of Puerto Rico: Restoring Growth.* Brookings, OR: Brookings Institution Press.

Bureau of Economic Analysis, U.S. Department of Commerce. http://www.bea.gov.

Caban, P. 1989. "Industrial Transformation and Labor Relations in Puerto Rico: From 'Operation Bootstrap' to the 1970s." *Journal of Latin American Studies* 21 (3): 559–91.

Central Bank of Costa Rica. http://www.bccr.fi.cr/indicadores_economicos_

CINDE. 2006. "Historic Overview of Foreign Direct Investments in Costa Rica." http://www.cinde.org.

Clark, M. A. 1997. "Transnational Alliances and Development Policy in Latin America: Nontraditional Export Promotion in Costa Rica." *Latin American Research Review* 32 (2): 71–97.

Dietz, J. 1976. "The Puerto Rican Political Economy." *Latin American Perspectives* 3 (3) Summer: 3–16.

———. 1982. "Puerto Rico in the 1970s and 1980s: Crisis of the Development Model." *Journal of Economic Issues* 16 (2): 497.

Edwards, F. L. 1981. "The New International Banking Facility: A Study in Regulatory Frustration." *Journal of World Business* 16: 4.

Freeman, A. C., and R. B. Freeman. 1991. "Minimum Wages in Puerto Rico: Textbook Case of a Wage Floor?" NBER Working Paper 3759, National Bureau of Economic Research, Cambridge, MA.

Garcia, E. P. 1984. "Puerto Rico: The Making of a Corporate Paradise." *Multinational Monitor* 5 (10&11) October/November.

Gindling, T. H., and J. D. Trejos. 2002. *Changing Earnings Inequality in Costa Rica, 1976–99: Evolution and Causes*. Baltimore, MD: University of Maryland.

Goss, J., and D. Pacheco. 1999. "Comparative Globalization and the State in Costa Rica and Thailand." *Journal of Contemporary Asia* 29 (4): 516–35.

Heston, Alan, Robert Summers, and Bettina Aten. 2006. Penn World Table Version 6.2. Center for International Comparisons of Production, Income and Prices at the University of Pennsylvania.

Hexner, J. T., and G. Jenkins. 1998. *Puerto Rico: The Economics and Fiscal Dimensions*. Citizens Educational Foundation, Puerto-Rico Herald, 2 (3). http://www.puertorico-herald.org/issues/vol2n03/hexner-jenkins.html.

Huang, Y. 2003. "Entrepreneurship in Asia and Foreign Direct Investment—Reflection for China from India, Taiwan, Hong Kong, Singapore, and Malaysia." PowerPoint presentation to the MIT Sloan Asian Business Club, September 5, 2003.

International Labour Organization. 2014. *ILOSTAT Database*. http://www.ilo.org/ilostat/faces/home/statisticaldata?_afrLoop=1235748998261282#%40%3F_afrLoop%3D1235748998261282%26_adf.ctrl-state%3D583dp37r4_134.

Irwin, D. A. 2005. "The Rise of US Anti-Dumping Activity in Historical Perspective." *The World Economy* 28 (5): 651–68.

Obando, J. C. 2006. "Patterns of Wage Inequality in Costa Rica during the Structural Change: 1976–2004." Working Paper 36, University of Texas Inequality Project, Austin, Texas.

OECD (Organisation for Economic Co-operation and Development). 2006. "OECD Economic Outlook 80." http://www.oecd.org.

Oxford Latin American Economic History Database. http://moxlad.fcs.edu.uy.

Rivera-Batiz, F. L. 1998. *Island Paradox: Puerto Rico in the 1990s*. Russell Sage Foundation Publications, 1990 Census Research Series. Vol. 4. New York City: Russell Sage Foundation.

Rodríguez-Clare, A. 2001. "Costa Rica's Development Strategy Based on Human Capital and Technology: How It Got There, the Impact of Intel, and Lessons for Other Countries." *Journal of Human Development* 2 (2): 311–24.

Rodríguez-Clare, A., M. Saenz, and A. Trejos. 2003. "Economic Growth in Costa Rica: 1950–2000." Research Department Working Paper, Inter-American Development Bank, Washington, DC.

Sanchez-Acochea, D. 2006. *Development Trajectories and New Comparative Advantages: Costa Rica and the Dominican Republic under Globalization.* University of London.

Seligson, M. A., and E. Muller. 1987. "Democratic Stability and Economic Crisis: Costa Rica 1978–83." *International Studies Quarterly* 31 (3): 301–26.

UNECLAC (United Nations Economic Commission for Latin America and Caribbean). 2004. "The Convergent/Divergent Economic Trajectories of Puerto Rico and the United States." Publications 2004, No. LC/CAR/L.11, May 3, 2004. http://www.cepal .org/publicaciones/xml/3/14803/L0011.pdf.

Wilson, B. M. 1994. "When Social Democrats Choose Neoliberal Economic Policies: The Case of Costa Rica." *Comparative Politics* 26 (2).

World Bank. 2007. *Doing Business 2007: How to Reform?* Washington, DC: World Bank.

CHAPTER 9

Why Is Haiti Poorer Than the Dominican Republic?

Aleksander Łaszek

This pair of countries is particularly interesting because of their many similarities—Haitians and Dominicans live on the same island, Hispaniola, separated only by an arbitrarily drawn frontier (see table 9.1). Also, until 1950 the history of both countries ran a similar course, abounding in protracted power struggles and frequent periods of domestic instability. As regards the economy, in 1950 gross domestic product (GDP) per capita was almost identical in Haiti and the Dominican Republic. Fifty years on, Haiti has many of the characteristics of a failed state; meanwhile, the Dominican Republic boasts an income per head that is almost five times the size of its neighbor's.[1]

The Pace of Economic Growth

In 1950 GDP per capita of the countries we are analyzing was very similar—1,051 GK\$ in Haiti versus 1,027 GK\$[2] in the Dominican Republic (Maddison 2007). Both countries were ethnically homogenous[3] and had no advanced industry. There was only a difference in their agricultural structures—Haitian farms were far smaller than the plantations prevailing in the Dominican Republic.[4] Turning to natural conditions, these were also very similar—climatic differences between the eastern and western side of the island were negligible.

Likewise, technical and social infrastructure was on a par in both countries—in the previous years, both countries had been occupied by the United States.[5] They had emerged from this period with a network of roads, a trained army, and constitutions written in Washington. The structure of both economies was also similar; they were agricultural countries, and exporters of coffee, sugar, sisal, or cocoa. Politically, in 1950 the Dominican Republic was under the dictatorship of Rafael L. Trujillo, while Haiti was undergoing a period of power struggles that ended, in the mid-1950s, with the ascent to power of the Duvalier family (Congress 2001a, 2001b). Despite all the similarities, the paths of the two countries soon diverged. From 1950 on, for the next half-century the Dominican

Republic's GDP per capita rose at an average rate of 2.62 percent,[6] while Haiti's fell at the rate of −0.56 percent.[4] After 50 years, the relation between GDP per capita of the two countries changed from 1:1 to 1:4.5 in favor of the Dominican Republic (see figure 9.1 for an overview of initial conditions in Haiti and the Dominican Republic in 1950).

Both countries' economic growth rates fluctuated heavily throughout the analyzed period (the standard deviation of both countries' growth rate amounted to approximately 5 percentage points). In some years Haiti developed faster, but except for a short period at the end of the 1980s, the Dominican Republic steadily posted markedly higher average growth (see figures 9.2 and 9.3).

Table 9.1 Conditions in Haiti and the Dominican Republic, 1950

	Haiti	Dominican Republic
Climate	Tropical	Tropical
Key trading partners	United States	United States
GDP per capita ($) starting level	1,051	1,027
Terms of trade changes	Similar	Similar
Population	3,097,000	2,353,000

Source: CIA Factbook database; Jaramillo and Sancak 2007; Maddison 2007.
Note: GDP = gross domestic product. Both countries were homogenous in terms of ethnic composition and language; they also shared a legacy of numerous coups and overthrows—between regaining independence in 1804 and the American intervention of 1915, Haiti had 33 heads of state. The Dominican Republic had 61 heads of state from declaring independence in 1844 to the American intervention in 1916.

Figure 9.1 Per Capita GDP: Haiti and the Dominican Republic in GK$, 1950–2000

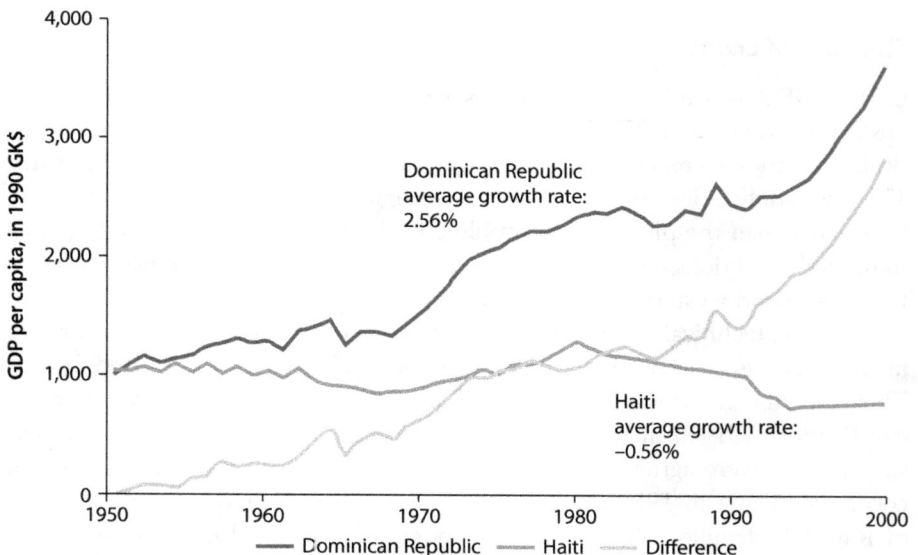

Source: Maddison 2007.
Note: GDP = gross domestic product; GK$ = Geary-Khamis international dollars, hypothetical unit of currency that has the same purchasing power parity that the U.S. dollar in the United States has at a given point of time; benchmarking year is 1990.

Figure 9.2 Per Capita GDP Growth in the Dominican Republic and Haiti, 1951–2003

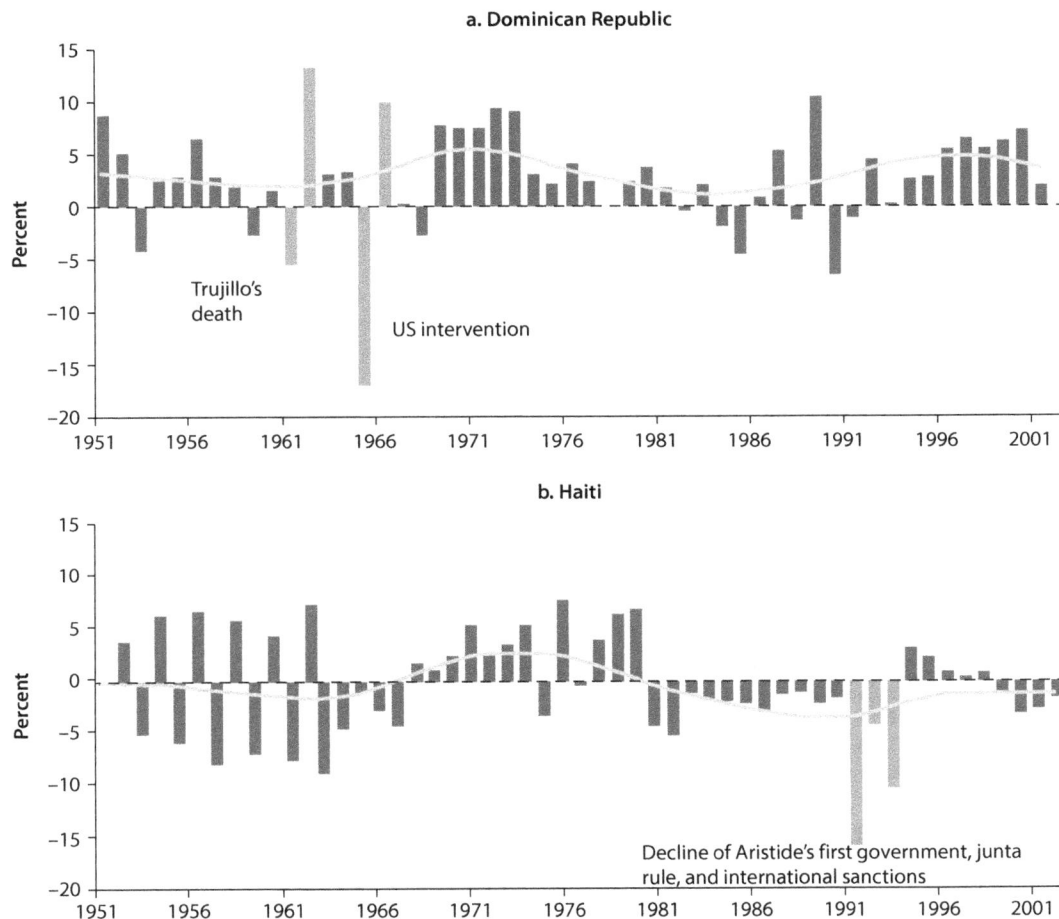

a. Dominican Republic

b. Haiti

Source: Based on Maddison 2007.
Note: GDP = gross domestic product. The bars represent the actual growth rates; the line—growth smoothed with HP filter (λ = 100).

- In the 1950s, under Trujillo, the Dominican Republic developed at a moderate pace of approximately 2 percent per year; in the same period, Haiti experienced sharp GDP fluctuations caused by changes in the prices of export commodities (sugar, coffee, cocoa) and ongoing power struggles. The situation lasted until the mid-1960s, when the Dominican Republic faced violent shocks triggered by the assassination of Trujillo in 1961; the ensuing social unrest ending with the election of Joaquín Balageur as president in 1966. Even though slumps in the Dominican GDP were large (−15 percent in 1965), growth tended to spring back as soon as the situation had calmed (+10 percent in 1966) (Congress 2001a, 2001b).

- From the mid-1960s both countries saw accelerated growth driven by favorable commodity export prices, inflow of foreign investment (particularly in

Figure 9.3 Trend in Per Capita GDP, 1951–2001

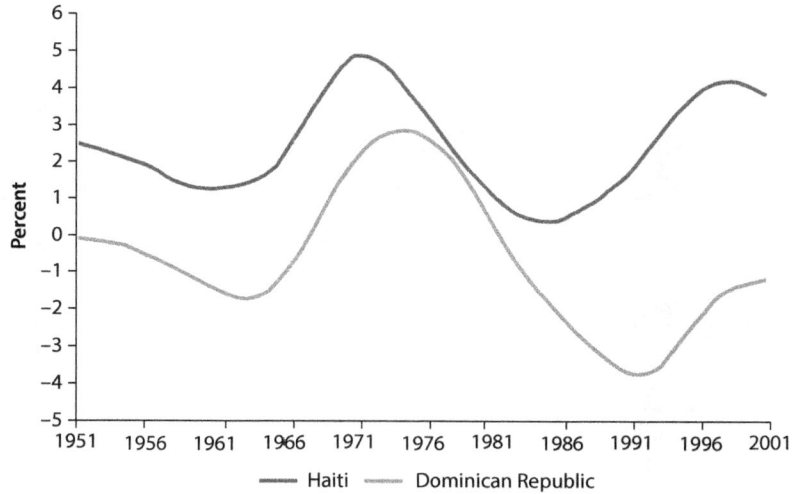

Source: Based on Maddison 2007.
Note: GDP = gross domestic product. The Hodrick-Prescott Lambda 100 filter, standard value for annual data.

the Dominican Republic), and an expanding tourist industry. Mining boomed in the Dominican Republic (nickel ore, bauxite, gold, silver). In 1973 the United States and other developed countries resumed, after a 10-year break, providing development aid to Haiti. But as of the mid-1970s, rising prices of oil combined with a decline in sugar prices started to exert a negative effect on the two island economies. Their external debt increased signifi-cantly (in 1973–79, Haiti's rose from 7 percent to 28 percent of GDP, and the Dominican Republic's from 20 percent to 29 percent; Congress 2001a, 2001b; World Development Indicators Online).

- At the beginning of the 1980s, both countries were hit by further oil price hikes, plunging sugar prices (to a 40-year low) and spurring problems in servicing external debt.[7] The Dominican government, in an attempt to avoid unpopular decisions, financed the deficit by printing money, triggering spiraling inflation (inflation went up from 5 percent in 1980 to 60 percent in 1988).[8] In Haiti, more underlying structural problems started to surface. Marc Bazin, appointed as the minister of finance in 1982, found that at least 36 percent of state revenue was appropriated by the ruling class (Bazin was promptly removed from office).[9] All-pervading corruption, nepotism, and a lack of progress in the democratization process led to cuts in development aid—previously one of the major sources of state revenue. At the same time, progressive deforestation and overexploitation of natural resources caused a decline in agricultural output. Mounting political chaos amid poverty translated into rising crime rates, lead-ing to a decline of the tourist sector (Congress 2001a, 2001b).

- The beginning of the 1990s brought a sudden GDP collapse in Haiti—the chaos following the overthrow of Jean-Bertrand Aristide's government and the sanctions imposed later[10] led to a decline in GDP per capita by 27 percent in 1991–94. Despite the restoration of democratic rule, the lifting of sanctions, and resumption of international aid, Haiti did not manage to make up for earlier setbacks. In the same period, the Dominican Republic struck an agreement with the International Monetary Fund (IMF), balanced the budget, contained inflation, and embarked on privatization of state-owned enterprises, thus overcoming the problems it had experienced in the 1980s and stepping on the path of accelerated economic growth (average GDP per capita growth in the 1990s was running at 4.5 percent; World Bank 2006a, 2006b).

To sum up, throughout the period under review, the Dominican Republic maintained an average GDP per capita growth rate more than 2 percentage points higher than Haiti's. Although in the mid-1970s growth in both countries started to decelerate sharply, at one stage becoming almost equal, by the mid-1980s the Dominican Republic was on a recovery path, whereas Haiti had embarked on a downward spiral. During the 1990s growth in the Dominican Republic picked up steadily, while the trend in Haiti changed only in the mid-1990s, but remained negative (that is, GDP per capita declines were increasingly smaller).

Both countries experienced numerous shocks and GDP per capita breakdowns, yet Haiti's overall performance cannot be explained by any single growth slump—it results from persistently lower growth in that country over many years. One exception is the 1991–94 slump, after which Haiti's GDP per capita, having hovered around $1,000 for 40 years, dropped to approximately $750 (in terms of 1990 Geary-Khamis dollars). Yet, even if we imagine that this bust did not occur, and Haiti had continued to post near-zero growth rates until the end of 1990s (which reflects the average of 1951–91),[11] in 2001 Haiti would still have been over 3.5 times poorer than the Dominican Republic ($3,723 vs. $1,000).

Differences in Economic Performance: Factors and Causes

Growth Accounting for the Years 1960–90

In the following growth accounting analysis, we omit the 1950s (due to the lack of data for Haiti) and the 1990s, when Haiti's economy collapsed. As economic busts of 1961 and 1965 in the Dominican Republic were politically conditioned, and economic activity sprang back to previous levels after political stability had been restored in 1966, we see no reason to disregard this period in our analysis.

The calculations are based on the Cobb-Douglas function with constant returns to scale. Capital contribution (α) was assumed at 0.4 (Young 1995), return on education at 0.1, and depreciation at 0.04 (Mahajan 2002). The level of capital in the starting year (1960) was calculated under the assumption of a 1.4 capital-to-GDP ratio in the Dominican Republic and 0.8 in Haiti (Nehru and Dhareshwar 1993).[12]

The contributions of change in capital, labor, and productivity to GDP growth in both countries was calculated based on the Sandeep Mahajan database (2002), comprising the longest time series for both countries (there are no data for Haiti relating to the 1950s). Poor reliability of the domestic statistical system has to be borne in mind (especially with respect to Haiti; see box 9.1 and Figure B9.1.1).

The results for several 10-year subperiods are presented in figure 9.4. The first three columns refer to decades, and the last one to the whole of the analyzed period, 1961–90. In the entire 1961–90 period, increase in capital was the key driver of growth in the Dominican Republic (1.78 percentage points),

---

Box 9.1 The Contribution of Investment to GDP in Haiti

The Haitian Institute of Statistics is underfunded and unable to fully meet its responsibilities. The methodology currently in place (SCN 1968) is outdated; work is in progress on implementing an upgraded version (SCN 1993). The available data are partial and often incomplete; moreover, various sources quote contradictory figures.

Data from the late 1990s are particularly problematic, with for example, the World Bank's "Key Development Data & Statistics" putting the contribution of investment to GDP in 2000 at almost 30 percent (which is striking, considering the country's poor condition). At the same time, according to the Sandeep Mahajan database (2002), also compiled by the World Bank, investment accounted for only 8 percent of GDP in that year, whereas the Penn World Table in turn quotes approximately 3 percent.

Figure B9.1.1 Share of Investment in GDP according to Different Databases

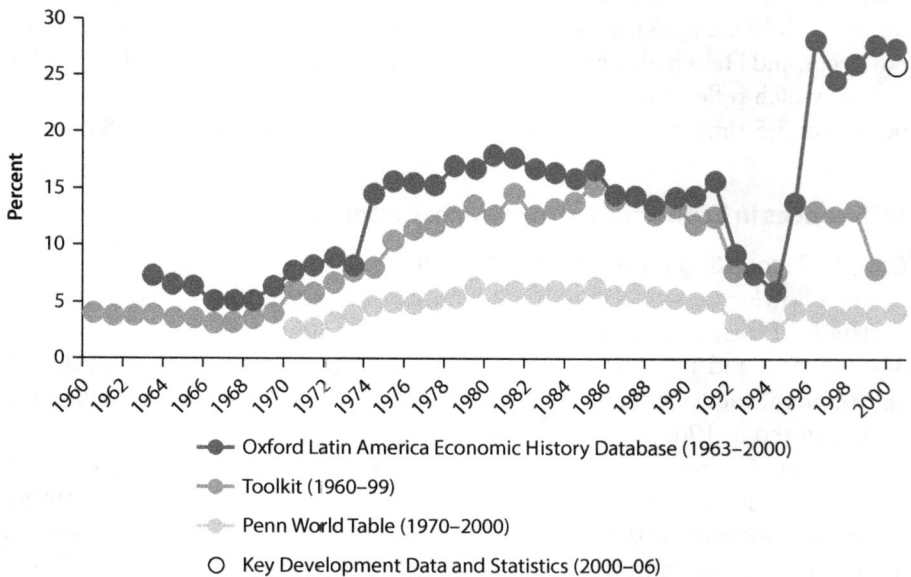

●— Oxford Latin America Economic History Database (1963–2000)

●— Toolkit (1960–99)

●— Penn World Table (1970–2000)

O   Key Development Data and Statistics (2000–06)

box continues next page

Box 9.1 The Contribution of Investment to GDP in Haiti *(continued)*

The Haitian Institute of Statistics and World Bank suggest two reasons for such a high figure for the share of investment in GDP:

- *Overestimated investment:* reported private investment is inflated for tax reasons; intermediate goods, registered as capital goods fall under different (more favorable) tax regulations; and public investment is boosted as all funds received from foreign sponsors (which account for a large part of Haiti's budget), regardless of their designation, are treated as investment.
- *Underestimated GDP:* the methodology and base year (1987) used do not account for, among others, the informal economy in communications and some parts of the construction sector. Further, the inflow of money transfers from the Haitian diaspora around the world is not included.

Figure 9.4 Contributions to Per Capita Growth: Haiti and the Dominican Republic, 1961–90

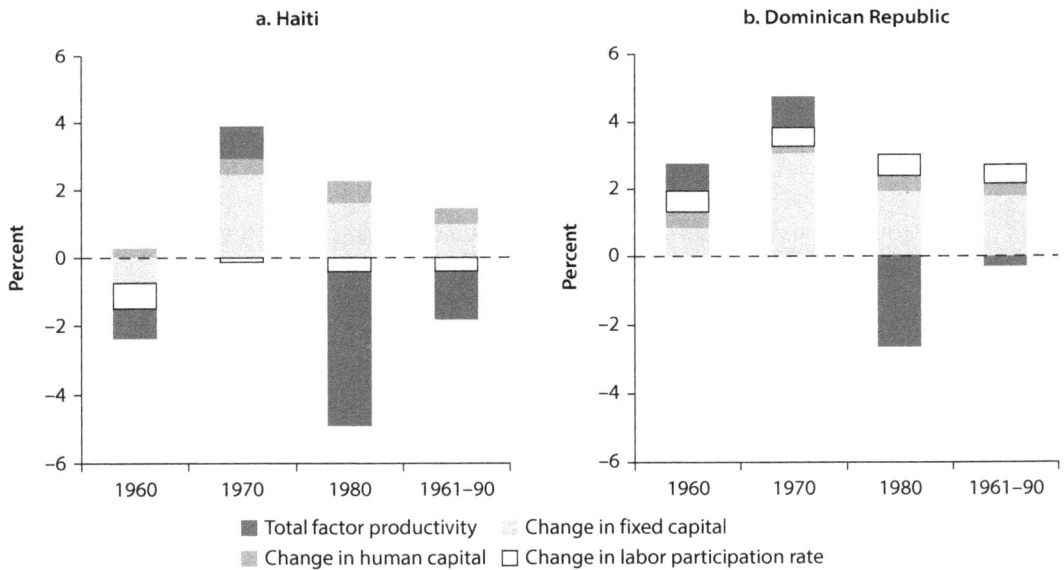

Source: Based on Maddison 2007 and Mahajan 2002.
Note: TFP = total factor productivity.

accounting for nearly three-fourths of overall growth. Smaller contributions were made by an increase in the working age population (0.56 percentage points), an increase in human capital (0.36 percentage points) and a marginal decline in efficiency (0.33 percentage points).[13] Also in Haiti, capital made the largest positive contribution to growth (1.01 percentage points); yet even in combination with the increase in human capital (0.44 percentage points) it could not outweigh a massive decline in productivity (−1.39 percentage points) and the shrinking size of the working age population (−0.4 percentage points).[14]

It suffices to analyze the first decade alone to see the differences between the two countries—in the Dominican Republic, all the components made a positive contribution to growth, in contrast to Haiti, where all the contributions except human capital were negative. In the 1970s and 1980s, the stock of capital in both countries was rising (in the 1970s, the arrival of petrodollars in the global markets and the partial opening of both countries to the world made borrowing abroad easier). In the 1980s both countries experienced significant productivity slumps (more severe than in Haiti). To recapitulate, 29 years of the Dominican Republic's growth was driven primarily by increments in capital. Haiti, apart from a short period of capital-driven growth in the 1970s, underwent subsequent periods of decline, with a particularly precipitous productivity drop in the 1980s.

Since investment is of prime importance to growth, we discuss it separately in the next section. The populations of both countries were similar throughout the period under examination. Yet, there was a difference in the working age population—in 1960[15] this share accounted for 57 percent of Haiti's and only 31 percent of the Dominican Republic's total populations, respectively.[16] In both cases this was connected with high fertility rates and a resultantly large share of youth. The difference narrowed over time, and in 2000, both countries had a similar share of working-age people—a little under 50 percent of the total population.[17] From the very outset, the Dominican Republic performed substantially better in terms of educational level. The average length of education in 1960 was 2.7 years in the Dominican Republic as against 0.8 in Haiti. Forty years later, the Dominican average had gone up to 4.9 years against Haiti's 2.8 years (Barro and Lee 2000). As regards the quality of education, as state structures disintegrated in Haiti, education was to a large extent taken over by private entities—Catholic or Protestant mission schools, and schools run by international organizations, local communities, or commercial enterprises. To take primary-level education as an example, state-run schools account for less than 10 percent of the total in Haiti (World Bank 2006b). Amid structural inefficiencies in the Ministry of Education, this translates into the inadequate supervision[18] of particular schools—approximately 70 percent of the schools do not hold the required permits and 60 percent of teachers lack requisite qualifications (World Bank 2006a, 2006b). In contrast, the Dominican Republic implemented reforms in the 1970s that, apart from increasing the number of students above primary age, introduced an instructional framework better aligned with the demands of a modern economy. The shortcomings of the Haitian education system were compounded by the "brain drain" phenomenon—in 2000 three-fourths of Haitians with a degree had emigrated to the United States (see table 9.2 for details on migration from Haiti and the Dominican Republic by level of education).[19]

Investment

Growth accounting highlights an increase in capital stock as one of the most important factors responsible for the development of the Dominican Republic.[20] Already in the early 1960s, investment per capita was double the figure of Haiti,

Table 9.2 Emigration to the United States, by Level of Education
Percent

	1980s	1990s	2000
Dominican Republic			
No education	1.7	1.7	1.8
Primary	12.5	8.9	18.0
Secondary	21.4	26.5	32.1
Tertiary	13.9	13.8	13.3
Haiti			
No education	0.3	0.8	0.6
Primary	9.6	10.5	15.7
Secondary	24.0	36.1	47.0
Tertiary	62.2	67.7	76.9

Source: Orozco 2002.
Note: Values are aggregated.

and in subsequent years the gap continued to widen. Steady absolute-terms investment growth in the Dominican Republic resulted both from the rising share of this component in GDP (in Haiti the contribution was continually low) and overall GDP growth, which was practically nonexistent in Haiti (Mahajan 2002). In both countries, private investment accounted for approximately three-fourths of total investment.

The most violent changes in investment levels (depicted in figure 9.5) are related to the sanctions imposed on a turbulent Haiti in the early 1990s and American intervention in the Dominican Republic in 1965.

Though data on the share of investment in Haiti's GDP in the 1950s is missing, time series are available for elements of infrastructure (roads, telephone lines) and production directly related to the investment process (cement, electric energy) in both countries. This affords a certain possibility of verifying the figures quoted in the national accounts.

The first graph in figure 9.6 indicates the total road network length (without breaking it down into paved and unpaved roads). The points in bold represent the available statistical data, while the others signify estimates for the years when no statistics were available.

Haiti and the Dominican Republic had a similar road network in 1950.[21] In the late 1950s the infrastructure of the Dominican Republic was gradually developed (under Trujillo). Later, in the late 1960s and early 1970s, there was another period of expansion, after which the road network stabilized at roughly 12,000 kilometers (km).[22] In the same period Haiti saw virtually no development in this area. This may testify to the weakness of the Haitian government, which failed to construct an adequate road network by its own means and to facilitate private sector investment in infrastructure. Apart from road length itself, there are partial data available on road quality—again, the Dominican Republic is at a clear advantage, with 6,224 km of paved roads out of the total of 12,600 km

Figure 9.5 Investment in Absolute Terms and as a Share of GDP, 1960–2000

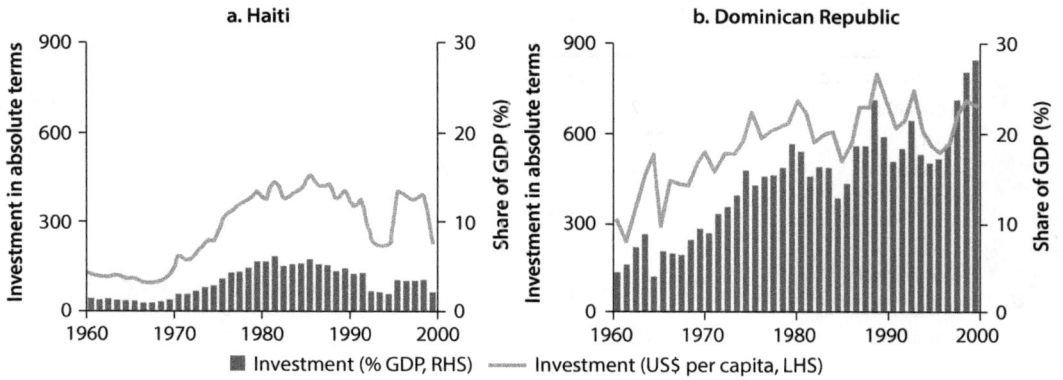

a. Haiti

b. Dominican Republic

■ Investment (% GDP, RHS)   ——— Investment (US$ per capita, LHS)

Source: Mahajan 2002; OxLAD database.
Note: GDP = gross domestic product; LHS = left axis; RHS = right axis.

Figure 9.6 Investment Outlays: Sanity Check, 1950–2000

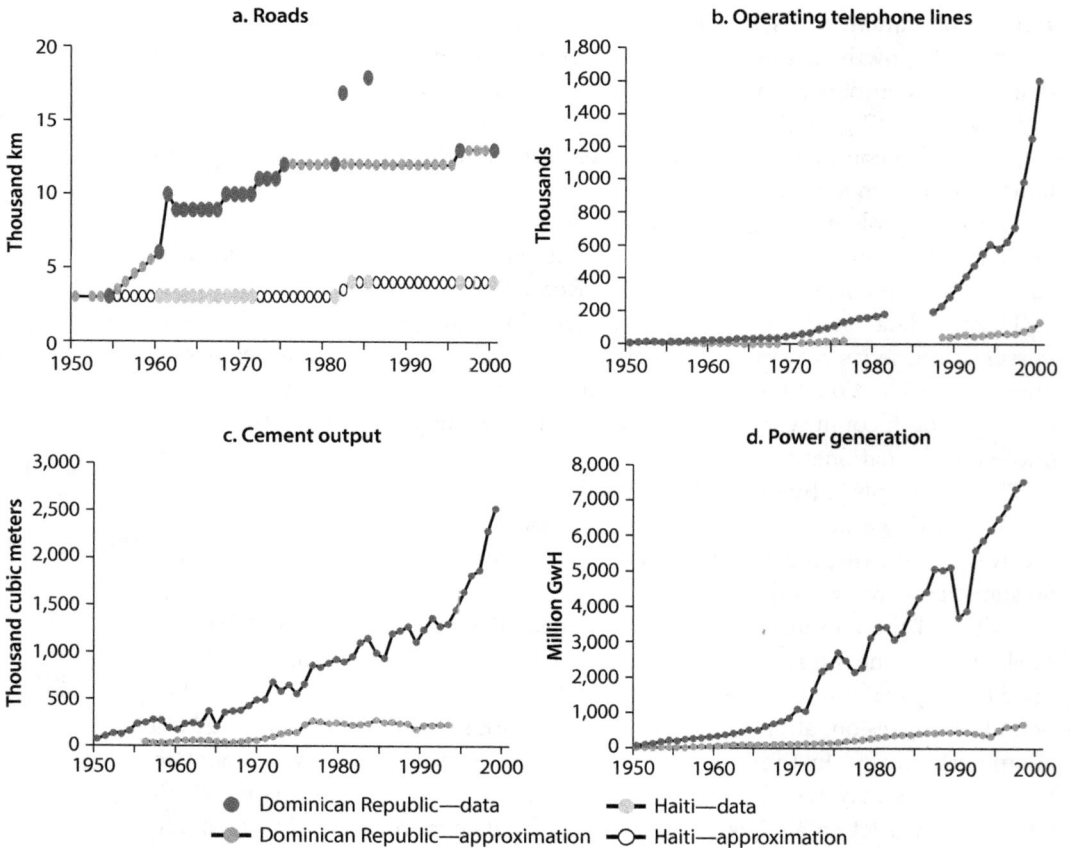

a. Roads

b. Operating telephone lines

c. Cement output

d. Power generation

● Dominican Republic—data   ●● Haiti—data
●— Dominican Republic—approximation   –○– Haiti—approximation

Sources: OxLAD database; Congress 2001a, 2001b; ECLAC 2001.
Note: A sanity test or sanity check is a basic test to quickly evaluate whether a claim or the result of a calculation can possibly be true.
GWh = gigawatt hour; km = kilometer.

(of Haiti's 4,160 km of roads, 1,011 km are paved).[23] Amid a tropical climate and mountainous terrain, a road network so severely underdeveloped makes parts of Haiti practically inaccessible during the rainy season.[24]

With respect to telephone lines, the Dominican Republic started off at a higher level (7,000 vs. 3,000 lines) and from the 1970s the difference grew at an accelerating pace. In the 1990s telecommunications was the fastest-growing sector of the Dominican economy.

Similarly, cement production may exemplify how little construction activity was taking place in Haiti—even in the 1950s and 1960s, when the wealth of the inhabitants of both countries was comparable, there was more construction going on in the Dominican Republic.[25]

Production of electric energy also reflects Haiti's stagnation and the Dominican Republic's development—even though the aftermath of the 1990–91 crisis cannot go unnoticed. At this point, it might be appropriate to once again highlight the development gap that has arisen between the two countries over 50 years. Although World Bank country reports (World Bank 2006a, 2006b) quote insufficient energy production as one of the constraints to growth for both Dominican Republic and Haiti, the analysis of figure 9.6 shows the magnitude of the difference.

Taking into account records on road development, cement production, and electricity generation it seems plausible that in the 1950s, too, the investment rate in the Dominican Republic was higher than in Haiti. Although data on this period are scant, one might speculate that the higher rate of investment in the Dominican Republic under Trujillo was an example of growth under "extractive institutions" (Acemoglu and Robinson 2012). In the following decades, however, the political institutions of the Dominican Republic became more inclusive and the investment rate grew further.

In ensuing decades the differences in the investment rate can, to a large extent, be attributed to differences in the legal system and property right protection. Although data for the 1960s and 1970s are limited, starting from 1980 more data on the quality of institutions in Haiti and the Dominican Republic are available. One such measure is a subindex, "legal system and property rights," that is part of the Fraser Institute's Economic Freedom index. It takes into account, among other factors, judicial independence, protection of property rights, legal enforcement of contracts, the reliability of police, and business costs of crime. During the whole period for which data are available, the Dominican Republic scored significantly better than Haiti (see figure 9.7).

Simple panel regression for Latin America countries in 1980–2009 confirms the importance of a nation's legal system and property rights to its investment rate (table 9.3). As far as other institutional variables are concerned, credit market regulations (consisting of, among other things, ownership of banks, interest rate regulations) turned out to be statistically significant as well, although their impact is much lower. From control variables (changes in terms of trade, inflation) only the variation of GDP growth (a measure of volatility) is statistically significant.

Figure 9.7 An Index of the Legal System and Property Rights in Haiti and the Dominican Republic, 1980–2005

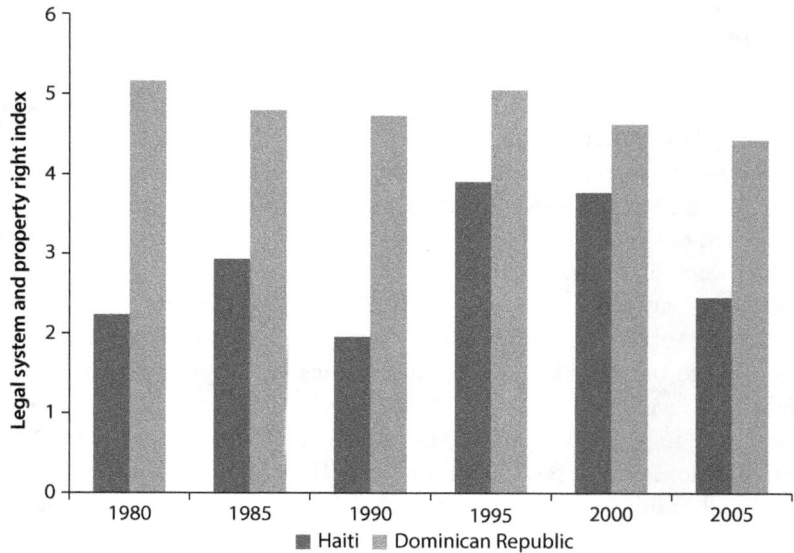

Source: Fraser Institute, Economic Freedom Network, http://www.freetheworld.com/.
Note: 0 = the worst; 10 = the best.

Table 9.3 Investment Rate Determinants

	Estimate	Standard error	t statistic	p
Const	14.67	1.80	8.15	<0.001***
GDP_var	−0.03	0.02	−1.69	0.093*
Credit regulation	0.27	0.14	1.85	0.067*
Legal system and property rights	1.12	0.27	4.12	<0.001***

Note: Random effects panel regression for eight Latin American countries across six five-year-long periods between 1980 and 2009. Dependent variable: investment rate (% GDP). Hausman test: $p = 0.18$. GDP = gross domestic product; Significance level: * = 10 percent, ** = 5 percent, *** = 1 percent

More than 90 percent of the difference in the investment rate in Haiti and the Dominican Republic during the period 1980–84 can be explained by the model shown in table 9.2 with differences in the legal system and property rights alone explaining over 80 percent of the difference. For the following period, the model explains about one-fourth of the differences between the countries. Poorer performance of the model after 1985 can be attributed to the subsequent coups, embargoes, and foreign interventions in Haiti (discussed in following section). The overall index of the legal system and property rights alone can explain nearly 40 percent of the differences between Haiti and the Dominican Republic during the period 1980–2009.

Political Stability, Internal Security, and Property Rights

While the level of investment explains, to a great extent, the Dominican Republic's growth, GDP slumps observed in Haiti are far more difficult to interpret. Models including economic variables (human capital, infrastructure, inflation, openness of the economy, changes in terms of trade, size of government spending, development of the financial sector, and so on) do not provide a satisfactory explanation for the scale of this phenomenon (Loayza, Fajnzylber, and Calderon 2004; World Bank 2006b). What seems of key importance is political stability, which, even when included in such models (as measured by for example, the ICRG),[26] having proved statistically significant, is played down due to the low values its coefficient tends to assume in estimation.[27]

An alternative measure could be constructed on the basis of the Polity IV index (see figure 9.8), which does not refer directly to stability, but to freedom in a given country (with 10 denoting full democracy, and –10 totalitarianism). By looking at the frequency and scale of system changes, we see how unstable a country Haiti has been. Since there is no hard evidence for democracy having a positive impact on the pace of economic growth, attention indeed should

Figure 9.8 Polity IV Index

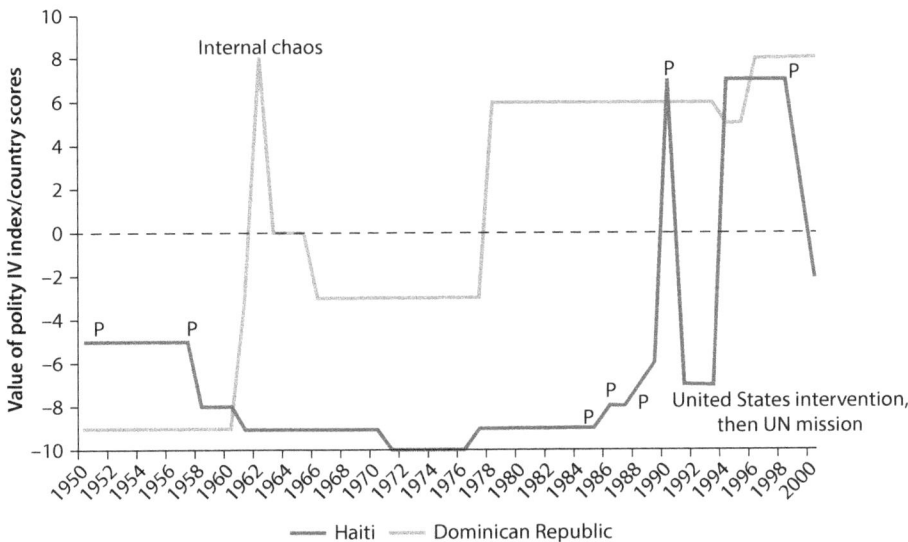

Source: Based on Polity IV (http://www.systemicpeace.org).
Note: In the Dominican Republic, the assassination of President Trujillo in 1961 started the period of internal chaos and frequent changes of governments, both trough coups and democratic elections. In 1965, the United States military intervened, enabling power seizure by Balageur.

In Haiti, overthrow of Baby Doc in 1986 started the period of military coups. Contrary to the earlier situation in the Dominican Republic, this time the United States intervened to restore democratically elected President Aristide. 10 = full democracy; –10 = totalitarianism; P = coup.

be focused on the frequency of changes to a political system (Jaramillo and Sancak 2007).[28]

Since gaining independence in the 19th century, both countries have experienced long periods of power struggles and permanent political turmoil. But in the Dominican Republic the situation changed in the 20th century. The American occupation, followed by the long rule of Trujillo, gave the country a degree of stability (albeit at the expense of brutal oppression). Simultaneously, foundations of domestic infrastructure were laid (roads, schools, development of the sugar industry).[29] After Trujillo's death (in 1961) a period of disruptive changes ensued—including the election of president Juan Bosch (1963), an American intervention (1966), and the election of Balaguer (1966). From that moment on the Dominican Republic enjoyed relative political stability under the authoritarian rule of Balaguer, and the country came to be perceived as a relatively predictable partner, despite its leader clinging to power (by means of electoral fraud and unlawful suppression of opposition) and often acting in a populist manner.[30] This was conducive to foreign investment, the inflow of tourists, and generally closer ties with the global economy. These trends strengthened toward the end of the 1970s (when Balaguer temporarily renounced power), to consolidate in the 1990s (when he withdrew from politics).

In contrast, the Duvalier regime in Haiti proved much less stable. The rule of the first Duvalier, Papa Doc, was relatively short (12 years as against Trujillo's 31) and focused entirely on brutally suppressing any sign of opposition. His successor, Baby Doc, assumed office at a very young age and proved to be a weak politician, incapable of properly controlling even his own entourage. Consequently, the already weak state structures went on to disintegrate and anarchy mounted in the country, finally erupting with full force after the president fled the island (1986). Except for a short interlude during the 1970s (the early years of Baby Doc's rule), investors shunned Haiti as a country too unstable to launch any business venture, and tourists avoided it. One period that especially stands out is the latter half of the 1980s, when system changes became particularly radical and were accompanied by frequent coups—coinciding with the country's worst economic performance in the whole analyzed half century.

Amid frequent and violent changes of power, it was impossible to establish a state governed by the rule of law. Besides the index of the legal system and property rights (provided in figure 9.7), one can quote more recent research showing the atrophy of the official law system in Haiti combined with a convoluted structure of property rights. Hernando de Soto (2002) estimates that 97 percent of rural and 68 percent of urban property is owned without official titles. In this highly corrupt[31] and bureaucratic state, it is extremely difficult—as well as time consuming—to obtain an official ownership title (de Soto notes that to purchase land legally it is necessary to complete 111 bureaucratic procedures that may easily take 19 years, effectively discouraging citizens from legalizing their assets). On the other hand, even though more than half of the Haitian population is illiterate, all persons interviewed by de Soto's team held diverse informal proofs of ownership (most of these have no backing in the statutes, yet are recognized by Haitians). This testifies to a strong need to document one's property as well as the substantial potential of local communities to self-organize as they attempt to replace the state in areas where it has failed most acutely.

Irrespective of the quality of law, it is hardly enforceable at the moment—after the army was disbanded in 1995, the only official forces of law and order in this country of 9 million was a 2,000-strong police force (2004) and the UNO stabilization mission numbering 8,000 troops (2007).[32] The weakness of state structures combined with the extreme poverty prevailing in Haiti has led to a substantial rise in crime levels. Unfortunately, the statistics of international organizations (Interpol, UNO) do not comprise figures on Haiti. The situation is illustrated indirectly by U.S. Department of State recommendations, strongly advising against any visits to Haiti. The country is depicted as devoid of "safe places," where protests and riots may break out at any time and turn into uncontrolled bursts of violence. The blockades cropping up at regular intervals may cut off vast regions of the country for extended periods. Not only individuals, but also companies and organizations can fall prey to this violence—feuds between companies may involve the use of force (cases of forceful takeovers have also been seen). The problem of violence affects both urban and rural areas. And while this refers to the current situation (2008), it has been similar at least since the mid-1990s.[33]

On the other hand, the Dominican Republic, notwithstanding rising crime rates in the 1980s (due to internal economic problems combined with a fast-developing illicit drug trade), continues to boast fairly low crime figures in comparison to highly developed countries. In Crime and Society, a comparative criminology tour of the world index representing crime levels following the approach of the U.S. Federal Bureau of Investigation,[34] is used to benchmark the Dominican Republic against other countries. The index in 1998 stood at 175 for the Dominican Republic (compared to 1,709 in Japan, a country with a low crime rate; and 4,123 in the United States, a country with a high one). Although there were fairly many murders per 100,000 inhabitants in the Dominican Republic (15.8 versus 1.1 in Japan and 5.5 in the United States), the country did much better in the assault category (28.4 as against 23.7 in Japan and 323.6 in the United States), as well as burglary (22.6 as against 233 in Japan and 728.4 in the United States) or car theft (14 as against 44.2 in Japan and 414 in the United States). The U.S. Department of State warns tourists against theft and other minor crimes in this nation, yet it does not discourage a visit to the Dominican Republic as it does in the case of Haiti. In the Dominican Republic, crime is concentrated in urban areas.[35]

Current (2007) rankings by different institutions (for example, Foreign Policy[36]) often classify Haiti as a failed state, unable to effectively exercise power over the territory it controls. Earlier, weak state institutions had already started to degenerate with the weakening of the Duvalier regime in the 1980s, and to disintegrate at a later stage, alongside frequent government changes and military coups. The institutional void that opened was filled by gangs—often connected with drug traffickers—on the one hand, and by different forms of citizen-organized groups on the other.

Puzzles of Economic Growth • http://dx.doi.org/10.1596/978-1-4648-0325-3

Openness

Both countries lack precise figures on tourism at the beginning of the period under review. But Fuller (1999) provides a rough proxy of tourist activity: in the 1960s *Fodor's Guide to the Caribbean*[37] devoted only nine pages to the Dominican Republic, describing it as a place of little interest from a tourist's point of view. It was contrasted with Haiti (29 pages), described as definitely worth visiting. In 2000 the Dominican Republic received 2,978,000 visitors while Haiti received only 140,000 (see figure 9.9). At the moment, tourism generates only 7 percent (and indirectly, a further 13–15 percent) of the Dominican GDP,[38] which amounts to nearly $1,000 per capita—more than the entire per capita GDP of Haiti.

The history of tourism on the island of Hispaniola reflects both countries' path of development. In spite of Haiti's slight advantage at the outset, the 1970s brought an increasingly fast expansion of the tourist sector in the Dominican Republic—the Ministry of Tourism, created in 1970, and the tourism promotion agency INFRATOUR both launched promotional campaigns in the United States, on the one hand, and initiated investment in public infrastructure in prospective resorts, on the other.[39] Those activities became particularly intensive after 1978 and the victory of the PRD party[40] in the parliamentary elections. At the same time, tax incentives were created, along with legal inducements to stimulate the development of the tourism industry.[41] Hotels and restaurants were predominantly privately owned (a distinguishing feature in the region— foreign investors held only 21 percent of all hotel rooms, against the average of 65 percent in the whole of the Caribbean). Also, Haiti saw a rising number of visitors in that period, peaking at 300,000 in 1980.

Figure 9.9 Number of Tourists Visiting Haiti and the Dominican Republic, 1978–2000

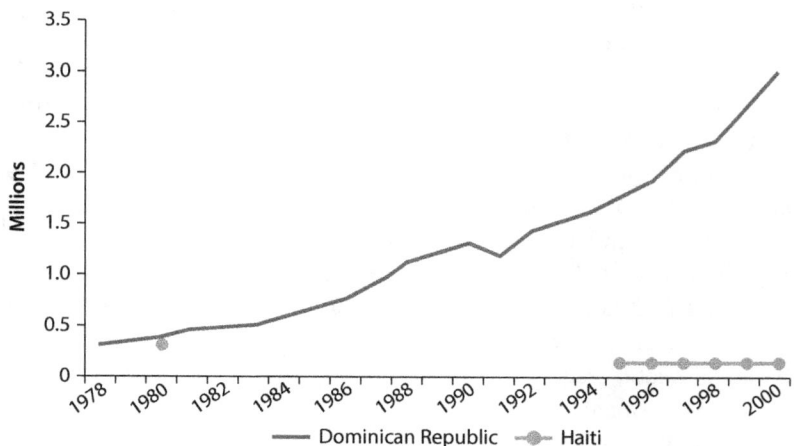

Source: World Tourism Organization database.

In the 1980s tourism in the two countries developed along two different paths—owing to very low prices (half the level of, for example, Cancun or Puerto Rico), the Dominican Republic attracted an increasing number of visitors. At the same time conditions in Haiti—haunted by political instability and frequent riots characteristic of the final period of Jean Claude Duvalier's rule, along with the chaos that ensued after his escape—proved a strong disincentive for tourists. This resulted in a gradual decline of the sector, with the number of hotel rooms shrinking from 3,000 in 1981 to 1,500 seven years later, combined with a marked deterioration in the more broadly understood tourist infrastructure. Apart from objective factors, tourism in Haiti was hurt by word of mouth that branded Haiti as a breeding ground for the HIV virus, effectively repelling a substantial proportion of tourists (Congress 2001b).

The 1990s brought a further decline in tourism in Haiti, marred by internal strife and international sanctions—and the sector's continued growth in the Dominican Republic. In the latter case, development also took on a qualitative character—whereas in the 1980s the sector's expansion was driven exclusively by price (the Dominican Republic had the lowest percentage of repeat visits, which is a measure of tourists' satisfaction), in the 1990s, due to further investment, tourism offers became far more enticing. This bore fruit as the number of visitors increased.

In some studies devoted to the tourist industry in the Dominican Republic, it is criticized for being only loosely connected to the rest of the economy and being characterized by high import intensity and the transfer of profits abroad (possibly owing to a substantial number of tax reliefs). Nevertheless, comparative analysis between Haiti and the Dominican Republic shows that, notwithstanding its flaws, tourism grew in the Dominican Republic, whereas Haiti, despite a greater[42] starting potential, failed to take advantage of opportunity.

Besides tourism, another material difference between Haiti and the Dominican Republic concerns free trade zones (embracing mainly assembly plants and the clothing industry). Even though toward the end of the 1970s they started to crop up on both sides of the border, the fall of the Duvalier regime, and the subsequent coups and sanctions led to a total closure of free trade zones in Haiti.[43] At the same time, free trade zones in the Dominican Republic continued to develop until as recently as 2000, with their workforce peaking at 200,000.[44]

Similar to the country's tourist sector, the Dominican free trade zones were criticized for their weak integration with the rest of the economy, high import intensity, and cases of unsafe conditions for local employees. But once again a comparative analysis shows that in contrast to Haiti, the Dominican Republic was able to take advantage of the development potential offered by these free trade zones.

The well-developed tourist sector and free trade zones also account, to a large extent, for the advantage of the Dominican Republic over Haiti in terms of exports volume (free trade zones alone generate almost three-fourths of goods exported by the Dominican Republic; see figure 9.10) and, consequently, for the degree of openness of the economy as measured by the sum of exports

Figure 9.10 Dominican Republic: Exports of Goods and Services, 1993–2005

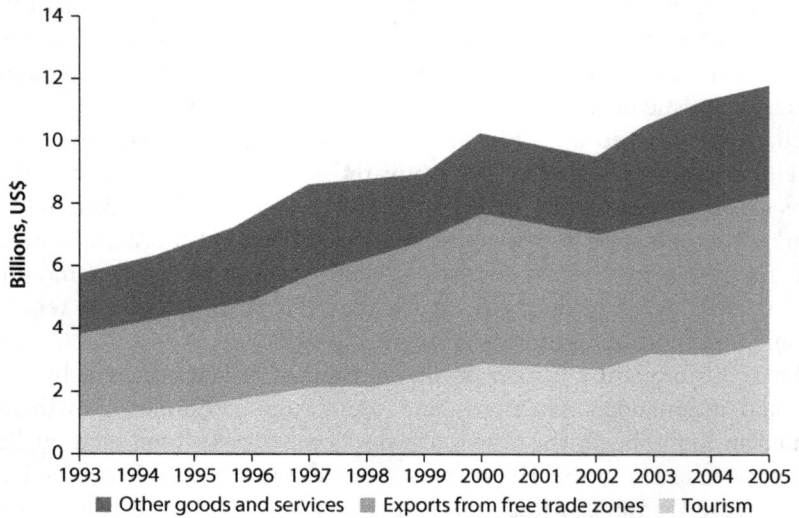

Legend: Other goods and services ■ Exports from free trade zones ■ Tourism

Source: Foreign Sector Statistics, Central Bank of the Dominican Republic: http://www.bancentral.gov
.do:8080/english/statistics.asp?a=Foreign_Secto.

Figure 9.11 Openness of the Two Economies (Exports + Imports as a Percentage of GDP), 1950–2000

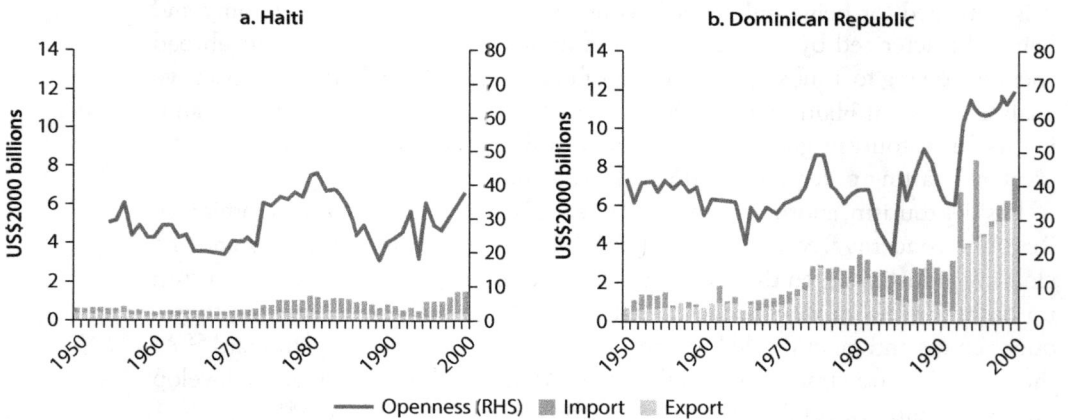

a. Haiti

b. Dominican Republic

Legend: —— Openness (RHS) ■ Import ■ Export

Source: OxLAD, IMF. databases
Note: GDP = gross domestic product; RHS = right axis.

and imports (the assembly plants operating in the free trade zones also generate high imports) in relation to GDP (see figure 9.11).

Inflow of Foreign Funds

Both countries saw a large (in relation to GDP) inflow of funds from abroad during the study period. Three basic types of inflows should be mentioned: remittances from emigrants, foreign direct investment (FDI), and official development aid.

In 1970–2000 funds transferred to the analyzed countries totaled $28 billion in the case of the Dominican Republic and $10 billion in Haiti (in both cases, at 2000 exchange rates). The largest portion of these flows were emigrants' remittances—currently there are approximately 2 million Haitians and 2 million Dominicans living abroad in the United States and Europe (as well as approximately 0.5 million Haitians in the Dominican Republic). Their remittances accounted for 12–14 percent of the Dominican, and over 25 percent of the Haitian GDP (see figure 9.12).

In both countries, households receiving transfers from abroad dedicated most of these funds to everyday expenses—this was particularly important in Haiti, where they were practically the only social security protecting the population from starvation. The second key item on the expenditure side in both countries is education—it may indicate, that the inhabitants of both countries understand the significance of education for their children's future development.[45] Finally, even though 4–5 percent devoted to new or existing business ventures seems relatively little, with the volume of transfers taken into account, it adds up to $850 million in the Dominican Republic and to $270 million in Haiti (which is comparable

Figure 9.12 Transfers from Abroad (1970–2010, Cumulated, in Dollars from 2000)

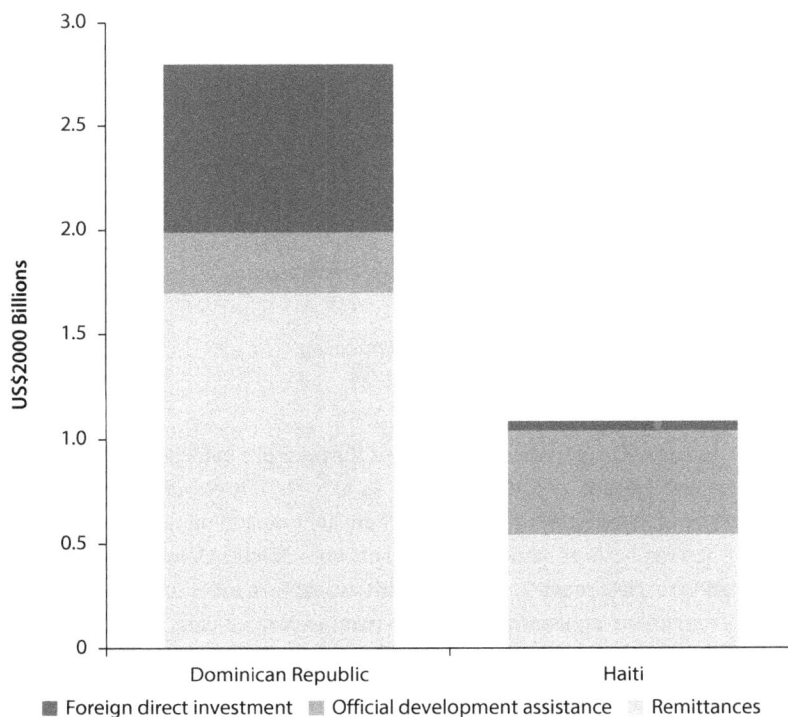

Source: Data on Remittances from Abroad are from Worldbank: http://www.worldbank.org/migration; data on ODA are from OECD.stat database (dataset: Dataset: DAC2a Official Development Assistance_ Disbursemnts); data on FDI flows are from UNCTAD database: http://unctadstat.unctad.org/ data series: Foregn Direct Investment indicators - 200 countries 1970–2003.

with total FDI in Haiti, that is, $410 million). The experience of the region's countries—as well as more thorough studies of the Dominican Republic—point to foreign funds being one of the strongest drivers of domestic investment (see box 9.2 for discussion of the link between remittances inflows and private investment in the Dominican Republic). Over time, the foreign inflow increased strongly during 1990s (see figure 9.13), as burgeoning diasporas were able to send ever-increasing amounts (Orozco 2006).

Another important source of foreign funds is development aid. Almost throughout the entire period discussed, Haiti received higher amounts (in absolute terms) than the Dominican Republic (see figure 9.14). The highest sums were received during the short period of democratization following Aristide's return to the country in 1994 (see figure 9.14). There is no detailed research showing to what extent this aid stimulated growth in Haiti, and international experience in this area is inconclusive.

The third source of foreign funds is FDI. Since 1970 foreign investors have clearly favored the Dominican Republic (see figure 9.15). With almost an identical location and quite similar labor costs in the 1970s, the decisive factors here seem to be the amount of bureaucratic barriers and the broadly understood

---

Box 9.2 Remittances from Abroad and Investment

An interesting attempt to explain changes in the contribution of investment to GDP is included in a World Bank study (2006a). The authors developed a model which, after being estimated, takes on the following form:

$$\ln\frac{private\,investment}{GDP} = -3,3 - 0,39\ln\frac{public\,investment}{GDP} + 3,16\Delta GDP - 0,16 price$$
$$+ 8,12\ \ln\left(1 + \frac{remittances}{GDP}\right)$$

where ΔGDP denotes GDP growth rate and price is the price of capital goods relative to wages. All parameters are relevant, and the signs are as expected. A crowding-out effect can be observed (rising public investment squeezes out private investment), yet the item of greatest significance is the remittances made by immigrants from abroad. Unfortunately, running this sort of calculation for Haiti proved unfeasible—the available number of observations (10) was too small to estimate the equations in a reliable manner. Nevertheless, a simplest correlation coefficient sufficed to indicate different patterns than in the Dominican Republic. While in the latter the correlation of investment and remittances (in 1970–2000) reached nearly 0.9, in Haiti it was −0.25. The negative sign may surprise, yet it is the product of a few troubled years in the late 1990s—in 1970–95, it was 0.74.

Source: World Bank 2006a.

Figure 9.13 Remittances from Abroad, 1970–2000

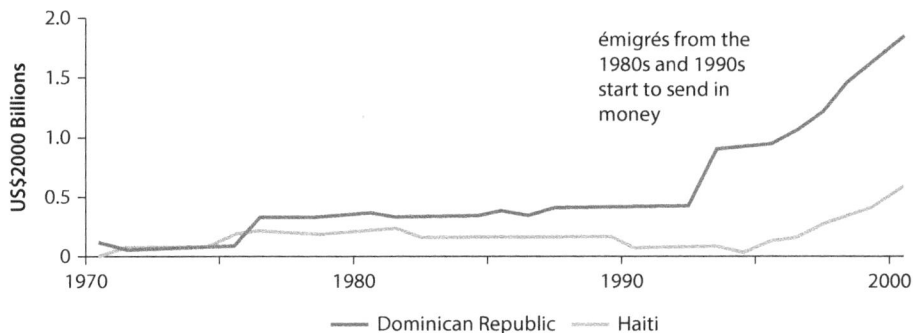

émigrés from the
1980s and 1990s
start to send in
money

Dominican Republic — Haiti

Source: World Bank. http://www.worldbank.org/migration.

Figure 9.14 Official Development Aid, 1970–2010

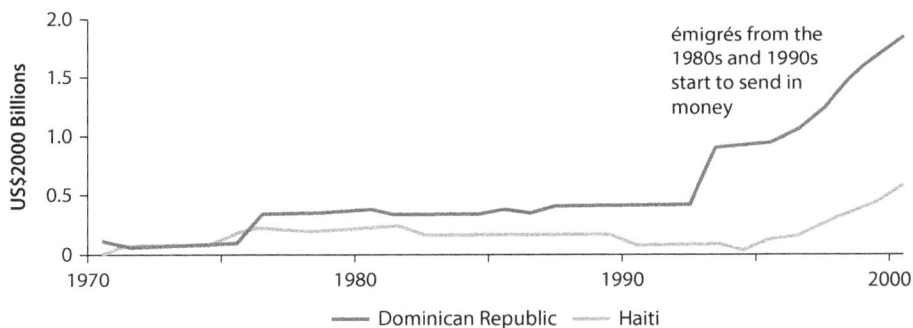

émigrés from the
1980s and 1990s
start to send in
money

Dominican Republic — Haiti

Source: OECD Dataset: DAC2a Official Development Assistance_Disbursemnts). http://stats.oecd.org/Index.aspx?DataSet
Code=TABLE2A, http://stats.oecd.org/OECDStat_Metadata/ShowMetadata.ashx?Dataset=TABLE2A.

Figure 9.15 Foreign Direct Investment (FDI)

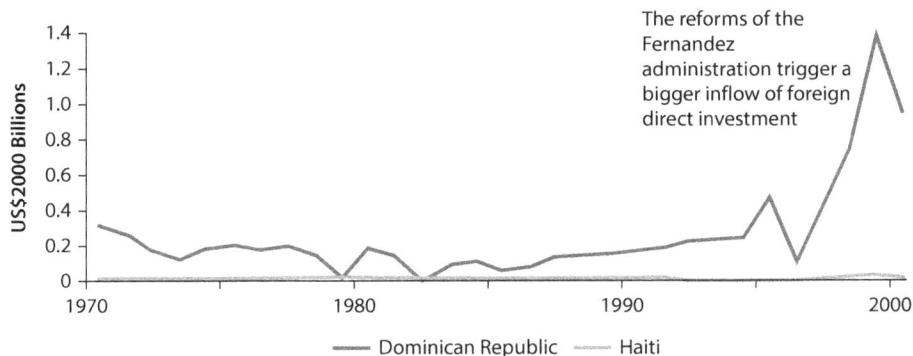

The reforms of the
Fernandez
administration trigger a
bigger inflow of foreign
direct investment

Dominican Republic — Haiti

Source: UNCTAD. http://unctadstat.unctad.org/EN.

country risks. When discussing FDI we must note that besides the injection of funds, it facilitates the transfer of technical and organizational knowledge often unavailable in the country of investment.

Summary and Conclusions

In the Dominican Republic, a modicum of predictability, political stability, and protection of property rights have been conducive to investment and helped make better use of the country's natural trump cards—cheap labor, pristine beaches, and the proximity of the United States. The free trade zones and the tourist sector alone, both drawing on these resources, account for roughly one-third of the difference in the levels of GDP per capita between Haiti and the Dominican Republic.

Haiti, despite possessing the same trump cards, was not able to benefit from them. Frequent power changes, rising crime, and the progressive decline of the state discouraged citizens from investing, while foreign investors and tourists alike started to avoid the nation. As state institutions disintegrated, the crime rate in Haiti shot to levels much higher than those in the Dominican Republic (in a 2006 Gallup survey, the question "have you been mugged in the last 12 months?" received an affirmative answer from 30 percent of Haitian respondents and 11 percent from Dominican respondents).

Back in 1950 the two countries shared similar technical and social infrastructure, yet as state structures in Haiti gradually decomposed (and those in the Dominican Republic developed, however slowly), differences started building up. In the period discussed, investment in the Dominican Republic (on average 19 percent of GDP) far exceeded that in Haiti (9 percent of GDP).[46] Also, the Dominican Republic developed its road network (12,600 km)—gaining a clear edge on Haiti (4,200 km), where many areas are still difficult to access. Simultaneously, due to an efficient education system, the population of the Dominican Republic is far better educated (16 percent of the population over 15 years of age is illiterate) than that of Haiti (50 percent).

The Dominican Republic's political stability paved the way for the development of the country's economic cooperation with other countries. Haiti, with its frequent and violent power changes, could not be perceived as a credible partner. Thanks to the development of the tourist sector, the Dominican Republic succeeded in attracting nearly 3 million tourists in 2000 (when Haiti had 140,000). At the same time, the aggregate value of FDI in the Dominican Republic amounted to $5.2 billion (as against $0.22 million in Haiti). Over the analyzed period, the Dominican Republic gradually shifted away from its role as a sugar exporter and developed an industry capable of selling export goods worth $5.7 billion in 2010 (while, in Haiti, this figure was $0.3 million).

The extreme poverty prevailing in Haiti today makes the country politically unstable and vulnerable to external shocks, thus impeding any attempt to restore the basic state institutions required for the country to develop. Combined with rural overpopulation, poverty has led to overexploitation of the Haitian forests (only 4 percent of the total area is currently forested, as against almost 30 percent in the Dominican Republic), making the country even more vulnerable to hurricane destruction as well as other natural disasters. The deficiencies that come with poverty were drastically exposed by the 2010 earthquake. Poorly constructed and maintained buildings (or and slums) easily collapsed during the earthquake, while the lack of infrastructure and emergency services impeded rescue operations. The death toll of Haitian earthquake exceeds 100,000 people[47]; in a more developed country the death toll of earthquake of similar magnitude would most probably it be significantly lower.

But even before the earthquake the life in Haiti was hard—in 2006 the question "have you been hungry during the last 12 months?" was answered in the affirmative by 72 percent of Haitian respondents, as compared with 36 percent of Dominican respondents.[48]

Notes

1. This chapter was written in 2009, one year before deadly earthquake which claimed the lives of over 100 thousands of Haitians and further widened the gap between Haiti and the Dominican Republic.

2. GK$—Geary-Khamis international dollar is a hypothetical unit of currency that has the same purchasing power parity that U.S. dollar in the United States at a given point of time; benchmarking year is 1990.

3. While there were divisions based on race in both countries, these were never as strong as, for example, the ethnic conflicts in Africa.

4. Haiti gained independence as a result of a slave rebellion that triggered a total collapse of the plantation system. In the Dominican Republic the proclamation of independence did not entail any violent changes to the ownership structure, and the plantation system was not abandoned (Congress 2001a, 200b).

5. Haiti in 1916–34, the Dominican Republic in 1916–24; after American troops were formally retrieved, American advisers stayed behind.

6. GDP per capita geometric mean, after Maddison (2007).

7. In addition, in 1979 the Dominican Republic was affected by hurricanes David and Frederic, resulting in losses of over of $1.8 billion (in 1998 prices; IDB 2000). Moreover, import quotas for Dominican sugar were introduced by the United States as of 1981 (Congress 2001a).

8. During this period, the Dominican Republic experienced inflation levels significantly higher than Haiti; however, amid other, much more acute problems in Haiti, a healthy currency did not translate into faster economic growth than in the Dominican Republic. In the case of these two countries, differences in monetary policy do not explain performance differences.

9. Throughout the analyzed period, the Dominican Republic posted a higher share of government expenditure in GDP (approximately 15–20 percent) than Haiti (approximately 10–15 percent). The exception is the 1980s, when, due to the shrinking GDP, the share of government spending in Haiti's GDP rose to 25 percent. But given Haiti's underlying problems, fiscal policy alone cannot explain such a large difference in the two countries' economic performance after 50 years.

10. The initial sanctions imposed by the United States and the Organisation of American States (OAS) were subsequently stepped up—in May 1994 the UNO imposed an embargo on all goods except humanitarian aid.

11. The precise average was 0.023 percent.

12. The value for Haiti is quoted directly after Nehru-Dhareshwar (1993); for the Dominican Republic, the available data for earlier years additionally enabled a calculation of capital as a function of previous investment.

13. Factor productivity defined as Solow's residual (TFP).

14. Recalculating using a lower depreciation rate or α value would have no impact on the conclusions—capital was the main source of growth in the Dominican Republic, and the productivity decline the biggest constraint for Haiti.

15. No data for the 1950s.

16. Such a large difference may raise doubt, yet the data are quoted after the World Bank and comply with the figures included in the study by the U.S. Library of Congress.

17. Working age, according to World Bank data, is 15–64 years of age. In the case of Haiti, it is pointless to analyze the number of the employed/jobless due to the size of informal economy—the official unemployment rate has occasionally exceeded 70 percent.

18. The absence of supervision is not necessarily wrong in itself—quality verification can sometimes be left to market forces (a more fundamental question, and one exceeding the scope of this study is to what extent the state should, for example, determine the core curriculum or resolve controversies, such as the clash of the theory of evolution and creationism); yet in Haiti, neither the former nor the latter function properly (the market needs competition, which is nonexistent in the educational sector in Haiti).

19. This is not a new phenomenon; in the 1960s it was already observed that more Haitians with a degree in medicine worked in Montreal alone than in the whole of Haiti (Congress 2001a).

20. Also in the 1990s, the period not included in our growth accounting analysis in the previous section (due to the scale of economic shocks in Haiti), investment in the Dominican Republic, despite the rising significance of productivity, remained an important source of growth. Growth accounting for the Dominican Republic in the 1990s is as follows: TFP increase, 2.2 percentage points; increase in capital stock, 1.1 percentage points; working age population increase, 0.6 percentage points; and human capital growth, 0.3 percentage points.

21. In 1937 Haiti had an even more extensive road network—2,000 km as against 1,000 km in the Dominican Republic.

22. According to OxLAD, in 1983 the total road length in the Dominican Republic increased to 17,000 km (compared to 12,000 km in the previous year), yet the data from the early 1990s put this figure again at 12,000 km (a level more or less consistent until today). Since both had a 50 percent increase in their road networks in one year and a fall—unconfirmed by other descriptive sources—back to 12,000 km seems rather unlikely, the two observations (1983 and 1985) have been omitted. The time series available in OxLAD are compiled from various sources, which is why such uncharacteristic observations may result from error made at the stage of data input or may result from the different definitions of a road encountered in various reference works (unpaved road, temporary road, and so on).

23. CIA Factbook, 1999 data.

24. In studies dealing with the American occupation it has been highlighted that the roads built at that time were of a concentric nature, connecting the capital with the rest of the country, while direct connections between the regions were underdeveloped. Considering the marginal amount of investment in the road network since that time, it can be assumed that the situation has remained more or less the same.

25. Road construction does not seem to account for the entire difference.

26. International Credit Risk Guide.

27. This could be related to the linear character of most such models and the nonlinear influence of political stability on economic growth—a certain minimum level of stability is a necessary, but not satisfactory, condition for economic growth to take place.

28. Although such an index has worked well in estimations by Jaramillo and Sancak (2007), it turned out to be statistically insignificant when it comes to the models explaining the investment rate. Still, the sign indicates that a greater number of political changes might have a negative impact on the investment rate.

29. The effectiveness of these projects is a separate issue. Yet, in a comparative analysis of Haiti versus the Dominican Republic it is important to note that in the Dominican Republic something was being developed, while in Haiti nothing happened.

30. In particular, toward the end of the 1980s, when he suspended talks with the IMF and continued financing the budget deficit by printing money. The main sources of the deficit were widely and arbitrarily granted tax breaks and subsidies for unprofitable state-owned enterprises.

31. No precise data are available for the years 1950–2000. In the Corruption Perceptions Index listings compiled by Transparency International, Haiti first features in 2002 in the 89th position (out of 102). In the same year the Dominican Republic ranked in 59th position.

32. The 2010 earthquake, that happened after this book was written, has further weakened institutions of Haitian state. The jury is still out weather international support in the aftermath of the earthquake will provide sufficient impulse to strengthen rule of law in Haiti in longer term.

33. More detailed description of situation in both Haiti and the Dominican Republic can be found in Crime and Society, A Comparative Criminology Tour of the World (http://www-rohan.sdsu.edu/faculty/rwinslow/namerica/dominican_republic.html.)

34. This index is constructed on data comprising: murders, forcible rapes, robberies, aggravated assaults, burglaries, larcenies-thefts, and motor vehicle thefts.

35. From Crime and Society, A Comparative Criminology Tour of the World.

36. In a list of bankrupt states compiled by *Foreign Policy*, Haiti features among 11 countries in the worst position. In terms of World Bank Worldwide Governance indicators Haiti during the most of the 1996–2012 period, for which data are available, was in lowest percentile in terms of government effectiveness, rule of law, control of corruption. In terms of Voice & Accountability, Political Stability and Absence of Violence and Regulatory Quality Haiti scores were between first and second percentile most of the time.

37. Fodor's is the largest publisher of guidebooks in English.

38. See the World Bank 2006a; World Tourism Organization (WTO) estimates for 1996 post a similar figure—putting 20.5 percent of GDP down to tourism (Michelitsch 2001).

39. In Puerto Plata alone, $74 million was invested in 1974–82.

40. The Dominican Revolutionary Party—a center-left party established in 1939. Its candidate Juan Bosch, after winning the presidential election in 1962, was deposed as a result of a coup. The party opposed Balaguer's rule and, in 1978, its candidate, Antonio Guzman, became president.

41. The Tourist Law of 1970 introduced exemptions from income taxes and inducements in importing goods needed to develop the sector.

42. Even though both countries are very similar in terms of geography, Haiti seems to offer a more interesting and exotic culture with many French influences and unique folklore and religion (voodoo).

43. At the beginning of the 1980s, they employed up to 80,000 people and, in 1991, only 33,000. They disappeared altogether by 1994 (Congress 2001b).

44. In the 21st century this trend has slowed down to the point of reversal—as a member of the WTO, the Dominican Republic has to apply equal treatment to all enterprises in the economy. At the same time, firms operating outside the free trade zone have been growing at an increasingly fast rate (Congress 2001a; World Bank 2006a).

45. According to survey by Inter-American Development Bank in 2007, money received as remittances was, excluding daily expanses, most frequently spend on education (29% of respondents), followed by start a business (25%). Similar survey in the Dominican Republic from 2004 (IDB and B&A 2004) brought similar results: remittances were spend mainly on daily needs (60% respondents) followed by investment in education (17%) and starting a business (5%).

46. Years 1960–2000 for both countries due to the lack of data for Haiti in the 1950s.

47. The official figure is 316,000 dead, but other estimates suggest substantially lower number of casualties, even as low as fewer than 100,000. http://earthquake.usgs.gov/earthquakes/world/most_destructive.php.

48. After the completion of the present study, Haiti was one of the first developing countries to experience riots triggered by the 2008 food price rises.

Bibliography

Publications

Acemoglu, D., and J. Robinson. 2012. *Why Nations Fail: The Origin of Power, Prosperity and Poverty*. New York: Crown Business.

Barro, R. J., and J-W. Lee. 2000. "International Data on Educational Attainment: Updates and Implications." CID Working Paper 42 (April), Harvard University.

Congress. 2001a. *A Country Study: Dominican Republic*. Library of Congress Call No. F1934.D64. Washington, DC.

———. 2001b. *A Country Study: Haiti*. Library of Congress Call No. F1934.D64. Washington, DC.

de Soto, H. 2002. *Tajemnica kapitału* [The Mystery of Capital]. Warsaw: Fijor Publishing.

ECLAC (Economic Commission for Latin America and the Caribbean). 2001. *Statistical Yearbook for Latin America and the Caribbean 2001*. UN ECLAC, Chile; http://www.eclac.org/publicaciones/xml/1/9641/indice.pdf; http://www.eclac.org/cgi-bin/getProd.asp?xml=/publicaciones/xml/1/9641/P9641.xml&xsl=/deype/tpl-i/p9f.xsl&base=/tpl-i/top-bottom.xslt.

Fuller, A. 1999. *Tourism Development in the Dominican Republic, Growth, Costs, Benefits and Choices.* Rutgers University.

Heston, A., R. Summers, and B. Aten. 2006. "Penn World Table Version 6.2." Center for International Comparisons of Production, Income and Prices, University of Pennsylvania.

IDB (Inter-American Development Bank). 2000. "A Matter of Development: How to Reduce Vulnerability in the Face of Natural Disasters." Seminar hand-outs, IDB, New Orleans.

IDB (Inter-American Development Bank) and B&A (Bendixen & Amandi). 2004. "Remittances and the Dominican Republic: Survey of Recipients in the Dominican Republic, Survey of Senders in the United States." IDB Publications 7499.

———. 2007. "Haiti Remittance Survey." http://idbdocs.iadb.org/wsdocs/getdocument .aspx?docnum=35119349.

Jaramillo, L., and C. Sancak. 2007. "Growth in the Dominican Republic and Haiti: Why Has the Grass Been Greener on One Side of Hispaniola?" IMF Working Paper III, International Monetary Fund, Washington, DC.

Loayza, N., P. Fajnzylber, and C. Calderon. 2004. *Economic Growth in Latin America and the Caribbean: Stylized Facts, Explanations, and Forecasts.* eBook 2004. http://hdl .handle.net/10986/7315.

Michelitsch, V. 2001. *Dominican Republic: Approaches Toward a Sustainable Tourism Development—A Strategic Concept.* Heilbronn, Germany: Fachhochshcule Heilbronn.

Nehru, V., and A. Dhareshwar. 1993. "A New Database on Physical Capital Stock: Sources, Methodology and Results." *Revista de Analisis Economica* 8 (1): 37–59.

Orozco, M. 2002. "Remittances to Latin America and its Effect on Development." Presentation available at http://publications.iadb.org/handle/11319/812?locale -attribute=en.

———. 2006. "Understanding the Remittance Economy in Haiti." Inter-American Dialogue Paper commissioned by the World Bank, Washington, DC, March 15.

World Bank. 2005. *Dominican Republic Review of Trade and Labor Competitiveness.* Washington, DC: World Bank.

———. 2006a. "The World Foundations of Growth and Competitiveness, Dominican Republic." Country Economic Memorandum, World Bank, Washington, DC.

———. 2006b. "Haiti: Options and Opportunities for Inclusive Growth." Country Economic Memorandum, World Bank, Washington, DC.

World Tourism Organization—papers on tourist traffic in the Dominican Republic and Haiti made available for the purposes of this study.

Young, A. 1995. "The Tyranny of Numbers: Confronting the Statistical Realities of the East Asian Growth Experience." *Quarterly Journal of Economics* 110 (3): 641–80.

Databases

Central Bank of the Dominican Republic. http://www.bancentral.gov.do/english/statistics .asp?a=Foreign_Sector.

CIA (Central Intelligence Agency) Factbook. https://www.cia.gov/library/publications /the-world-factbook/.

Crime and Society, a Comparative Criminology Tour of the World: http://www-rohan .sdsu.edu/faculty/rwinslow/namerica/dominican_republic.html.

Fraser Institute, Economic Freedom Network. http://www.freetheworld.com/.

Maddison. 2007. "Historical Statistics for the World Economy: 1–2003 AD." http://www
.ggdc.net/maddison/maddison-project/home.htm.

Mahajan, S. 2002. "TFP Toolkit." http://info.worldbank.org/etools/docs/library/86435/ses1
.1percent5Ftfptoolkitjune2003.xls.

OxLAD (The Oxford Latin American Economic History Database).

World Bank. "World Development Indicators Online." http://go.worldbank.org
/6HAYAHG8H0.

———. "Worldwide Governance Indicators." http://info.worldbank.org/governance/wgi
/index.aspx#home.

CHAPTER 10

How Has China Outpaced India?

Paweł Kozub

This chapter attempts to explain the reasons why the gap in gross domestic product (GDP) per capita between China and India reached 79 percent in the years 1978–2001.[1]

China and India attract attention because of their size and impact on the global economy. They account for 40 percent of the world's working age population and for 18 percent of total GDP (as measured by purchasing power parity, PPP; Aha and Xie 2004). Over the past two decades economic growth in both the Chinese and Indian economies has markedly outpaced growth in other countries in the world.

Until 1978 the two countries' economic growth differed only slightly (see figure 10.1). Today's gap is the result of markedly faster average economic growth in China than India since 1987. In the years 1978–2001 annual per capita GDP growth averaged 10.1 percent in China and 7.2 percent in India.[2]

In the period under review, fluctuations in growth were similar in both countries. Neither experienced an economic slump. There were a few years when China largely outperformed India (1979, 1991, 1992), but this is not the reason for today's gap in per capita income (see figure 10.2).

Thus, the differences in GDP growth cannot be attributed to internal or external shocks. The large size of both economies coupled with their limited openness (in China at the beginning and in India throughout the entire period), made them resilient to external shocks. On the other hand, shock intensification driven by natural disasters was similar in both countries, and their impact on GDP was limited due to the countries' area and population size (figure 10.3). Neither of the analyzed countries faced any major economic slump as a result of macroeconomic policy.

GDP growth per capita in both countries in the analyzed period was mainly driven by the improved productivity and capital formation:

- Growth in the productivity[3] boosted the average GDP growth per capita by 0.6 percentage points (60.4 percent of total growth) in China and by 4.4 percentage points (60.7 percent) in India.[4]

Figure 10.1 GDP Per Capita: China and India, 1950–2001

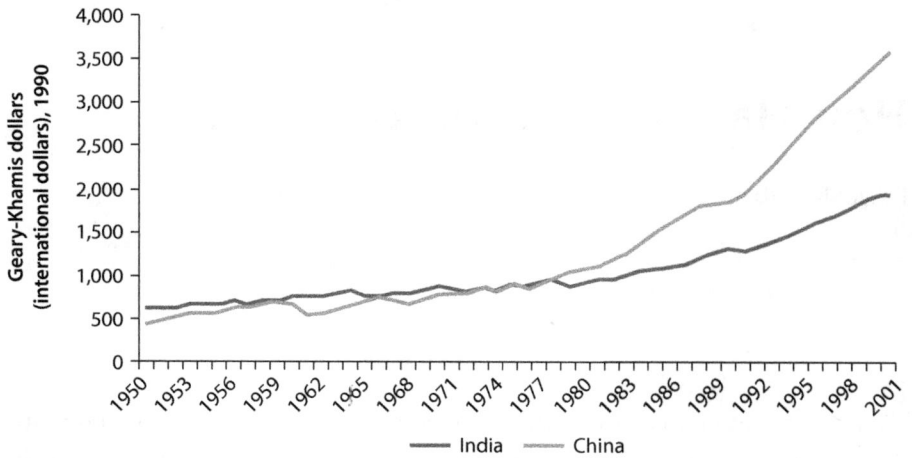

Source: Maddison 2004.
Note: GDP = gross domestic product.

Figure 10.2 GDP Growth Per Capita in China and India, 1978–2000

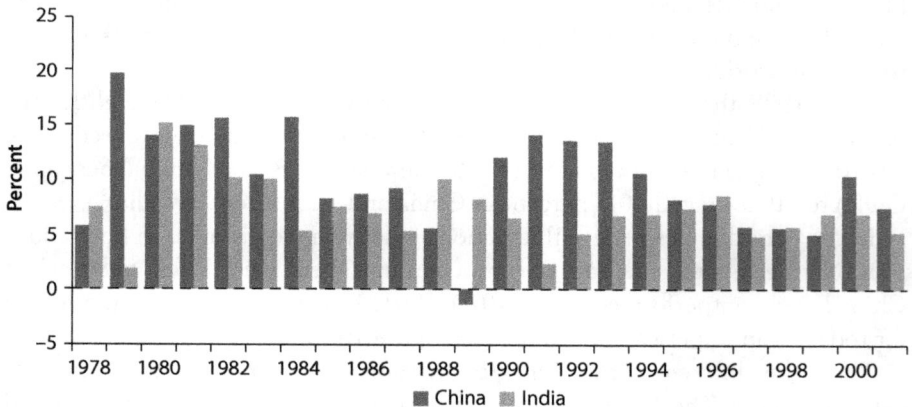

Source: Penn World Table 6.2.
Note: GDP = gross domestic product. Decline in per capita GDP growth in China in 1989 is suggested by PENN data only.
Figures derived from other sources (World Development Indicators, Maddison) point to a slight 2.5 percent growth. A more
in-depth analysis of statistical data on China may be found in Young (2000).

- The number of people employed in China's agricultural sector (with relatively low productivity) declined from 61 percent in 1981 to 45 percent in 2001 (Aha and Xie 2004). The same indicator, measured over the same period, in India fell from 67 percent to 58.5 percent.

- Capital expenditure accounted for 3.1 percentage points (30.7 percent of aggregate growth) of average per capita GDP growth in China in the years 1978–2011 and for 1.2 percentage points (16.2 percent of aggregate growth)

Figure 10.3 The Average Annual Impact of Natural Disasters on the Economy, 1980–2005

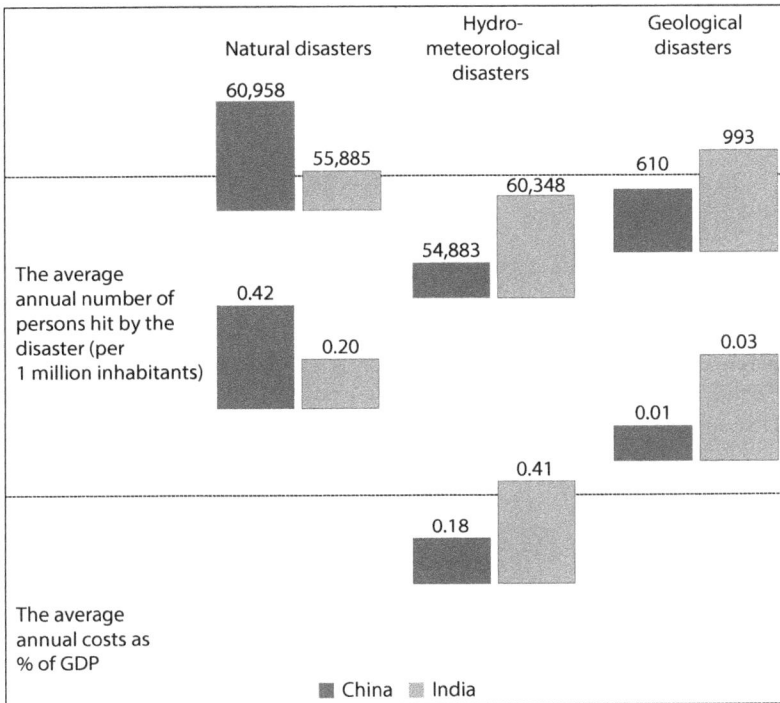

Source: Maple Croft Maps.
Note: GDP = gross domestic product.

in India. The share of growth accounting for capital expenditure between the period 1978–89 and the period 1990–2001 increased from 0.8 percentage points to 1.6 percentage points (over the same period, China saw the share of capital-driven growth increase from 2.9 percentage points to 3.4).

- As China's growth accelerated after 1978, both investment and savings largely outstripped those recorded in India (see figure 10.4). In 1978 savings accounted for 37.7 percent of GDP in China and only 19.1 percent of GDP in India. In 2001 this difference was even larger: in China, savings accounted for 40.9 percent of GDP, and in India for 21.7 percent.

- Capital per capita rose significantly faster in China than in India. Yet, its productivity in India was higher and did not undergo any major fluctuations after the onset of economic reforms, whereas in China it continued on a downward trend.

- Changes in labor force quality (measured by years of education completed) accounted for 0.9 percentage points of per capita GDP growth (8.7 percent of aggregate growth) in China and for 1.6 percentage points (22.7 percent of aggregate growth) in India. In China the average number of years of education

Figure 10.4 Savings, Investments, and Capital Productivity

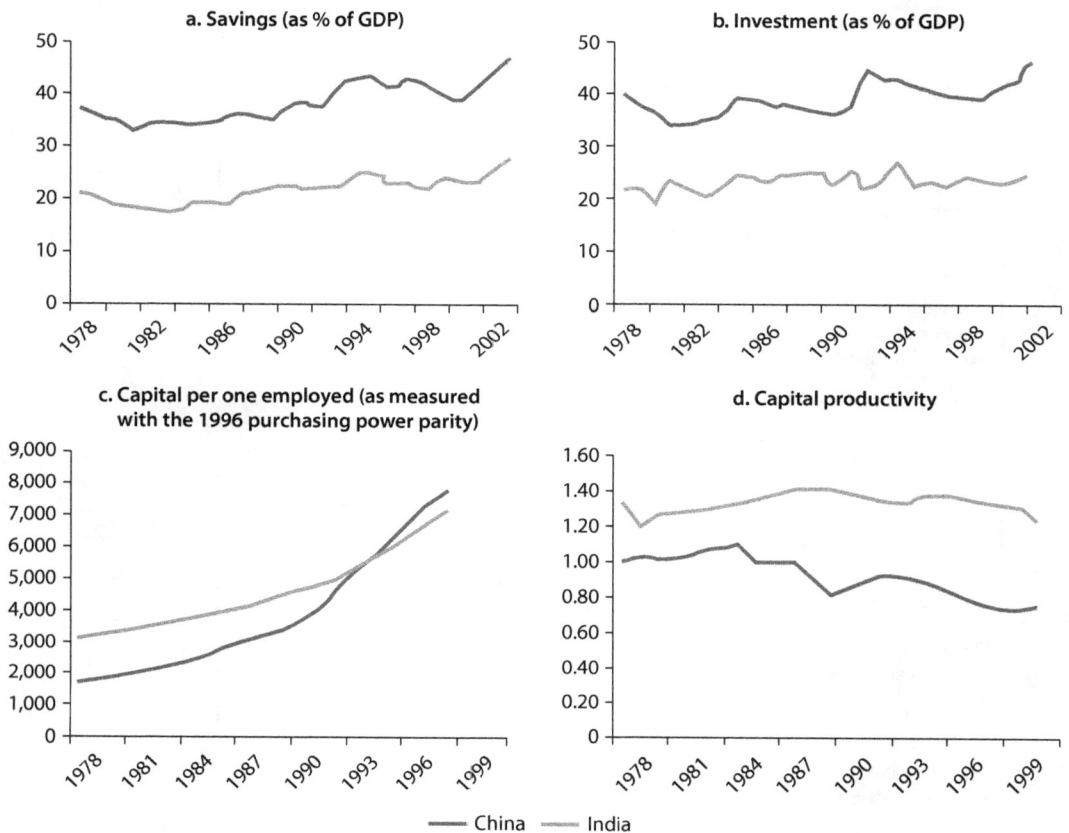

Source: Panels a and b: Compilations based on World Development Indicators 2004, Reserve Bank of India Database on Indian Economy (http://www.rbi.org.in/scripts/statistics.aspx). Panels c and d: Heston, Summers, and Aten 2006.
Note: Calculated as GDP/capital ratio; GDP = gross domestic product.

outstrips that in India (in 2000, 6.4 years as against 4.1 years in India). Also the illiteracy level is considerably lower (6 percent as compared to 35 percent in India; World Development Indicators 2004). The contribution of improved labor force quality (as measured by the number of years of education completed) to per capita GDP growth in India exceeds that in China mainly because it started from a very low point in India (see figure 10.5).

- However according to other studies the significance of improved productivity for economic growth was slightly below of those calculations. Hu and Khan (1996) estimate that it accounted for approximately 3.9 percentage points (42 percent) of average GDP growth in China in the years 1979–94. The World Bank (1997) ascribes 3.7 percentage points (43 percent) of GDP growth to productivity in the years 1978–95, and the Organisation for Economic Co-operation and Development (OECD 2005) 3.7 percentage points (30 percent) in the years 1983–2003. In the case of India, O'Neill (2007) estimates that labor productivity is the factor behind the 24.5 percent growth in the 1980s and 22.9 percent growth in the 1990s. Bosworth and Collins (2007) estimate the contribution of increased productivity to GDP growth per employee at 1.6 percentage points (40 percent) in the years 1978–2004.

Differences in Economic Performance: Factors and Causes

There are no significant differences in the economic growth fluctuations observed in China and India in the years 1978–2001. This leads us to conclude that shocks were not a major driving force behind differences in economic growth.

Figure 10.5 Decomposition of Economic Growth in China and India

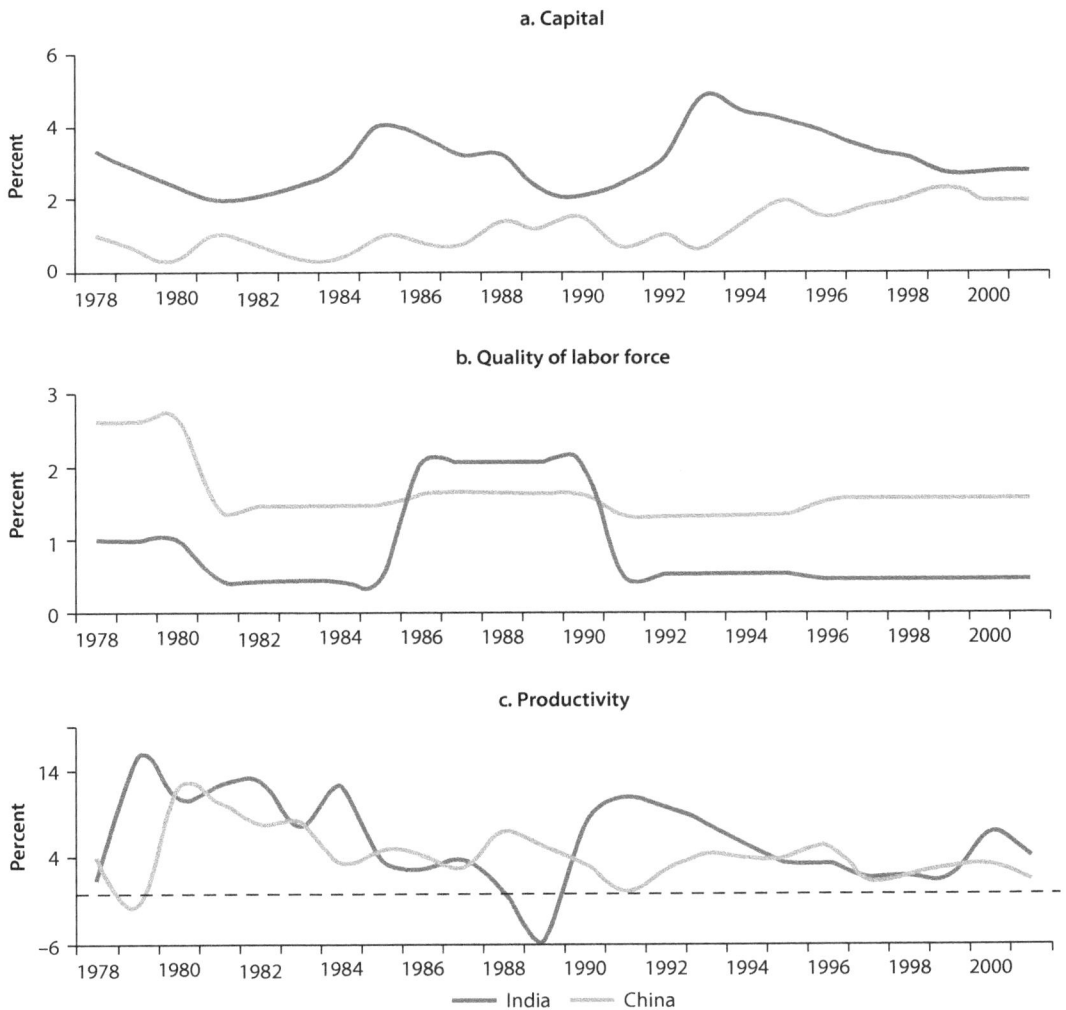

figure continues next page

Figure 10.5 Decomposition of Economic Growth in China and India *(continued)*

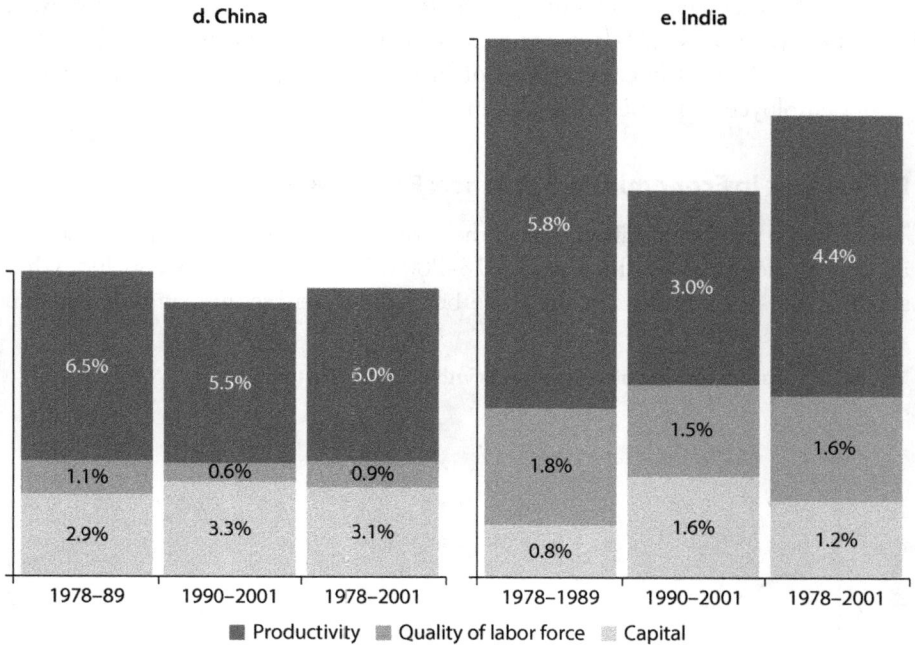

d. China   e. India

Productivity ▧ Quality of labor force ▧ Capital

Source: Based on Penn World Table 6.2, Barro-Lee Education Database.

This chapter therefore focuses on systematic growth forces determined by institutions and institutional reforms.

The major reasons for the launch of China's reforms was the low effectiveness of its centrally planned economy—and not the collapse of the Chinese political system. Economic reforms were launched by the Communist Party after the takeover of the Party's leadership by Deng Xiaoping, even as the Party maintained full political power. The first changes, enabling the private sector to develop, concerned urban areas.

In 1977, inhabitants of Fengyang Andhu Province spontaneously launched a reform of the land ownership system. The province authorities agreed to give land to farmers under a certain form of lease. Under this lease system, the state authorities kept possession of the land that was leased to farmers. Farmers were allowed to plant and cultivate any products they wished, and sell their surplus on the market. This system was approved by the government and implemented all over China. In 1983 the system covered 93 percent of rural areas (Jianglin and Jie 2000). The wide use of this system boosted food production.

At the end of the 1970s, the government allowed for the establishment of township-village enterprises (TVEs).[5] TVEs were collective or semi-private enterprises operating under market rules. Some of them gained considerable autonomy from local authorities (Wenzhou Province), while others actually remained under the government's full control (for example, Wuxi Province). In 1990 TVEs employed 100 million people—over three times as much as in

1978—and accounted for one-third of China's GDP (Jianglin and Jie 2000). The success of TVEs resulted from their freedom (relative to state-owned enterprises) to choose production types and methods. They were allowed to operate in industrial sectors unrelated to agriculture that had previously been reserved for state-owned enterprises only.

The launch of agricultural reforms presented a number of benefits. First, the reforms benefited most of society and improved the quality of life of the poorest. Second, their results encouraged the Communist Party to extend the reform program. For example, as TVEs became more competitive than state-owned enterprises, this increased pressure to implement yet more reforms. Third, increasing household income in rural areas boosted growth in the industrial goods market. Fourth, farmers who were allowed to migrate to urban areas were becoming cheap labor for industry. On the other hand, burgeoning food production made it possible to keep food prices in cities at a low level. But in subsequent years (after 1985) output growth in the agriculture industry declined, a trend that might have been caused by farmers' uncertainty about their ownership title to the land they had leased. In addition, the government made considerable cuts in its expenditure on agricultural infrastructure (in 1994 investment accounted for a mere 58 percent of 1978 investment; Sachs and Woo 1997).

The main difference between China's reforms in the 1990s and those implemented in the 1980s was their approach to the free market. In the period 1978–93 the market was just a mechanism supporting the centrally planned economy. After 1993 reforms were aimed to entirely replace central planning—the existing economic coordination mechanism—with the free market (even if it was called the "socialist market economy"). TVEs ceased to be the main driving force of the economy and many were privatized. TVE privatization was accelerated in 1998 by constitutional amendments recognizing ownership titles. As a result, TVEs did not need as much protection from local authorities. Quasi-private enterprises were gradually becoming exclusively private ones. Additionally, markets for many different goods changed from seller-dominated markets to buyer-oriented markets, which undermined the profitability of many TVEs. More thorough reforms of the financial system also provided local bank branches with more autonomy from local authorities, which made it more difficult for TVEs to obtain bank loans. The local authorities, fearing the decline in tax revenues transferred to the central budget, supported rather than hindered TVE privatization, thus boosting their profitability. In the 1990s agriculture went through another wave of privatization—local authorities privatized over half a million TVEs (Li and Rozelle 2000). As a result of this and previous waves of privatization, over 90 percent of TVEs were privatized by 1999. This, in turn, significantly improved the TVEs' effectiveness and increased proceeds to local government budgets (Li and Rozelle 2000). Privatization related to the growth of quasi-private enterprises lead to the development of a strictly private sector. However, the majority of enterprises were sold to managers and employees, which reduced privatization proceeds and the potential transfer of new knowledge and technologies resulting from acquisitions by external investors.

Puzzles of Economic Growth • http://dx.doi.org/10.1596/978-1-4648-0325-3

In 1984, China started to enhance the autonomy of state-owned enterprises. To solve the low wage problem, the government promoted the contract responsibility system (Qian 2001)—which made manager wages somewhat dependent on corporate profits. Under the system, company managers were endowed with more responsibility, and guaranteed employment gave way to negotiated contracts. By 1989 this system was put in place in almost all state-owned enterprises. Yet, their profitability continued on a downward trend. Average profits before tax (per unit of capital) in state-owned enterprises went down from 24.2 percent in 1978 to 12.4 percent in 1990 (Qian 2001). This was partly due to the higher competitiveness of private enterprises, but also reflected the insurmountable difficulties encountered in attempts to increase the effectiveness of state-owned enterprises.

In 1993, China launched reforms aimed to transform state-controlled enterprises into independent ones. In this period the output of private and quasi-private enterprises accounted for as much as 48.8 percent of GDP (Sun 2006). Thanks to the issue of shares, state-owned enterprises were initially provided with external capital. Yet, massive sale of state-owned enterprises started in China as late as in 1995 and focused mainly on smaller enterprises. Approximately 1,000 of the largest companies remained state owned. Ownership diversification in large state-owned enterprises started in 1999 (state control still being in place), yet, it failed to bring the expected results: enterprises remained under state control.

A profitability analysis of state-owned enterprises (before and after their partial privatization, without control being taken over by private investors) shows that those firms were not becoming more profitable as a result of privatization (Xiao 2005).

Thus, in a relatively short period of time, China managed to develop strong private and quasi-private sectors whose contribution to GDP reached 68.6 percent in 1999 (see figure 10.6), and whose productivity grew considerably faster than in the government sector (Sachs and Woo 1997).

Privatization

In the 1970s, 15 branches of engineering industry in India were allowed to expand their production capacity, so far limited by administrative decisions. In the mid-1980s deregulation covered a further 25 branches of industry (Panagariya 2004). Large enterprises were allowed to operate in industries previously reserved for small and medium-sized enterprises (SMEs) and to import technologies. Yet, in India private businesses were supposedly subject to very strict regulation.

Although India has never introduced complete nationalization, similar to Chinese, quasi-private and government entities prevailed in the country—until the second half of the 1990s—in all industrial sectors (OECD 1996). In 1996 state-owned enterprises controlled 55 percent of capital and accounted for 25 percent of GDP in agricultural sectors (OECD 1996). Reforms in the state-owned enterprise sector, launched as late as the early 1990s, mainly involved the withdrawal of barriers of entry to selected monopolized sectors and limited access to public funds as well as the deregulation of supposedly private companies.[6]

Figure 10.6 Contribution of Companies to China's GDP, Depending on the Form of Enterprise, 1991–2000

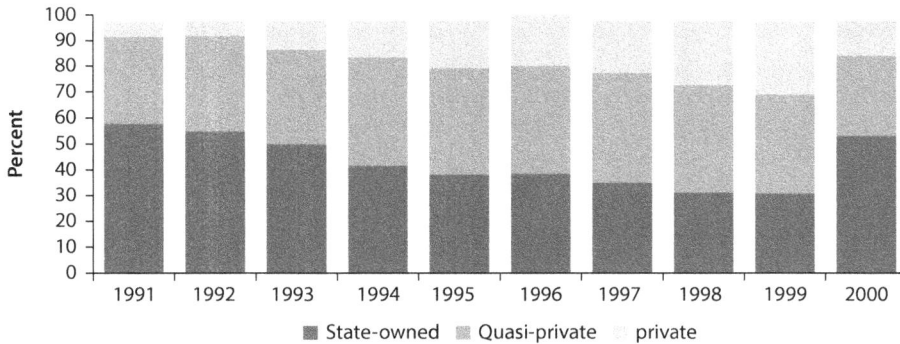

Source: Sun 2006.
Note: GDP = gross domestic product. Higher contribution of state-owned companies in 2000 was driven by the changed methodology used by Chinese statistical authorities in estimating the contribution of particular ownership sectors to GDP.

In 1991–2003, only 3 percent of enterprises were partly privatized (with government holding more than 50 percent of shares; Kaur 2004). Only 1.13 percent of state-owned enterprises were subject to full privatization over the same period (Kaur 2004). Foreign enterprises were allowed to acquire private enterprises as late as in 1998.

The restrictions on land acquisition on market terms by individuals and businesses, introduced in 1976, are still in place. They concern, among other things, the size of the land held in freehold. In case an enterprise or an individual bought more land than permitted by the law, they were obliged to sell it to the state government at a price far below the market price (Kaur 2004, 10).

Hindered privatization is one of the reasons why India's economic growth has been less robust than China's. As in China, the private enterprise sector experienced much faster productivity growth than the state-owned enterprise sector. In the years 1994–2002 the aggregate value added per employee grew in India at a rate of 9.9 percent as compared to the 5.6 percent growth in value added in the public sector (see figure 10.7). At the end of this period, value added per employee reached $10.4 thousand as compared to a mere $5.6 thousand recorded in the public sector. Yet to create an additional unit of production, private sector companies needed to invest twice as much as state-owned companies.

Liberalization of Goods and Services
In China in the period before 1978 the prices of all goods and services were centrally administered. At the start of the reform period, the government allowed for simultaneous operation of two pricing systems, that is, market prices and prices set by China's State Planning Committee. Yet, market prices had to oscillate within a specific range (±20 percent of government prices; Jianglin and Jie 2000). Centrally set prices applied up to a certain output amount

Figure 10.7 The Productivity of Enterprises in India

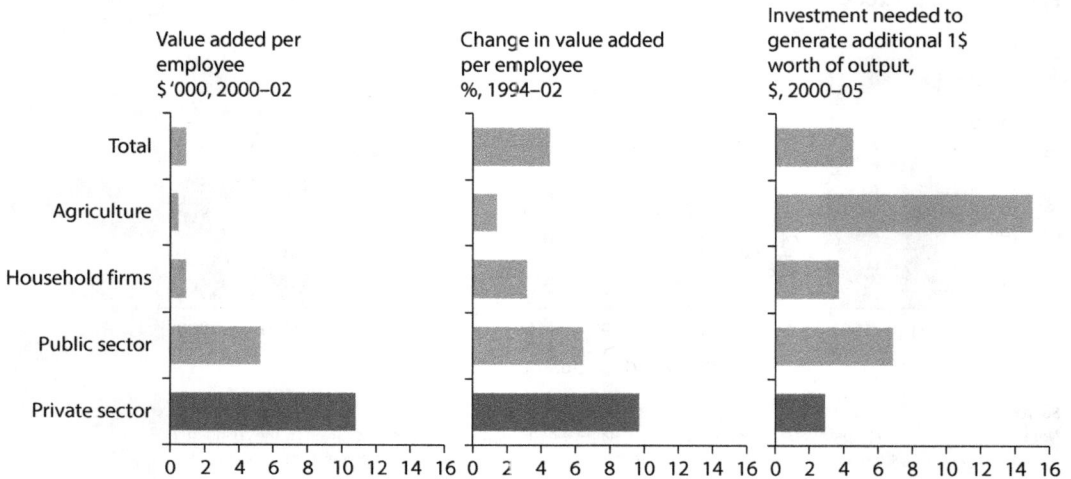

Source: McKinsey 2006a.

determined by the State Planning Committee. Above this limit, enterprises could sell goods at market prices. This provided companies with an incentive to expand their production. Availability of goods increased and difficulties with the acquisition of production materials eased. The weakness of the above system was the creation of a so-called double quality—goods manufactured to be sold at government prices were lower in quality than those sold in the market. The dual-track price system was abolished in 1985, allowing for the emergence of inflation which, coupled with dissatisfaction about growing corruption and fraud, was one of the driving forces behind the student movement and the Tiananmen Square protests in 1989. In the years 1989 and 1990 GDP growth stood at 2.2 percent and 3.1 percent, respectively. In 1992, Deng Xiaoping made a speech saying that the free market economy was not in conflict with the socialist regime. Free market reforms were implemented at an accelerated rate. The Chinese economy became increasingly more open to global economies (see figure 10.8).

In India, the government controlled prices of agricultural produce and industrial products until 1997. Prices of all main agricultural products were announced each year. The government also arranged for their purchase by government agencies (Bajpai, Jian, and Sachs 1997). Then, via the public distribution system, it provided six categories of major goods below market prices. At the end of the 1990s, this system was gradually phased out—mainly due to the declining number of people using the public distribution system, as a result of the low quality of products it offered. Yet, the price reform has never been completed. Throughout the analyzed period, the government's price control hindered the transfer of production factors to sectors where they would have been most effectively used.

Figure 10.8 Price Control System in China

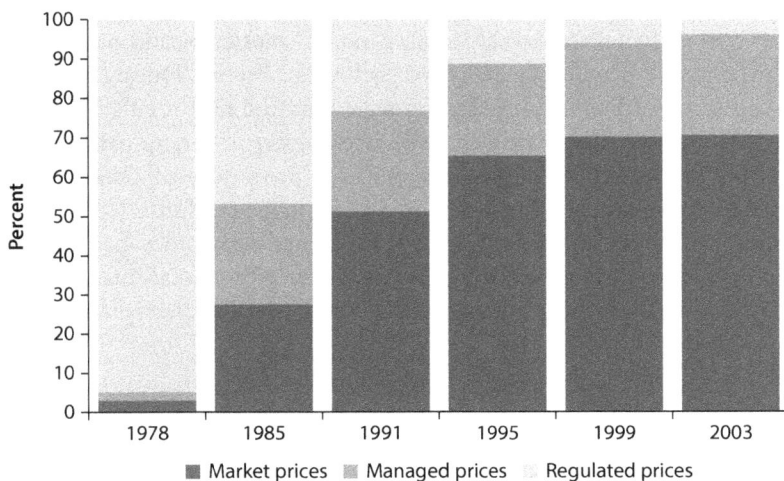

Source: Based on OECD 2005.

Labor Market Reforms

By the 1980s farmers in China worked on land allocated to them, and urban migration was banned. Industrial workers worked in the same plant for their lifetimes and were not made redundant even if the enterprise faced financial problems. Young people reaching working age were assigned to companies depending on the centralized plan. Neither enterprises nor employees had any motivation to search for appropriate employees/jobs or to compete in the labor market.

In 1980 city inhabitants were given the freedom to search for jobs on their own. At the same time, enterprises, including state-owned enterprises, were allowed more freedom to determine the size of their labor force and to set wages (Bajpai, Jian, and Sachs 1997). In the mid-1980s China put in place the so-called contract employment system that replaced lifetime employment. These reforms were further enhanced in 1994. The government allowed for an increase in the number of contract employees (employed on the basis of labor contracts concluded for a definite period of time) in the total number of the employed. Redundancies in state-owned enterprises became a lawful measure. Although restrictions on the domestic migration of Chinese employees were upheld, they were typically not respected. Urban migration continued to boost labor supply in cities, and, a result, halted the growth of labor cost growth. At the same time, immigration made it possible to curb overemployment in agriculture, and, consequently, enhance labor productivity in this sector. Finally, it limited the share of employment in low-productivity sectors (agriculture) to the benefit of sectors with higher productivity (industry, services).[7] The number of the employed in agriculture went down from 61 percent in 1981 to 45 percent in 2001 (Aha and Xie 2004; in India this number slid in the same period from 67 percent to 58.5 percent).

In India economic reforms were hardly linked with more flexible labor regulations. Before 1978 labor regulations were even less stringent than in the analyzed period. Layoffs were subject to a month's notice period, and a severance pay of 50 percent of monthly salary for each year of work. During the following two decades more than 40 various acts were adopted that regulated wages, layoffs, or trade unions' operations. In 2002 every enterprise employing more than 100 persons had to go through a complicated procedure of obtaining various licenses and permits to be able to lay off an employee (Deloitte Research 2006). To circumvent these and other restrictions many companies had recourse to contract employees. Moreover, they gave preference to capital-intensive production methods to limit employment. India's potential for cheap labor remained largely unused.

Foreign Direct Investment

In 1979 China adopted an act that formally allowed foreign capital companies to operate in China. In May 1980 the Chinese government chose four cities (Shenzen, Zhuhai, Santou, and Xianmen) for the purpose of setting up special economic zones. In 1984 similar privileges were granted to another 14 cities.[8] These areas had been traditionally involved in foreign trade and were located in China's Eastern Coastal Provinces. Special economic zones were largely separated from the rest of the country. At the beginning, the government supported them through additional investments in infrastructure, tax exemptions, and more market-oriented methods of foreign exchange.

In the years 1979–89 joint ventures in which Chinese companies had majority ownership accounted for 42 percent of foreign direct investment (FDI). In 1999 more than half the FDI were 100 percent foreign capital investments. This shift confirms China's extensive opening to foreign investors. According to the OECD, the main factors driving FDI in China included fast economic growth, low labor costs, well-developed infrastructure (mainly in the special economic zones), an exports-promoting policy, and an expansionary institutional and regulatory system.[9]

In the 1980s India remained practically closed to FDI. The country opened up more to FDI in 1991. At that time, India introduced equal treatment of domestic and foreign businesses. Also many restrictions on entry into the market were relaxed. The telecommunications market serves as an example. Its liberalization in 1993 lowered the costs of services by 90 percent, and supported the development of computer services and offshoring (Aha and Xie 2004). In the 1990s the Indian government automatically granted consent to foreign investment amounting to up to 51 percent of capital in the majority of industry branches. Foreign investments of up to 100 percent of capital were also subject to fewer restrictions, yet remained under government control. In certain sectors, the Indian government tried to use special incentives such as tax exemptions to encourage foreign investments.

Yet, incentive measures set up for foreign investors in India were not as farreaching as in China. Until 2012 many branches of industry were monopolized by the state or reserved for small-sized enterprises. Moreover, measures designed to facilitate the inflow of FDI at the national level were not supported by any relaxation of administrative restrictions at the state level. The time necessary to comply with all the formalities involved in starting a business in India was significantly longer than in China. According to the McKinsey consulting company, these formalities would take up at least two to three years in India as compared to 6–12 months in China (Virmani 2004). Based on interviews with large investors, the A.T. Kearney consulting company pointed to bureaucratic procedures and ineffective operation of institutions as the key obstacle to investment projects in India (Virmani 2004). Poorly developed road and power generation and distribution infrastructure were identified as another major problem (see figure 10.9).[10] Another deterrent to foreign investment in India were inflexible labor regulations and an ineffective judicial system.

As a result of the introduced changes, China managed to attract a considerable volume of FDI (see figure 10.10). In 1993 FDI inflows to China reached 6.7 percent of GDP, and remained at levels exceeding 4 percent of GDP in subsequent years. At the same time, this figure stood at approximately 0.5 percent of GDP in India.

As a result, aggregate foreign investment in China in 2001 reached 30 percent of GDP as compared to a mere 4 percent of GDP in India. As estimated by the International Monetary Fund (IMF) in China, inflows of FDI accounted for 2.2 percentage points of GDP growth in the 1990s (Tseng and Zebregs 2002), while the major contributor to GDP growth was rising productivity

Figure 10.9 Energy Losses during Power Distribution to Final Users

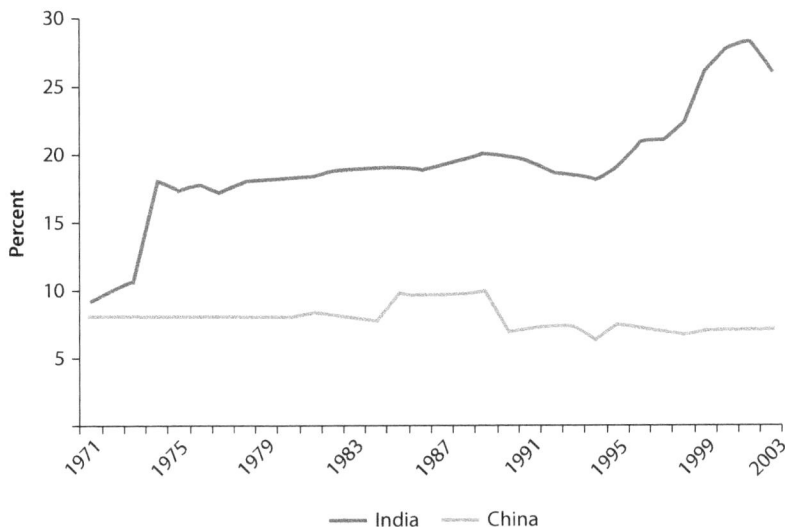

Source: World Development Indicators database.

Figure 10.10 Foreign Direct Investment in China and India

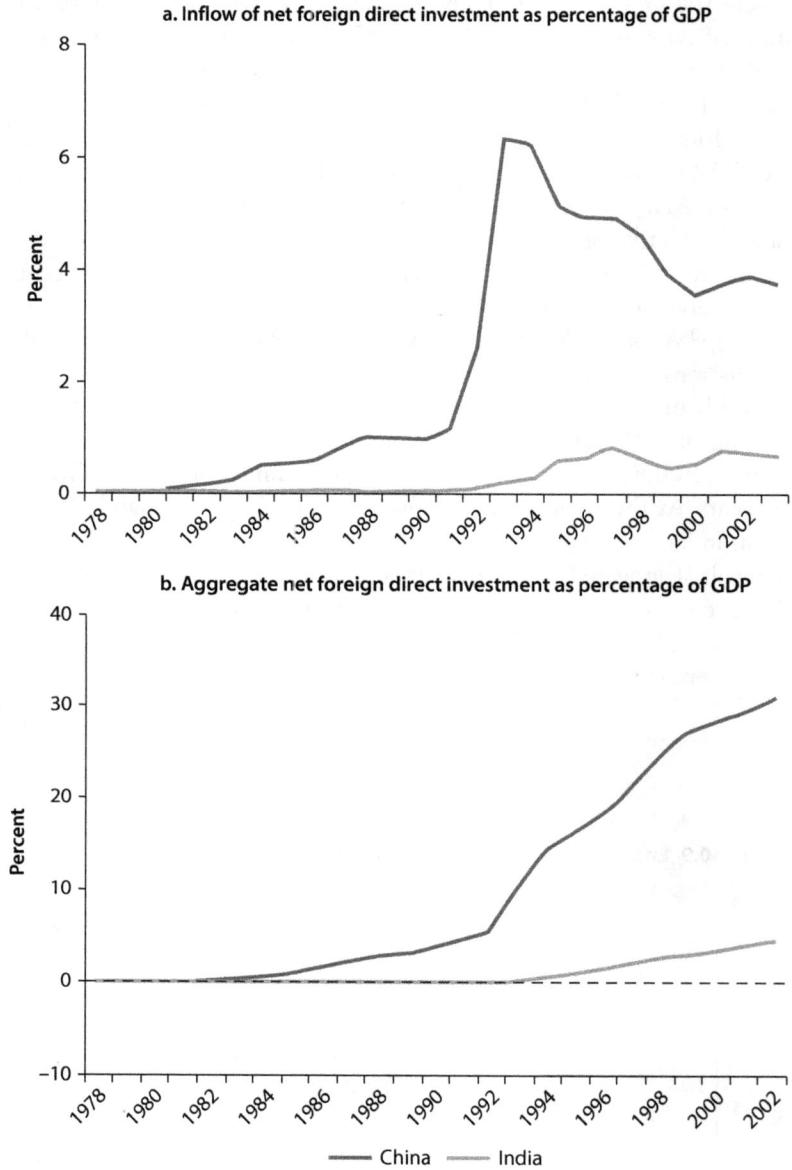

a. Inflow of net foreign direct investment as percentage of GDP

b. Aggregate net foreign direct investment as percentage of GDP

——— China ——— India

Source: World Development Indicators database.
Note: GDP = gross domestic product.

(2.5 percentage points). On the other hand, due to its limited scale, FDI was of lesser importance to economic growth. Yet, it should be remembered that FDI was directed toward the services sector, which is a considerably less-capital-intensive than industry. In other words, capital outlays in services translate into larger production growth than in industry.

Opening to Foreign Trade

China opened up more than India not only to FDI inflow, but also to foreign trade (see figure 10.11). Thus, the country could capitalize on its competitive advantages more and draw on the transfer of technology and knowledge fueled by international trade.

By the 1970s China's exports and imports were planned by the Central Planning Committee, and all proceeds from exports were transferred to the Treasury Department. The reforms launched at the end of the 1970s opened the Chinese economy to foreign trade. The state monopoly over foreign trade was gradually broken. At the beginning, only some enterprises were licensed to engage in foreign trade, but by the start of the 1990s the majority of businesses were permitted to sell their products abroad. As China was set to join the World Trade Organization (WTO) in the 1990s, it gradually eased restrictions imposed on tariff-free trade and even reduced customs. The average tariff weighted with the value of imports (of particular types of goods) went down from 10 percent in the years 1985-89 to approximately 3 percent in the years 1995–2000. Customs proceeds fell from 30 percent of total tax receipts in the mid-1990s to a mere 6 percent in 1999.

In India the first economic reforms launched in the 1980s did not trigger foreign trade liberalization. The only positive change was the fact that the list of goods allowed to be imported was replaced with a list of goods whose import was prohibited or restricted. All goods not included in the new list could be traded internationally without any restrictions. The Indian government also reduced the number of goods that could be imported by state-owned enterprises only. Yet, it maintained high customs duties. In 1980 all export profits were exempted from tax (Panagariya 2004), and exporters were exempted from import customs.

Figure 10.11 Import Obstacles in China and India

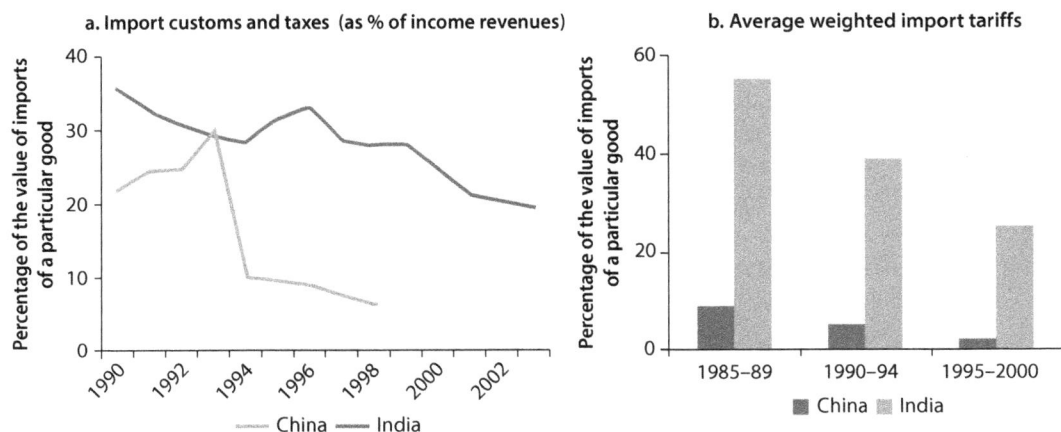

Source: World Development Indicators Database (panel a); Aha and Xie 2004 (panel b).

Import subsidies soared from $922 million in 1980 to $1,594 million in 1987 (Acharya and others 2003).

It was only with the 1991 reforms that India opened up to international trade. The average tariff weighted by the value of imported goods slid from 54 percent in the years 1985–89 to 25 percent in the years 1995–2000. The share of import customs in total tax receipts declined from 35 percent in 1991 to 21 percent in 2003. In 1995 India joined the WTO.

Until 1979 the circulation and holding of foreign currency were completely prohibited in China. At the onset of the reforms, China set the exchange rate based on prices compared to the average value of the basket of main currencies, tourist expenditure, transportation costs, and export values (Lin 1997). China allowed full convertibility of the Chinese yuan in 1996, yet, its exchange rate continued to be controlled by the central bank. In 2005 China revalued the Chinese yuan by 2.1 percent and allowed for daily fluctuations of 0.3 percent. Yet, it did not decide to unpeg the exchange rate (see figure 10.12).

The Indian government revalued the rupee by 22 percent in 1992, and introduced the Liberalized Exchange Rate System. Thus, a double-track exchange rate system was adopted, allowing exporters to sell up to 60 percent of foreign currency stock on the free market. By the end of 1994, the double-track exchange rate system had been abolished, and the Liberalized Exchange Rate System was replaced by the Unified Exchange Rate. Thus, the Indian rupee was made fully convertible for the Indian current account. Yet, for a long time, Indian citizens could not have any personal foreign currency holdings. The nominal exchange rate of the rupee in the years 1978–2001 continued to depreciate against the American dollar by 8.0 percent annually, which was close to the yuan depreciation of an average of 7.5 percent annually[11] (however depreciations of both currencies were driven by different developments).

Real exchange rate fluctuations against the American dollar were, from the point of view of price competitiveness of domestic goods in the global marketplace, more favorable in the case of the Chinese yuan than the Indian rupee (see figures 10.12 and 10.13). This happened as inflation declined in China down to the level observed in the second half of the 1990s. Yet, inflation rates—and, consequently, real exchange rate fluctuations—were not considerably different in the two nations. As such, they cannot explain differences in the economic performance and export growth.

In the years 1978–2001 two levels of inflation in China may be distinguished (see figure 10.14). The years 1978–95 were marked by rising inflation. As a result of price controls at the onset of the reforms, there was no open inflation. It started with the abolishment of price control. It was additionally fueled by the inflow of foreign capital and an ensuing rise in money supply driven by the central bank's purchases of foreign currency (Bajpai, Jian, and Sachs 1997). In 1995 foreign currency purchases hit their record high in the analyzed period, reaching 19.9 percent. Then, in 1996–2001, inflation was close to 0 percent. This decline resulted from a tightened monetary policy, a prohibition on monetizing the fiscal deficit, the reduced inflow of foreign

Figure 10.12 History of the Chinese Yuan

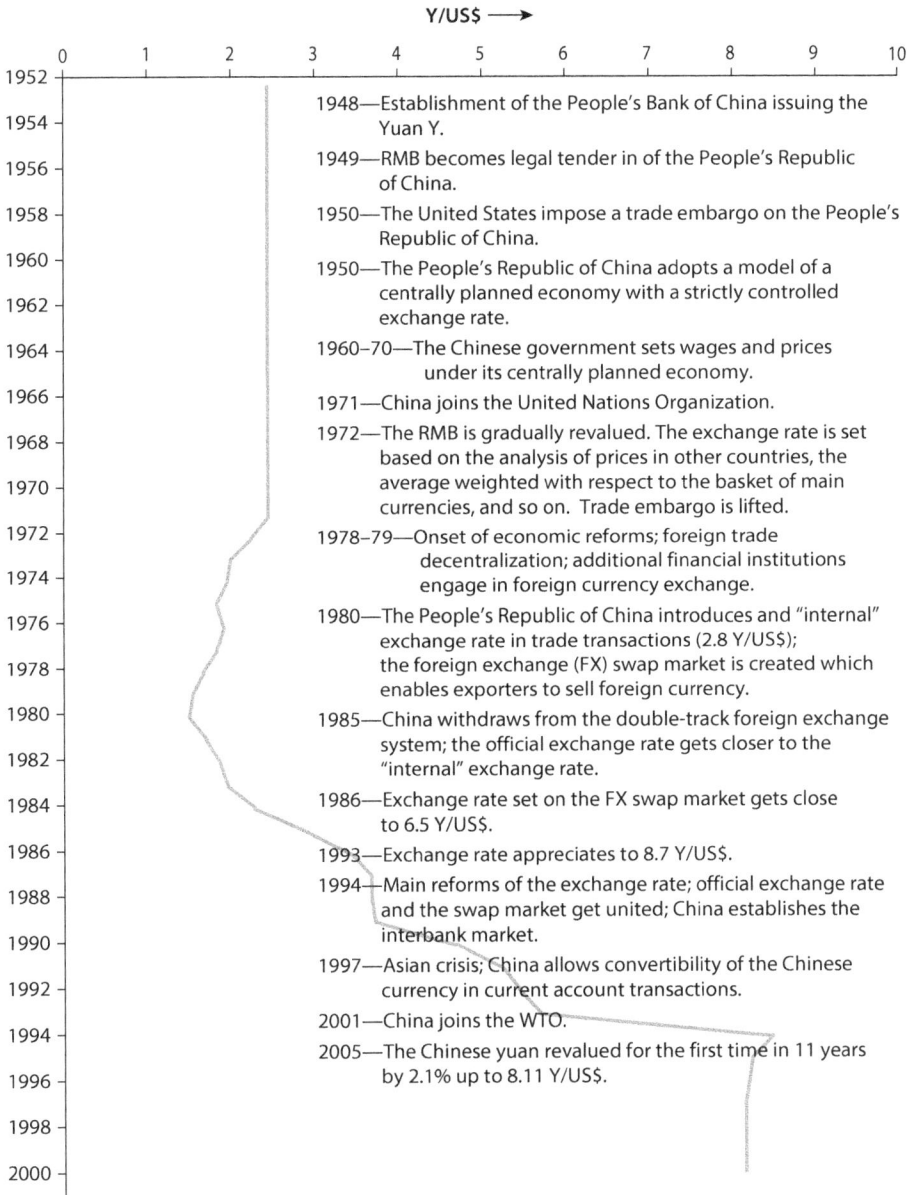

Y/US$ ⟶

| 0 | 1 | 2 | 3 | 4 | 5 | 6 | 7 | 8 | 9 | 10 |

1952
1954
1956
1958
1960
1962
1964
1966
1968
1970
1972
1974
1976
1978
1980
1982
1984
1986
1988
1990
1992
1994
1996
1998
2000

1948—Establishment of the People's Bank of China issuing the Yuan Y.

1949—RMB becomes legal tender in of the People's Republic of China.

1950—The United States impose a trade embargo on the People's Republic of China.

1950—The People's Republic of China adopts a model of a centrally planned economy with a strictly controlled exchange rate.

1960–70—The Chinese government sets wages and prices under its centrally planned economy.

1971—China joins the United Nations Organization.

1972—The RMB is gradually revalued. The exchange rate is set based on the analysis of prices in other countries, the average weighted with respect to the basket of main currencies, and so on. Trade embargo is lifted.

1978–79—Onset of economic reforms; foreign trade decentralization; additional financial institutions engage in foreign currency exchange.

1980—The People's Republic of China introduces and "internal" exchange rate in trade transactions (2.8 Y/US$); the foreign exchange (FX) swap market is created which enables exporters to sell foreign currency.

1985—China withdraws from the double-track foreign exchange system; the official exchange rate gets closer to the "internal" exchange rate.

1986—Exchange rate set on the FX swap market gets close to 6.5 Y/US$.

1993—Exchange rate appreciates to 8.7 Y/US$.

1994—Main reforms of the exchange rate; official exchange rate and the swap market get united; China establishes the interbank market.

1997—Asian crisis; China allows convertibility of the Chinese currency in current account transactions.

2001—China joins the WTO.

2005—The Chinese yuan revalued for the first time in 11 years by 2.1% up to 8.11 Y/US$.

Sources: Penn World Table 6.2; Aha and Xie 2004.

capital in the aftermath of the Asian crisis, the economy's higher production capacity, and demand that outpaced growth.

In the period following 1978, India's inflation edged up to 15 percent and continued to exceed 10 percent until 1981. It rose again to 12 percent in the years 1990–91, that is, during the budget crisis. The following years saw inflation sink

Puzzles of Economic Growth • http://dx.doi.org/10.1596/978-1-4648-0325-3

Figure 10.13 History of the Indian Rupee

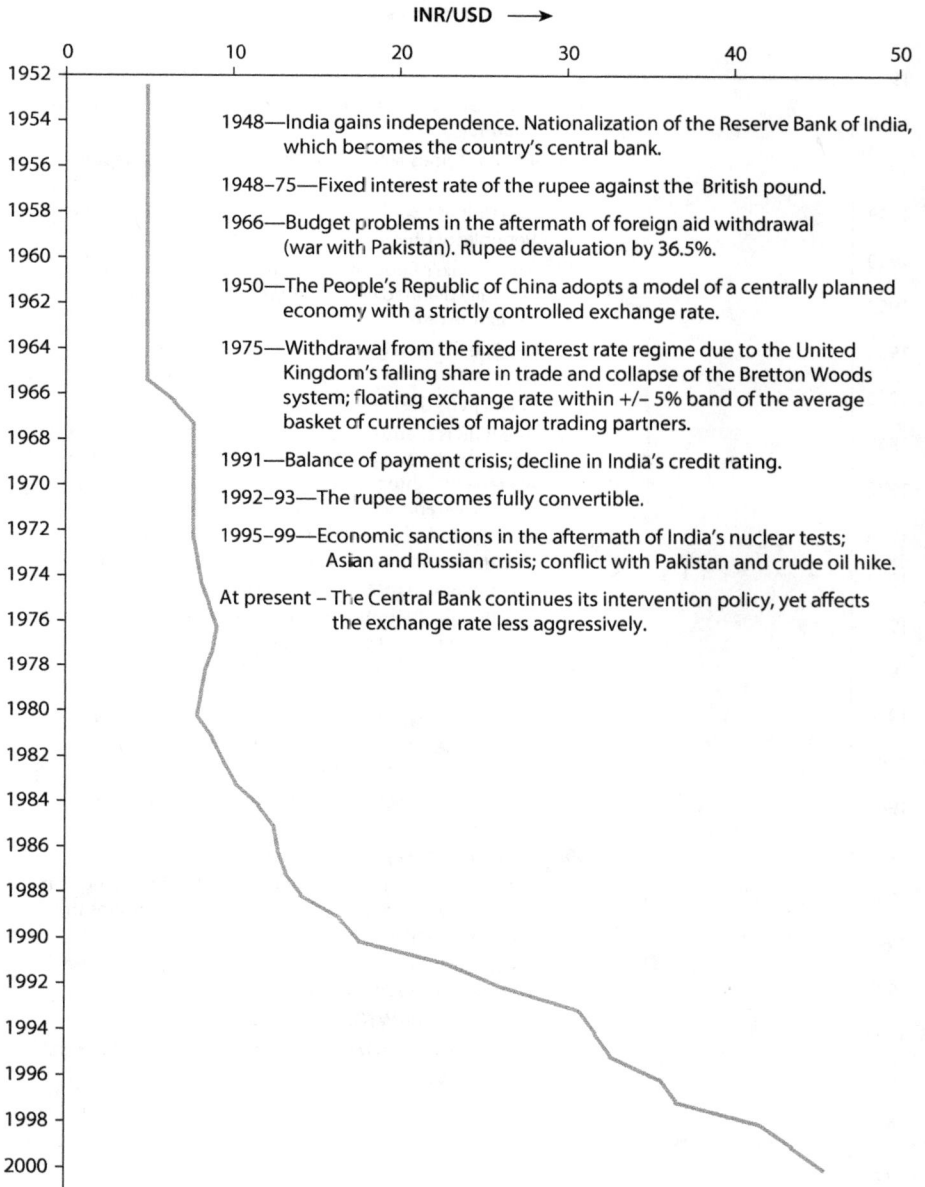

INR/USD ⟶

```
        0          10          20          30          40          50
1952 ┼────────────┼────────────┼────────────┼────────────┼────────────┤
1954 ┤          1948—India gains independence. Nationalization of the Reserve Bank of India,
                    which becomes the country's central bank.
1956 ┤
           1948–75—Fixed interest rate of the rupee against the British pound.
1958 ┤
           1966—Budget problems in the aftermath of foreign aid withdrawal
1960 ┤            (war with Pakistan). Rupee devaluation by 36.5%.

1962 ┤     1950—The People's Republic of China adopts a model of a centrally planned
                    economy with a strictly controlled exchange rate.
1964 ┤
           1975—Withdrawal from the fixed interest rate regime due to the United
1966 ┤            Kingdom's falling share in trade and collapse of the Bretton Woods
                    system; floating exchange rate within +/– 5% band of the average
1968 ┤            basket of currencies of major trading partners.

1970 ┤     1991—Balance of payment crisis; decline in India's credit rating.

1972 ┤     1992–93—The rupee becomes fully convertible.

1974 ┤     1995–99—Economic sanctions in the aftermath of India's nuclear tests;
                    Asian and Russian crisis; conflict with Pakistan and crude oil hike.
1976 ┤
           At present – The Central Bank continues its intervention policy, yet affects
1978 ┤            the exchange rate less aggressively.
1980 ┤
1982 ┤
1984 ┤
1986 ┤
1988 ┤
1990 ┤
1992 ┤
1994 ┤
1996 ┤
1998 ┤
2000 ┤
```

Sources: Penn World Table 6.2; Aha and Xie 2004.

again below 5 percent. Initially, inflation was fueled by a high fiscal deficit, largely monetized (Bajpai, Jian, and Sachs 1997). In the 1990s, on the other hand, inflation was driven by price control system reforms, periodic rises in government-controlled cereal prices, and larger inflows of foreign capital (Bajpai, Jian, and Sachs 1997), rather than by India's bad fiscal condition. Deficit monetization was

Figure 10.14 Inflation Rate (Year-on-Year Changes in GDP Deflator)

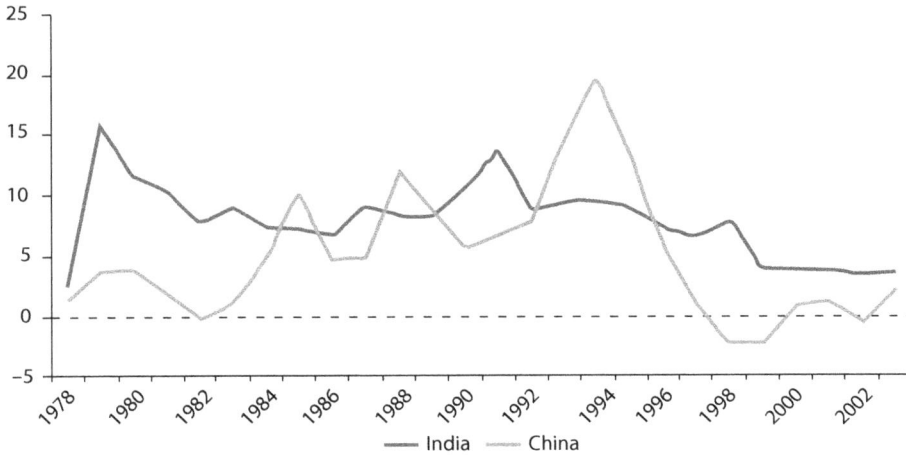

Source: Based on World Development Indicators database.
Note: GDP = gross domestic product.

halted and price stability was given priority among the central bank's objectives (Mohan 2006).

China performed much better in the process of catching up with the global economy (see figure 10.15). The openness of the Chinese economy—as measured by the ratio of total exports and imports to GDP—soared from 9.26 percent in 1978 to reach 49 percent in 2000 (Penn World Table 6.2). Over the same time, this index in India rose from 13.32 percent to 30.5 percent (Penn World Table 6.2). In 2005 China's shares in global trade accounted for 5.2 percent as compared to India's share at the level of 0.9 percent (Aha and Xie 2004).

Fiscal Position

The first reforms in China resulted in a drastic weakening of China's fiscal position. According to the IMF's estimates, public expenditure was slashed from 31.7 percent of GDP at the onset of the reform period to 20 percent of GDP in 1991—mainly through cuts in widely understood social expenditure (including spending on education and health care). Limited budget spending, coupled with rapid GDP growth in the 1980s and 1990s, urged people to increase savings. The role of foresight as an incentive to save increased. At the same time, expenditure cuts were combined with state finance centralization. Chinese provinces were obliged to transfer certain amounts of taxes to the central government budget, yet were allowed to keep the rest of generated income. They could not set tax rates but were authorized to set their own expenses. At the beginning of the 1990s, fiscal decentralization considerably boosted competition between local government units and provinces.

In 1994, the tax reforms were launched. A clear distinction was made between local and central government taxes, and the tax collection system

Figure 10.15 Exports and Imports in China and India

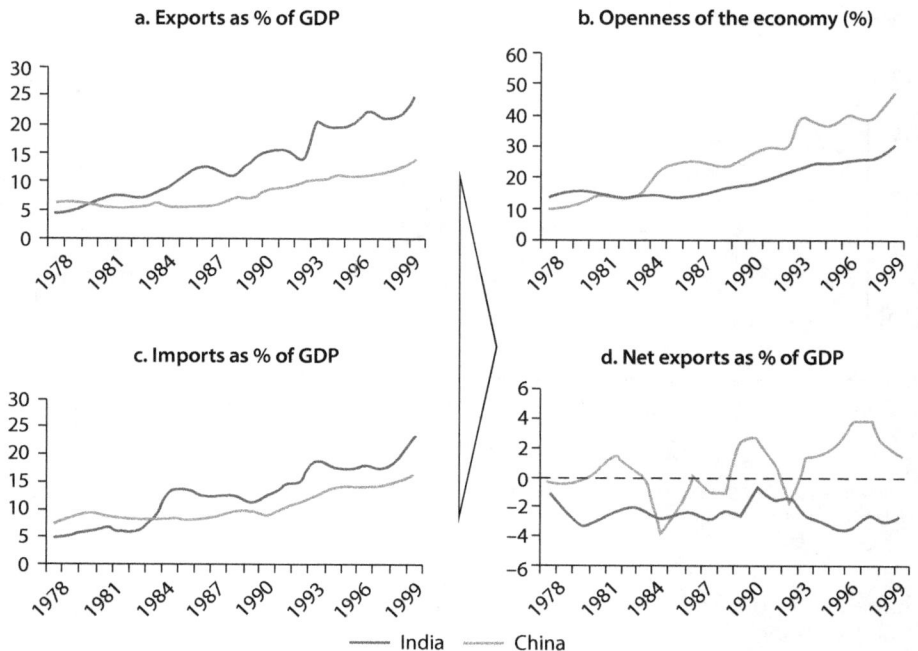

a. Exports as % of GDP

b. Openness of the economy (%)

c. Imports as % of GDP

d. Net exports as % of GDP

India   China

Source: Based on Penn World Table 6.2.
Note: GDP = gross domestic product.

was modernized. The reforms also involved the introduction of a 17 percent value added tax (VAT). In 1995 a new budget law was adopted prohibiting the government from borrowing money from the central bank. It still was not possible for local government units to set tax rates or issue public bonds (OECD 2006). Thanks to China's sound public finance, the country's investments in infrastructure considerably surpassed India's (figure 10.16) (for example, the value of China's road investments for years 1993–2003 years amounted to $34 billion annually as compared to a mere $2 billion–$3 billion in India; Aha and Xie 2004).

In the analyzed period, India's public expenditure generally ranged from 25 percent to 30 percent of GDP. India's higher public expenditure level as compared to China's resulted from higher spending on national defense, fuel subsidies to farmers, social spending, the pension system, and public debt servicing (Aha and others 2006). India's government spending was much less efficient than China's. Despite a higher ratio of expenditure to GDP throughout most of the analyzed period, India trailed behind China in terms of all social indicators and infrastructure quality.

The fact that public expenditure in India exceeded that in China led, in the first place, to higher taxes. These, in turn, drove the higher costs of industrial goods in India (Aha and Xie 2004). Additionally, the Indian tax system was intricate and ineffective (for example, out of 363 million people employed in

Figure 10.16 Expenditure on Road Construction

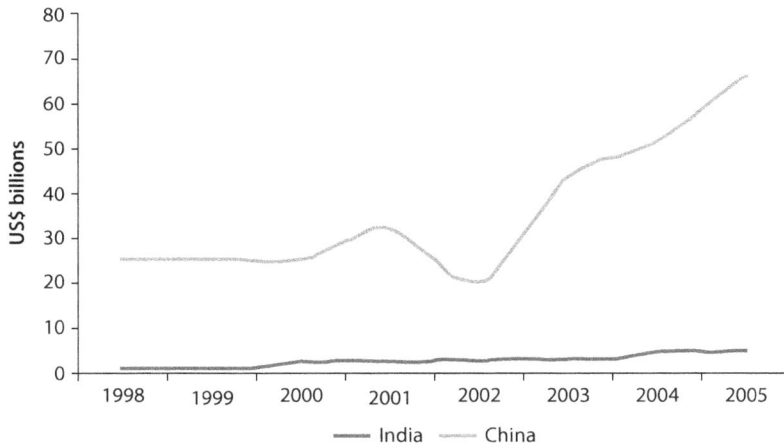

Source: Aha and others 2006, 42.

Figure 10.17 Fiscal Deficit

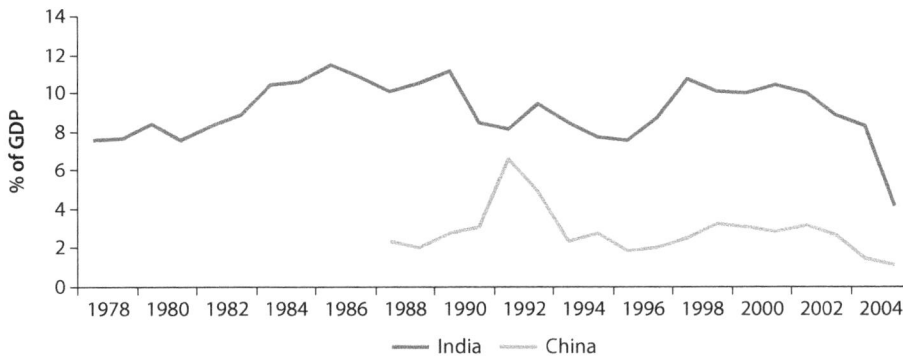

Sources: World Development Indicators Database: Asia Development Bank Database, Reserve Bank of India Database on Indian Economy.
Note: GDP = gross domestic product; Data for China in 1978–88 are not available.

2005 only 30.9 million filed annual tax returns; the number of taxpayers paying taxes was even smaller). Consequently, the difference in tax rates between India and China was much bigger than the difference in tax revenues. A complicated and nontransparent tax system resulted in disturbances in production factor allocation and, in consequence, dragged down India's productivity (Poirson 2006). High tax rates had a negative impact on the extent of production factor utilization, including, in particular, employment (Poirson 2006).

Second, India's higher expenditure was combined with a high fiscal deficit that crowded out private investment (see figure 10.17). In the 1980s the investment rate posted a slight rise in the public sector and declined in the private sector (Panagariya 2004). Growing debt service costs (a result of the high

Figure 10.18 Public Sector Deficit: India and China, 1990–2003

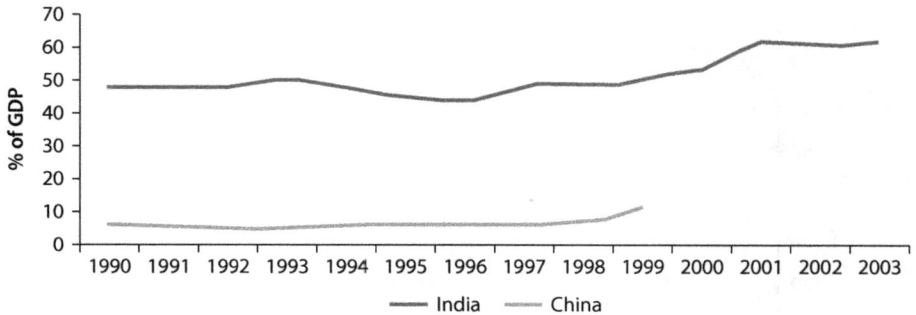

Source: World Development Indicators Database.
Note: GDP = gross domestic product.

deficit), crowded out investment in infrastructure and health care and education (IMF 2000). In 1999 India's fiscal deficit exceeded 11.2 percent of GDP,[12] and threatened the country's solvency. The need to curb the deficit helped drive the reforms launched in India in the 1990s (Rodrik and Subramanian 2004).

The balance-of-payments crisis was contained by the end of 1993. Yet, India did not manage to reduce its deficit in a sustainable manner. Instead the deficit rose again in subsequent years—to reach 10.4 percent in 2000 (Rodrik and Subramanian 2004). The budgets of some Indian states were behind the overall high deficit. Meanwhile rising expenditures in the budgets of some Indian states were mainly related to noninvestment expenses such as spending on pension benefits and administrative services (Aha and others 2006). Potentially growth-boosting public spending went down from 17.1 percent of GDP in 1991 to 14.2 percent in 2006 (Aha and others 2006).

The reforms of China's and India's financial systems—systems responsible for the squandering of huge sums—were delayed and inconsistent. Yet, contrary to India's, the Chinese financial system was effective in mobilizing savings.

Until the 1980s China had practically no market financial system in place. In 1983 the nation started to build its two-tier banking system. The People's Bank of China started to function as the central bank, and four newly established commercial banks took charge of economic affairs. Initially, each specialized in one sector only. Yet, starting from 1984 banks were allowed to establish their branches to operate in sectors previously reserved for their competitors. At the same time, enterprises were gradually allowed to keep accounts at more than one bank. Correspondingly, the banks' autonomy increased as well. As a result, part of the lending was directed to the more profitable private enterprises (Yueh 2003).

Yet, the overwhelming majority of loans was granted to state-owned enterprises—in 1997 a mere 10.4 percent of loans were granted to private companies, although they accounted for 56.5 percent of industrial output (McKinsey 2006a). With the government's support it was easier for them to get loans (even if they unable to repay them), especially as the government maintained its dominant position in the banking sector—in 1997 state-owned banks controlled 93 percent of the banking sector assets (Jianglin and Jie 2000). Chinese banks faced problems with lending money to private companies, not only because of government intervention, but because of the poorly developed credit information system. The first credit information bureau was launched in early 2006. Previously, banks did not collect this type of information. Direct funding (through the issue of shares) also supported state-owned enterprises. For a long time, only state-owned companies could issue shares. The absence of appropriate standards, the strong influence of the government, and (since 1984) the influence of local authorities on lending, increased corruption and led to a high share of bad loans among total loans. In 1993 local banks ceased to be supervised by local branches of the central bank, and control was exercised wholly by headquarters. In 1995 the law on the central bank was adopted, curtailing the influence of local authorities on credit decisions. Despite these measures, in 2001 bad loans accounted for 30 percent of banks' loan portfolios (McKinsey 2006a).[13]

In 1981, capital market construction got under way. First government bonds were issued. In 1984 the corporate bond market was established, but due to complex regulations only state-owned companies and banks operated in this market. In 1990 and 1991 stock exchanges were established in Shanghai and Shenzhen. In the late 1990s they became the main channel of "partial" privatization of state-owned enterprises. Due to its small size (market capitalization of 17 percent of GDP in 2004) the capital market did not offer any alternative to the inefficient banking system (see figure 10.19). Also, the bond market remained very small, as it was almost exclusively limited to government securities. Ineffective and restrictive regulations preventing access to the bond market were the main reason for its poor development. The absence of an adequate accounting system and proper rating agencies also made bond issuance difficult

Figure 10.19 Value of Particular Components of the Chinese Financial System, 1994–2004

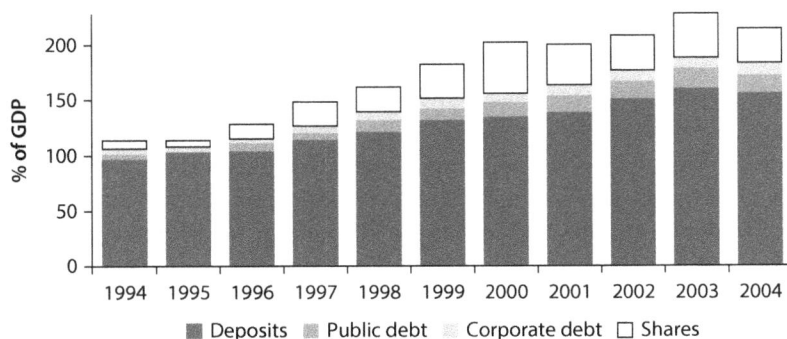

Source: McKinsey 2006a.
Note: GDP = gross domestic product.

Figure 10.20 Real Interest Rates in China and India, 1980–2002

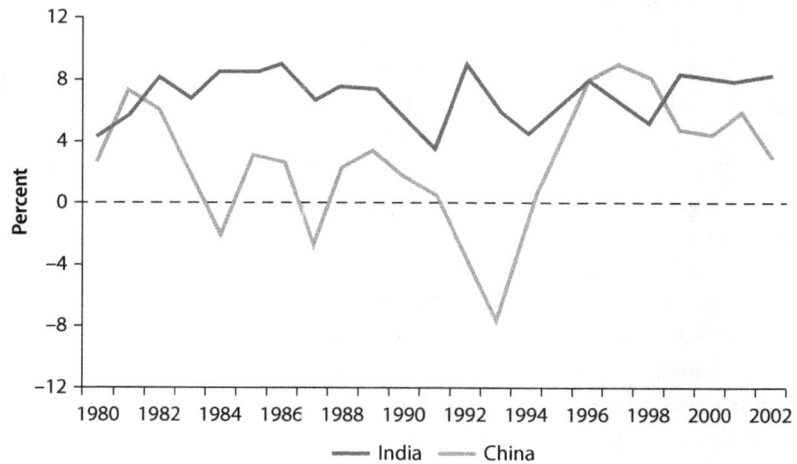

Source: World Development Indicators database.

and expensive. As a result of all these limitations, companies acquired only some 10 percent of their capital through bond issue (in India this figure stood at 13 percent).[14]

In the early 1970s all Indian banks were state owned. The government forced them to finance the deficit (this was reflected in the central bank's rise of the so-called liquidity ratio[15] from 25 percent to 34 percent) and grant loans to so-called priority sectors.

They were to receive at least 40 percent of all loans. Moreover, regulations on debt issuance by private companies made it all but impossible to use this form of capital. Liberalization of the financial system was launched in the 1990s. India's central bank introduced stricter capital adequacy requirements, and reduced the required share of cash and government securities in assets (yet, these requirements continued to be strict—banks were required to hold 25 percent of assets in government bonds). The banking market became subject to competition. Yet, the share of state-owned banks in lending did not fall significantly—it was down to 73 percent in 2005 (McKinsey 2006b). It got easier for Indian companies to raise capital and issue securities abroad (see figure 10.21). These changes had a positive impact on the productivity growth of production factors (Prasad 2005). Yet, foreign banks still found it difficult to enter the financial sector, and the banking system directed most of its funds to rather unproductive sectors of the economy. Lending to "priority" sectors was reduced, albeit only slightly—from 40 percent to 36 percent.[16] In 2004, 57 percent of loans went to state-owned enterprises or agriculture. Banks' low efficiency discouraged people to deposit their savings with banks. Although households saved on average almost 28 percent of their income, only half of their savings were deposited at banks.[17] This boosted the cost of capital—even if measured in terms of real interest rates on loans, from which most of the

Figure 10.21 Value of Particular Segments of the Financial System in India, 1994–2004

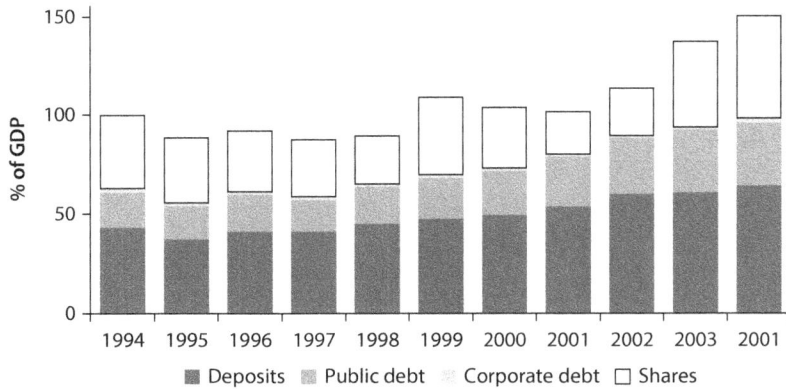

Source: McKinsey 2006b.
Note: GDP = gross domestic product.

companies were cut off. The high cost of capital, in turn, could be one reason India's investment level was low compared to that China's (see figure 10.20).

The Indian capital market, despite the fact that it is one of the oldest in the world (the stock exchange was established in Mumbai in 1875), lost its position in the years 1950–80. At the beginning of the 1980s, only 3.2 percent of household savings were invested in securities (Acharya and others 2003). The government increased its importance as a source of capital for enterprises (thanks to partial deregulation of the capital market). In 2003 India ranked second in the world for its number of listed companies—nearly 6,000 (of which approximately 40 percent, however, were not engaged in any trade). Unlike the stock market, which was the fastest-growing segment of the financial market in India, the corporate bond market remained small (with a value of approximately 2 percent of GDP)—mainly due to regulatory restrictions.

Growth differences between China and India are also partially related to the inadequate rule of law in China (though it is also insufficient in India, due to widespread corruption and the lethargy of courts).

China did not establish a rule of law that would limit the possibility of state interference in the operation of business and households. But such interference was limited anyhow, as the amount of information available to the state was reduced (Qian 2001). With the launch of the first reforms enabling cash transactions (until 1978 their value was limited to approximately $20.00), the ratio of the currency in circulation to GDP rose to 13 percent in 1990 (Qian 2001). The state did not control cash transactions and, consequently, did not receive any information on the actual income generated by such transactions. In addition, the development of the informal financial market allowed assets and profits to be maintained outside state control. Yet, the size of this private market was not large as compared to the entire economy.

Puzzles of Economic Growth • http://dx.doi.org/10.1596/978-1-4648-0325-3

The Chinese judicial system, though formally independent from the government, has always been ineffective and strongly connected with local authorities.
The expansion of businesses across Chinese provinces was curbed by corrupt
judges and officials protecting local businesses. Although the Chinese legal
system expanded significantly over the analyzed period (as is evident in the
growth in the number of lawyers in China—from 5,500 in 1981 to 110,000 in
1998—though only 20 percent of lawyers and even fewer judges hold a formal
university degree and have studied law), it was no match for the Indian one. Yet,
the effectiveness of the Indian judicial system was still low—it often took several
years to resolve legal disputes.

Summary and Conclusions

Until 1978 both India and China developed at a similar rate of growth. Yet,
starting from 1978, with the end of the Cultural Revolution in China, per capita
GDP growth in China was much higher than in India. It stood at 10.1 percent
as compared to 7.2 percent in India. This chapter aims to explain the reasons for
such a difference.

No significant differences in *growth homogeneity* between the two countries
made it possible to use growth accounting. Per capita GDP growth in both
countries was, for the most part, supported by improved productivity driven
by production factors. More pronounced differences between the two countries
were seen in the contribution of capital investment to growth capital.

Faster growth in the productivity of production factors in China than in India
resulted from much more comprehensive and deeper structural reforms that
strengthened growth-propelling institutions. It should be noted that in many
areas, the scope of economic freedom in China continued to be more limited
than in India, where all the institutions related to the operation of a free market
did not have to be built from scratch. China is an example of a country where
high GDP growth was driven by the scale of expansion of economic freedom,
rather than its final level (which is still low). There are several reasons why, in
the analyzed period, India's growth was outpaced by China:

- *The economy was privatized faster.* In both countries, private enterprises were
  characterized by higher and faster growing productivity than state-owned
  enterprises. Although, at the end of the period, the share of the private sector in China's GDP was lower than in India, it had to be built from scratch.
  In India the importance of the public sector hardly changed over the period.
  Moreover, most private sector companies, stifled by excessive regulations and
  administrative constraints, were, in fact, quasi-private enterprises.

- *Prices were released faster.* As a result, they provided reliable information
  about the cost-effectiveness of production factors be used in different areas.
  At the beginning of the 20th century, only 3.7 percent of China's prices
  were set by the government. In India the price reform is still incomplete.

Puzzles of Economic Growth • http://dx.doi.org/10.1596/978-1-4648-0325-3

As of 1997 the government still controlled the prices of most agricultural and industrial products.

- *The labor market underwent much deeper reforms*, allowing labor transfer to more productive sectors of the economy and to businesses. China reduced labor costs, and made it radically easier to dismiss and hire employees in all types of businesses. Continuous urban migration curbed upward pressure on wages, which boosted the competitiveness of Chinese enterprises, and ensured the nation's deeper integration with the global economy. Urban migration also directly increased the productivity of production factors as, on the one hand, it reduced excessive employment in agriculture/labor productivity growth in the sector, and, on the other, limited agriculture's share in employment. This low productivity sector was replaced by more productive sectors. At the same time, India introduced additional regulations aimed to make wages more rigid, dismissals more difficult, and trade unions stronger. These rigidities boosted labor costs and limited labor mobility. This also intensified the incentives to introduce capital-intensive methods of production. As a result, India's cheap labor potential remained unused.

- *The economy was opened up to international trade and FDI faster and to a greater extent.* International trade and foreign investment brought to China previously nonexistent competition and enabled the transfer of technology. India decided to open its economy only after the 1991 budget crisis, and its liberalization was not as far-reaching as in China. Even now, to enter the Indian market it is necessary to wade through a very complicated procedure. Potential costs of investment are also boosted by rigid labor laws, the intricate tax system, and poor road and power infrastructure.

- *The state's fiscal position was drastically limited and fiscal competition among China's provinces was introduced* (yet, provinces could not set tax amounts individually). On the one hand, this raised the efficiency of public spending—China outpaces India in all social and infrastructural indicators. On the other hand, this helped to reduce the fiscal burden, and—thanks to the country's low deficit—limit uncertainty as to its value in the future. In India even the 1991 budget crisis did not prompt any sustainable reduction in public spending. Growing debt service costs displaced spending on infrastructure, education, and health care. India's complex and nontransparent tax system impaired the profitability of production factor utilization to a larger extent than in China. Sound public finances also allowed China to invest in infrastructure much more than in India.

Economic reforms also explain at least some of the differences between China and India in terms of capital expenditure growth:

- Savings in China were driven by demographic changes. The ratio of the non-working-age to working-age populations decreased from 79 percent in 1970 to

49 percent in 2003 (as compared to a decline from 79 percent to 61 percent in India). Yet, growing uncertainty associated with the reforms was also of considerable importance. Foresight as an incentive to save gained in importance as social security was reduced. On the one hand, job security was gone; on the other, social spending was dramatically cut.

- India's public finances did not undergo any changes that improved the incentive to save. At the same time, a high budget deficit absorbed a large portion of private savings and increased investment risk.

- China's greater integration with the global economy improved its ability to capitalize on specialization and large-scale operations, and consequently increased the profits of Chinese enterprises. These were also increased by other reforms, including China's move toward a more flexible labor market (workers' urban migration was curbed by rising labor costs), reduced tax burdens, and privatization (which reduced the squandering of funds, a commonplace in state-owned enterprises). Thus, businesses had both funds (their share in domestic savings was greater than that of households) as well as the incentive to invest them. China recorded more domestic and foreign investment. In India, on the other hand, the inflow of FDI started in the late 1990s and was directed mainly toward the services sector, which is characterized by low capital needs.

Notes

1. The end date, that is, 2001, was chosen owing to data availability. If comparable data series for subsequent periods were at hand, they were used in the analysis.

2. All data concerning economic growth presented in this study have been based on the Penn World Tables 6.2 data, unless specified otherwise. Yet, objective assessment of economic growth in both countries, especially China, is problematic. Data derived from the World Development Indicators (WDI), Maddison (2004), PWT 6.2, and China's official data may, in some cases, differ considerably. An in-depth analysis of China's statistical data and related limitations are presented in Young (2000).

3. Measured as the Solow residual.

4. Author's own calculations based on the Solow Neoclassical Growth Model.

5. This distinction between private and quasi-private enterprises is based on Balcerowicz (1997). Private enterprises are defined as those with nonpublic owners, holding capitalist ownership rights, and enjoying considerable autonomy from the state. Quasi-private enterprises meet the first two of these conditions, but their autonomy is largely limited by government regulations. Thus, enterprises' control rights are limited despite their cash flow rights being preserved.

6. Thanks to the announcement of the Industrial Policy Statement in 1996, which reduced the number of sectors previously monopolized by the public sector from 17 to 8.

7. For example, IMF (2006) observes that 1.0 percentage points of the average growth is ascribed to a labor shift from agriculture to industry, and 0.5 percentage points to a labor shift from agriculture to services. A similar analysis—with similar results—was carried out by Holz (2005).

8. The so-called *open coastal cities*.

9. Tax exemptions, too, especially in the special economic zones, were of considerable importance. Despite the 1994 introduction of a uniform tax system for both domestic and foreign companies, the latter were granted minimum five-year tax exemptions. China also offered a 40 percent refund of paid taxes to foreign companies provided they reinvested their profits in China over a minimum five-year period instead of transferring them abroad. A detailed analysis of investment incentives to foreign investors may be found in Tseng and Zebregs (2002).

10. A detailed description of investments may be found in annex III.

11. Penn World Tables 6.2.

12. Reserve Bank of India Database, http://www.rbi.org.in/scripts/statistics.aspx.

13. In recent years, there was a significant improvement in the banking system, mainly thanks to better supervision but also institutional investments. In 2005 foreign banks invested $18 billion in the Chinese market. There is a marked improvement in terms of the share of bad loans, risk management, and accounting standards. The China Regulatory Banking Commission introduced a series of institutional changes to strengthen the banking system. Classification of bad loans was put in place, restrictions on the amount of the cost of credit were lifted, and the minimum rate of return on deposits was introduced. Yet, bad loans continue to be a problem; the consulting company McKinsey estimates that should China's financial institutions perform better, GDP would increase by $259 billion (McKinsey 2006a).

14. Data from 2004 (McKinsey 2006a).

15. Liquidity ratio determines the percentage of deposits to be collateralized in the form of cash and government securities.

16. This leads to a situation where over 30 percent of bank assets are invested in government bonds. In China this figure was 3 percent in 2004 (see Prasad 2005, 38).

17. The rest is invested mainly in real estate and small family-run or local businesses. Additionally, there is an extensive system of informal financial intermediaries. Indian statistics do not include bank account savings accounts in total deposits.

Bibliography

Acharya, S., I. Ahluwalia, K. L. Krishna, and I. Patnaik. 2003. "India Economic Growth 1950–2000." Global Research Project on Growth, Indian Council for Research on International Economic Relations, Oxford University Press.

Aha, C., and A. Xie. 2004. *India and China: New Tigers of Asia*, Part I. Special Economic Analysis, Morgan Stanley, New York.

Aha, C., A. Xie, S. S. Roach, M. Sheth, and D. Yam. 2006. *India and China: New Tigers of Asia*, Part II. Special Economic Analysis, Morgan Stanley, New York.

Asian Development Bank Database. https://sdbs.adb.org/sdbs/index.jsp.

Bajpai, N., T. Jian, and J. D. Sachs.1997. "Economic Reforms in China and India: Selected Issues in Industrial Policy." Development Discussion Paper 580, Harvard Institute for International Development, Harvard.

Balcerowicz, L.1997. *Socjalizm, kapitalizm, transformacja*. Warsaw, Poland: PWN.

Bosworth, B., and S. M. Collins. 2007. "Accounting for Growth: Comparing India and China." Working Paper 12943, Brookings Institution and National Bureau of Economic Research, Washington, DC, and Cambridge, MA.

Deloitte Research. 2006. "China and India, the Reality beyond the Hype." Deloitte Consulting.

Heston, A., R. Summers, and B. Aten. 2006. "Penn World Table Version 6.2." Center for International Comparisons of Production, Income and Prices, University of Pennsylvania.

Holz, C. A. 2005. "China's Economic Growth 1978–2025: What We Know Today about China's Economic Growth Tomorrow." Social Science Division, Hong Kong University of Science & Technology.

Hu, Z., and M. Khan. 1996. "Why is China Growing So Fast?" IMF Working Paper 96/75, International Monetary Fund, Washington, DC.

IMF (International Monetary Fund). 2000. *India Recent Economic Development*. IMF Country Report 00/155, IMF, Washington, DC.

———. 2005a. *World Economic Outlook*. Washington, DC: IMF.

———. 2005b. "When Do Institutions Change?" Chapter 3, Building Institutions, IMF, Washington, DC, September.

———. 2006. *World Economic Outlook*. Washington, DC: IMF.

Jianglin, Z., and T. Jie. 2000. "Explaining Growth: The Case of China." Working Paper, Institute of Asia-Pacific Studies.

Kaur, S. 2004. "Privatization and Public Enterprise Reform: A Suggestive Action Plan." ASARC Working Paper, Australian National University, Canberra, Australia.

Li, H., and S. Rozelle. 2000. "Privatizing Rural China: Insider Privatization, Innovative Contracts, and the Performance of Township Enterprise." Working Paper, The Chinese University of Hong Kong.

Lin, G. 1997. "On the Exchange Rate of the RMB." University of International Business and Economics Press, China (quoted after: Aha and others 2006, 60).

Maddison, A. 2004. *The World Economy: Historical Statistics*, Maddison Project, University of Groningen, the Netherlands.

McKinsey. 2006a. *Putting China's Capital to Work: The Value of Financial System Reform*. McKinsey Global Institute, New York.

———. 2006b. *Accelerating India's Growth through Financial System Reform*. McKinsey Global Institute, New York.

Mohan, R. 2006. "Financial Sector and Monetary Policy Reforms—Indian Experience." Working Paper, Conference on Economic Policy in Asia, Stanford University.

OECD (Organisation for Economic Co-operation and Development). 1996. *Foreign Direct Investment in India*. Paris: OECD.

———. 2000. "Main Determinants and Impacts of Foreign Direct Investment on China's Economy." Working Paper on International Investment 2000/4, Directorate for Fiscal, Financial and Enterprise Affairs, OECD, Paris.

———. 2005. *Economic Surveys China 2005*. Paris: OECD.

———. 2006. *Challenges for China's Public Spending: Toward Greater Effectiveness and Equity*. Paris: OECD.

O'Neill, J. 2007. "BRICS and Beyond." Goldman Sachs. www.goldmansachs.com /our-thinking/archive/BRICs-and-Beyond.html.

Panagariya, A. 2004. "India in the 1980s and 1990s: A Triumph of Reforms." IMF Working Paper WP/04/43, International Monetary Fund, Washington, DC.

Poddar, T., and E. Yi. 2007. "India's Rising Growth Potential." Global Economics Paper 152, Goldman Sachs, New York.

Poirson, H. 2006. "The Tax System in India: Could Reform Spur Growth?" IMF Working Paper WP/06/93, International Monetary Fund, Washington, DC.

Prasad, G. S. 2005. "Competition in Indian Banking." IMF Working Paper WP/05/141, International Monetary Fund, Washington, DC.

Qian, Y. 2001. "How Reforms Worked in China." Department of Economics, University of California, Berkeley.

RBI Database on Indian Economy. http://www.rbi.org.in/scripts/statistics.aspx.

Rodrik, D., and A. Subramanian. 2004. "From Hindu Growth to Productivity Surge, the Mystery of the Indian Growth Transition." IMF Staff Papers 52, International Monetary Fund, Washington, DC.

Sachs, J. D., and W. T. Woo. 1997. "Understanding China's Economic Performance." NBER Working Papers 5939, National Bureau of Economic Research, Cambridge, MA.

Sun, M. 2006. "Regional Inequality in China, 1978–2006." Department of Geography, University of California, Los Angeles.

Ter-Minassian, T. 2006. "Intergovernmental Fiscal Relations in China." Working Paper, Conference on Economic Policy in Asia, Stanford University, Stanford, CA, June.

Tseng, W., and H. Zebregs. 2002. *Foreign Direct Investment in China: Some Lessons for Other Countries*. Washington, DC: International Monetary Fund.

Virmani, A. 2004. "Foreign Direct Investment Reform." Indian Council for Research on International Economic Relations, New Delhi.

World Bank. 1997. *China 2020: Development Challenges in the New Century*. Washington, DC: World Bank.

World Bank. 2004. *World Development Indicators*. Washington, DC: World Bank.

Xiao, S. 2005. "Share Issue Privatization in China: Theory and Evidence-Change of Control Matters." Department of Economics, Vanderbilt University.

Young, A. 2000. "Gold into Base Metals: Productivity Growth in the People's Republic of China during the Reform Period." NBER Working Paper 7856, National Bureau of Economic Research, Cambridge, MA.

Yueh, L. Y. 2003. "China's Economic Growth with WTO Accession: Is It Sustainable?" Asia Program Working Paper 1, Royal Institute of International Affairs, London, May.

CHAPTER 11

Why Has Pakistan Developed More Slowly Than Indonesia?

Filip Berkowski

Both Indonesia and Pakistan share not only a similar number of inhabitants (with marked ethnic differences), but also the same religion (these are the two countries with the largest number of Muslims)[1] and a similar history. After many years of colonial rule under the Netherlands and Great Britain, respectively, both gained independence in the 20th century. Both had to solve border problems and build their institutional framework from scratch (amid numerous internal conflicts, as the shape of their territory was determined by the shape of the land held by the former colonial rulers rather than by the people living on the territory).

In 1965 both countries had an almost identical per capita gross domestic product (GDP; in Pakistan it was 1 percent below Indonesian GDP). In 2004 per capita GDP in Indonesia was almost 50 percent more than in Pakistan. Yet, our GDP analysis starts in 1961; in the years 1961–65 Pakistan developed faster than Indonesia, contrary to the years 1966–2004 (see figure 11.1).

In the years 1965–2004 the average annual per capita GDP growth in Indonesia stood at 3.62 percent and exceeded Pakistan's (2.55 percent) by 1.06 percentage points.

Our analysis of economic growth in Indonesia and Pakistan covers the years 1966–96, thus leaving out the effect of the 1997 Asian crisis. The main factor behind Indonesia's rapid economic growth in this period was the expansion of physical capital (investment), which accounted for almost 74 percent of the country's economic growth. Investment expansion in Indonesia (in particular, in the 1970s and 1980s) was driven by public investment financed with income from crude oil sales. Growth in physical capital in Pakistan accounted for 52 percent of per capita GDP growth in this country, and its pace of growth accounted for a mere 33 percent of growth recorded in Indonesia. A considerable part of Pakistani economic growth may be attributed to the improved productivity of production factors. The contribution of total factor productivity (TFP) to per capita GDP growth in Indonesia was 30 percent lower than in Pakistan (see figure 11.1; table 11.1).[2]

Figure 11.1 Average Annual GDP Per Capita in Indonesia and Pakistan, 1960–2004

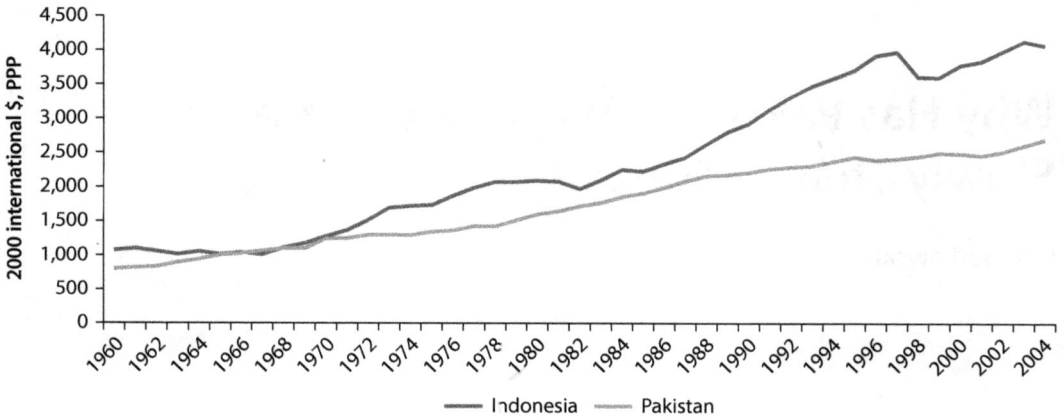

Source: Based on Penn World Table 6.2.
Note: GDP =gross domestic product; PPP = purchasing power parity.

Table 11.1 Results of Growth Accounting for Indonesia and Pakistan, 1966–96
Percent

	y	A	k	n
Indonesia				
Growth rate	4.4	1.70	6.61	0.61
Contribution to growth		19.04	74.07	6.89
Pakistan				
Growth rate	2.7	2.09	2.17	−0.13
Contribution to growth		50.61	52.50	−3.12

Source: Based on Penn World Table 6.2.
Note: y = per capita GDP; A = total factor productivity; k = change in capital outlays per capita; n = change in number of people working.

The growth rate of labor productivity was similar in both countries: 2.7 percent in Indonesia and 3.0 percent in Pakistan. In Indonesia it differed significantly across sectors. The fastest output growth per one employed person was seen in industry (an average growth of 4.4 percent annually as compared to a 0.8 percent growth in agriculture and 1.2 percent growth in services), with the highest growth seen at the beginning. As a result, in 2002 it exceeded more than nine times the labor productivity in industry and three times the labor productivity in services. Such large disparities in labor productivity led to considerable differences in income levels. The share of industry in GDP increased four times (up to 44 percent in 2002). This growth was largely driven by rising crude oil prices in the international commodity markets observed in the 1970s.[3] In Pakistan labor productivity growth was considerably less diversified (it ranged from 2.4 percent in agriculture and services to 2.8 percent in industry). There were also differences in labor productivity, yet considerably less pronounced than in

Indonesia (where in 2002 labor productivity in agriculture and industry constituted 39 percent and 77 percent, respectively, of labor productivity in services).

Both countries witnessed considerable changes in the structure of employment—
an outflow of the workforce from agriculture to the services sector (and in
Indonesia also to industry, although to a much lesser extent—the percentage of
persons employed in industry fell from 8 percent in 1960 to 14 percent in 2002).
The percentage of persons in agriculture dropped from 73 percent in 1960 to
less than 50 percent in 2002 in Indonesia, and from 60 percent to slightly over
40 percent in Pakistan.

The labor participation rates of working-age adults differed in both countries,
as did the percentage of persons of working age in the total population. The labor
participation rate climbed by an average of 0.15 percent annually in Indonesia and
slid by 0.11 percent in Pakistan. Moreover, the percentage of persons of productive age in the total population increased from 57 percent in 1960 to 66 percent
in 2000 in Indonesia and remained at a steady 55 percent level in Pakistan.

In the years 1961–2004 economic growth was unsteady in both Indonesia
and Pakistan. Especially, per capita GDP growth in Indonesia was volatile (see
table 11.2).

- In the years 1961–65, Pakistan developed extremely dynamically, whereas
  Indonesia experienced an economic collapse with an average annual GDP
  decline of 1.05 percent per capita.
- In the years 1966–87—a period marked by crude oil slumps—the Indonesian
  crisis was headed off, and the average annual GDP per capita reached 5.68
  percent. This was 3 percentage points more than in Pakistan, whose economy,
  after a successful start in the early 1960s, had slowed down considerably.
- In the years 1979–86, per capita GDP growth in Indonesia slowed down considerably, reaching a mere 1.7 percent on an annual basis. Pakistan, on the

Table 11.2 Average Annual Per Capita GDP Growth in Indonesia and Pakistan, 1960–2004

| Years | Average annual change in per capita GDP | | | Per capita GDP in Pakistan |
	Indonesia (%)	Pakistan (%)	Change in %	Per capita GDP in Indonesia (at the beginning of the period, %)
1960–65	−1.05	4.65	−5.69	75
1966–78	5.86	2.72	3.13	99
1979–86	1.70	3.96	−2.26	73
1987–96	5.48	1.54	3.94	86
1997–98	−9.12	1.22	−10.34	61
1999–2004	2.48	1.57	0.91	69
2004	n.a.	n.a.	n.a.	66
1965–2004	3.62	2.55	1.06	—

Source: Based on Penn World Table 6.2.
Note: GDP = gross domestic product.
 n.a. = not applicable; — = not available.

other hand, posted a more robust growth, exceeding 2 percentage points, out-
pacing Indonesia in terms of per capita GDP growth.

- Neither country experienced any external shocks in the period 1987–96,
  which marked another reversal in their situation. The average annual growth
  rate in Indonesia reached almost 5.5 percent. Consequently, Indonesia continued to develop faster than Pakistan, whose GDP growth per capita went down
  to 2.4 percentage points as compared with the previous period.
- The year 1997 was primarily marked by a considerable GDP decline in
  Indonesia, driven by the Asian currency crisis. In the years 1997–98 the Pakistani
  economy also ran into stagnation, after the preceding mediocre 10-year period.
- The years 1999–2004 brought economic recovery both to Indonesia
  (2.48 percent) and to Pakistan (1.54 percent). Over the last three years of this
  period, the annual GDP growth per capita in Pakistan stood at 4.99 percent—
  the highest level since gaining independence in 1947.

Differences in Economic Performance: Factors and Causes

The Years 1961–65

In the years 1961–65 Pakistan's robust economic growth was accompanied by
recession in Indonesia. The key to understanding such considerable differences
in per capita GDP growth lies in an analysis of the economic policy pursued.

As a result of the nationalization of private Dutch enterprises initiated by
workers in Indonesia, the share of public ownership in GDP generation increased
considerably, to reach more than 35 percent in 1960. By 1957 the government
took over 300 Dutch plantations and 300 financial, commercial, and public
utility sector enterprises (Frederick and Worden 1993). The financial sector was
not only nationalized but also consolidated—five major banks were merged
(Frederick and Worden 1993). Former Dutch management boards of private
enterprises were replaced by public servants of the Sukarno administration and
military officers lacking, for the most part, the necessary knowledge or experience of running these enterprises.

The new eight-year plan of economic growth launched by the Sukarno government in 1959 assumed a significant increase (12-fold increase as compared with
the previous plan) in public expenditure (primarily on investment in a nationalized economy). Poor tax collection combined with the corrupt practices of
civil servants dramatically boosted expenditure and increased the public finance
deficit.[4] At the beginning of the 1960s almost half of public expenditure was
financed with the central bank's loans, which consequently led to a rapid price
increase. In 1996 the inflation rate exceeded 1,500 percent (Temple 2001, see
figure 11.2), and external debt rose considerably.[5] Debt-servicing costs resulting
from loans granted by both Western countries and the Soviet Union rapidly surpassed the limits of the Sukarno government, putting the country at the edge of
bankruptcy (Temple 2001, 4). An economic crisis broke out, highlighting weaknesses in Indonesia's stabilizing institutions. In the years 1960–65 the Indonesian
economy continued to shrink by an average of 1 percent on an annual basis.

Figure 11.2 GDP Deflator in Indonesia and Pakistan, 1967–78

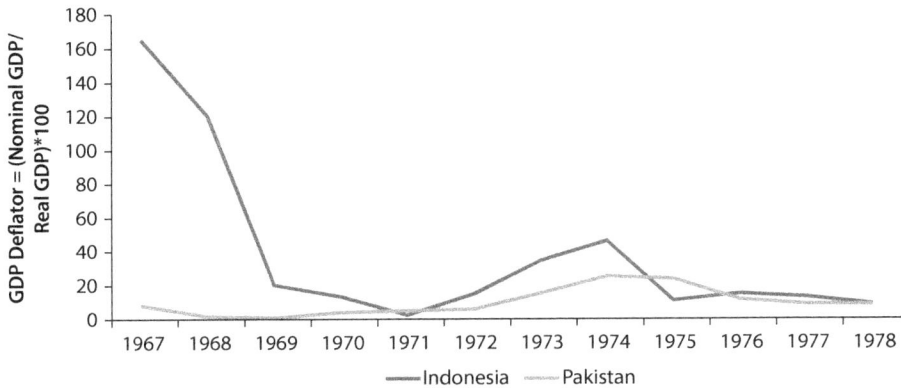

Source: Based on World Development Indicators 2006 (http://data.worldbank.org/products/data-books/WDI-2006).
Note: GDP = gross domestic product.

Contrary to Indonesia, the years 1960–65 brought changes supporting eco-nomic growth in Pakistan. Apart from investment in public infrastructure, which was supposed to supplement private investments, the government did not inter-fere with other sectors of the economy. In 1960 the share of public ownership in GDP stood at 12.8 percent and was almost three times lower than in Indonesia. State ownership was limited to the armament industry, water power plants, railway, telephony, telegraphy, and radiotelephony (a sector rather unattractive to private investors at that time; Blood 1995). In the 1960s budget expenses accounted for 11.6 percent of the Pakistani GDP amid income at a level of 13.1 percent of GDP. Public finance surplus was maintained despite the absence of any formal rules. This was also the case for inflation, which continued at a low level despite the fact that the central bank was totally controlled by the govern-ment. The government's minor participation in the economy—combined with fiscal discipline and low, one-digit inflation—contributed to high per capita GDP, exceeding 4.6 percent on an annual basis.

The key factor differentiating the economic performance of both countries was the character of the dictators in power (Sukarno in Indonesia and Ayub Khan in Pakistan) rather than the power of the institutions.

The Years 1966–78

The years 1965–78 were marked by robust economic growth in Indonesia and economic downturn in Pakistan. During these years the analyzed countries launched different reforms to their institutional systems, in the process affecting their growth. Also, the 1973 surge in oil prices was a major factor behind differ-ences in economic growth.

The Indonesian economic crisis in 1965 helped the head of the military forces, General Suharto, to take over political power. With the help (and financial aid) of the International Monetary Fund (IMF), an economic stabilization program was prepared. Lower budget expenses and money supply control helped to rapidly curb high inflation (Hill 2000). To prevent the recurrence of economic collapse, at the end of the Sukarno regime a balanced budget rule was introduced (Hamada 2003). However, from an institutional point of view, the balanced budget rule was rather a fiction as it allowed deficit financing items (external debt and foreign aid) to be labeled as income (Boediono 1990) and an introduction of more disciplined fiscal policy was a result of General Suharto's actions rather than the rule itself. Until 1973 General Suharto pursued a relatively liberal trade policy, and in 1970 proceeded with capital inflow liberalization (Hill 2000). Moreover, he intensified competition in the financial sector and reinstated the right to establish new commercial banks and broke down the banking conglomerate created under Sukarno's dictatorship (Frederick and Worden 1993). Also, a number of foreign banks were permitted to operate in Indonesia. The stabilization and liberalization programs proved a success. In the years 1966–71 per capita GDP was on the rise—at a level of about 5 percent a year.

The period 1966–78 was also one of political turmoil in Pakistan: civil war and social conflicts raged. As a result of the 1971 Pakistani civil war, Eastern Pakistan, supported by India and the Soviet Union, separated from Pakistan proper and created an independent state—Bangladesh (Blood 1995). On the other hand, civil riots and demonstrations triggered among the poor in Pakistan resulted in, among other things, the introduction of minimum wages; the establishment of labor unions; the approval of a new, more progressive tax system; and wage increases for the worst paid (apart from changes in labor productivity; Blood 1995).

In 1962 Indonesia became a member of the Organization of the Petroleum Exporting Countries (OPEC). The 1970s oil crises, driven by restricted oil production (being, in turn, the consequence of measures taken by OPEC), largely contributed to Indonesia's robust economic growth. The public sector's income generated by oil sales, which in 1972 accounted for 4 percent of GDP, surged to almost 7.7 percent of GDP in 1974 and to 13.3 percent of GDP in 1980 (Hill 2000). The contribution of rising crude oil prices to average annual GDP growth in the years 1973–80 may be estimated at 1.46 percentage points. Without oil price increases, the years 1974, 1979, and 1980 would have brought a decline in per capita GDP. This estimate fails to account for the indirect effects of the oil crises, capital expenditures in industry sector financed by income from crude oil sales and following increase in exports of industrial products. Public sector spending intended to boost economic growth (for the most part, investment in industry and services) increased from 6.5 percent of GDP in 1973 to nearly 13 percent of GDP in 1975, and remained at the level of 11–13 percent of GDP until 1985. Yet, the effectiveness of this investment was doubtful (see later in this chapter).

The 1970s crude oil shocks had no significant impact on the pace of economic growth in Pakistan, although the country was an oil importer. Due to a low level of development and the small contribution of industry to GDP growth, the country's demand for oil was small: crude oil consumed during a year (amid high crude oil prices in 1980) amounted to a mere 2.0 percent of GDP.[6]

Pakistan adopted a growth strategy similar to that pursued in Indonesia—financing large-scale investments from public funds, except that the financing beneficiaries were state-owned enterprises, and not government-linked yet private conglomerates as in Indonesia (in Indonesia private conglomerates were more market driven than state-owned enterprises in Pakistan, which affected changes in labor productivity growth in industry in both countries). As a result, in the years 1966–78 public expenditure in both countries increased to a similar level—from 10 percent to 23 percent of GDP in Indonesia and from 11 percent to 25 percent of GDP in Pakistan. In Indonesia the deficit reached approximately 2–4 percent of GDP, and public debt approximately 30 percent of GDP. Growth in expenditure was largely financed with income from crude oil sales and foreign aid (other budget expenditure rose from 4.2 percent to 7.3 percent). In Pakistan growing public expenditure increased the deficit (to 7 percent of GDP), a significant change from the small surplus maintained in the 1960s. Public debt reached 72 percent of GDP in 1973 to level off at approximately 60 percent of GDP.

Pakistan's nationalization program, launched at the beginning of the 1970s, largely contributed to its economic downturn. In 1972, under Zulfikar Ali Bhutto's[7] leadership, 32 large manufacturing plants in major branches of industry—namely steel, iron, metal, heavy, vehicle manufacturing, agricultural machinery, chemical, petrochemical, and cement—were nationalized, as well as public utilities. Also, the entire insurance, transport, mills, and textile industries as well as the oil processing and distribution network were nationalized. In 1974 nationalization involved all commercial banks. As a result of the nationalization process, after 1972, private capital fled the country. In 1973 the value of private investment in the industry accounted for half, and in 1978 only one-third of 1970 levels (Sakr 1993).

Investors who chose to leave their capital in the country invested mainly in real estate and small-scale manufacturing plants. Construction of almost all new factories was financed by the government, which also established new state-owned companies operating as rice or cotton exporters. As a result of nationalization, the contribution of the Pakistani public sector to GDP rose from 12.8 percent in 1960 to 17.8 percent in 1970 and 37.1 percent in 1980. State-owned enterprises, promoting the government-run social equality policy, were not able to retain highly qualified technical staff and management. The qualified workforce emigrated mainly to Great Britain (Blood 1995). This, combined with the government's wage increase policy (not hinged on labor productivity), deepened the inefficiency of the public sector—these inefficiencies in Pakistan expanded to a larger degree than in Indonesia.

In agriculture, in turn, the government introduced restrictions on the size of agricultural production and increased the rights and security of land tenants. These limited the development opportunities of large farms, the only entities in agriculture (especially after 1972 and following a 57 percent devaluation of the rupee) to generate substantial profits (Ahmed 1994).

Puzzles of Economic Growth • http://dx.doi.org/10.1596/978-1-4648-0325-3

Fraser Institute's index of legal structure and security of property rights ranked Pakistan at 2.2 points in 1970, 1.5 in 1975, and 2.5 points in 1980. The index fell in the case of Indonesia—from 4.4 in 1970 to 3.7 in 1975 and 3.4 points in 1980.

Meanwhile, Indonesia's economy was dominated by private conglomerates holding a privileged, often monopolistic position. The largest of them controlled almost all sectors of the Indonesian economy.[8]

Business success depended on an entrepreneur's good relations with the Suharto administration. As a result of the government industrialization programs implemented with the use of conglomerates, industry developed in isolation from international markets. Indonesian industry was not in a position to face foreign competition; Indonesian exports of industrial products did not exceed 1 percent of GDP. The next measure undertaken by the Suharto administration was to tighten trade regulations so that expensive Indonesian industrial goods could find buyers in the domestic market.

The privileged position of the conglomerates disturbed the development of the financial sector. Many private banks had connections with the conglomerates and they granted loans to related parties only. Moreover, the sector was still dominated by state-owned banks (their share in the aggregate assets of the banking sector in 1975 reached almost 70 percent).[9] Their lending activity largely involved the performance of government programs aimed to support select economic activities. Low-interest loans called "liquidity credits," subsidized by the central bank at the end of the 1970s, accounted for almost 50 percent of the loans granted by state-owned banks.

Private conglomerates followed the rules of the economy to a much greater degree than state-owned enterprises. This may explain Indonesia's much higher labor productivity growth in industry, compared with Pakistan. At the same time, however, as conglomerates were more profit sensitive than state-owned enterprises, their privileged position was a much stronger shock for other sectors. On the one hand, the rapid growth of labor productivity in conglomerates (and therefore wage growth) drew the qualified workforce away from other sectors. On the other hand, conglomerates could solicit the government to support them more effectively than state-owned enterprises—at the expense of other sectors.

The Years 1979–86

In the years 1979–86, the Pakistani economy accelerated to reach an average annual per capita GDP growth of 4 percent. But in Indonesia, where in the years 1974–78 a number of changes were introduced limiting economic freedom and competition, the average annual per capita GDP stood at a mere 1.7 percent (as compared to 5.9 percent in the previous period).

Their economic plight, caused by the statist Bhutto rule, made Pakistanis aware of the need for reforms (Khan, Qayyum, and Sheikh 2005). A new government, headed by Mohammad Zia ul-Haq (in charge since 1978) introduced a constitutional guarantee that Pakistan would not see the nationalization of the early 1970s again, and that possible expropriations—limited to special cases only—would be carried out against fair compensation. The private sector was given rights comparable to those enjoyed by the public sector, and private businesses gained almost complete freedom in choosing the investment sector (only a few sectors were supposed to remain fully state controlled; Blood 1995). The financial sector was liberalized, and banking supervision was strengthened (Khan, Qayyum, and Sheikh 2005).

Despite the fact that in the analyzed period the contribution of public ownership to GDP growth in Pakistan was higher than in Indonesia, the Pakistani GDP followed a gradual (albeit slow) downward trend (from 37.1 percent in 1980 to 33.7 percent in 1990)—in contrast to Indonesia, where state participation in the economy increased (from 26.4 percent to 29 percent of GDP). In Pakistan, as a consequence of free-market reforms, competition increased, at a time when the Indonesian market was still dominated by privileged Indonesian conglomerates.

The rapid economic growth in Pakistan was also thanks to the partially lifted foreign trade restrictions. In Indonesia the economic openness indicator, defined as the share of exports and imports in GDP (excluding oil exports), remained stable and lower than the level in Pakistan.

In Pakistan in the early 1980s import tariffs were lowered and a large portion of nontariff restrictions were lifted (in 1981 nearly 41 percent of industrial value added output was protected by import bans, and a further 22 percent by other forms of import restrictions; Siddiqui and Kemal 2002, see table 11.3). More liberal trade policy was aimed, on the one hand, to increase the competitive pressure on the domestic industry, and, on the other hand, to facilitate access thereof to foreign commodities and intermediate goods. The economic openness indicator rose from 32 percent of GDP in 1979 to 35 percent of GDP in 1986.

In Indonesia in the early 1980s, almost 1,500 goods (accounting for approximately 35 percent of import value) were subject to import quotas or could be imported by holders of government licenses only (Frederick and Worden 1993). Import licenses for specific goods were often granted to particular enterprises. Apart from nontariff barriers to trade, import duties were also common–they reached as much as 200 percent of the value of goods not subject to the licensing system (Frederick and Worden 1993). Nontariff barriers were used in all branches of industry, particularly in textiles, chemicals, and paper products. Complex trade regulations triggered corruption among the customs authorities

Table 11.3 Structure of Customs Tariffs in Pakistan, 1980–85

Percent

Years	Imports of processed products	Imports of commodities
1980–81	28.42	13.97
1984–85	17.66	12.94

Source: Based on Siddiqui and Kemal 2002.

Puzzles of Economic Growth • http://dx.doi.org/10.1596/978-1-4648-0325-3

involved in evaluating import values and levying customs duties. The openness indicator, net of crude oil, fell from 32 percent of GDP in 1979 to 30 percent of GDP in 1986.

The rise in Indonesia's external debt in the analyzed period—from 28 percent to 69 percent of GDP—revealed the weaknesses of its stabilizing institutions. Although Pakistani external debt also remained high (48 percent of GDP in 1986), its growth was not that critical (since 1979 it had increased by 2 percent of GDP).

Economic failures made the Suharto government aware of the need for reform. Changes introduced at the end of the analyzed period were not conducive to growth acceleration in the period up to 1986. Yet, they created more favorable growth conditions in the years 1987–96.

- In the face of falling oil prices, the Indonesian government reduced budget expenditure significantly (from 25 percent to 21 percent of GDP in 1986) and postponed and finally withdrew from a number of large projects (government investment fell from 13 percent of GDP in 1979 to 8 percent of GDP in 1986).[10]

- In 1983 a financial sector reform program was launched that aimed to transform the corrupt and government-controlled sector into a source of competitive lending based on interest rates determined by market forces.[11] Credit quotas were abolished, and national banks were allowed to introduce market-based interest rates (Hamada 2003). Although the central bank continued to subsidize loans used to finance key political investment decisions, many preferential loan programs were closed (their share in loans extended by state-owned banks fell from about 50 percent to 33 percent in 1988). On the other hand, limits continued to be applied to the number of private banks and state-owned enterprises who could place their deposits with state-owned banks only (Frederick and Worden 1993).

- In the years 1985–86 foreign trade liberalization was also initiated. The Customs Clearance Office was closed down and its responsibilities were taken over by a Swiss company, Société Générale de Surveillance. One month after the change, Indonesian importers noted an average 20 percent reduction in import costs (Frederick and Worden 1993). As the amendments aimed to liberalize foreign trade fueled the Indonesian economy at a later time, they are more thoroughly analyzed in the next section, focusing on sources of economic growth in the years 1987–96.

The Years 1987–96

Although both analyzed countries carried out free market reforms in 1987–96, only Indonesia saw rapid economic growth.

Free market reforms that strengthened propelling institutions (which drove Indonesia's growth in the period 1987–96) were started in 1985 and continued in subsequent years. (Mackie and Sjahrir 1989; Frederick and Worden 1993). They concerned, in particular:

- The liberalization of foreign trade.
- The partial elimination of privileges enjoyed by conglomerates.
- Financial sector reforms.

In 1985, under the General Agreement on Tariffs and Trade (GATT) regime, Indonesia pledged not to use certain export subsidies (Frederick and Worden 1993). In May 1986 a decision was made to refund import duties levied on commodities and intermediate products imported to Indonesia to be used in the production of export goods. Domestic exporters were allowed to import commodities and intermediate products that had once been subject to licenses. Also, regulations restricting the inflow of foreign direct investment (FDI) were eased. As a result, FDI inflow increased from 0.5 percent of GDP in 1987 to almost 1.5 percent of GDP in the early 1990s and more than 2.5 percent of GDP in the mid-1990s. In November 1988 a large number of nontariff barriers on imports were abolished, and duty tariffs were simplified. The share of industrial production protected by nontariff barriers in Indonesia decreased from 50 percent in 1986 to 35 percent in 1988 (Frederick and Worden 1993). In 1990 there were nontariff barriers on 660 products, as compared with 1,500 products two years earlier. The maximum customs tariff was 40 percent as compared to the 200 percent tariff in the early 1980s (Frederick and Worden 1993).

In 1991 the agreement with Société Générale de Surveillance was extended. Under the agreement, Société Générale de Surveillance was to assign customs tariffs to particular goods. In 1992 the Association of Southeast Asian Nations Free Trade Area (AFTA) was established (Hill 2000;[12] the Association of Southeast Asian Nations is a regional political and economic organization founded in August 1967 by Indonesia, the Philippines, Malaysia, Singapore, and Thailand). As a result of these changes—and strong economic growth among Indonesia's major political and trading partners—the economic openness indicator, with oil trade excluded, increased from 33 percent of GDP in 1987 to 45 percent of GDP in 1996. Exports of industrial products increased from 6 percent of GDP in 1987 to 15 percent in 1993 and 14 percent in 1996.

Conglomerates gradually started to lose their privileged position as monopolies in steel and plastic industries were broken up in 1988. Licenses for the production and marketing of the steel and plastic, previously granted to conglomerates only, were abolished. At the end of the 1980s, conglomerates lost their privileged position in foreign trade (the export licensing system was abolished) and financial aid for government-run development programs (as a result of public expenditure on development having declined from 7.4 percent in 1987 to 4.3 percent of GDP in 1996).[13] In the 1980s the Chamber of Commerce and Industry (Kadin) was established as a group of small and medium-sized companies not participating in the government distribution of petrodollars. In 1987 this organization, which opposed a monopoly-based economy, became an official party in contacts between businesses and the government.

As part of the financial sector's liberalization, October 1988 saw the imposition of limits on loans extended to entities controlled by bank shareholders (which forced banks controlled by the conglomerates to search for new clients). Moreover, the formalities involved in setting up new banks were considerably simplified and all existing domestic banks were given freedom to open new branches (see table 11.4, which illustrates changes in the structure of banking sector assets). State-owned enterprises were allowed to invest up to 50 percent of their funds in private banks. Also, the reserve requirement for commercial banks was reduced from 15 percent to 2 percent of liabilities (Hill 2000).[14] Foreign investors, whose interest in a company listed in Jakarta could reach up to 49 percent of its share capital, were allowed to enter the Jakarta Stock Exchange (Frederick and Worden 1993). The number of companies listed on the Jakarta Stock Exchange increased from 24 in 1988 to 125 in 1991 (Hill 2000).

In 1988–91 the Pakistani government lowered custom duties levied on 1,134 goods (and increased custom duties levied on 462 goods), reducing the maximum customs tariff from 225 percent to 100 percent and then to 65 percent in 1995 (Siddiqui and Kemal 2002). At the same time, the number of customs tariffs also fell from 17 to 10. The country's economic openness indicator rose from 34 percent of GDP in 1987 to 39 percent of GDP in 1990 and remained at a similar level in subsequent years.

With the government's consent, in 1991 the National Bank of Pakistan was allowed to issue licenses for the establishment of new private commercial banks. Within three years, the central bank exercised that right on 10 occasions. In addition, by 1994 Pakistan had opened 21 branches of foreign banks such as the Bank of America, Citibank, and American Express. Foreign banks conducted operations through 61 branches, located mainly in Karachi.

In 1992, 20 enterprises and 2 commercial banks were privatized (Blood 1995). In 1994 the government began to break up state-owned monopolies in the insurance, telecommunications, transport, port services, airlines, power plants, and road construction sectors. Apart from the government's key areas of business,

Table 11.4 Composition of the Total Assets of the Commercial Banks Sector in Indonesia, 1987–96

Percent

	1987	1988	1989	1990	1991	1992	1993	1994	1995	1996
State owned	64.7	63.0	54.8	48.7	50.9	51.8	47.0	42.1	39.7	36.5
Private domestic	21.9	24.0	31.9	36.2	38.2	36.8	41.2	45.9	47.8	51.8
Private foreign	5.8	5.1	5.5	7.4	8.5	8.4	9.2	9.5	9.8	9.2
Regional banks for development	7.7	8.0	7.8	7.7	3.0	2.9	3.2	3.2	3.2	2.8

Source: Hamada 2003.

Note: During the analyzed period (1987–96), Pakistan also launched a series of reforms.

private investors gained complete freedom to invest capital without needing to obtain the government's license. Inflow of FDI was again allowed. In the years 1987–96 FDI increased from 0.4 percent to 1.5 percent of GDP.

In the analyzed period the approach of Indonesia and Pakistan to their public finances significantly differs, as discussed below.

Indonesia consistently reduced budget expenditure, from 21.3 percent in 1987 to 13.0 percent of GDP in 1996 (see figure 11.3). This was the government's response to falling income from oil exports and reduced foreign aid. Yet, revenue declined more slowly than expenditure. As a result, the budget deficit narrowed gradually, and starting from 1994 (for the first time in the history of Indonesia) budget surpluses were achieved. Due to public debt reduction, debt-servicing costs also decreased (from 6.4 percent to 4.1 percent of GDP), which improved public finances.

In the years 1987–96 Pakistan failed to match its budget expenditure with budget revenues and to broaden the tax base. Although spending was reduced from 26.0 percent to 22.3 percent of GDP, with income at about 17.5 percent of GDP, the deficit remained at dangerously high levels (reaching, in some years, as much as 8.0 percent of GDP, see figure 11.4).

The fiscal imbalance forced the government to withdraw from the majority of its domestic development programs (spending on domestic development programs fell from 8.1 percent to 3.5 percent of GDP over the years 1987–96). Also the current expenditure budget was reduced from 4.8 percent of GDP in 1987 to 2 percent of GDP in 1996. The arms race with India (national defense spending amounted to 6.0–7.5 percent of GDP) was not abandoned, which had a negative impact on economic growth (Yildirm and Ocal 2003). Chronic deficits boosted debt-servicing costs by nearly 90 percent, to reach 10.9 percent of

Figure 11.3 Public Sector Expenditure and Revenue as a Percentage of GDP in Indonesia, 1987–96

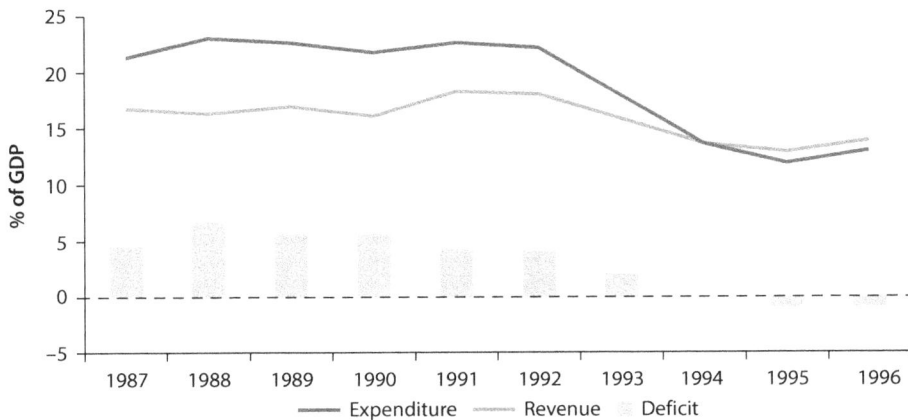

Sources: Based on Hill 2000 and World Bank 2007.
Note: GDP = gross domestic product.

Figure 11.4 Public Sector Expenditure and Receipts as a Percentage of GDP in Pakistan, 1987–96

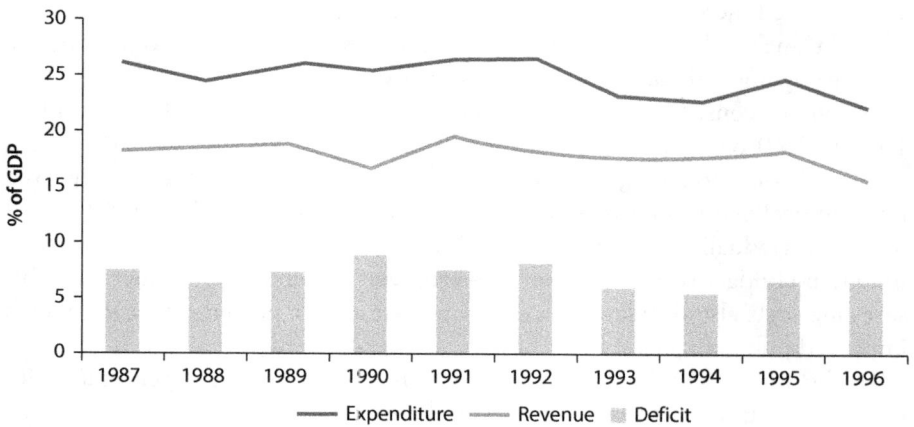

Sources: Based on Pasha 1992; Fiscal Development, Pakistan Economic Survey 2006-07.
Note: GDP = gross domestic product.

GDP in 1996. Together with the expenditure on the army, debt-servicing costs accounted for as much as 75 percent of the total budget expenditure.

Although both the analyzed countries carried out liberal reforms in the years 1987–96, only Indonesia saw rapid economic growth. The lower growth rate in Pakistan was the result of rising debt and related debt-servicing costs combined with persistent budget deficits.

The Years 1997–2004

The 1997 Asian financial crisis interrupted the region's nearly 30-year-long dynamic growth. Indonesia, whose per capita GDP fell in just one year by more than 9 percent, was the hardest-hit country in Southeast Asia. A serious economic collapse, though not driven by the Asian crisis, was also observed in Pakistan. While GDP decline in Indonesia was sudden and unexpected, the economic crisis in Pakistan was the result of a long-term accumulation of imbalances—particularly in public finances.

Before the crisis, Indonesia showed no symptoms of the looming foreign exchange crisis (Hill 2000). In the 1990s the public sector significantly cut back its expenditure (to approximately 15 percent of GDP). As a result, starting in 1994, public finances recorded a slight surplus. Until 1997 inflation had remained stable at 8–9 percent. The current account deficit was relatively low (just before the onset of the crisis it was about half that of Thailand, where the crisis broke out). There were no signs of any significant revaluation of the rupee, or (until mid-1997) loss of investor confidence in the rupee and the Indonesian stock exchange. Until the very beginning of the crisis, ratings of Indonesia were positive and showed gradual improvement. Financial indicators pointed to the good condition of Indonesian companies (the crisis was not preceded by wage increases exceeding labor productivity growth). The real estate market showed no symptoms of asset bubbles.

The key factor behind the financial crisis in Southeast Asia was mainly international investors' doubt that the exchange rates of currency in countries affected by the crisis were stable. Three factors widened the scope of the crisis in Indonesia at the time it broke out:

- A major mistake in crisis management: the abrupt closure of 16 banks, which—on the back of rupee devaluation, withdrawal of deposits, and interest rate hikes—lost their liquidity.[15] This immediately undermined the credibility of the entire banking system in Indonesia (Lane 1999, 279–85).
- In the face of the crisis, President Suharto attempted, by all possible means, to defend his family's private economic interests. Thus, Suharto's conduct led to a loss of confidence in the regime and its ability to manage the deepening crisis (Lane 1999).
- The undemocratic political system and growing corruption limited opportunities to obtain external aid, including that from the IMF (Lane 1999).

Political instability, combined with strong depreciation of the Indonesian rupee, led to capital outflow and, consequently, falls in stock market indices, further dramatic depreciation of the rupee, a leap in inflation, and a public debt explosion. In 1998–99 even the FDI balance was negative. Indonesia's main stock market index represented only 15 percent of its mid-1997 value in March 1999. On March 31, 1998, the value of the rupee accounted for only 28 percent of its value as recorded in mid-1997 (the decline was twice that in other crisis-stricken countries). Up to mid-1998, prices almost doubled, and until 1999 public debt increased four times. At the end of 1999, it reached almost 100 percent of GDP. The crisis highlighted the weaknesses of the stabilizing institutions in Indonesia.

The crisis in Pakistan broke out in 1998. Although the imbalance in the economy had continued to build up over the years, its occurrence was accelerated by successful nuclear tests conducted on May 31, 1998, in response to India's nuclear tests (*The Economist* 1998). Most Western countries, including the United States, in protest to the tests, stopped their aid and investment in Pakistan, introducing, at the same time, economic sanctions (*The Economist* 1998).

A few days after the nuclear tests, the government, fearing a run on the state-owned banks and a massive outflow of foreign currency deposits, froze accounts totaling $11 billion of funds deposited with local banks. The Pakistani rupee depreciated sharply. This resulted in a 25 percent difference between the official and market exchange rate. Pakistanis working abroad ceased sending money home through banks. According to the government's official estimates (which were understated figures according independent experts), in 1998 there was a shortage of a total of $3.5 billion to finance imports and service foreign debt (*The Economist* 1998). Pakistan was on the verge of bankruptcy and close to ceasing service of its foreign debt. To narrow the gap in financing, the spread between buying and selling rates of foreign currencies was extended, thereby raising the cost of imports. Higher prices of imported goods (particularly oil) combined with an increase in the price of public utility services, boosted inflationary pressures, and, on the other, reduced the total supply. Cuts in government expenditure on development hindered growth in aggregate demand.

The 1998 crisis was the result of economic problems piling up over time. For many years, the government of Pakistan kept long-lasting budget deficits of 6–8 percent of GDP. The size of the public debt reached 100 percent of GDP, and three-quarters of budget expenditure was allocated to the country's army and debt servicing. Only an estimated 1 million out of more than 140 million people in Pakistan paid any income taxes. State-owned commercial banks were burdened with loans worth $3.4 billion granted to state-owned enterprises that were refusing to pay them back (*The Economist* 1998).

Ultimately, the crisis in Pakistan did not result in any significant reduction in per capita GDP, proving to be significantly milder than in Indonesia. In response to the economic downturn in both countries, changes were introduced to put their national economies back on the path of development. By and large, this was a success.[16]

Riots and deepening chaos in Indonesia forced President Suharto to resign from office in May 1998, prompting the beginning of democratic rule, called *reformasi* (Pritchett, Sumarto, and Suryahadi 2002). The priorities of the new government were to limit the social impact of the crisis and ensure recovery of the banking sector:

- The most important social programs included (Pritchett, Sumarto, and Suryahadi 2002): sale of subsidized rice to the poor, programs to increase employment, student scholarships and grants for schools, and subsidized health care. Although these programs were not addressed to everybody but designed for specific groups, they significantly boosted public spending—from 16 percent of GDP in 1999 to 22 percent of GDP in 2001 and approximately 19 percent of GDP in subsequent years. Despite rising expenses, due to higher tax receipts it was possible to maintain a balance in public finances. The deficit did not exceed 1–2 percent of GDP, and in 2000 even a slight surplus was observed. As a result, public debt fell from 97 percent in 1999 to 46 percent of GDP in 2005.

- In January 1998 the Indonesian government established the Indonesian Bank Restructuring Agency (IBRA; Fane and McLeod 2002). The sector's restructuring plans were based on the experience of Sweden in the years 1991–94. They were limited to the financial support to some insolvent banks and mergers (and, possibly, liquidation) of the remaining ones. All seven state-owned banks were recapitalized. Four of them merged into Mandiri Bank, which (with 30 percent of bank deposits) became the largest bank in Indonesia. Private banks were subject to an independent audit. As a result of audit, banks were split into: (1) institutions not requiring any additional capital; (2) institutions that, if recapitalized, could continue their operations; and (3) banks destined for liquidation. The analysis also allowed the IBRA to choose the appropriate restructuring method out of three options: (1) immediate sale to a strategic investor, (2) liquidation, or (3) partial or total nationalization (Fane and McLeod 2002).

Moreover, the government continued to pursue a liberal trade policy and did not limit the freedom of capital movements. After 2001 high inflation was limited to a few percentage points per year. All this strengthened incentives to invest. Growth in private investment, particularly FDI, became one of the main drivers behind economic recovery after the financial crisis (Sjöholm 2000).

Pakistan, mired deep in the crisis, also saw dramatic political changes. In 1999 General Pervez Musharraf took over power. Then, in cooperation with the IMF and World Bank, a program of economic stabilization and structural reforms was developed. It provided for tax reform, privatization, restructuring of the financial sector, trade liberalization, and deregulation (Husain 2007):

- To reduce fiscal deficit, the sales tax was reduced and most government subsidies were withdrawn. Contrary to the previous announcements, there were no cuts in military expenditures. Spending cuts (from 18.7 percent in 1999 to 17.2 percent in 2004), were driven by the falling costs of debt service following an agreement with the Paris Club on the government's foreign debt restructuring. As a result, the deficit fell from 5.2 percent in 1999 to 2.4 percent in 2003 and 3.4 percent in 2004. The country's debt, which exceeded 100 percent of GDP in 1999, was reduced to 62 percent over a six-year period.

- Monetary policy was also tightened. In 1999–2000 money supply growth did not exceed 9 percent. In 2001 the inflation dropped to a several percentage points. This led to a gradual reduction in interest rates, which soon reached a single-digit figure, affecting growth in lending to private companies (Husain 2004).

- The tax system was largely simplified, which helped streamline the multitude of taxes and considerably reduce contacts between tax collection agencies and taxpayers, thus limiting corruption and improving tax collection. At the same, tax rates were cut.

- In 2002–05 the largest state-owned companies were sold.

- The petrochemical, banking, telecommunications, and power sectors were privatized. Foreign investors were invited to participate in the privatization process and were allowed to invest and withdraw capital from Pakistan without any limitations. Restrictions on portfolio investments were also lifted.

- The financial sector was opened up to competition. Private banks (domestic and foreign) increased their share in total assets of the banking sector to more than 80 percent. The central bank ceased to control interest rates in an administrative way and began to influence them through standard monetary policy instruments. Banking and financial supervision authorities, beyond government control, were formed, enjoying quasi-judicial powers.

- The maximum customs tariff was slashed from 225 percent in 1990 to 25 percent in 2000, while the average customs tariff was cut from 65 percent to 11 percent (Husain 2007). The customs duty calculation method was largely simplified, and the number of different customs duty tariffs was reduced to four. Almost all import quotas were cancelled, with the exception of safety- and health-threatening products, and those that were in conflict with Islamic morals. By June 2004 duty-exempt "statutory contracts" granted to selected industries were cancelled. In the same time customs tariffs on 4,000 products used in industry were reduced. Pakistan's trade policy in 1999–2004 was classified by the World Bank as among the least restrictive in South Asia (Husain 2004).

- Deregulation allowed the market to freely determine prices of crude oil and petroleum products, natural gas, energy, and agricultural products. At the same time, independent regulatory agencies, free from government control, were established and enjoyed the exclusive right to set these prices. Their CEOs and board members could not be dismissed by the executive power before the end of their term of office (Husain 2007).

The aforementioned reform program strengthened not only those stabilizing institutions whose weaknesses were responsible for the 1998 crisis, but also the propelling institutions. In Pakistan the so-called transition effect appeared—growth had accelerated considerably before the reconstruction of the institutional system was completed. In 2002–04, for the first time in history, annual per capita GDP growth reached 5 percent.

Summary and Conclusions

This chapter aims to explain differences in the rates of economic growth in Indonesia and Pakistan in the years 1961–2004. During this period, neither country recorded stable economic growth. Figures 11.5 and 11.6 summarize main events in both countries and their impact on GDP per capita.

The decline in Indonesia's per capita GDP in the early 1960s was the consequence of industry nationalization in the late 1950s and 1960s as well as irresponsible fiscal policy. As monetary policy was subordinated to fiscal policy, this resulted in hyperinflation in 1965. As a result of strict control of money supply and budget deficit reduction, by 1968 Indonesia had managed to stabilize its economy, creating foundations for rapid economic growth in the 1970s. Rising oil prices (Indonesia was one of the largest oil exporters worldwide) were conducive to a sharp increase in budget revenues used to finance

Figure 11.5 Main Reasons for Fluctuations in Per Capita GDP Growth in Indonesia, 1961–2004

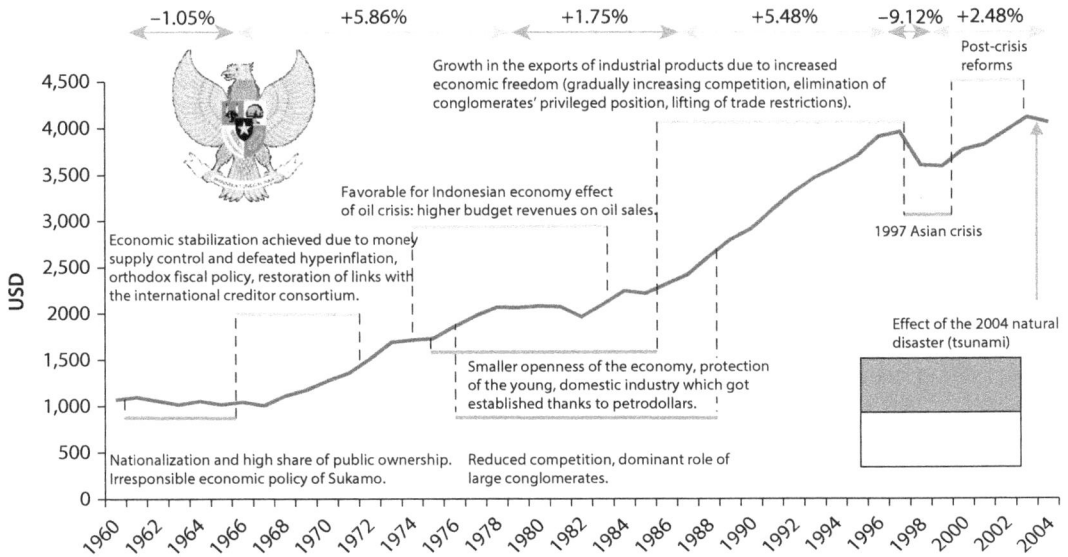

−1.05%   +5.86%   +1.75%   +5.48%   −9.12% +2.48%

Growth in the exports of industrial products due to increased
economic freedom (gradually increasing competition, elimination of
conglomerates' privileged position, lifting of trade restrictions).

Post-crisis
reforms

Favorable for Indonesian economy effect
of oil crisis: higher budget revenues on oil sales.

Economic stabilization achieved due to money
supply control and defeated hyperinflation,
orthodox fiscal policy, restoration of links with
the international creditor consortium.

1997 Asian crisis

Effect of the 2004 natural
disaster (tsunami)

Smaller openness of the economy, protection
of the young, domestic industry which got
established thanks to petrodollars.

Nationalization and high share of public ownership.   Reduced competition, dominant role of
Irresponsible economic policy of Sukamo.   large conglomerates.

Sources: Based on information in this publication. Figures presenting per capita gross domestic product (GDP) growth in Indonesia and Pakistan
are based on Penn World Table 6.2.

Figure 11.6 Main Reasons for Fluctuations in Per Capita GDP Growth in Pakistan, 1961–2004

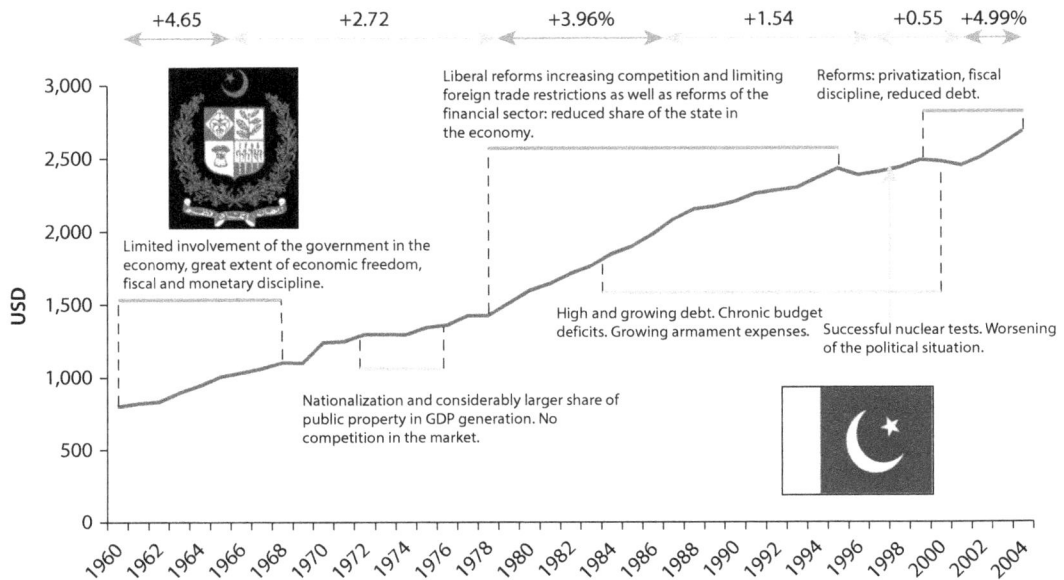

+4.65   +2.72   +3.96%   +1.54   +0.55 +4.99%

Liberal reforms increasing competition and limiting   Reforms: privatization, fiscal
foreign trade restrictions as well as reforms of the   discipline, reduced debt.
financial sector: reduced share of the state in
the economy.

Limited involvement of the government in the
economy, great extent of economic freedom,
fiscal and monetary discipline.

High and growing debt. Chronic budget
deficits. Growing armament expenses.   Successful nuclear tests. Worsening
of the political situation.

Nationalization and considerably larger share of
public property in GDP generation. No
competition in the market.

Sources: Based on information in this publication. Figures presenting per capita gross domestic product (GDP) growth in Indonesia and Pakistan
are based on Penn World Table 6.2.

investment in the industry. Yet, industrial development was accompanied by the return of protectionism, supported mainly by the growing power of Indonesian conglomerates. Lack of competition in the domestic market, resulting from the conglomerates' privileged position—combined with foreign trade restrictions—led to a decline in economic growth in the first half of the 1980s. Poor economic performance forced the government to launch market reforms at the end of the 1980s and into the 1990s. Cuts in public spending, mainly in subsidies to conglomerates, helped to improve the condition of public finances, despite sharp declines in oil revenues after 1986. As conglomerates' privileged position was curtailed and foreign trade liberalized, there was a significant increase in export production—which in 1987–96 was one of the key drivers of rapid growth. Yet, rapid growth was interrupted by the Asian crisis of 1997. Errors in crisis management (the closure of many banks without any distinct criteria) undermined confidence in the banking sector. This move, and resulting political instability, spurred a deep decline in per capita GDP. The country reembarked on the growth path in 1999, when a new democratic administration began a program of macroeconomic stabilization and a restructuring of the financial sector.

Rapid economic growth in Pakistan in the early 1960s was mainly due to the state's minor participation in the economy, a wide range of economic freedom, and fiscal and monetary discipline—maintained despite the absence of institutional constraints. Dynamic development ended with nationalization in the early 1970s; almost all industry became state owned. Competition in agriculture, the largest contributor to GDP, was also restricted. As a result of investments in industry (of similar magnitude as in Indonesia, despite the lack of oil revenues) a surplus in public finances changed into a deep deficit, additionally aggravated by armament spending. In response to poor economic performance, in 1978 Pakistan started to gradually lift restrictions on foreign trade, reduce the state's role in the economy, and strengthen the protection of property rights. These changes boosted economic growth in the 1980s, but were not accompanied by any reduction in the public finance imbalance. High expenditure on armed forces in conjunction with a narrow tax base resulted, despite reduced subsidies to companies, in large and chronic deficits and growing public debt. Payment of interest on public debt forced Pakistan to curb other expenditure, with the exception of national defense spending. Only the looming bankruptcy of the state, following the cuts in foreign aid in response to nuclear tests carried out by Pakistan, forced the government to strengthen public finance discipline. Macroeconomic stabilization in 1999–2004 was accompanied by structural reforms, including privatization, liberalization of foreign trade, capital movements, and deregulation. These contributed to rapid growth in 2002–04.

In both countries changes in GDP growth were strongly correlated with political changes, driven by a reversal in economic policy and by the shape of institutions—including, in particular, those determining ownership structure, the extent of competition in the domestic market, and the degree of freedom in foreign trade. Both countries went through periods of limited economic freedom, yet the restrictions imposed in Pakistan were more far-reaching than those in Indonesia. Stabilizing institutions did not see any major changes in either country, but their weaknesses were responsible for the occurrence and depth of their economic collapse.

In sum, Indonesia's better economic performance, relative to that of Pakistan, may be attributed to institutional differences. The external shocks of oil price surges undoubtedly had a significant impact on Indonesia's economic performance (among others, by distorting the structure of the economy, as manifested by the huge difference in labor productivity across sectors). Yet, the size of the shocks, as compared to the scale of the Indonesian economy, does not fully explain Indonesia's economic growth in the years 1973–81 (at least directly—that is, disregarding its impact on economic policy).

Notes

1. Religion plays an important role in both countries. As provided by the 1956 Constitution, Pakistan is an Islamic republic. On the other hand, Indonesia is a secular state where the tenets of Islam do not dictate the country's legal framework.

2. The results of this author's growth analysis are close to the results obtained by other authors in their studies quoted in this chapter.

3. Growth in global oil prices contributed to the increased share of industry in GDP in the following two ways. First, growing income from oil sales prompted the petrochemical industry's rising share in GDP. This effect accounted for 48 percent of growth in the industry's contribution to GDP in the years 1970–80. Second, the bulk of income from crude oil sales transferred to the Indonesian budget was intended to finance investment in industry. In the years 1970–80 this effect accounted for a 35 percent rise in industry's share in the Indonesian GDP. The total growth in industry's share from 18.7 percent of GDP in 1970 to 41.7 percent in 1980 was fueled by the 1970s oil crises.

4. In 1966, as a result of Sukarno's rule, Indonesian budget expenditure exceeded 9.3 percent of GDP, amid budget receipts of 4.3 percent of GDP (Hill 2000, 43–64).

5. Temple (2001) points to the growing foreign debt. Yet, there are no precise data concerning the 1960–65 debt.

6. The author's estimate based on the Official Energy Statistics of the U.S. Government (http://www.eia.gov/petroleum/data.cfm), Energy Information Agency, and Penn World Tables 6.2 (Heston, Summers, and Aten 2006).

7. Bhutto came to power in 1971, taking advantage of President Yahya Khan's resignation.

8. For example, the largest Indonesian conglomerate in the 1970s in terms of income, Liem Sioe Liong, managed approximately 450 companies in the financial sector, automotive sector, cement production, and agricultural industry.

9. The author's estimate, based on Hill (2000).

10. For the sake of comparison, Pakistani budget expenditure in the years 1979–87 followed an upward trend. Between 1981 and 1987 it rose from 19.7 percent to 25.9 percent of GDP. Higher expenditure on armament (as a result of the Indian-Pakistani conflict—an increase from 5.4 percent to 7.3 percent of GDP) and rising costs of public debt service (growth to 5 percent of GDP) were the factors behind its growth. To finance rising expenditure, two traditional Islamic taxes

were imposed—Zakat and Ushr. Zakat is an annually paid tax in the amount of 2.5 percent of assets, intended to be given as aid to the poor, whereas Ushr is a 5 percent tax on agricultural production paid by the owner or tenant of farming land (see Blood 1995).

11. See Temple 2001; moreover, in the year 1979–87 Pakistan continued to record long-lasting budget deficits, averaging 7 percent of GDP.

12. AFTA concerned only industrial goods exclusive of capital goods.

13. Yet, conglomerates managed to adapt to the new environment quite rapidly. For example, the Bimantara Group controlled by Suharto's son lost its exclusive license to import plastics; yet, it soon managed to acquire shares in the sectors previously closed to private investors (that is, broadcasting and the petrochemical industry; see, for example, Frederick and Worden 1993).

14. Yet, not all the changes improved the efficiency of capital allocation by the financial sector. In 1990 a requirement was introduced according to which a minimum of 20 percent of lending had to be offered to small enterprises (see Frederick and Worden 1993).

15. Banks (both private and public) were closed down after being identified as insolvent. Yet, no precise insolvency criteria was defined (see Lane 1999).

16. Fall in per capita GDP in 2004 was partly connected with losses caused by the tsunami. Economic costs of the 2004 tsunami in Indonesia were described in detail in *Indonesia: Preliminary Damage and Loss Assessment, The December 26, 2004 Natural Disaster*, The Consultative Group on Indonesia, January 19–20, 2005.

Bibliography

Ahmed, S. 1994. *Explaining Pakistan's High Growth Performance over the Past Two Decades*. South Asia Country Department III, World Bank, Washington, DC. http://econ .worldbank.org/external/default/main?pagePK=64210502&theSitePK=544849&piP K=64210520&menuPK=64166093&entityID=000009265_3970716141607.

Blood, P. 1995. *Pakistan: A Country Study*. 6th ed. Washington, DC: Federal Research Division, Library of Congress.

Boediono. 1990. "Fiscal Policy in Indonesia." Paper presented to the Second Convention of the East Asian Economic Association, Bandung, Indonesia.

The Economist. 1998. "Pakistan Takes a Beating." http://www.economist.com/node/161886.

Fane, G., and R. H. McLeod. 2002. "Banking Collapse and Restructuring in Indonesia, 1997–2001." *Cato Journal* 22 (2), 277–95.

Fiscal Development, Pakistan Economic Survey 2006–07, June 2007.

Frederick, W. H., and R. L. Worden. 1993. *Indonesia: A Country Study*. 5th ed. Washington, DC: Federal Research Division, Library of Congress.

Hamada, M. 2003. "Transformation of the Financial Sector in Indonesia." Institute of Developing Economies Research Paper 6, September. https://ir.ide.go.jp/dspace /handle/2344/814.

Hill, H. 2000. *The Indonesian Economy*. Cambridge, U.K.: Cambridge University Press.

Husain, I. 2004. "Pakistan's Economic Progress since 2000: False Dawn or a Promising Stat?" A Paper presented at a Seminar at the Paul H. Nitze School of Advanced and International Studies (SAIS), Johns Hopkins University, Washington, DC, October 6.

———. 2007. "Economy of Pakistan: Past, Present and Future." Keynote address at the Conference on Islamization and the Pakistani Economy held at the Woodrow Wilson Center, Washington, DC, January 27.

Khan, A., A. Qayyum, and S. Sheikh. 2005. "Financial Development and Economic Growth: The Case of Pakistan." *The Pakistan Development Review* 44 (4): 819–37. Pakistan Institute of Development Economics. http://ideas.repec.org/p/pra/mprapa/2145.html.

Lane, T. 1999. *IMF-Supported Programs in Indonesia, Korea, and Thailand: A Preliminary Assessment*. Washington, DC: International Monetary Fund.

Mackie, J., and Sjahrir. 1989. "Survey of Recent Developments." *Bulletin of Indonesian Economic Studies* 25 (3): 3–34.

Pasha, H. A. 1992. "Fiscal Policy in Pakistan." Research Report 1. http://www.econbiz.de/Record/fiscal-policy-in-pakistan-pasha-hafiz/10000973816.

Pritchett, L., S. Sumarto, and A. Suryahadi. 2002. "Targeted Programs in an Economic Crisis: Empirical Findings from the Experience of Indonesia." SMERU Research Institute, October. http://www.hks.harvard.edu/fs/lpritch/Poverty%20-%20docs/3%20The%20targeting%20of%20Safety%20Net%20programs/TargetedProgramSSN.pdf.

Sakr, K. 1993. "Determinants of Private Investment in Pakistan." IMF Working Paper WP/93/30, International Monetary Fund, Washington, DC.

Siddiqui, R., and A. R. Kemal. 2002. "Remittances, Trade Liberalization, and Poverty Reduction in Pakistan: The Role of Excluded Variables in Poverty Change Analysis, Globalisation and Poverty." http://mpra.ub.uni-muenchen.de/4228/.

Sjöholm, F. 2000. "Economic Recovery in Indonesia: The Challenge of Combining FDI and Regional Development." Department of Economics, National University of Singapore. http://swopec.hhs.se/hastef/papers/hastef0347.pdf.

Temple, J. 2001. "Growing into Trouble: Indonesia after 1966." Department of Economics, University of Bristol, U.K. and CEPR. http://www.efm.bris.ac.uk/economics/working_papers/pdffiles/dp01522.pdf.

The Consultative Group on Indonesia. 2005. "Indonesia: Preliminary Damage and Loss Assessment: The December 26, 2004, Natural Disaster." January 19–20.

World Bank. 2007. "Indonesia Public Expenditure Review 2007." Office Jakarta, World Bank, February.

Yildirm, J., and N. Ocal. 2003. *Arms Race and Economic Growth: Case of India and Pakistan*. Gazi University. http://www.researchgate.net/publication/24078275_ARMS_RACE_AND_ECONOMIC_GROWTH_THE_CASE_OF_INDIA_AND_PAKISTAN.

CHAPTER 12

Conclusions

Leszek Balcerowicz and Andrzej Rzońca

In this concluding chapter of *Puzzles of Economic Growth* we shall first present the main results of the comparative studies outlined in chapters 3–11, then provide general conclusions on the basis of all of these studies.

In chapter 3 the author argues that the difference in the level of per capita income between Australia and New Zealand, as observed in the period between 1975 and 2002, can be traced down to two periods of economic downturn in New Zealand—in 1975–80 and in 1987–92. These periods of economic downturn—in particular that of 1975–80—were primarily the consequence of external shocks. On the one hand, the price of oil imported by New Zealand rocketed, and on the other, following the accession of the United Kingdom to the European Economic Community (EEC), the privileges in trade with the country's major partner disappeared (Australia was a net exporter of crude oil, and the share of its exports destined for the United Kingdom was considerably lower). New Zealand's macroeconomic policy proved an additional source of disturbance—until the mid-1980s that policy was not constrained by any form of institutionally imposed discipline. After the first oil crisis, the public finance deficit increased in both countries—a trend that was stronger and longer lasting in New Zealand than in Australia. In addition, New Zealand's deficit, which persisted until the mid-1980s, could be and was monetized, perpetuating inflation that was further enhanced by oil shocks. It was only brought down to a low level after 1990, when the central bank was given independence. In the second period of economic downturn, New Zealand was forced to increase the tax burden. Due to the high initial deficit, the government could not allow automatic stabilizers to operate. Furthermore the 10-year delay in relation to Australia in implementing reforms limiting state interference in the economy made it impossible for New Zealand to adjust public spending to decreasing tax revenues.

As described in chapter 4, a collapse of economic growth had a major impact on the difference in the levels of per capita income in *Switzerland* and *Austria* in the second half of 20th century. In Switzerland economic downturns were observed in 1974–76 and 1991–96, both times following a slowdown in the global economy and turmoil in the global financial markets, the demand for the

Swiss franc increased, as it was regarded as a safe currency. The large scale of this increase, as compared to the size of the Swiss economy, resulted in a strong appreciation of the Swiss franc. A strengthening of the Swiss franc weakened the price competitiveness of Swiss goods in international markets during periods of increased price sensitivity (as overall drops in income prompted customers to look for savings and attach more importance to prices). A collapse in economic growth was exacerbated by the country's procyclical fiscal policy. This procyclical character resulted, among other things, from the nation's tax structure—specifically, the long period (two to four years) allowed between the generation of income and the obligation to pay income taxes. Taxes on the high income generated in periods of prosperity might be required during periods of recession.

But Switzerland's decreasing advantage over Austria in terms of per capita income cannot be attributed solely to these periods of economic slowdown. In the 1990s Austria grew faster than Switzerland (even if periods of economic slowdown in Switzerland are not taken into consideration). European integration (and formal commitments related thereto) on the one hand, and competitive pressure on the other, resulted in the following: strong goods market deregulation in Austria as compared to Switzerland (including network industries), greater openness to foreign competition, and privatization of the large sector of state-owned enterprises which, in accordance with European Union (EU) requirements, could no longer benefit from state aid. The prospect of introducing the euro encouraged Austria to strengthen fiscal discipline, and significantly reduce public spending, which (in the light of some research) activated non-Keynesian effects—that is, it led to an increase in aggregate demand and, as a result, gross domestic product (GDP) growth in the short term. Finally, the introduction of a single European currency contributed to further deepening of foreign trade, which was higher than the average for the euro zone (and strengthened technology transfer resulting thereof, as well as enhanced competition and expanded opportunities for specialization and benefits of large-scale production). In a referendum in 1992 Switzerland rejected accession to the European Economic Area (EEA). The government strove to mitigate the negative economic effects of this decision by bilateral agreements, but Switzerland adopted the main principles on which the EEA is founded only in 2002. Still later, it concluded negotiations on the liberalization of trade in agricultural products, in 2004.

Chapter 5 which is devoted to the political transformation from centrally planned economies to free market democracies of Estonia and Slovenia, author shows the importance—in the short and long term—of initial conditions in deciding subsequent economic growth. Estonia's economic situation was then much more difficult than Slovenia's. This manifested itself, among other ways, in a much stronger dependence on the market of the former USSR (in both exports and imports) and a much larger deformation of prices and—as a consequence—of the structure of the economy. Such challenges first led to a very large drop in GDP, much more significant in Estonia than in Slovenia. At the same time, incentives were created for policy makers to carry out radical free-market reforms quickly. From 1995 the Estonian economy grew significantly faster than the Slovenian economy. Without policy makers' appropriate attitudes and skills, these reforms would not have been possible. In the majority of the former republics of the USSR—where initial economic conditions were similar to Estonia's—reforms were delayed.

By 1992 all Estonian prices had been released, with the exception of energy and housing prices. In Slovenia the process of price liberalization was much slower. Estonia refrained from any tariff protection of the domestic market. Privatization was carried out quickly and with the significant participation of strategic investors. Privatization vouchers distributed, to citizens, were used primarily for the acquisition of flats. Consequently, and as opposed to Slovenia, Estonia avoided the dispersion of shares in privatized companies, which would slow or even prevent their rapid and profound restructuring. The labor market became more flexible and the eligibility criteria and amount of employment benefits were tightened. In Slovenia the labor market was much more rigid—there were restrictions on redundancies and a high minimum wage, high unemployment benefits, and benefits for people leaving the labor market were maintained. In Estonia, due to a decline of social spending in relation to GDP, the tax burden was gradually reduced. In Slovenia taxes were not only higher than in Estonia, but also their structure—for example, the variety of personal income tax rates and high social security contributions—discouraged entrepreneurial behavior. Estonia built an efficient administration and the country managed to avoid bureaucratic barriers impeding entrepreneurship. The scope of free market reforms was so wide that EU membership meant that Estonia had to abandon certain reforms: for example, it had to introduce duties and raise the minimum wage. On the other hand, Estonia failed to establish institutions that were strong enough to ensure the stability of the economy. Their weaknesses became evident after 2004. The introduction of a currency board and—consequently—the abandonment of an independent monetary policy led to a credit explosion, and Estonia became more credible from the point of view of investors and interest rates dropped to a level close to the level of interest rates in the euro area. Fiscal policy was designed to stabilize the economy. Despite the establishment of the Stabilization Reserve Fund, an institution that invested public savings abroad and was thus supposed to inhibit credit growth, the state saved only part of the windfall tax revenues arising from an increase in demand that rose faster than the economy's productive capacity (the structural balance declined in 2004–07).

The difference in the level of per capita income between *Spain* and *Mexico*, analyzed in chapter 6, began to emerge after 1961, when Spain opened up to international trade, whereas Mexico pursued its protectionist policies by both increasing tariffs and tightening nontariff restrictions. Following Spain's decision to liberate imports, the transfer of technologies from abroad intensified. Spain also benefited from a broad stream of foreign direct investment (FDI).

Mexico's position in relation to Spain was further weakened by the crises of 1982, 1986, and 1995. The first two crises occurred due to reckless macroeconomic policies, reflecting the weakness of the institutions responsible for the country's economic stability.

The first of these crises in Mexico, in 1982, was the consequence of policies pursued under the banner of "redistribution together with growth." Lack of institutional constraints to ensure fiscal discipline allowed a public finance deficit to balloon in a period when the country's budget was supplied with extraordinary revenues from oil exports. This deficit was covered primarily by loans contracted abroad or by forcing the central bank—fully dependent on the government—to print fiat money. The monetization of the deficit generated high inflation, which contributed to real appreciation of the domestic currency in the country's managed floating exchange rate system. The state's intervention in the banking sector—reflected, among other things, in forcing banks to invest a high and growing proportion of deposits in government securities and providing loans to state-owned enterprises at a reduced price (which was further lowered by soaring inflation)—significantly weakened the profitability of the sector and made the financial market shallower, thus forcing not only private companies, but also the government to borrow from abroad. The increase in interest rates in developed countries dramatically increased the cost of servicing foreign debt. In 1982 Mexico refused to pay off its debt. The country nationalized its banks, further weakened by runaway inflation, which reduced the real value of loans to a greater extent than it did the value of deposits, the majority of which were in dollars.

The earthquake of 1985 and plummeting oil prices a year later contributed to the crisis of 1986. But its primary source was the inconsistent implementation of economic stabilization, which resulted in a large deficit in public finances and high inflation. The economy did not stabilize until the late 1980s and the beginning of the 1990s. For the first time since the 1950s, a surplus in public finance had been observed and a fixed exchange rate helped reduce inflation to a single-digit level. A liberalization program was also introduced at that time (for instance, restrictions on FDI were lifted and a free trade agreement was signed with the United States and Canada), and hundreds of state-owned enterprises were sold. The crisis of 1995 was the consequence of an error in macroeconomic policy, which postponed the devaluation of the national currency despite rising external imbalances (as a result of the private sector's foreign loans; Spain managed to avoid this mistake when its currency came under pressure in 1992–93). An unfortunate coincidence also had its impact on the 1995 crisis in Mexico—political turmoil (the Zapatista rebellion and a number of political assassinations) undermined investor confidence in the country. The negative effects of the currency crisis intensified the banking crisis, which resulted from incomplete reforms of the stabilizing institutions. There was no properly functioning banking supervision system. The banks, which were privatized without the participation of any foreign banks, were unable to properly assess risks. Bank owners, hoping to recover capital, invested in them as soon as possible, as they feared that following the presidential election all the free-market reforms pursued thus far might be reversed. Conversely, the turmoil in the foreign exchange market in 1992 and 1993 did not adversely affect the Spanish banking sector. Banking supervision had been strengthened from the late 1970s. The Spanish crisis that began in 2008 comes to show that—just as in the case of Estonia—an effective mechanism inhibiting the growth of credit must be introduced following the abandonment of an independent monetary policy. That mechanism is badly needed in countries which grow faster than the area from which they "import" their monetary policy, as faster growth raises their natural interest rate.

Crude oil has been a curse—at least for some time now—for República Bolivariana de Venezuela, to an even greater extent than for Mexico. On the other hand, *Chile* exemplifies how a powerful primary sector does not necessarily destabilize the economy. The economic growth of these two countries is analyzed in chapter 7. In República Bolivariana de Venezuela surges in revenues—generated through oil exports following the oil shocks of the 1970s—prompted increased state intervention in the economy. A program of major public investment in the corporate sector was launched. Both the oil and steel sectors were nationalized. Following the country's accession to the Andean Pact, private companies saw their investment opportunities limited only to those sectors of economy in which República Bolivariana de Venezuela was to specialize (within the framework of the pact). The public finance deficit soared (until the 1970s, despite the lack of institutional constraints ensuring fiscal discipline, public finance had remained balanced). After a drop in oil prices in the early 1980s, the deficit rose to such a level that the government monetized it. The monetization of the deficit resulted in an inflation-and-devaluation spiral (before the oil shocks, despite the central bank's formal dependence on the government, the bolivar was one of the world's most stable currencies). Unsuccessful attempts to stabilize the economy intensified the public conviction that the deteriorating quality of life was the consequence of reforms. Social conflicts were further fueled by large income disparities, as the share of the remuneration of capital in total income grew, while the share of labor remuneration decreased. Such development was a result of growing macroeconomic instability, as it led to an increasing risk premium taken into consideration in the cost of renting capital. Social conflicts paved the way for populist politicians.

In 1973 the Chilean economy's collapse prompted a shift away from statism. A military coup sparked radical reforms that stabilized the economy and broadened the scope of individual economic freedom. In the following four years, the gigantic deficit in public finances was reduced to zero, and the tax system was simplified. Value added tax (VAT) became the major source of tax revenues, as it weakened the incentives for productive behavior to a lesser extent than other types of taxes. All nontariff restrictions on foreign trade were abolished and a single tariff rate was introduced. The PAYG[1] pension system was replaced by the funded pension scheme. Enterprises that had been nationalized by Allende went through a process of reprivatization and the majority of banks were privatized. Administrative control of interest rates was abandoned and restrictions on granting loans were eliminated. The labor market became more flexible through, among other things, lowering the cost of redundancies.

But in the early 1980s the economy collapsed again. This was the result of errors in the country's economic policy. The fixed exchange rate, combined with the price indexation of wages, had delayed a decline in inflation and—consequently—brought about a real appreciation of the domestic currency. Meanwhile some of the institutions responsible for the country's economic stability were weak, and had failed to build an effective oversight system of the banking sector. These factors were compounded by external shocks. On the one hand, to reduce inflation, developed countries raised interest rates, which significantly increased the cost of servicing the Chilean external debt; on the other, a decrease in demand for raw materials led to a drop in copper prices in the global market and to a reduction in Chile's revenues from exports, affecting the country's ability to repay its foreign debt. The outbreak of the crisis, however, did not lead to the abandonment of the country's free-market reforms. On the contrary, the privatization of the copper sector was completed and competition was introduced. The sources of the crisis were quickly removed: price indexation of wages was abolished, a managed floating exchange rate was introduced, and banking supervision was strengthened. An increase in copper prices helped the country to overcome the economic crisis. The high income generated through its exports was used to cover the cost of rescuing the banks. In subsequent years, windfall profits from the sale of copper were collected in a special fund, which reduced the impact of fluctuations in the global copper market on the national economy. From the mid-1980s Chile was the fastest-growing country in Latin America. In 2001, in terms of per capita income, Chile outpaced Argentina, which had been the region's wealthiest country for many years.

Until the 1970s Puerto Rico was Latin America and the Caribbean's economic tiger (in chapter 8 the country's economic results are compared to those of *Costa Rica*). In 1960 per capita income in Puerto Rico was slightly lower than in Costa Rica, whereas by 1973 it rose by more than 40 percent. Puerto Rico's dynamic growth since the 1970s was possible due to the country's opening to foreign trade and the inflow of FDI. In the same period, the government of Costa Rica pursued forced the industrialization of sectors that competed with imports. As a result, capital expenditure in Costa Rica grew faster than in Puerto Rico, but was accompanied by a decline in the productivity of the factors of production.

In 1974–81 the economic growth of Puerto Rico collapsed. It was partly due to oil shocks that hit the energy-intensive economy of the island heavily. The economy's high energy intensity was the consequence of major investments in capital-intensive technologies, including in the petrochemical sector. The crisis was deepened when, on the basis of a decision of the U.S. Congress, Puerto Rico was covered by American minimum wage regulations, which further reduced the price competitiveness of the island's labor-intensive sectors. These sectors suffered another shock following the extension of American social transfer programs to Puerto Rico—they became a valid alternative to employment for less productive workers. In the early 1980s transfers from the federal budget amounted to a quarter of the disposable income of an average Puerto Rican citizen.

In Costa Rica economic growth collapsed in 1982–91 as a consequence of a debt crisis. Just as in the case of Mexico and República Bolivariana de Venezuela, the extraordinary budget revenues in the 1970s (whose source in Costa Rica was the "coffee boom" of 1975–79) led to an explosion of public spending and a large public finance deficit, covered by foreign loans. The collapse of public finances occurred when coffee prices plummeted and developed countries began to raise interest rates to reduce inflation. The crisis was further deepened when devaluation of the exchange rate was postponed, despite high inflation and capital flight from Costa Rica. But unlike other Latin American countries, Costa Rica did not delay stabilization reforms. A floating exchange rate was introduced, wages in the public sector were frozen, and taxes were raised—which quickly brought the deficit down to a manageable level.

Structural reforms were initiated, such as the liberalization of foreign trade (Costa Rica joined the General Agreement on Tariffs and Trade [GATT] in 1990) and the privatization of CODESA (an inefficient state-owned conglomerate). These reforms bore fruit in the 1990s. Although the propelling institutions in Costa Rica remained all in all weaker than those of Puerto Rico (the legal protection of property was not properly strengthened, many areas were monopolized by inefficient state-owned enterprises, public spending remained inflated, and a double-digit inflation rate continued), the Costa Rican economy grew slightly faster than the Puerto Rican. Although, thanks to tax reliefs (not only local, but also granted by the U.S. Congress), Puerto Rico managed to attract a lot of investment in high-tech sectors, this failed to offset the negative economic impact of a high minimum wage and high social benefits of that period—even though these were mostly funded by the United States, and therefore did not result in tax increases that could have weakened the incentives for productive behavior. Despite Puerto Rico's "tiger" episode of 1960–70, between 1961 and 2003 the territory managed to reduce the economic gap to the United States only slightly—it remained poorer than Mississippi, the poorest U.S. state.

Chapter 9 presents an analysis of the experiences of the Dominican Republic and Haiti, and shows the importance of political stability (or lack thereof) and the fundamental security of persons and property for a country's economic performance. The Dominican Republic took advantage (at least when compared with Haiti) of its geographical location and natural conditions, which were conducive to the development of tourism. In 2000 the Dominican Republic attracted 21 times more tourists than Haiti. Although the level of development of the two countries was similar back in 1950, the current level of per capita income in the Dominican Republic is over four times higher than in Haiti.

With the exception of the 1970s, the Haitian economy has been steadily shrinking for 50 years. Political instability contributed to Haiti developing several of the characteristics of a failed state. The state does not fulfill its basic functions, such as ensuring public order, and the crime rate is about three times higher than in the Dominican Republic. The state is also not interested in those spheres that contribute to the country's development: for instance, the road network in this country is three times shorter than the road network of the Dominican Republic, and the percentage of illiteracy among adults is over three times higher. The uncertain and low profitability of investments has reduced their contribution to GDP to very low levels. The people earn their living through exploiting the environment: for example, almost all of the country's forests have been cut down. As a result, the island has become even more sensitive to the frequent hurricanes typical of this region as well as other natural disasters. The deficiencies that come with poverty were drastically exposed by the 2010 earthquake. Poorly constructed and maintained buildings easily collapsed during the earthquake, while the lack of infrastructure and emergency services impeded rescue operations. The death toll of Haitian earthquake exceeds 100,000 people[2]; in better developed country the death toll of earthquake of similar magnitude would most probably be significantly lower.

Two of the world's most populous countries, China and India, were also among the fastest-growing economies of the last 30 years. No study of economic growth can overlook these two countries. But during this period the Chinese economy grew much faster than the economy of India, with differences outlined in chapter 10.

Structural reforms in China were much broader and deeper than in India (and began roughly 10 years earlier). China privatized a large percentage of its state-owned enterprises, although their contribution to GDP remained higher than in India. In India the government waived its control over only approximately 1 percent of state-owned enterprises. In China most prices were freed at least partially. At the beginning of the analyzed period all prices in China were regulated; by the end of the period, the state controlled only 4 percent of prices. In India almost until the end of the analyzed period, most prices of industrial and agricultural products were subject to administrative control. China lifted the majority of restrictions on dismissing and hiring staff in all types of businesses. In India new restrictions were introduced in this area and the position of trade unions against employers was strengthened. China liberalized foreign trade faster and to a larger extent and the country opened much more widely to foreign investment, which in the 1990s became the driving force of the economy (especially of Chinese exports). After the 1991 budget crisis, India began opening its economy to trade and foreign investment, but the process was slow. China rapidly and dramatically reduced the fiscal position of the state. In the early 1990s public spending dropped from over 30 percent to below 20 percent of GDP. India failed to permanently reduce public spending, even after the budget crisis of 1991 (in the analyzed period, public spending ranged between 25 percent and 30 percent of GDP). The rising costs of debt servicing, as a result of a chronic budget deficit, began to dominate and eliminate potential pro-development spending on infrastructure or education. The structure of the Indian tax system remained complex and nontransparent to a much greater extent than in China.

Even though free-market reforms in China were broader and deeper than in India, in many areas individual economic freedom in China remained more limited. This was due to the country's high initial level of state interference in the economy. The rapid growth of the Chinese economy was not so much the consequence of the newly broadened scope of individual economic freedom, but the result of the scale of its increase following a number of reforms aimed at strengthening the institutions that were propelling the economy.

In chapter 11 the examples of Indonesia and Pakistan show the interdependence of economic policy and economic growth. The two countries developed in similar ways. Rapid economic growth led to the expansion of the state. Increasing government intervention resulted in a deterioration of economic performance. The difficult economic situation forced the government to partially withdraw from its interventionist policies. Free-market reforms led to the acceleration of economic growth, which completed the cycle.

In the 1950s and 1960s Indonesia nationalized its industry. An extremely expansionary fiscal policy was pursued. The result—a large deficit in the public finances—was monetized, which led to hyperinflation. In the first half of the 1960s, the Indonesian economy was dwindling; in the same period, Pakistan developed dynamically. The state's interference in the economy consisted mainly in investing in infrastructure. The contribution of state-owned enterprises to the GDP of Pakistan was three times lower than in Indonesia. Despite the lack of institutional constraints providing macroeconomic policy discipline (including an independent central bank), a surplus in public finances and a low rate of inflation were maintained. In Indonesia the economic downturn led to the collapse of one dictatorship and the emergence of another. The new dictator stabilized the economy by reducing the deficit and curbing inflation. Foreign trade and capital flows were also liberalized. These changes allowed Indonesia to grow rapidly in the 1970s. This rapid growth was boosted by the rise in oil prices—Indonesia became one of the world's biggest oil exporters. At the same time, however, a very significant increase in state revenues from oil exports prompted a further expansion of state intervention in the economy. Thus, generated revenue was used to invest in industry, which was also to be "protected" against foreign competition.

In Pakistan the rapid growth of the economy was interrupted in the 1970s, when the development of large farms was limited and almost the entire industry was nationalized. Meanwhile, the government introduced a program to invest in industry—and on a scale comparable with Indonesia. But since Pakistan did not have—as opposed to Indonesia—any oil revenues, this decision led to an immense deficit in the public finances.

Indonesia's economy, following the recurrence of protectionism and with a domestic market dominated by conglomerates, experienced a slowdown in the 1980s. Economic problems forced the government to introduce market reforms in the late 1980s and the beginning of the 1990s. Foreign trade was freed and some of the privileges previously awarded to conglomerates were abolished. The reduction of subsidies for conglomerates helped reduce the deficit in public finances, despite a drop in income generated from the sale of oil after 1986. (Indonesia managed to avoid a fiscal crisis, which distinguished it from Mexico and República Bolivariana de Venezuela—two other major oil exporters outlined in this book.) These changes accelerated the country's economic growth in the 1990s.

In Pakistan the strong state intervention in the economy in the 1970s also led to problems. As the scale of the intervention was larger than in Indonesia, and Pakistan did not have any oil revenues, problems emerged earlier and were more profound. Therefore, trade liberalization and privatization were initiated as early as the late 1970s. In addition, the constitution guaranteed that the country's industry would never be nationalized. Free-market reforms, even though introduced gradually and to a very limited extent (for example, public finances were not strengthened), helped Pakistan develop in the 1980s at a faster pace than Indonesia.

The rapid economic growth of Indonesia, initiated by free-market reforms introduced in the late 1980s and the beginning of the 1990s, was interrupted by the Asian crisis. Errors in managing the crisis (lack of clear rules for granting/refusing financial support for troubled banks and companies) and the resulting political turmoil led to an economic downturn that was deeper than in other Asian countries, despite Indonesia's smaller initial imbalances. Indonesia managed to overcome the crisis owing to a program of economic stabilization and the process of restructuring financial institutions introduced by the democratic government.

Pakistan also suffered a crisis in the late 1990s, even though its course was not as dramatic as in the case of Indonesia. In 1998 the country was on the edge of a fiscal crisis, due to the country's arms race with India—and a narrow tax base that was responsible for the chronically high deficit in the country's public finances. Economic sanctions following Pakistan's nuclear tests left the country deprived of any foreign aid, and the handling of debt became problematic. After a military coup, a program aimed at stabilizing the economy was introduced, and structural reforms were accelerated and deepened.

Throughout that period, Indonesia grew faster than Pakistan, as its phases of state expansion in the described cycle were generally less intense, and consequently, the propelling institutions were on average stronger. In addition, Indonesia covered direct expansion costs with proceeds from the sale of crude oil, while Pakistan was incurring further debts. The interest on the public debt and the arms race with India limited the Pakistani state's capability to fulfill its basic functions.

Table 12.1 summarizes the results of the various empirical studies in chapters 3–11, separating the relative importance for economic growth of both: the shocks (as well as the economic policy and institutions responsible for stability), and the differences and changes in the propelling institutions in the analyzed countries.

Let us now formulate more general conclusions on the basis of the content of the present publication.

Shocks Matter

The conducted empirical studies suggest the strong influence of shocks on the economic performance of almost all analyzed countries. Shocks played an important role in New Zealand, Switzerland, Estonia, Slovenia, Mexico, Chile, República Bolivariana de Venezuela, Puerto Rico, Costa Rica, the Dominican Republic, Haiti, Pakistan, and Indonesia. The experience of these countries shows that rapid and long-term growth requires the avoidance of frequent or deep

Table 12.1 Economic Growth and Its Drivers: An Overview of the Country Pairs Analyzed in This Book

Countries and periods	Differences in economic growth	Main reasons for differences in economic growth
Australia and New Zealand, 1971–2002	1971–74—per capita income similar in both countries. 2001—per capita income 34 percent higher in Australia than in New Zealand.	1. The difference in per capita income can be explained by the two periods of economic slowdown in New Zealand: • The collapse of 1975–80 was the result of a negative external shock: a clear deterioration in the terms of trade (an oil shock) and a decline in exports to the United Kingdom following the loss of trade privileges after its accession to the European Economic Community (EEC) (Australia was a net exporter of oil, and the United Kingdom had a much smaller share in its exports). • The collapse of 1987–92 was mainly the consequence of the removing of imbalances caused by the expansionary fiscal and monetary policy of the previous years (tensions in Australian public finances did not reach the same proportions as those in New Zealand, and efforts were started earlier to eliminate them). 2. Differences in propelling institutions were minimal; however, throughout the analyzed period New Zealand maintained a stronger state grip on the fiscal system, which might have inhibited the growth of the country.
Austria and Switzerland, 1971–2003	1971—per capita income in Austria at 64 percent of per capita income in Switzerland. 2002—per capita income in Austria at 96 percent of per capita income in Switzerland.	1. Periods of slow growth in Switzerland explain the difference in its growth rates in relation to Austria in 1971–2003. If they were to be excluded from the calculation, the difference would fall to 0.2 percentage points. They were caused by the strong appreciation of the Swiss franc during the slowdown in the global economy and exacerbated by the procyclical fiscal policy and monetary policy errors, which allowed for greater inflation fluctuations. 2. Austria's deep reforms (carried out in 1991–2000) that were aimed at strengthening the country's propelling institutions also contributed to reducing the gap between Switzerland and Austria in terms of per capita income. Austria weakened the fiscal position of the state, liberalized its foreign trade and the goods market, and conducted privatization reforms.
Estonia and Slovenia, 1990–2004	1990—per capita income 25 percent lower in Estonia than in Slovenia. 2004—per capita income 32 percent lower in Estonia than in Slovenia.	1. The collapse of growth had a much more serious impact on economic growth in Estonia than in Slovenia. • In 1991–94 the collapse of trade relations with the former USSR led to a significant shock for the relative position of Estonia. Slovenia was much less dependent on the markets of the socialist countries. If the scale of the economic slowdown in Estonia in 1991–94 had been similar to its scale in Slovenia, the average annual growth rate of per capita income in 1990–2004 would have been over 2 percentage points higher than the actual rate and over 1.5 percentage points higher than in Slovenia. • Estonia was also more strongly affected by the Russian crisis of 1998 than Slovenia. In 1990–2004 the average growth rate of Estonia decreased by 0.2–0.4 percentage points. • The third dramatic economic slump began in Estonia in 2007: the effects of the global crisis enhanced the effects of the collapse of the credit boom after 2000 caused by low interest rates (currency board) in the absence of a sufficiently restrictive fiscal and supervisory policy. 2. In 1995–2004 Estonia increased its per capita income much faster than Slovenia (4.7 percent vs. 3.3 percent) due to a number of wider-ranging and radical reforms strengthening the propelling institutions: radical external and internal economic liberalization, privatization, and the establishment of a competent public administration.

table continues next page

Table 12.1 **Economic Growth and Its Drivers: An Overview of the Country Pairs Analyzed in This Book** *(continued)*

Countries and periods	Differences in economic growth	Main reasons for differences in economic growth
Spain and Mexico 1960–2001	1960—per capita income similar in both countries. 2001—per capita income 125 percent higher in Spain than in Mexico.	1. The main reason for Mexico's economic lag in relation to Spain were the economic crises in 1982, 1986, and 1995, resulting mainly from an expansionary fiscal policy, high levels of foreign debt, excessive real appreciation of the peso, and a weak system of banking supervision. These errors in macroeconomic policy reflected the weaknesses of the institutions responsible for economic stability. If the years of gross domestic product (GDP) decline in Mexico were replaced with the growth pace of Spain in the same period, the average growth rate of GDP in 1978–2001 there would be 3.0 percent, as compared to the actual 1.2 percent and 2.4 percent in Spain. Therefore, the economic crises in Mexico explain the growth in the gap in per capita GDP in that period in relation to Spain. 2. This gap, however, had already begun to grow in 1961–71, when per capita income in Spain grew by an average of 5.5 percent, and in Mexico by 3 percent. The main reason for the difference in the growth rate was, on the one hand, the liberalization of foreign trade in Spain (which attracted foreign capital and enabled large investments in the country's industry) and, on the other, increased protectionism in Mexico.
Chile and Venezuela, RB, 1971–2003	1971—per capita income 9 percent lower in Chile than in Venezuela, RB. 2003—per capita income 95 percent higher in Chile than in Venezuela, RB.	1. Both Venezuela, RB, and Chile experienced crashes in the analyzed period; their scope and size ranks among the largest in the world's economic history of the 20th century: • In the entire period after 1977, Venezuela, RB, was hit by recurring crises caused by increasing levels of public spending and foreign debt, as well as the monetization of the budget deficit. This macroeconomic policy reflected the weaknesses of institutions responsible for economic stability. • Chile was hit by a deep economic crisis in 1973–75 as a result of the earlier fiscal expansion, rapid inflation, and general disorganization of the economy. The second profound crisis took place in 1982–83 and was the result of an excessive appreciation of the peso and the liberalization of the banking sector without a prior strengthening of supervision of this sector. Since then Chile has maintained a steady and relatively fast economic growth—a result of the strengthening of the institutions responsible for the country's economic stability and prudent macroeconomic policies. 2. Since the beginning of the 1970s, Venezuela, RB, weakened its institutions: it increased the share of state-owned enterprises in the economy and limited private investment opportunities, including foreign investment. It weakened the protection of private property, due to, among others, large-scale corruption. In Chile extensive and radical reforms were introduced after 1974, which strongly reinforced propelling institutions: the majority of state-owned enterprises were privatized, economic competition was strengthened, the tax and pension systems were reformed, and the protection of property rights was enhanced. The state fiscal policy was limited.

table continues next page

Table 12.1 Economic Growth and Its Drivers: An Overview of the Country Pairs Analyzed in This Book *(continued)*

Countries and periods	Differences in economic growth	Main reasons for differences in economic growth
Puerto Rico and Costa Rica, 1961—2003	1961—per capita income similar in both countries. 2003—per capita income 33 percent lower in Costa Rica than in Puerto Rico.	1. The difference in the scale and consequences of economic shocks is not a major cause of the large difference in per capita income between Puerto Rico and Costa Rica. In both countries, economic growth was severely limited by subsequent shocks: • In Puerto Rico they were observed in 1974 and 1979 and were connected with the oil shocks and the raising of the minimum wage to the U.S. level, as well as a radical increase in social transfers financed from the federal budget. • In Costa Rica a breakdown of growth was observed in 1982 as a result of an earlier explosion of budget spending and the related accumulation of foreign debt. A sharp increase in public spending reflected the weaknesses of the stabilizing institutions. 2. The significant difference in per capita income can be explained by the strength of the propelling institutions and its changes: • The difference occurred mainly in the period until 1973, when Puerto Rico took advantage of the openness to foreign trade and the inflow of foreign direct investment (FDI), as well as the effective protection of property rights, while Costa Rica pursued the opposite strategy—industrialization focused on import substitution. Since the 1970s growth in Puerto Rico was constrained mainly by the country's inclusion in federal social programs and the introduction of the federal minimum wage, which resulted in a low employment level. • An acceleration of growth in Costa Rica in the 1990s was possible following the lowering of barriers to foreign trade. The positive effects of these changes were, however, limited by, among other factors, the excessively strong fiscal position of the state and the existence of a number of state-owned monopolies.
The Dominican Republic and Haiti, 1950–2000	1950—per capita income similar in both countries. 2000—per capita income about 378 percent higher in the Dominican Republic than in Haiti.	1. Both countries have experienced a number of severe economic shocks. 2. The main reason, however, for the radical differences in per capita income lies in the propelling institutions: • The fundamental political stability of the Dominican Republic—and, consequently, a significantly higher level of security for persons and property—attracted much greater investment, including foreign investment in the export and tourism sectors. • In Haiti extreme political instability and the ensuing collapse of the state apparatus, in the absence of sufficiently strong traditional social structures to ensure basic security, lowered the level of protection of persons and property to such an extent that investments in the country were minimal and tourists avoided the country.
China and India, 1978–2001	1978—per capita income similar in both countries. 2001—per capita income 79 percent higher in China than in India.	1. No dramatic economic collapse (defined as a decrease of GDP) was observed in either of the two countries in the analyzed period. 2. The reasons for significantly faster growth in per capita income in China as compared to India stem from differences in the scale of reforms aimed at strengthening the propelling institutions. • In China a larger number of state-owned enterprises were privatized, the majority of prices were freed, the country was opened up to foreign trade and FDI, a much more flexible labor market was created, and the relationship of social transfers to GDP was dramatically lowered. Following these reforms, China managed to significantly increase savings and investment, carry out large-scale reallocation of labor from the less-productive sector of agriculture to industry, and open its economy to the world to a larger extent than India.

table continues next page

Table 12.1 Economic Growth and Its Drivers: An Overview of the Country Pairs Analyzed in This Book *(continued)*

Countries and periods	Differences in economic growth	Main reasons for differences in economic growth
Indonesia and Pakistan, 1965–2004	1965—per capita income similar in both countries. 2004—per capita income about 52 percent higher in Indonesia than in Pakistan.	1. Indonesia suffered a much stronger economic downturn than Pakistan in the analyzed period. In 1997–98 its per capita GDP was shrinking at a rate of over 9 percent per year. 2. The reasons for the emergence of Indonesia's clear economic advantage over Pakistan in terms of per capita income are the strength and changes of its propelling institutions. The two countries experienced periods of both expansion of statism and economic liberalization. In Indonesia, however, the temporary expansion of statism took place on a smaller scale, and therefore the institutions were on average stronger. Besides, the "excesses" of economic policy were financed from the sale of crude oil, and not—as in Pakistan—with debt whose servicing was so expensive that the state could no longer finance its basic functions.

economic shocks. It can therefore be concluded that the analysis of economic growth should be focused to a much greater extent on its dependence on shocks. This conclusion is confirmed by three subsequent observations.

Although economic shocks occurred in a majority of the analyzed countries, their strength and frequency was not the same everywhere. Variations in both the strength and frequency of shocks explain the gap in per capita income that emerged in 1975–2002 between Australia and New Zealand and in 1978–2001 between Mexico and Spain. Shocks of differing strength helped close the gap between Switzerland and Austria, as well as widen the gap between Estonia and Slovenia. They also reduced the average rate at which Indonesia outpaced Pakistan in 1966–2004, and delayed by about 10 years the moment when Chile outstripped República Bolivariana de Venezuela in terms of per capita income.

Shocks do not result solely, or even mainly, from bad luck. Purely external shocks (that is, those that were neither caused nor aggravated by national economic policy) affected only one of the analyzed countries: Estonia in 1991–94 and in 1998.

Other shocks were caused or aggravated by a lack of discipline in fiscal or monetary policy, which was often accompanied by borrowing from abroad, and sometimes by a weak system of banking supervision. Shocks caused or aggravated by national economic policy, mainly macroeconomic, occurred in New Zealand in 1975–80 and 1987–92; in Switzerland in 1974–76 and 1991–96; in Mexico in 1982, 1986, and 1995; in Chile in the first half of the 1970s and in 1982–83; in Puerto Rico in 1974 and 1979; in Costa Rica in 1982; repeatedly in the Dominican Republic, Haiti, and República Bolivariana de Venezuela; in Indonesia in 1966 and 1997–98; and in Pakistan in 1998. The majority of the analyzed countries suffered serious breakdowns of growth caused or intensified by their national economic policies. This shows how serious a problem the weakness of national institutions responsible for economic stability was in those countries. The causes of this weakness have yet to be sufficiently explored. They of particular interest in the case

Puzzles of Economic Growth • http://dx.doi.org/10.1596/978-1-4648-0325-3

of societies with a democratic form of government, which provides the ability to impose the necessary restrictions on decision makers.

Institutional Weaknesses Take Time to Counterbalance

The weakness of stabilizing institutions in many countries is an important research problem whose scope goes beyond the field of political economy. In-depth research should be carried out not only to investigate failures to strengthen weak stabilizing institutions (even though each society pays a high price for the weakness of its institutions) but also which institutions in particular would allow for the effective limiting of both the frequency and strength of shocks. Our knowledge in this subject is very limited, as proven by the current global financial crisis and the scale of economic collapse in Spain and Estonia, countries that—as mentioned in this book—attempted to introduce institutional reforms aimed at protecting them, long before the crisis.

Countries vary considerably not only in terms of economic shocks and, consequently, the institutions responsible for the stability of the economy, but also in terms of the propelling institutions and the directions of their change. Only some of the reforms discussed in this book strengthened the analyzed countries, while many deepened their weakness. The first category includes the market-oriented reforms in Australia and, later, in New Zealand; the liberalization and privatization in Austria in 1991–2000; the radical reforms in Estonia in 1991 and the gradual reforms in Slovenia; the liberalization of foreign trade and inflow of FDI in Spain in 1961–71; the radical reforms in Chile since the mid-1970s; the reform in Costa Rica after the crisis of 1982; the reforms in Mexico since the late 1980s; the systematic reforms in China since the late 1970s and, albeit less consistently, in India; as well as the cyclic liberalization in Indonesia and Pakistan. In the second category, there is the crawling (and, in the last few years, accelerated) growth of statism in República Bolivariana de Venezuela since the 1970s, the eruption of statism in Chile in the early 1970s, the policy of import substitution in Costa Rica and Mexico until the 1980s, and the periodic increases of statism in Indonesia and Pakistan in 1965–2000.

The strength of shocks does not minimize the importance of the propelling institutions for a country's economic growth. The results of empirical research presented in this book show that reform packages that clearly strengthened these institutions led to a significant acceleration in economic growth, and that institutional changes that weaken these institutions inhibit growth. As a result, differences in the progress or scale of changes in these institutions explain to a large extent (and sometimes entirely) the increasing (or decreasing) difference in per capita income between the analyzed pairs of countries. The difference in per capita income between Australia and New Zealand following shocks would have been even higher if New Zealand had not decided to pursue free-market reforms in the 1980s—reforms that Australia had introduced 10 years earlier.

Austria reduced the gap that separated it from Switzerland following its liberalization and privatization process in 1991–2000. The radical free-market reforms introduced in Estonia in 1991 helped to offset the effects of shocks that had affected the country more adversely than those that had impacted Slovenia. In the 1960s Spain's per capita income overtook that of Mexico as Spain liberalized foreign trade and the inflow of FDI (while Mexico increased its level of protectionism).

The dramatic increase of differences in the strength of the propelling institutions in Chile and República Bolivariana de Venezuela after 1975 allowed Chile to first catch up, and then, in 1993–2003, outstrip República Bolivariana de Venezuela in terms of per capita income. While Chile moved from a chaotic socialist economy to a market economy open to competition with a limited fiscal role of the state, República Bolivariana de Venezuela increased the share of the public sector in the economy—and the operating conditions for private businesses deteriorated in the country.

Puerto Rico's advantage over Costa Rica in terms of per capita income in 1961–2003 can be fully explained by its earlier and greater openness to trade and foreign investment, and a better structure combined with a higher level of protection of property rights (through its relations with the United States). It should be noted that the economic growth of Puerto Rico would have been faster and this advantage would have been more significant, if excessive social transfers and a high minimum wage had not resulted in a low level of employment.

The vast difference in the level of per capita income between the Dominican Republic and Haiti in 1950–2000 resulted mainly from differences in the level of protection of people and property rights. The huge difference in per capita income that grew in 1978–2001 between the two giants China and India, accompanied by the rapid growth of both countries, can be explained by China's larger-scale liberalization and privatization, including its opening to foreign trade and FDI. Importantly, China relaxed its fiscal policy, reducing the scope of the welfare state, while India maintained both at a level relatively high for a developing country. Finally, the fact that Indonesia, despite the deep economic downturn in 1997–98, outpaced Pakistan in terms of per capita income 1965–2004, can be explained by the fact that, despite all the fluctuations in the strength of the propelling institutions in both countries, Indonesia's were generally stronger simply because the changes aimed at weakening them were less drastic.

From the case studies in this book, we may conclude that the most important propelling institutions (that is, institutions whose diversity and variability have an important impact on the long-term growth rate) include:

- The ownership structure of the economy, and more specifically, the participation of the state in the ownership of enterprises.
- The structure of property rights, in particular the freedom of private enterprise.
- The level of protection of private property rights (and persons)—including corruption, which can be regarded as a factor limiting these rights.
- The intensity of competition between suppliers, strongly influenced by the opening of the economy to foreign trade and FDI.
- The state's fiscal position, which is strengthened mainly by an increase in social spending in relation to GDP.

Empirical studies confirm that, in some cases, key propelling institutions condemn a country to sluggish growth (or even to the stagnation or decline of GDP), regardless of the conditions of other institutions. Such institutional barriers to development include, for example: lack of protection of people and property in Haiti (due to, among other things, chronic public finance problems and high levels of corruption); the state's large share of ownership of companies in República Bolivariana de Venezuela and Costa Rica, and (until recently) in Pakistan; the state's strong fiscal position in Costa Rica; and, finally, the high social transfers in Puerto Rico. The existence of these barriers seriously constrained economic growth in these, despite the strength of other propelling institutions—as in Puerto Rico—and any reforms aimed to reduce these institutions' weaknesses. Such reforms were introduced in all of the listed countries except in Haiti, including in República Bolivariana de Venezuela in the early 1990s.

Growth Spurts Do Not Necessarily Dictate Trends

Finally, the analysis in this book shows that in some cases—as a result of a prior institutional system constraining the economy—specific, temporary mechanisms of growth may work to release such constraints. Their operation is accompanied by particularly quick growth if, on the one hand, the earlier constraints are particularly large and, on the other, they are quickly removed. But for such growth to be sustainable, it must be based on innovation. A sufficiently wide-ranging package of reforms is necessary both to quickly remove past barriers and to trigger growth based on innovation. This seems to correspond to the characteristics of institutional change in Chile after 1975, in Estonia since 1991, and in China since the late 1970s. We refer hesitantly to the example of China, in spite of the radical free-market reforms that were introduced there, as the scale of the original constraints was so great that specific growth mechanisms could increase the growth rate for a longer time and more considerably than in most other countries. Time will tell if the weaknesses of the Chinese economy, not eradicated despite the reforms, will change into barriers to growth. In some other examples, specific mechanisms of growth remain "dormant." They may prove exceptionally strong in Puerto Rico and República Bolivariana de Venezuela. An economic policy that creates constraints (such as the social transfers that reduced employment in Puerto Rico and the statism that lowered the overall efficiency of the economy in República Bolivariana de Venezuela) inhibits economic growth. But if this policy direction is reversed, growth may be accelerated in the short term as the past cumulative barriers are removed.

Notes

1. In pay-as-you-go pension system benefits are paid directly from current workers' contributions and taxes.
2. The official figure is 316,000 dead, but other estimates suggest substantially lower number of casualties. http://earthquake.usgs.gov/earthquakes/world/most _destructive.php.

Environmental Benefits Statement

green
press
INITIATIVE

www.ingramcontent.com/pod-product-compliance
Lightning Source LLC
Chambersburg PA
CBHW082135210326
41599CB00031B/5986